The Earthscan Reader on World Transport Policy and Practice

Edited by

John Whitelegg
and
Gary Haq

Earthscan Publications Ltd
London • Sterling, VA

First published in the UK and USA in 2003 by
Earthscan Publications Ltd

ISBN: 1 85383 851 9 (paperback)
        1 85383 850 0 (hardback)

Typesetting by Denis Dalinnik, Minsk, Belarus
Printed and bound by Creative Print and Design Wales, Ebbw Vale
Cover design by Andrew Corbett

For a full list of publications please contact:

Earthscan Publications Ltd
120 Pentonville Road
London, N1 9JN, UK
Tel: +44 (0)20 7278 0433
Fax: +44 (0)20 7278 1142
Email: earthinfo@earthscan.co.uk
Web: **www.earthscan.co.uk**

22883 Quicksilver Drive, Sterling, VA 20166–2012, USA

A catalogue record for this book is available from the British Library

Library of Congress Cataloging-in-Publication data applied for

Earthscan is an editorially independent subsidiary of Kogan Page Ltd and publishes in association
with WWF-UK and the International Institute for Environment and Development

This book is printed on elemental chlorine-free paper

Contents

Part 1 Introduction

Part 2 Transport in Africa

Part 3 Transport in Asia

Part 4 Transport in Australia

Part 5 Transport in Europe

Part 6 Transport in Latin America

Part 7 Transport in North America

Part 8 Transport in the Middle East

Part 9 Visioning Change

List of Tables, Figures and Boxes

Tables

Figures

Boxes

About the Authors

Eddie Akinyemi is a senior staff member at the International Institute for Infrastructural, Hydraulic and Environmental Engineering (IHE) in The Netherlands. IHE is an international institute for scientific research and postgraduate education and training in the fields of water, environment and transport. He has over 20 years of experience in scientific research, education and consulting in transport and road engineering internationally. He has published over 30 papers in journals and presented numerous papers at many international conferences. His key research topics include traffic management for rapidly developing cities, operationalization of the concepts of mobility, accessibility and sustainable transport development and the environmental capacity of roads.

Paul Barter is a visiting fellow at the Department of Geography, National University of Singapore, where he undertakes research on the linkages and interactions of urban transport with sustainable development, social justice, urban space and morphology. His work has a particular focus on urban transport policy and practice in Asia and the developing world. He initially pursued these interests through several collaborative projects while associated with the Institute for Sustainability and Technology Policy at Murdoch University, Western Australia. He was co-founder and coordinator from 1995 to 2000 of an international information-sharing and advocacy network, the Sustainable Transport Action Network for Asia and the Pacific (SUSTRAN Network) which was based in Malaysia (and now Indonesia). He is still an information services coordinator for the network on a voluntary basis.

Eli Ben-Michael is a graduate in psychology and is enrolled in studies for a master of philosophy degree at the Hebrew University. He has published research on the health impacts of exposures to ionizing radiation in nuclear workers, non-ionizing radiation and radar, organochlorine exposures and the effects of raised speed limits on case fatality.

Dipankar Chakraborti is director of the School of Environmental Studies, Jadavpur University, Kolkata, India. He has undertaken research on air pollution, groundwater pollution and fluoride poisoning in West Bengal and India. He holds three patents on techniques for arsenic removal, has written ten chapters in books and monographs and authored and co-authored more than 250 papers in international journals. He is a visiting professor at a number of universities in Austria, Belgium, the People's Republic of China, Spain and Venezuela.

Martin Dietrich is a conservation biologist based in Germany, where he specializes in aquatic habitats. He has pioneered the interaction between ecologists and social scientists on sustainability issues and co-organized a symposium on 'Ecological economics: integrating ecology and socio-economic development' during the 1998 INTECOL congress in Florence, Italy. He is a grass-roots activist within the German Friends of the Earth (BUND – Bund für Umwelt und Naturschutz Deutschland).

Elaine Fletcher is a US journalist and transport researcher based in Jerusalem. She corresponds for the Washington, DC-based Newhouse News Service and is the author of a number of documents on transport policy in Israel and the Palestinian territories, including *Transport, Environment and Social Equity* published by the Tel Aviv-based Adva Institute. She is a member of the board of directors of the Israeli-based Committee for Public Transport. At present she is the editor of the Israeli bi-monthly magazine *ERETZ*.

Ralph Gakenheimer is professor of urban planning at the Department of Urban Studies and Planning, Massachusetts Institute of Technology (MIT), USA. He specializes in problems of cities in developing countries which are experiencing rapid motorization and land development. He is currently undertaking research in Latin America, China and India.

Gary Ginsberg is the director of Medical Technology Assessment Sector, Ministry of Health, Jerusalem, Israel. He has 30 years of experience of working as a health economist in the UK, US and Israeli health services. His research interests include quantifying, in both epidemiological and economic terms, the costs and benefits of health effects on morbidity and mortality of new technologies such as vaccinations, new pharmaceuticals, bicycle-helmet laws, new roads and new travel modalities, such as electric cars or the expansion of the train system.

Frazer Goodwin is a policy officer at the European Federation for Transport and Environment (T&E) based in Brussels, Belgium. T&E is the umbrella organization for environmental non-governmental organizations across the continent and acts as Europe's voice for a sustainable transport future. He has been with T&E for more than five years and has campaigned on a range of transport policies, from vehicle emission and fuel quality standards to pricing policy and infrastructure decision-making. His background is in human ecology, which he studied in Huddersfield and Brussels.

Gary Haq is a research associate of the Stockholm Environment Institute at York (SEI-Y), University of York, UK, where he undertakes research on urban environment issues and methodologies for environmental and sustainability assessment. His current research focuses on urban air quality management and transport in Europe and Asia. He is author of the book *Towards Sustainable Transport Planning: A Comparison between Britain and The Netherlands* (Avebury, 1997). He coordinates the Implementing Sustainability Research group at SEI-Y and is a member of the UNEP/WHO Steering Group for Air Pollution in the Megacities of Asia (APMA) project.

Mayer Hillman is senior fellow emeritus at the Policy Studies Institute (PSI) (formerly PEP), London, England, which is considered to be one of the UK's leading independent research organizations in the economic and social policy domains. From 1970 to 1991 he was the head of the institute's Environment and Quality of Life Research Programme and, since then, he has been senior fellow emeritus of PSI. His studies have been concerned with transport, urban planning, energy conservation, health promotion, road safety and environment policies. He is the author or co-author of many publications on the subject of his research.

John Howe is an independent transport sector consultant based in Oxford, UK. He has spent his entire professional career working on the transport sector in developing countries as a researcher, academic and consultant. From 1991 to 2001 he was professor of Transport Engineering at the International Institute for Infrastructural, Hydraulic and Environmental Engineering, Delft, The Netherlands. He has a special interest in all aspects of rural transport and its influence on poverty alleviation.

Jad Isaac is the director general of the Applied Research Institute (ARIJ) which is a leading Palestinian institute that conducts research on agriculture, environment and water based in Jerusalem, Israel. He is the former dean of science at Bethlehem University. He has published several articles and books in his field of interest including *The Environmental Profile for the West Bank* (Applied Research Institute, 1996) and the *Atlas of Palestine* (Applied Research Institute, 2000).

Jeff Kenworthy is associate professor in sustainable settlements at the Institute for Sustainability and Technology Policy, Murdoch University, Perth, Western Australia. He has been involved in transport research for 22 years, focusing on international comparisons of land use and urban transport systems. He is best known for his books which include *Cities and Automobile Dependence: An International Sourcebook* (with Peter Newman) (Ashgate, 1989); *Sustainability and Cities: Overcoming Automobile Dependence* (with Peter Newman) (Island Press, 1999); *An International Sourcebook of Automobile Dependence in Cities, 1960–1990* (with Felix Laube and Peter Newman) (University of Press of Colorado, 2000); and *The UITP Millennium Cities Database for Sustainable Transport* (with Felix Laube) (UITP, 2001).

Ian Ker is director of integrated policy at the Department for Planning and Infrastructure, Western Australia where he is responsible for the development of methodology and processes for improving decision-making with regard to infrastructure investment. He has worked in most areas of transport, including policy development, planning and research in relation to freight transport, railways, ports and shipping, bicycles, travel demand management, climate change and access for people with disabilities. In all this he has sought to apply robust evaluation concepts and principles to decision-making, often in the face of limited data and lack of established methodology, whilst having a keen eye on opportunities to make change happen. He has worked for such diverse organizations as the British Road Federation, the Australian Road Research Board and Bikewest, and has also been a member of the Conservation Council of Western Australia.

Meleckidzedeck Khayesi is lecturer in the Department of Geography, Kenyatta University, Nairobi, Kenya. He teaches transport geography, human geography, quantitative techniques, geography of development and geography of Africa. His research interests and experience in the field of transport and environment include rural household travel patterns, rural accessibility, road safety, the small-scale transport sector (in particular the mini-bus or *matatu*) and sustainable transport.

Philip Laird is an associate professor in the School of Mathematics and Applied Statistics, University of Wollongong, Australia and an adjunct fellow of the Centre for Resource and Environmental Studies, Australian National University, Canberra. He is a member of the Chartered Institute of Transport and a companion of the Institution of Engineers, Australia. He is involved in land transport research and consulting, has served on various transport advisory committees and was recently national chairman of the railway technical society of Australasia.

Christopher Leo is a professor of politics at the University of Winnipeg, Canada and adjunct professor of city planning at the University of Manitoba. He has been researching, teaching and writing about urban planning and the politics of urban planning for more than 20 years. More recently, his primary research interest has been the politics of urban planning. He has undertaken research on metropolitan growth management in Portland, Oregon, and elsewhere; downtown redevelopment; inner-city decay and social isolation; and a comparative study of North American and European urban planning.

Todd Litman is director of the Victoria Transport Policy Institute, Canada, which is an organization dedicated to developing innovative tools for transportation decision-making. He has worked on numerous studies that evaluate the full benefits of transportation alternatives such as transit, pedestrian and bicycle improvements, land use management and market reforms. He has written several guides and technical manuals dealing with transportation planning issues. He is an active member of the Institute of Transportation Engineers, the Transportation Research Board (a section of the US National Academy of Sciences) and the Centre for Sustainable Transportation. He lectures on transport and land use planning at the University of Victoria, British Columbia.

Hanna Maoh is the head of the GIS and Remote Sensing Unit at the Applied Research Institute (ARIJ) which is a leading Palestinian institute that conducts research into agriculture, environment and water based in Jerusalem, Israel. He coordinated Phase II (1999–2000) of a German-funded project on GIS tools and GIS-based models for sustainable transport in Israel and Palestine. His research interests include land use management, urban planning and development and spatial analysis and transport modelling.

Paul Mees is a lecturer in urban planning in the Faculty of Architecture and Planning, University of Melbourne, Australia and is president of Melbourne's Public Transport Users Association. He is the author of the book *A Very Public Solution: Transport in the*

Dispersed City (Melbourne University Press, 2000). His research interests include the operation of public transport in dispersed cities and sustainable regional transport planning.

Peter Newman is professor of city policy at Murdoch University, and director of the Sustainability Unit, Department of Premier and Cabinet, Western Australia Government. He has published extensively on transport and sustainability in cities. He is actively involved in government and is best known for his work on reviving the Perth rail system. In addition, he is visiting professor of city and regional planning at the University of Pennsylvania, Philadelphia, USA.

Rudolf Pfleiderer is an electrical engineer who is now retired in Germany. He is an activist in the German environmental movement. He used to be a guest member of a committee of the German Road and Transportation Research Association, but he was expelled as a result of his criticism of the cost–benefit analyses used for the German Federal Transportation Plan.

Stephen Reingold is a research student at the Center for Injury Prevention, Unit of Occupational and Environmental Medicine, Hebrew University–Hadassah, School of Public Health and Community Medicine in Jerusalem, Israel. His research interests include preventive medicine and injury prevention. He has contributed to several past and current projects at the Center for Injury Prevention.

Ulrike Reutter is acting head of transport research at the Research Institute for Regional and Urban Development of the Federal State of North Rhine-Westphalia, Germany (ILS) (Institut für Landes und Stadtentwicklungsforschung des Landes Nordrhein-Westfalen). ILS is a state government institution which advises and assists decision-makers on regional and urban development policy matters. She is working on sustainable urban transport, land use and transport, traffic safety, mobility management, mobility of children and young people, car-free living, car-sharing, shopping and leisure traffic.

Oscar Reutter is a senior scientist at the Wuppertal Institute for Climate, Environment, Energy, which is an independent research institute, part of the Science Centre, North Rhine-Westphalia, Germany and belongs to the federal state of North Rhine-Westphalia. He works in sustainable transport issues and specializes in car-free lifestyles, car-independent mobility and car-free housing areas and urban districts. He is also a stand-in professor at the Department of Transportation Planning, University of Applied Sciences, Erfurt.

Elihu Richter heads both the Unit of Occupational and Environmental Medicine and the Center for Injury Prevention at the Hebrew University–Hadassah, School of Public Health and Community Medicine in Jerusalem, Israel, and has undertaken research on the effects of speed and speed limits, the use of speed cameras in Israel and around the world, drink driving, working conditions and fatigue in truck drivers, and the ethical implications of using cost–benefit criteria to evaluate transport policies. He co-founded and serves as scientific consultant to Metuna and the Committee for Public Transportation, two Israeli NGOs concerned with injury prevention and sustainable transportation. He is currently examining the public health impacts of superhighways on road deaths, air and water pollution, and socio-economic differentials in access to mobility.

Preston Schiller is adjunct to the Center for Canadian–American Studies and Huxley Environmental College, Western Washington University, USA. He has written and worked on transportation policy issues for the Sierra Club, the Chesapeake Bay Foundation and the Surface Transportation Policy Project (Washington, DC). He also tries to teach students and colleagues how to walk, cycle and use public transport.

Paul Tranter is currently a senior lecturer in geography at University College, Australian Defence Force Academy, University of New South Wales, Canberra, which is committed to providing students with a balanced and liberal university education. His research interests include the study of sustainable cities and transport systems, and child-friendly cities. He has conducted research in Australia (Sydney and Canberra) and New Zealand (Christchurch) on children's independent mobility and access to their local environments. He has examined urban transport practices in a number of European countries, and has examined the importance of streets as places for people rather than simply as movement corridors for cars. He is currently examining the implications for healthy transport policy of Canberra's V8 Supercar race, held in the parliamentary zone of Australia's national capital.

Eduardo Vasconcellos is an associate director of the National Association of Public Transport (Associação Nacional de Transportes Públicos, ANTP) in Brazil, which is an NGO devoted to urban public transport and continuously involved with policy discussions at the federal, regional and municipal levels. He has been working and teaching on transport and traffic planning and engineering issues since 1975. He received his PhD in public policy from the University of São Paulo and conducted his post-doctoral research in transport planning in developing countries at Cornell University in the USA. He has published several papers in international transport journals and is author of the book *Urban Transport, Environment and Equity: The Case for Developing Countries* (Earthscan, 2001).

John Whitelegg is professor and research leader for the Implementing Sustainability Group at the Stockholm Environment Institute at York, University of York, UK. He is also managing director of EcoLogica, a consultancy mainly dealing with transport planning and sustainable development issues. His main interests include the fundamental restructuring of transport supply and demand to reflect sustainability principles and to deliver health objectives through transport policy globally. He has specific interests in urban planning in Asian cities and in the developed world, in the links between transport infrastructure investment and economic progress, and in the human rights and ethical issues surrounding transport policy. He is also editor of the journal *World Transport Policy & Practice*. More recently he has studied environmental issues related to the continued growth in aviation and has experience in working with organizations to bring about reductions in car use. Much of this work involves detailed public participation exercises.

Chris Zegras is a research associate with the Laboratory for Energy and Environment and the Cooperative Mobility Program at the Massachusetts Institute of Technology (MIT), USA. His work focuses primarily on urban transportation issues in the less industrialized regions of the world. He worked with the International Institute for Energy Conservation (IIEC) analysing policy and technology options for addressing transportation's environmental impacts. He has been an advisor to the government of Peru and the World Bank, among other institutions.

Acknowledgements

World transport policy and practice has never before experienced such a volatile mixture of doom-ridden forecasts, radical ideas and an overwhelming tide of political and popular opinion that things simply cannot continue in the same way as they have done in the past. The need to address transport issues has never been so great as it is now at the beginning of the 21st century. Increasing car ownership, concentration of populations, and economic activity in large urban centres cause a number of problems for urban city dwellers. Air and noise pollution, vibration, community severance, road traffic accidents, loss of mobility for the elderly and the young, disease, psychological impairment, hazardous waste, polluted run-off and enormous financial costs are issues that need to be resolved in the development of future regional transport policy and practice.

This *Earthscan Reader on World Transport Policy and Practice* includes a large number of topics, regions, places, innovative solutions and policy suggestions, but inevitably there are still gaps. Our objective has been to create a base-line, set down markers and to accelerate a process of debate, comparison, challenge, diffusion and awareness of the simplicity of sustainable transport scenarios. Transport is still in the vanguard of non-sustainability and this book is about breaking the logjam and setting transport on course towards a socially just and inclusive destination worldwide.

We owe a great deal to the many individuals from around the world who have contributed to this reader. In particular we would like to thank the seven authors who prepared an overview of transport policy and problems in their region. We thank Enrique Peñalosa for sharing with us his own personal experiences of implementing sustainable transport practices in Bogotá, Colombia, in the Foreword to this book.

In the preparation of the book we would like to thank Pascal Desmond for assisting in contacting the contributors from around the world and in some cases acting as a detective, tracking down those authors who have moved organization. Very special thanks go to Isobel Devane who gave up her spare time to assist in the editing of this book.

Thank you also to Jonathan Sinclair Wilson, Tamsin Langrishe and Akan Leander at Earthscan for their cooperation and patience.

At the Stockholm Environment Institute (SEI) at York we would like to thank Erik Willis for preparing the figures for publication and Lisetta Tripodi for advising us on the formatting of the book.

The book was prepared as part of the SEI's Sustainable Development Studies Programme. We would like to thank all the members of the Implementing Sustainability Group for allowing us to undertake this project as part of the group's work programme.

The mission of SEI is to support decision-making and induce change towards sustainable development around the world by providing integrative knowledge that bridges science and policy in the field of environment and development. We believe this reader makes a important contribution to the SEI mission.

John Whitelegg and Gary Haq
Stockholm Environment Institute
York, UK

List of Acronyms and Abbreviations

ABS	Australian Bureau of Statistics
ADB	Asian Development Bank
ARIJ	Applied Research Institute, Jerusalem
ASSIST	African Programme of Advisory, Support, Information Services and Training (ILO)
BIDS	Bangladesh Institute of Development Studies
BMA	Bangkok Metropolitan Administration
BSOM	benzene soluble organic matter
BTE	Bureau of Transport Economics (Australia)
BUND	Bund für Umwelt und Naturschutz Deutschland (Friends of the Earth, Germany)
CAFE	corporate average fuel efficiency (USA)
CBD	central business district
CBS	Central Bureau for Statistics (The Netherlands)
CDM	Clean Development Mechanism
CEC	Commission of the European Communities
CEE	central and eastern Europe
CHI	Canadian Highways International
CMA	census metropolitan area
CMC	Calcutta Municipal Corporation
CO	carbon monoxide
CO_2	carbon dioxide
COE	certificate of entitlement (Singapore)
CPRE	Council for the Protection of Rural England
CSO	car-sharing organization
dB(A)	decibel
DoT	Department of Transport (UK)
DPWH	Department of Public Works and Highways (Metro Manila)
DTLR	Department of Transport, Local Government and the Regions (UK)
EBPP	Energy Best Practice Programme (UK)
ECMT	European Conference of Ministers of Transport
EEA	European Environment Agency
EIB	European Investment Bank
ERTA	Expressway and Rapid Transit Authority (Bangkok)
ESD	ecologically sustainable development
EU	European Union

EVS	Einkommens und Verbrauchsstichprobe (income and consumption sampling, Germany)
GDP	gross domestic product
GHG	greenhouse gas
GIS	geographical information systems
GNP	gross national product
GOB	government of Bangladesh
GTZ	Gesellschaft für Technische Zusammenarbeit
ha	hectare
HC	hydrocarbon
HGV	heavy goods vehicle
HIV	human immunodeficiency virus
HOV	high occupancy vehicle
ICBS	Israeli Census Bureau of Statistics
IEA	International Energy Agency
IFPRI	International Food Policy Research Institute
IHE	International Institute for Infrastructural, Hydraulic and Environmental Engineering
IIEC	International Institute for Energy Conservation
ILO	International Labour Organization
IMF	International Monetary Fund
IPCC	Intergovernmental Panel on Climate Change
IPPUC	Curitiba Institute for Urban Planning and Research (Brazil)
ISTEA	Inter-modal Surface Transportation Efficiency Act (USA)
ITDP	Institute for Transportation and Development Policy (USA)
JICA	Japanese International Cooperation Agency
KIP	Kampung Improvement Programme (Indonesia)
kph	kilometres per hour
MIST	Maidstone Integrated Sustainable Transport (UK)
MIT	Massachusetts Institute of Technology
mt/c	megatonnes of carbon
N_2O	nitrous oxide
NAO	National Audit Office
NGO	non-governmental organization
NMT	non-motorized transport
OFIS	Ozone Fine Structure model
NO_2	nitrogen dioxide
NO_x	nitrogen oxides
NTPT	National Transport Planning Taskforce (Australia)
O_3	ozone
OECD	Organisation for Economic Co-operation and Development
PAH	polynuclear aromatic hydrocarbons
PCPME	per capita per month expenditure
pkm	passenger kilometres
PM	particulate matter
PPG 13	Planning Policy Guidance Note 13: Transport (UK)

PQLI	physical quality of life index
R&D	research and development
RTA	road traffic accident
RSN	Road Safety Network (Kenya)
SEI	Stockholm Environment Institute
SO_2	sulphur dioxide
SOV	single occupancy vehicle
SO_x	sulphur oxides
SPM	suspended particulate matter
SRT	State Railway of Thailand
SSA	site-specific advice
SSATP	Sub-Saharan African Transport Programme
SUV	sports utility vehicle
TDRI	Thailand Development Research Institute
tkm	tonne(s) per kilometre
TRL	Transport Research Laboratory (UK)
TSP	total suspended particulate(s)
UAQAM	Urban Air Quality Assessment Model
UN	United Nations
UNCHS	United Nations Centre for Human Settlements (now UN-Habitat)
UNCSD	United Nations Commission for Sustainable Development
UNDP	United Nations Development Programme
UNEP	United Nations Environment Programme
UNESCAP	United Nations Economic and Social Commission for Asia and the South Pacific
UN-Habitat	United Nations Human Settlements Programme (formerly UNCHS)
UPI	Umwelt und Prognose Institut
USAID	United States Agency for International Development
US DOT	United States Department of Transportation
VAT	valued added tax
vkm	vehicle kilometres
vkt	vehicle kilometres travelled
VOCs	volatile organic compounds
WA	Western Australia
WB	World Bank
WBCSD	World Business Council for Sustainable Development
WHO	World Health Organization
WRI	World Resources Institute
WTO	World Trade Organization

Foreword

The papers presented in this book are valuable contributions to the analysis of one of the most difficult development challenges: urban transport. For a variety of reasons the book is of particular importance for cities in developing countries. While sanitation, health, education and employment tend to improve through economic development, transport problems tend to worsen. There are also no successful development models to be followed, particularly models within the developing countries' investment possibilities; and even if resources were unlimited it is questionable whether the developed countries' model should be followed.

Over the next 25 years the urban population in developing countries is expected to increase to 2 billion. While cities in the developed world may have more than 650 cars per 1000 inhabitants, developing country counterparts have fewer than 200 and, in most cases, fewer than 100. Unchecked, the combined effect of population growth and motorization can create severe quality of life problems. Moreover, almost by definition, in developing-country cities only a minority of the population use private cars for daily transport. Road transport absorbs massive public investments for the building and maintenance of road infrastructure; creates congestion which affects the mobility of the bus-riding majority; causes air and noise pollution; and results in road arteries, primarily for private vehicle users, becoming obstacles to lower income pedestrians.

Urban transport is a political rather than a technical issue. The technical aspects are simple. The difficult decisions relate to who is going to benefit from the models adopted. Do we dare create a transport model different from that in the so-called advanced world cities? Do we dare create a transport system that gives priority to the needs of the poor majority rather than the automobile-owning minority? Are we trying to find the most efficient, economical way to move a city's population, as cleanly and comfortably as possible? Or are we just trying to minimize traffic jams for the upper classes?

Thousands of kilometres of road can be found in many developing-country cities. If private cars are kept off the streets during peak hours every day, it is easy to structure an efficient, low cost bus system which could transport all citizens with speed and dignity. The technical solution is simple. The challenge, of course, is political: to remove cars and non-system buses from the streets. The removal of private cars from the streets sounds radical and strange. Over the last 80 years we have been developing cities for increased car mobility rather than for pedestrians' and children's happiness and safety. Just for a moment, let's imagine a city as follows:

Car use is banned during six peak hours every weekday. During those hours everybody uses public transport or bicycles for his or her mobility. All citizens, regardless of their socio-economic standing, meet as equals on trains, buses or bicycles. There is little air and noise pollution. There is a park only a short distance from any home. Large tree-lined pedestrian avenues cross the city in all directions, and there are as many exclusively pedestrian streets as roads for vehicles. There is as much space for pedestrians as road space.

At first it is difficult to think differently because we are subject to the most pernicious kind of imperialism: self-imposed cultural imperialism.

Developing-country cities are different in aspects such as:

• income inequality;
• poverty;
• illegal housing development with a lack of basic infrastructure and public space;
• scarcity of public funds;
• density;
• climate; and
• low motorization – only a minority of households own a car, and an even smaller minority of people use cars for daily mobility.

For the aforementioned reasons, and because developed-country cities have failed in many ways, we must create a different city model for a different way of living.

We cannot talk about urban transport until we know what kind of city we want. If we want a city for people, and particularly for children, road infrastructure must be limited and car use restricted. Any street with motor vehicles is dangerous to children, but more so if it is a multi-lane artery or a high velocity road. Such arteries become fences that separate segments of the city and isolate people, thus dehumanizing the city.

The unsustainable nature of car-based transport is illustrated by the fact that the problem becomes worse as societies grow richer. Unless car use is restricted severely, society will be worse instead of better, resulting in:

• more traffic jams;
• more noise;
• more air pollution;
• more health problems;
• more low density city expansion and suburban development; and
• more expenditure on road building and maintenance that benefits primarily the car-owning upper middle classes. In a poor city such as Delhi, road building and improvement in order to relieve congestion are very regressive. Scarce government resources are taken up, leaving the needs of the poor untended.

All the national constitutions in the world, and of course the Universal Declaration of Human Rights, are based upon the equality of all citizens before the law and the state. If all citizens are equal, the public good or the good of the majority must prevail as the guiding criteria for governmental decisions. When only a minority use motor vehicles for their mobility, as is the case in developing-country cities, is there any doubt that the public good would be served if private car use were severely restricted, such as not allowing it during peak hours?

Trying to solve traffic problems by building more extensive roads is like trying to put out a fire with petrol. In the USA, time lost due to traffic congestion increases every year, despite enormous highways. A new highway stimulates new development around it, particularly at its extremes, and thus generates its own traffic. Let us imagine a new ten-lane highway from the centre of a city to any location on its outskirts. Immediately after it is completed, or even before, new housing projects, shopping malls and factories are built around the new road and in the countryside near its extreme. The new road stimulates urban expansion, lower densities and longer trips. Ten years after the road is built, traffic jams are just as bad as ever, but now average trips are longer. For traffic considerations, doubling the number of vehicles is the same as having the original number of vehicles travelling twice the distance.

If car use is not restricted there will be traffic congestion. This will cause a greater pressure to invest in more and larger road infrastructure, which in turn stimulates low density suburban development. Low density US-type suburban development, or any kind of development that reduces population densities, creates the following problems:

- extensive and inefficient land use;
- difficulties in providing low cost, high frequency public transport;
- exclusion of non-drivers, such as the poor, children and the elderly, who depend on public transport, walking and cycling; and
- deserted, lonely streets.

Do we want to create a city for children and the elderly, and therefore for every other human being, or a city for automobiles? The important questions are not about engineering, but about ways of living.

Most developing-country cities have relatively high population densities, not as a result of good planning but because of a lack of cars and resources to build extensive roads. Such high density is an asset. It provides people with their main source of enjoyment – being close to other people – and it facilitates high quality, low cost public transport. High density implies relatively short distances and, thus, low transport costs. More importantly, it means that a high frequency public transit system can work efficiently. Developing-country cities should, at all costs, try to avoid suburban development, which will probably be sought by some higher income citizens.

In October 2000, the people of Bogotá in Colombia voted in a referendum to exclude cars from the streets every weekday between 6am and 9am and 4.30pm and 7.30pm from January 2015 onwards. Constitutional interpretations later demanded a higher voter turnout for the referendum to provide a legal mandate. Nevertheless, it proved that it is possible for people to conceive a different, perhaps better, city for themselves, and other ways of organizing city life and city transport. Beyond the environmental advantages of a city that moves basically without cars, the economic implications are significant. The private savings on garages, vehicle depreciation and fuel can be spent on other goods.

A city may follow a more timid approach and simply structure an excellent bus-based transit system on exclusive lanes without restricting automobile use. But why should the rest of society tolerate that car-using minority which generates noise, air pollution and other costs to society?

The public savings on road construction and maintenance, traffic police, and hospital costs of people injured in traffic accidents can be used not only to provide excellent public transport, but also for schools, libraries and parks, to mention but a few things. Of course, people could always own cars to use at off-peak hours or to travel to the countryside at weekends; or they could simply rent them when necessary. Free from the pressure to find ever more room for cars, authorities can concentrate on more citizen-orientated endeavours such as creating more public pedestrian space.

A city such as that proposed here would become a world example of sustainability, quality of life, social justice and social integration. In addition, it would become extremely attractive to highly qualified professionals and investors. If in the past capital investments were attracted by subsidies of different sorts, in the new knowledge economy perhaps the most crucial competitive factor is urban quality of life.

Let us imagine that 1000 wealthy individuals in a large city decide to use private helicopters for their daily transport. Helicopters are very loud. Why should the rest of society forego its silence when the atmosphere belongs to all of us? Why should the majority suffer noise pollution for the benefit of the minority? Yet the car-using minority generates heavier costs for the majority than helicopters would, because cars destroy the common silence, pollute the air and require extremely costly road space and infrastructure, which absorb public funds that could be used to meet the needs of the poor. The most important point illustrated by the helicopter example is that while it would be possible for a few hundred people to use helicopters for their transport, it would be impossible for everyone in a city to do so. The same happens with private cars. While only an upper middle class minority use cars, despite enormous costs and injustice, the system works. But it would not be possible for every citizen to use a private car for his or her mobility, or there would be gridlock and high velocity roads would destroy the city's human qualities and structure.

During my term as mayor of Bogotá we implemented several schemes to reduce car use. Through a tag number system, 40 per cent of all cars had to be off the streets during peak hours for two days every week. This reduced daily travel times by about 58 minutes and lowered pollution levels. Petrol consumption went down by 10.3 per cent.

Bogotá has had a tradition of *Ciclovia*, the closing of main arteries to motor vehicle traffic for seven hours every Sunday so that people can use the roads for cycling, jogging and meeting up. The total amount of road space closed to traffic has doubled: now 120km of main city arteries are closed to motor vehicles. Approximately 2 million people come out every weekend in a marvellous community-building celebration. A new tradition was started, closing the same 120km on a night close to Christmas, allowing citizens to come out and see the Christmas lights decorating the city. Almost half the city's population, nearly 3 million people of all ages and social standings, take advantage of this and the exercise creates a sense of belonging and community.

Another collective adventure was the car-free day. One Thursday, the city (of nearly 7 million inhabitants) went to work leaving all cars at home. The experiment ran smoothly, with 98 per cent of people going to school and work as usual by bus, bicycle or taxi. People enjoyed the adventure. Afterwards, in the referendum of October 2000, approximately 64 per cent of voters approved establishing a car-free day on the first

Thursday of February every year. Polls taken the day after the 2002 car-free day found that 82.7 per cent of the population supported the concept. The importance of the exercise, beyond transportation or the environment, has to do with social integration, as people of all socio-economic conditions meet as equals on their bicycles or on public transport.

More than 300km of protected bicycle paths were built, and usage is increasing steadily. Moreover, bike paths are a symbol of respect for human dignity and of a more egalitarian city, as are high quality pavements. Both show that a city is for *its people* and not for the motor vehicles of its upper classes, as it is so often the case. Bicycles can also provide very efficient feeder systems to mass transit.

All that I have described here was important in order to change the attitude of our people towards their city. However, what dramatically improved the quality of life and gave citizens confidence in a better future was the implementation of a bus-based transit system. Starting from scratch and inspired by the system in Curitiba, Brazil, we were able to design and build the infrastructure, identify the private partners that would operate it, remove the thousands of buses that previously used the roads, and had the system in operation within three years. Today the incipient system, which we called TransMilenio, accounts for more than 540,000 daily trips, and the main line carries more than 50,000 passengers per hour, more than many rail systems. TransMilenio users are saving an average of 223 hours annually; 9 per cent of them used to go to work by car.

Although the system is bus-based, its operation is similar to that of a rail-based system. Articulated buses operate on exclusive bus-ways, using one or two lanes in each direction. Passengers board the buses only at stations. They buy a ticket when they enter the station or in stores outside. In this way, when the bus arrives and opens its two doors simultaneously with the station doors, a hundred passengers can exit and a hundred may enter in seconds. The bus floor is at the same level as that of the station, making entering and exiting the bus a rapid and safe operation, as well as making the buses fully accessible to the disabled.

TransMilenio uses articulated 165-passenger buses with clean diesel engines that comply with Euro II vehicle emission standards. Contractual arrangements guarantee that the buses are clean and well lit, and are replaced before they are in less than perfect shape. Drivers wear uniforms and have to complete training courses. While some buses stop at all stations, others operate express routes with limited stops. Passengers can change from a local to an express bus on the same ticket; they can also change from a bus on one route to another on a different route without any extra cost. Although feeder buses do not use exclusive bus lanes and share streets with the rest of the traffic, they do give people in marginal neighbourhoods access to the system. TransMilenio buses run in the middle of the road and not on the sides, so that vehicles entering and exiting driveways or delivery vehicles do not become obstacles. Also, in this way, just one station is required in each place instead of one in each direction. Passengers access most stations through disabled-friendly pedestrian bridges. Although TransMilenio is the fastest way to move around in Bogotá today, it could be made even faster at a low cost by building underpasses for the buses at busy intersections. This can easily be done at any time in the future. There is nothing technically complex about TransMilenio. The issue is whether a city is ready to remove cars from several lanes of its main arteries in order to assign them exclusively to articulated buses. If the common good is to prevail over private interests, it is very clear that this must be done.

The main advantage of TransMilenio over rail systems is its low cost. Our public investments were US$5 million per kilometre. Even though this cost is high, we chose not only to build a transit artery but also to dramatically improve the public pedestrian space around it with sidewalks, plazas and trees to enhance the city's quality of life and to attract more users to the system. Operating costs are also low. While almost all rail systems in the world require operational subsidies at US$0.40 per passenger, TransMilenio's private operators not only cover their costs but also make a profit. With problems of malnutrition, lack of clean water, sewage, schools, parks and paved roads, developing-country cities cannot afford costly rail transit systems. There are too many critical investments required for the poor that would be left unattended if expensive rail solutions were chosen. Often the political attraction of rail projects, or the financial facilities offered by the vendor countries, lead local or national governments to acquire sophisticated subway systems. But at US$100 million or more per kilometre, and given that they are usually unable to generate sufficient revenues to cover even their operating costs, such systems are an enormous financial drain for developing-country cities. With resources of that magnitude, basic water and sewage infrastructure, schools, housing projects or huge parks to improve the quality of life of many generations could be created.

Often the upper classes in developing countries insist on rail systems because they oppose bus systems' use of space, which they would rather have for their private cars. Generally they prefer subways, not because they use them, but simply because they imagine that by putting the poor underground traffic problems will go away. Rail- or bus-based surface transport systems are more humane. It is much nicer to travel while looking at buildings, people, trees and stores than to travel underground like a rodent. When rail systems are chosen in developing-country cities, limited funds only permit building a few lines, which rarely serve more than 15 per cent of daily trips. Buses serve the rest of public transport trips. In all developing-country cities the majority of public transport is bus-based.

The local government of Bogotá built TransMilenio's infrastructure for passenger transport users, just as roads are built for private car use. We have established a 20 per cent tax surcharge on all petrol sold in the city, and half of it, approximately US$40 million annually, goes in to TransMilenio infrastructure investment. If the national government contributed approximately US$100 million annually in this way, then we could have TransMilenio moving more than 80 per cent of the city's population by 2015. The buses are privately owned and operated, but it is not the case that just anyone can be an operator. Only owners of the former buses that operated chaotically can participate in the bids to own and operate the new buses. All the contractors are private: large bus operators, feeder bus operators, ticketing system operators and the financial fiduciary who handles the money. The public company receives just 5 per cent of the system's income. Bus operators share in the system's income according to the number of kilometres their buses have travelled.

We have been building cities more for the use of the motor vehicle than for pedestrians. It is now time to give more importance to public pedestrian space than to motor vehicle roads. As mayor, I was almost impeached for getting cars off the pavements (where they were often parked), sometimes carving special bays for them out of the pavement. At first it may appear that pavements are a frivolous issue in a developing country; but the privations of low income people are not really felt during working hours – it is during leisure hours that the differences are felt. While higher income people have cars, clubs, country houses, theatres, restaurants and vacations, for the poor, public space is the only alternative to television. Parks, plazas, pedestrian streets and pavements are essential for social justice. High quality pavements are the most basic element of respect for human dignity, and of consideration for society's vulnerable members such as the poor, the elderly and children. Images of high-rise apartment blocks and highways are frequently used to portray a city's advance. In fact, in urban terms, a city is more civilized not when it has highways, but when a child on a tricycle is able to move about everywhere with ease and safety.

This book is an important contribution to the construction of a new paradigm of urban structure and urban transport. Particularly in cities in the developing world, there is still time to address the challenge of mobility in a more socially and environmentally sustainable manner than has been the case in Western nations. If radical changes are not implemented (as could be the case judging from current international experience) transport problems will become the most serious obstacles to quality of life and competitiveness in developing-country cities in the near future.

Enrique Peñalosa

Enrique Peñalosa is currently a visiting scholar at New York University. He was formerly mayor of Bogotá, Colombia (1998–2001), where he was responsible for promoting a city model that gave priority to children and public spaces, restricting private car use and providing more facilities for pedestrians and cyclists.

Part 1

Introduction

1

The Global Transport Problem: Same Issues but a Different Place

John Whitelegg and Gary Haq

Introduction

The global transport problem has now reached crisis proportions. The simplest everyday activities, involving no more than gaining access to work, education, recreation, shopping, friends, relatives and medical services, now consume a significant proportion of natural, financial, environmental and human resources. A useful way of visualizing the depth of the crisis would be to describe the policy that has created the global outcomes discussed in this book. Transport policies are either non-existent or cast in the general context of reducing road traffic congestion, reducing road traffic accidents (RTAs) and increasing levels of economic activity. The global outcomes of transport are normally at odds with these policy objectives and it is informative to undertake a backcasting exercise. What are the policies that would have produced the transport problems we are now dealing with? These policies would include the following:

- encouraging as many people as possible to make as many journeys as possible by car on the assumption that government will always find the cash to build the roads, tunnels, flyovers and bridges;
- providing as much government subsidy and encouragement as possible to car-based transport through loans, grants, road building, cheap fuel and every other expenditure that can be diverted into supporting this system (health care, policing, the courts system);
- ignoring the enormous advantages of walking and cycling for conferring health benefits, achieving accessibility at low cost and enhancing the aesthetics and ethics of the city;
- trying to ensure that children get as little exercise as possible and therefore become more unhealthy as a result of being carried everywhere in cars;
- encouraging as much use as possible of very large cars (ideally up to 2 tonnes in weight) by one person only;
- encouraging as many cars as possible to fill up the available road space (always in short supply in cities) so that these cars disrupt buses, making them an unattractive option and making life very difficult for pedestrians and cyclists;
- encouraging as many cars as possible to pollute the air, increase noise levels and kill children;

- donating as much land as possible to keeping this system going, especially if that land is needed for food production;
- always ensuring that wealthy groups and middle class groups are well looked after, with enough road space, parking and public expenditure; and
- always ensuring that pedestrians are inconvenienced as much as possible when trying to cross roads, making very sure that cars are never delayed by even a couple of seconds in order to give pedestrians easy road crossing possibilities.

No country in the world has a transport policy that even remotely resembles this ten-point plan. At the same time, every country in the world has achieved all or most of the policy objectives described in this list. The enormous power of the images sold by 'automobility', in combination with the political power of car builders and road builders, has produced a global system of 'auto-dependency' that has transformed the simple everyday experience of making contact with something into a perverse and damaging industry that consumes space, time, resources and people. The scale of the environmental damage caused by automobility is only surpassed by the damage to human rights. The rights of children to move around freely in most societies have been seriously curbed by the car; millions of people are subjected to harassment, forcible relocation and an assault on their senses by road, rail and airport projects; and the rights of future generations are seriously compromised by the profligate use of fossil fuels and its associated greenhouse gas (GHG) emissions.

In the remainder of this chapter we will set the scene for this *Earthscan Reader on World Transport Policy and Practice* by giving a brief introduction to the most important themes that are taken up in subsequent chapters. Some of these issues will then be revisited in Chapter 25, where new directions for world transport policy and practice will be outlined. The main themes to be covered are:

- growth in demand for transport;
- resource use;
- GHGs;
- urban air pollution and noise;
- health impacts; and
- RTAs.

Growth in Demand for Road Transport

Global passenger car production reached a record 40.9 million vehicles in 2000 (see Figure 1.1) (Worldwatch Institute, 2001). Each one of these passenger cars carries with it an 'ecological rucksack' (ie, consequential waste and resource use) of at least 25 tonnes of discarded material. Each one consumes fossil fuel energy and produces GHG emissions, and each one denies pedestrians and cyclists a fair chance of independent mobility and accessibility in congested cities. Each vehicle is 'responsible' for the loss of 820 hours of human life (UPI, 1999). The size of the global vehicle fleet has grown significantly over the past 50 years. In 2000 the global passenger fleet was approxi-

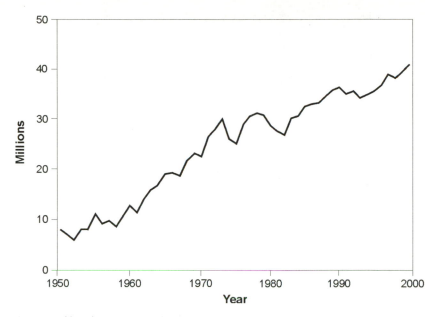

Source: Worldwatch Institute (2001)

Figure 1.1 *Global vehicle production, 1950 to 2000*

mately 532 million vehicles (see Figure 1.2). The Heidelberg-based organization Umwelt und Prognose Institut (UPI) has forecast that by 2030 the global car population will be 2.3 billion (UPI, 1995).

Of the total global fleet of 40.9 million motor vehicles, 47 per cent were produced in Japan, the USA and Germany. By 2005 Brazil, China and India are forecast to increase their production of passenger cars by 78 per cent, from 2.6 million (2000) to 4.6 million (2005) (Worldwatch Institute, 2001).

There are now 11.5 people per car in the world, but this average disguises huge discrepancies between developed and developing countries. In Europe and North America there are 2–3 people per car, and in India and China there are 224 and 279 people per car, respectively. In the USA and Australia the market is increasingly dominated by very large sports utility vehicles (SUVs), which are fuel-greedy and polluting. These vehicles have reduced the overall fuel efficiency of the fleet in these countries, with corresponding increases in GHG emissions.

The annual distance travelled by each person on the planet has also been increasing. The average global growth rate of passenger kilometres (pkm) travelled has been rising by 4.6 per cent each year (see Table 1.1). In 1997, total pkm travelled in the industralized regions roughly equalled total travel in other regions. During the period 1950–1997, total distance travelled in industrialized regions increased fivefold compared to 1950. Developing countries have been also increasing their rate of travel, but on a per capita basis industrialized regions still travel six times further, at 16,645pkm compared to 2,627pkm.

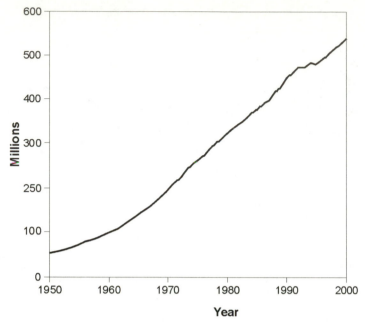

Source: Worldwatch Institute (2001)

Figure 1.2 *Global vehicle fleet, 1950 to 2000*

Table 1.1 *Growth in global passenger kilometres travelled*

	1950		1997		Average annual growth rate 1950–1997	
	Per capita	Total (billions)	Per capita	Total (billions)	Per capita	Total
Industralized regions	4479	2628	16,645	14,951	2.8%	3.8%
Other regions	373	717	2627	12,998	4.2%	6.4%
World	1334	3345	4781	27,949	2.8%	4.6%

Source: WBCSD (2001)

High rates of growth of car ownership and use are now becoming a common experience in many poorer countries of the world. The number of cars registered in Delhi grew from 1,830,000 in 1990 to 3,300,000 in 1999 (Japanese Bank for International Co-operation, 2002). Generally, motor vehicle ownership has increased in line with economic growth. High levels of motorization have been experienced in Asian countries such as Cambodia, China, the Philippines and South Korea, which have experienced high economic growth rates. As shown in Figure 1.3, despite the growth in global motorization, cities in the developing world are still dependent on public transport and

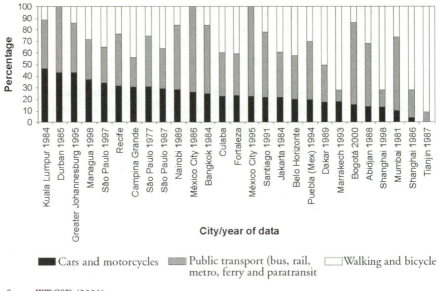

Source: WBCSD (2001)

Figure 1.3 *Modal share of transport in selected cities in the developing world*

on non-motorized means of transport such as walking and cycling (eg, Tianjin and Marrekech).

Globally, the supply of new transport infrastructure has increased steeply in recent years, with international financial institutions playing a key role in funding transportation infrastructure in developing countries. During 1983–1993 most of the loans of the World Bank were directed at intercity transportation such as motorways. In the same period, the Bank lent approximately US$2.5 trillion to urban transport projects throughout the world. Of this total, 60 per cent funded road building and maintenance projects, 17 per cent funded bus and rail systems, 10 per cent funded traffic management and 14 per cent funded technical assistance (IIEC, 1996).

Much of this increase has been in poorer countries where only a small percentage of the population can benefit from major new highway projects. In Calcutta (officially renamed Kolkata from 1 January 2001) the Japanese government-funded flyovers have increased traffic volumes and congestion in areas of the city occupied by lower income groups and have involved the relocation of local residents and small local businesses. Other Kolkata road projects, such as the eastern metropolitan bypass, have served to increase the rate of suburbanization and urban sprawl, with the doubly damaging effect of increasing car use and depriving the city of valuable agricultural lands and wetlands in the east of the city.

New highway building is particularly rampant in Australia, which already has one of the highest rates of per capita GHG production in the world. Most Australian cities are building new freeways, tunnels and bridges and are oblivious to the arguments about car dependency and urban sprawl. The Queensland government is spending Aus$2.2 billion each year on major road projects and adding new capacity in areas like Brisbane, which already have many major new highways giving direct access to the city.

This rate of building and expenditure is adding to the numbers of cars making short distance local trips (50 per cent of all trips by car in Brisbane are less than 5km in length). It also damages the health of children. Similar projects are underway in Melbourne and Sydney, making Australian cities amongst the most unsustainable in the world.

Other world hot spots for accelerated road building are the rapidly developing economies of eastern Europe, eg Hungary, Romania, Poland and the Czech Republic.

Transport infrastructure and urban sprawl are inextricably linked. Cities in developing countries are currently undergoing a rapid expansion. The urban area of Santiago grew more than sixfold during the second half of the 20th century, while in 1995 the urban area of México City was 13 times greater than in 1940 (WBCSD, 2001). An increasing dependence on motorization means that more land will have to be set aside for road and transport infrastructure.

Kolkata, with its dense urban population, has 6 per cent of its total area devoted to roads. Los Angeles has 60 per cent of its land area devoted to highways. Cities with low densities and urban sprawl are very car-dependent and heavy users of fossil fuel in maintaining their everyday activity patterns. The average distance covered each day per capita in Perth (Western Australia (WA)) is 45km, whilst in Delft in The Netherlands it is 15km. Global trends are currently moving in the direction of more sprawl. This is very much the case in Australian cities, where auto-dependency is beginning to overtake the USA. Planning systems around the world are increasingly incapable of holding back the tide. Governments are keen to facilitate the development process and do not wish to erect barriers in the way of globalized manufacturing, warehousing, distribution and new housing. For all the differences that exist between cities like Kolkata and Perth (WA), the northward march of Perth's suburbs is almost identical to the eastward march of Kolkata's suburbs (such as Salt Lake City). In both cases, the lowered population densities, highway construction and sprawl add to car use, congestion and pollution.

The UK land use planning system recognizes this problem and tries to encourage new, higher density, mixed use communities. This has been largely swamped by the growth of traditional housing estates, which on a greenfield site in the north of England will generate seven new car trips per dwelling per day. The development of Perth (WA) has carried on apace in spite of the attempts to win more trips over to rail to the north of the city, and in spite of the success of Joondaloup in establishing a mixed use, subregional centre approximately 30km to the north of the Perth's central business district (CBD). Urban sprawl is likely to be the main cause of transportation difficulties over the next 20–30 years, and is also very resistant to policy intervention as governments like that of the UK stick to a globalized, privatized and free market development process.

Resource Use

Transport consumes a large amount of energy. Oil is expected to remain the primary source of energy for transport throughout the world. Over the next two decades, most of the growth in the demand for oil will come from the transport sector, where high rates of growth are expected and the potential for replacing oil with another fuel is limited (IEA, 2001).

Some oil analysts believe that world oil production will reach a peak sometime during this decade and then begin to fall when half of the ultimately recoverable reserve of oil has been consumed (Leech, 2001). Figure 1.4 presents future global oil output. This graph, known as the Hubbert Curve, is based on an ultimate recovery of 750 billion barrels of conventional oil. The graph depicts alternative scenarios of oil production. The 'swing' scenario assumes a price leap when the share of world production from a few Middle East countries reaches 30 per cent. This is expected to curb demand, leading to a plateau of output until the swing countries reach the midpoint of their depletion, when resource constraints force down output at the then depletion rate (Campbell, 1996).

When oil production does peak, analyses have suggested that oil production will fall each year by approximately 2.7 per cent, which is equivalent to 2 million barrels of oil a day. The daily production of oil currently stands at 74 million barrels. The International Energy Agency (IEA) predicts that oil reserves will be adequate to meet demand until 2020. After this period unconventional oil, such as oil from tar sands and oil shales, will play a growing role together with renewable energy and new technologies, such as hydrogen-based fuel cells.

By 2020 transportation fuels are expected to account for 57 per cent of total world oil consumption. Energy consumption for transportation is expected to increase by 4.8 per cent per year in the developing world. This is compared to an average annual

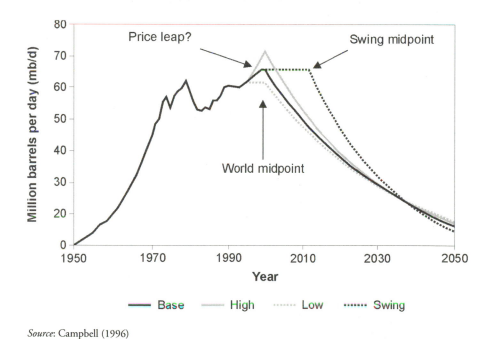

Source: Campbell (1996)

Figure 1.4 *Global oil output 1950–2050*

increase of 1.6 per cent in industrialized countries, where transport systems and infra-structure are established and levels of per capita car ownership are expected to reach saturation (IEO, 2001). Rapid growth in transportation energy use is expected to take place in developing Asia, which is expected to increase by 5.1 per cent per year between 1990 and 2020, and the Middle East and Central and South America, at 4.8 and 4.6 per cent per year, respectively (see Figure 1.5). Much of this growth is expected to be in personal car use and freight movement.

UPI (1995) have predicted that the fuel used for cars will increase from 650 mil-lion tonnes in the mid-1990s to 1.3 billion tonnes in 2030. The total amount of GHG emissions from this 2030 car fleet (trucks and aircraft are excluded) is 10 billion tonnes of carbon dioxide (CO_2) equivalent. This is more than enough to seriously disrupt glo-bal GHG reduction strategies. When aircraft and trucks are factored into the analysis, the prospects for GHG reduction look even more remote.

A technological system that requires at least 1 tonne of metal and plastics to move one person (weighing less than 100kg) a couple of kilometres on a journey to work or to buy a litre of milk is grossly inefficient. This is a materials-intensive technology that delivers very small parcels of work done for very large expenditures of materials, energy, effort and cash. The materials intensity of an average modern car has been calculated by UPI (1999) as presented in Table 1.2.

All this material has to be extracted from the ground and/or processed from other materials. At every stage in this global system of sourcing, manufacturing and assembly there are transport and energy costs and quantities of waste produced. Each car is responsible for 25 tonnes of waste accumulated throughout this cycle (UPI, 1999). This waste accumulates all over the world and is associated with land contamination and the pollution of surface water/acquifers.

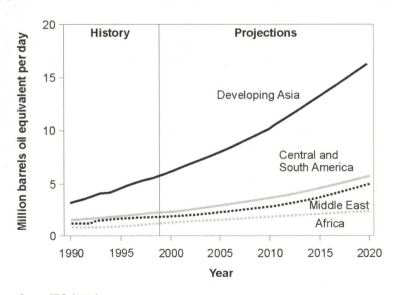

Source: IEO (2001)

Figure 1.5 *Transport energy consumption in the developing world by region,*
1990 to 2020

Table 1.2 *Material intensity of an average modern car*

Material type	Weight in tonnes
Steel	0.75
Copper	0.07
Other non-ferrous metal	0.01
Plastics	0.27
Tyres	0.04
Total weight	1.14

Source: UPI (1999)

A full materials analysis should also include the consequences of extracting and transporting crude oil. Data are scarce on this subject, though UPI (1999) refer to the pollution of the world's oceans by crude oil (including accidental spillage and routine washing out of tanks whilst at sea). This amounts to 13 litres of crude oil deposited in the oceans for every car. Land contamination is also a problem, and was the source of the environmental and political crisis in the Ogoni lands of Nigeria. In this case the oil companies themselves were responsible for considerable land and watercourse pollution and the leaders of the environmental movement opposing such pollution were executed by the Nigerian government.

Land-take for transport infrastructure is a key/headline indicator of the global impact of vehicles. German data (UPI, 1999) show that the total land requirement for vehicles, parking and road is 3800km^2, which is 60 per cent higher than the total requirement for all housing space for every German citizen. Each car requires 200m^2 of land allocation.

UPI (1995) predicts that by 2030 the global population of motor vehicles will require 200,000km^2 of land for highway and parking pace. Most of the time this land will be the most productive land in the poorer regions of the world, leading to a stark choice between 'car crop' and food crop. In a situation of increasing population numbers and pressure of space, valuable agricultural land will be allocated to cars and not to food production with severe consequences for poorer groups, health and social inequality. UPI (1995) estimates that the land needed for cars in 2030 will be equivalent to the land that could be used to feed 80 million people.

The situation in China with respect to cars and land is particularly serious (Worldwatch Institute, 2001). Car sales in China continue to rise at 15 per cent per year, while annual domestic bicycle sales fall as rich Chinese people give up their bikes for cars. Car ownership in China is expected to continue to increase, particularly as membership of the World Trade Organization (WTO) will force China to lower import tariffs, making cars cheaper (*The Times*, 2002).

If China were one day to achieve the Japanese car ownership rate of one car for every two people, it would have a fleet of 640 million compared with only 13 million today. Assuming 0.02 hectares of land are required per vehicle in China (the same as in Europe and Japan), a fleet of 640 million would require 13 million hectares of land, most of which would be cropland. This figure is over one half of China's current rice cropland, part of which it double-crops to produce 135 million tonnes of rice. What should China do? The choices are stark but the likelihood is that China will embark on the path towards auto-dependency, with all the problems that will flow from that choice.

Greenhouse Gases

Transport is the fastest-growing source of GHG emissions and the one area that most policy-makers find difficult to address (see Table 1.3). However, the transport sector is the least flexible because of its dependence on petroleum-based fuels, current entrenched travel lifestyles and lack of political will (IPCC, 2000). Emissions of CO_2 from all transport sectors are currently responsible for approximately 22 per cent of global carbon emissions from fossil fuel use.

Table 1.3 *Carbon emissions from fossil fuel in megatonnes of carbon*

Sector	Carbon emissions in MT (1995)	Percentage share	Average annual growth rate (%)	
			1971–1990	1990–1995
Industry	2370	43	1.7	0.4
Buildings:				
residential	1172	21	1.8	1.0
commercial	584	10	2.2	1.0
transport	1227	22	2.6	2.4
agriculture	223	4	3.8	0.8
All sectors	5576	100	2.0	1.0

Source: IPCC (2000)

Transportation is growing in all regions of the world. Air travel has been increasing faster than road travel. During the period 1960–1990, pkm in air travel increased by 9.5 per cent each year and air freight by 11.7 per cent. More recently this figure has fallen to 5–6 per cent. (IPCC, 2000).

The situation in Europe is characteristic of the global problem, though it is not as serious as the very large per capita emissions in the USA and Australia. Both these countries have refused to play a full cooperative role in the Kyoto process to reduce GHG emissions, and both are committed to a significant amount of auto-dependency and a distance-intensive, car-based lifestyle. Australia also has the world's highest per capita amount of road freight transport, and is very reluctant indeed to use the fiscal/taxation system to stimulate a more efficient use of road freight and a better balance of road and rail in delivering freight.

Carbon dioxide emissions from transport in the European Union (EU) increased by 47 per cent between 1985 and 2001. Other sectors increased by 4.2 per cent. More than 30 per cent of final energy in the EU is now consumed by transport. If this trend continues, the EU will not meet its Kyoto commitments.

Road transport is the main cause of this increase and contributed 84 per cent of the CO_2 emissions from transport in 1998. Carbon dioxide emissions from road freight are also expected to rise substantially, by 33 per cent between 1990 and 2010. Road transport is also a small but growing source of nitrous oxide (N_2O) emissions from passenger car catalysts. Emissions doubled between 1990 and 1998 to 7 per cent of total N_2O emissions.

In 1998, EU GHG emissions from international transport (aviation and shipping) amounted to 5 per cent of total EU emissions. Aviation emissions are expected to rise dramatically in future years and to account for about 20 per cent of GHG emissions by the year 2020 (Whitelegg, 2003).

Attempts to restrict or reduce GHGs from transport in Europe have largely failed. A voluntary agreement with the automobile industry to set an emission limit of 140g/km of CO_2 will reduce the rate of growth by a few percentage points but is more than compensated for by the increase in popularity of SUVs. Sports utility vehicles are large, heavy, four-wheel drive, jeep-like vehicles with poor fuel efficiency and high GHG emissions (more than 250g/km). Their market penetration is high in the USA and in Europe. Average vehicle occupancy is falling as more people choose to travel alone in their vehicles, thus increasing per capita GHG and cancelling out fuel efficiency gains.

Put crudely, European car transport is characterized by increasingly fewer people in increasingly heavier and more polluting vehicles. This is not a trend that can be influenced by technology but it can be influenced by pricing (Whitelegg, 2003).

Urban sprawl and logistic tendencies also exercise a powerful influence on GHGs. The UK has seen a substantial increase in car use for retailing, as it has moved towards the US-style 'mall' concept. Large shopping centres on the edges of cities (eg Meadow hall in Sheffield, the MetroCentre in Newcastle and the Trafford Centre in Manchester) have all proceeded on the basis of attracting shoppers from distances of over 100km to their thousands of car parking places. The impact on traditional retailing centres has been very negative: for example, Dudley (near Meadowhall) has lost about 40 per cent of its retail space, and shopping trips account for more miles travelled than commuter trips. Other European countries have resisted these trends. In Denmark, shopping is still conducted in traditional city centre retail outlets supported by local centres. Germany has also resisted these trends, but the accession states (such as Hungary and Poland) are moving very fast in the direction of the out-of-town centre. Urban sprawl has the potential to counteract and over-compensate for any technological gains made in fuel/engine efficiency and also any gains made by fiscal means (eg fuel taxation, congestion charging or car park charges). Without a radical change in the business/developer-driven agenda towards business parks, shopping malls and new models of suburbia, Europe will not meet Kyoto targets and will see a continuing growth in transport GHG emissions.

The European Environment Agency (EEA) in Copenhagen has addressed this issue and predicted that GHG emissions from transport will be 39 per cent above the 1990 levels by 2010 (EEA, 2001). This does not include the aviation GHG emissions which can be allocated to EU citizens on the basis of their air miles and are currently not counted in EU GHG inventories.

Road freight transport is of increasing concern due to its environmental impact and GHG emissions. The differences among regions of the world for the early 1990s

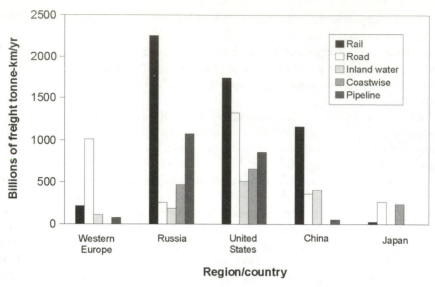

Source: US DOT (1997)

Note: Early 1990s – varies by country (1991, 1993 or 1994)

Figure 1.6 *Freight traffic in selected countries, early 1990s*

are shown in Figure 1.6. The USA had the most balanced distribution between different modes as well as the highest amount of freight traffic. In Russia, rail and pipelines carried high volumes of freight but there was little movement of freight by road. China had a higher volume of rail freight with roads and waterways playing an important role in freight distribution. In contrast, western Europe and Japan had relatively small amounts of rail freight and were highly dependent on road freight.

In the EU, road freight tonne kilometres increased by 29 per cent in the period 1990–1997 and road freight could increase by much more in the future. The road freight problem is essentially one of the spatial organization of production and logistic supply chains. Paradoxically, because logistics is so well organized and so sophisticated (just-in-time delivery, very short lead times, satellite tracking, reliability) it is now possible in Europe, at very low costs, to source a huge variety of raw material and semi-processed inputs into a production chain that is very fragmented in spatial terms. Essentially, the traditional barriers of the friction of distance and the cost of movement have been removed. It is now normal to move thousands of products over tens of thousands of kilometres in a highly efficient manner. The products will be delivered exactly where they are needed at the time they are needed. One of the best documented examples of this process is the case of the yoghurt pot (Boege, 1995). Boege made a study of yoghurt production at one factory in Stuttgart, Germany, and found that many different products and sub-products went into making the final consumer product. The final product was very transport intensive. Each 150g pot of yoghurt was responsible for moving one lorry 9.2m. Similar trends can be observed throughout food retailing (onions from Poland) and globally (onions on sale in UK supermarkets from New Zealand). Furniture and household products sold by IKEA throughout the EU are made up of parts sourced in eastern Europe (eg Poland), assembled at various places, in Europe, shipped to Sweden, shipped to the UK and so on. The distance intensity of such production processes is growing at an increasing rate, producing more GHG emissions.

Urban Air Pollution and Noise

Walking the streets of México City, Harare, London, Brisbane or Kolkata is a dreadful experience. Traffic levels, air pollution, noise pollution and danger are all at record levels and quality of life is very poor indeed. Only very exceptionally (as in the case of Bogotá described in the Foreword to this book by the main architect of the policy) is the policy response urgent enough and strong enough to deal with this problem.

Urban air pollution poses a significant threat to human health and the environment throughout both the developed and developing world (see Chapter 7). Worldwide, more than 1.5 billion people are exposed to levels of ambient air pollution that exceed maximum recommended levels, and an estimated 400,000 deaths each year are attributable to air pollution (Satterthwaite, 1999).

The issue of urban air quality is receiving more attention as an increasing share of the world's population now lives in urban centres and demands a cleaner urban environment. The United Nations (UN) estimates 4.9 billion inhabitants out of 8.1 billion will be living in cities throughout the world by 2030 compared to the current level of 2.9 billion out of 6.1 billion (UNCSD, 2001). High levels of urbanization have resulted in increasing urban air pollution due to transportation, energy production and industrial activity all concentrated in densely populated urban areas. The environmental impacts are particularly severe in cities of 10 million or more inhabitants, especially in countries that have a combination of intense industrial activity, large population density and high motor vehicle use. These cities have become known as 'megacities', and include cities such as Bangkok, Beijing, Buenos Aires, Delhi, Moscow, México City, Mumbai, London, Los Angeles, São Paulo, Seoul and Tokyo (UNEP/WHO, 1992).

The transport sector is a large contributor to urban air pollution, where particulate emissions from diesel vehicles can be very high, leaded petrol is still in use and where sunny conditions readily give rise to photochemical smog and to increased ozone (O_3) and nitrogen dioxide (NO_2) related health impacts.

Motor vehicles produce more air pollution than any other single human activity (WRI, 1997). Nearly 50 per cent of global carbon monoxide (CO), hydrocarbons (HCs) and NO_2 emissions from fossil fuel combustion come from petrol and diesel engines. In city centres and on congested streets, traffic can be responsible for 80–90 per cent of these pollutants. The situation is particularly severe in cities in the developing world.

In 1996, the total number of registered cars in the Asian and Pacific regions was approximately 127 million – 4.24 per cent higher than the previous year (UNEP, 2000). In the cities of Delhi and Manila, the number of cars has doubled every seven years. In southeast Asia the popularity of motorcycles and scooters, which have highly polluting two-stroke engines, together with high average vehicle age and poor maintenance, has led to more emissions per kilometre driven than in developed countries (Walsh, 1999).

In southeast Asia, two- or three-wheelers account for 50–90 per cent of the vehicle fleet. The main pollutants from two-stroke engines are HCs and particulate matter (PM). There is now a move from two-stroke to four-stroke engines in some Asian countries. The increase in the use of four-stroke engines results in higher emissions of nitrogen oxides (NO_x) but lower emissions of CO and HCs and an increase in fuel efficiency. Poor people tend to be more affected by pollution from two- or three-wheelers as they are unable to physically separate themselves from the source of pollution (WB/ADB, 2001).

Transport poses a major challenge to city authorities in improving the mobility of urban residents while enhancing the efficiency of transportation systems. The increase in the number of motor vehicles has not been matched by investment in infrastructure, and many cities are currently suffering from persistent traffic congestion. Cities such as Singapore, Hong Kong, Tokyo, Kuala Lumpur and Bangkok are now developing light rail and mass transit systems to reduce the pressure on the roads and provide an opportunity to reappraise city-wide transportation plans (UNESCAP, 2000).

Many countries are making progress in reducing vehicle emissions as a major source of urban air pollutants by phasing out leaded petrol, introducing stricter emissions standards and requiring new cars to be fitted with catalytic converters (Walsh, 1999). However, air pollution from motor vehicles continues to rise in spite of technological improvements. Technology cannot deliver significant improvements in air quality against a background of steep rises in car ownership and use.

Community noise pollution, especially from transport, is a far more serious environmental and health problem than traditionally recognized. Noisy environments can cause hearing impairment, raise blood pressure, increase the rate of cardiovascular disease and impair the learning ability of children, as well as provoke annoyance responses and changes in social behaviour. Transportation noise is the main source of environmental noise pollution, including road, rail and air traffic. The World Health Organization (WHO) recommends that noise levels should not exceed 55 decibels (dB(A)) and in some cases (eg at night or near schools) the thresholds should be much lower. In the EU approximately 40 per cent of the population is exposed to road traffic noise of 55dB(A) in the daytime and 20 per cent are exposed to levels exceeding 65dB(A) (WHO, 1999). In cities in developing countries, traffic noise levels alongside densely-travelled roads can reach 75–80dB(A) for 24 hours (WHO, 1999). Noise pollution is just as much a problem in affluent areas of southeast England and Australia as it is in México City and Kolkata – noise levels in Indian cities are frequently above 80dB(A).

Noise levels in all the world's cities are above recommended maximum levels and are still largely ignored as an environmental and public health problem. For example, in Karachi, the former capital city of Pakistan, undisciplined and erratic traffic can result in noise levels at $L_{Aeq\ (8-hour)}$[1] of 80–85dB(A) and can reach levels in excess of 140dB(A) during the peak rush hour at around 5pm (Zaidi, 1989). Motor engines, horns, loud music on public buses and rickshaws are responsible for 65 per cent of noise in Karachi. Rickshaws that do not have silencers produce noise levels of 100–110dB(A). A study of 14 different sites in Karachi showed that the average noise level ranged from 79–

80dB(A) in 11 of the sites (Bosan et al, 1995). Maximum noise levels at all sites exceed 100dB(A). The study showed that two people facing each other at a distance of 1.2m would have to shout to be intelligible and that communication was unsatisfactory. Audiograms of 587 males between the ages of 17 and 45 years old who worked as shop-keepers, vehicle drivers, builders and office assistants showed that 14.6 per cent of the subjects had significant hearing impairment at 3000–4000 Hertz. A study of traffic constables in Karachi showed that 82.8 per cent suffered from noise-induced hearing loss (Itrat and Zaidi, 1999). The study also showed that 33.3 per cent of rickshaw driv-ers and 56.9 per cent of shopkeepers who worked in noisy bazaars had hearing impairment.

A much more fundamental car-free and traffic reduction approach is needed to deal with this urgent public health problem in the cities of the developing world. The role of traditional, non-motorized transport (eg rickshaws in Kolkata) can play a major role in moving towards a more sustainable transportation system. However, developing-country governments are being encouraged and assisted in pursuing transport policies based on increased car dependency. The response to increasing rates of car ownership and traffic congestion has been expensive road building schemes, which have further encouraged motor vehicle use and dependency, causing adverse environmental and health impacts (Whitelegg and Williams, 2000).

Health Impacts of Transport

It is only very recently that the full extent of transport's negative impact on health has become clearer. In an ecological audit of the impact of cars on German society, UPI (1999) concluded that cars were responsible for 47,000 deaths each year and a range of other, less severe, health impacts. These are summarized in Table 1.4.

The volume of death and illness revealed in Table 1.4 puts the European transport problem into a very serious public health perspective. Transport is a major health prob-lem and should be addressed as much within a public health context as in a traditional transport/roads/highway context. All the deaths and injuries in Table 1.4 relate directly to cars and not to lorries or aircraft. Total deaths are about five times greater than RTA deaths.

The total amount of sickness and days in hospital, among other things, imposes a huge burden on the health services of European countries and this burden is not recov-ered from those who drive cars. The health impact is a huge human tragedy. With 15 million days of use of broncho-dilators, there is a huge problem for many children and families and the impact on physical activity, social activity, enjoyment of outdoor pur-suits, community and neighbourhood is incalculable. Health impacts in Europe in the 21st century are the direct equivalent of disease impacts in 19th-century cities, which required major re-engineering to provide clean drinking water and sewage systems.

Road traffic noise and noise from aircraft also create significant health problems (WHO, 1993). These health problems are generally understated in Europe, with an implicit assumption on the part of traffic engineers and planners that most people can get used to noise and, in any case, it is only a minor irritation and part of life in an

Table 1.4 *Health damage caused by cars, Germany 1996, annual totals*

	Number	Unit
Deaths from particulate pollution	25,500	deaths/pa
Deaths from lung cancer	8700	deaths/pa
Deaths from heart attacks	2000	deaths/pa
Deaths from summer smog	1900	deaths/pa
Deaths from road traffic accidents (RTAs)	8758	deaths/pa
	TOTAL 46,858	deaths/pa
Serious injuries (RTAs)	116,456	injured/pa
Light injuries (RTAs)	376,702	injured/pa
Chronic bronchitis (adults)	218,000	number of illnesses/pa
Invalidity due to chronic bronchitis	110	number of invalids/pa
Coughs	92,400,000	days/year
Bronchitis (children)	313,000	number of illnesses/pa
Bronchitis	1,440,000	number of illnesses/pa
Hospitalization (breathing problems)	600	number of hospitalizations/pa
Hospitalization (breathing problems)	9200	number of days of care/pa
Hospitalization (cardiovascular disease)	600	hospitalizations/pa
Hospitalization (cardiovascular disease)	8200	number of days of care/pa
Unavailable for work (not cancer)	24,600,000	days/pa
Asthma attacks (days with attacks)	14,000,000	days/pa
Asthma attacks (days with broncho-dilator)	15,000,000	days/pa

Source: UPI (1999)

advanced industrial society. This has to be rejected. Noise causes raised blood pressure, cardiovascular disease, a range of psychological problems and sleep disturbance, and it damages school age children if they are frequently exposed to noise in a learning environment. WHO (1999a) discusses the evidence that supports the contention that children exposed to noise learn less well and have reading abilities lower than is the case for children not in noisy environments. Studies around Heathrow airport in southeast England also point to damage to children living near the airport and under flight paths.

Children suffer in other ways as a result of the growth in car use and mobility. It is common in the UK, though less so in Germany, Denmark and The Netherlands, for children to be taken to school by car. Hillman et al (1990) drew attention to the serious impact of this tendency, especially in the loss of independent mobility on the part of young children. The consequences of this loss of independence and physical activity are that the UK has the highest rate of incidence of overweight and obesity amongst its 15 and 16 year olds. Children (and young adults) increasingly living a sedentary lifestyle with very little physical activity incur a health penalty. As they grow into full adulthood they are more likely to experience cardiovascular problems and specific illnesses such as diabetes. A National Audit Office investigation in the UK (NAO, 2001) has identified the importance of walking and cycling as a mechanism for reducing illness, reducing demands on the National Health Service and reducing the size of the growing bill for health care.

Traffic also damages community life and it is surprising that the frequently articulated comments of urban residents in European cities about the damage to neighbourhoods, community, social interaction and 'liveability' are so poorly researched and understood. In European transport we know far more about the skid resistance of different road surface materials than we do about how traffic deeply affects psychological and physical wellbeing in urban communities. The outstanding exception to this general rule is Donald Appleyard's work in San Francisco (Appleyard, 1981). Appleyard shows in a series of diagrams that heavily trafficked streets seriously impede social interaction to the extent that residents on these streets have much less social contact and fewer friends and acquaintances than do residents on lightly trafficked streets. This is not just a passing item of sociological interest. Isolation is keenly felt by elderly people and by parents with young children. Poor physical conditions reduce the attractiveness of urban living and contribute to economic decline, outmigration and the downward spiral of urban decay. Low levels of physical use of public space (ie, few people actually walking) increase the likelihood of crimes against the person and burglary. Cities are attractive when they are well used by people and cyclists (as is the case in Copenhagen) or very well 'policed' in the sense that there is a significant degree of general public surveillance, as is the case with German and Austrian tram systems. Travelling by tram through Dortmund or Bochum in Germany or Vienna in Austria provides ample opportunities for everyone to survey and oversee everyone else. The significant public presence is qualitatively and quantitatively different from that provided by car users who are in a very private and insulated world.

Studies of individual exposure to pollution (Rank et al, 2001) show that car occupants are exposed to two to four times as much pollution from vehicles as are cyclists. This finding is in some ways counter-intuitive and surprising, but is the result of cars following a very similar path through traffic to that followed by all other cars, and effectively driving in a 'tunnel of pollution'. This raises the very interesting and important conclusion that the car itself damages the health of car occupants. The conventional view is that cars are safer and more pleasant than cycling (often regarded as a dangerous activity). Scientific research shows that this is not the case and the growth of car use in Europe (especially in the number of children carried around by car) represents a significant public health problem, which is at least an example of direct correspondence between perpetrator and victim. Those who cause the problem suffer the consequences of that problem.

Data on health effects of exposure to air and noise pollution in developing countries paint a more serious picture. On a global scale, an estimated 200,000–570,000 deaths occur each year due to outdoor air pollution, which represents 0.1–1.1 per cent of annual deaths (WHO, 1997). Figures 1.7 to 1.9 show ambient levels of total suspended particulates (TSP), sulphur dioxide (SO_2) and NO_2 in selected major cities and megacities in Asia. The levels of TSP in a number of cities are three to four times those recommended by the WHO, while only a few large cities greatly exceed SO_2 and NO_x levels (UNESCAP, 2000). A study by Hong et al (2002) on air pollution and health impacts in Seoul showed an increase in the incidence of strokes as levels of PM, O_3, NO_x and sulphur oxides (SO_x) rose.

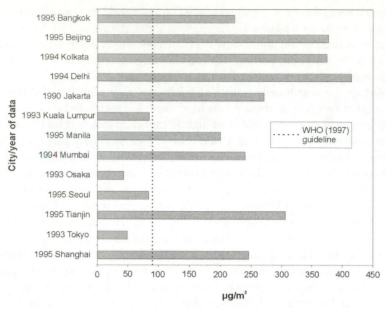

Source: WRI (1998)

Figure 1.7 *Mean annual concentration of total suspended particulate matter in selected major cities and megacities in Asia*

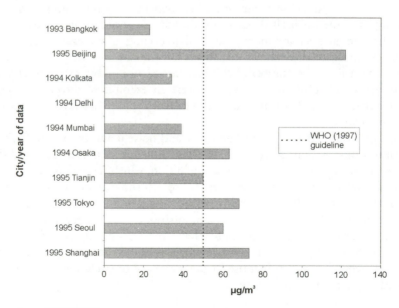

Source: WRI (1998)

Figure 1.8 *Mean annual concentration of sulphur dioxide in selected major cities and megacities in Asia*

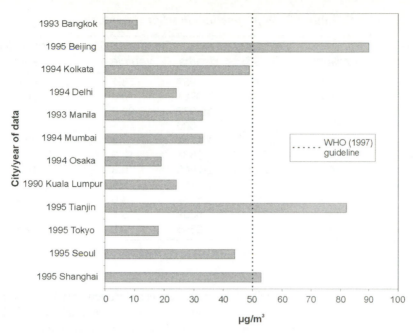

Source: WRI (1998)

Figure 1.9 *Mean annual concentration of nitrogen dioxide in selected major cities and megacities in Asia*

Road Traffic Accidents

In 1999, between 750,000 and 880,000 people died in road traffic accidents (RTAs) worldwide. A crude estimate of the annual cost of RTAs suggests a figure in excess of US$500 billion (TRL, 2000). The majority of these deaths (85 per cent) were in developing countries and countries in transition, where vehicle ownership levels are relatively low. Almost half of these RTAs occurred in the Asia Pacific region. Although developing and transitional countries own only 40 per cent of the world's motor vehicles they account for 86 per cent of its road fatalities. Africa and the Middle East/North Africa region own approximately 3 per cent of the world's vehicles, but account for almost three times the percentage of road deaths (TRL, 2000).

Road traffic accidents are a leading cause of death in economically active age groups. The WHO (1999b) estimated that in 1998 more children in Africa died from road crashes than from HIV/AIDS, and more young adults (aged between 15 and 44 years) were killed by road crashes than by malaria. In India, RTA deaths are 18 times higher than in Japan, amounting to 60,000 fatalities per year. Each year in the EU, 55,000 people are killed, 1.7 million injured and 150,000 permanently disabled as a result of RTAs. This is a huge price to pay for the achievement of moving around a little bit quicker and enjoying the convenience of the car for short distances. Table 1.5 shows the large variations that are to be found in RTA fatalities around the world.

Table 1.5 *Traffic fatalities in selected countries*

Country	Population (millions)	GNP/capita (US$)	Road deaths	Deaths/10,000 vehicles	Deaths/100,000 people
Ghana	18	398	987	73.1	5.6
South Africa	43	3170	9981	16.8	26.5
India	945	378	59,972	20.3	6.3
Bangalore	7	–	600	–	–
Thailand	60	2761	16,782	9.5	28.0
Vietnam	75	319	5581	10.6	7.4
Brazil	161	4859	26,903	10.3	16.7
Costa Rica	3	2695	260	5.5	7.6
Hungary	10	4489	1367	4.6	13.4
Poland	39	3597	6359	5.7	16.5
Romania	23	1406	2845	9.0	12.6

Note: All figures 1996, except South Africa (1994), India (1995) and Bangalore (2000)
Source: TRL (2000)

Road traffic accidents are not distributed equally between different social groups. In the UK, a child in the lowest socio-economic group is six times more likely to be killed or seriously injured than a child in the highest group. The cars of the rich and the powerful kill the children of the poor. In Hong Kong, 70 per cent of fatalities are pedestrians (TRL, 2000). In Kolkata, over 1000 pedestrians are killed each year. The vast majority of these deaths take place amongst the poorest and in environmental conditions where the needs of the pedestrian are recklessly disregarded. The worldwide attack on pedestrians by traffic is a human rights disaster made worse because it is so easily remedied. Pedestrian safety needs are well understood and require a systematic approach to:

*   pedestrian footpaths/pavements;
*   traffic speed/police monitoring and enforcement/prosecution;
*   road crossing facilities;
*   traffic bans/street closures;
*   10–15km per hour speed limitation in sensitive areas;
*   high quality access to public transport vehicles to protect users of buses and trams; and
*   dedicated, high quality pedestrian networks

This systematic approach is missing in Kolkata and it is also missing in the majority of rural areas in the UK and in Perth (WA). Neglecting the pedestrian whilst spending billions of tax dollars on new highways is a successful global industry.

Unwelt und Prognose Institut in Heidelberg has forecast that the global number of deaths from RTAs by the year 2030 will be 2.5 million per annum (UPI, 1995). This is a huge assault on quality of life and a major public health problem that still remains largely unaddressed as auto-dependence increases and motor vehicle manufacturers produce larger and more powerful vehicles. The number of injured RTA victims by 2030 will be 60 million per annum and the number of people handicapped for life will be 5.7 million per annum. For many of the world's poorer countries, where the majority of these tragedies will be concentrated, this loss of life and health also represents a significant fiscal drag on the economy.

Road traffic accidents in Germany have been subjected to an unusual and revealing calculation (UPI, 1999). Based on the analysis of the total number of hours of life lost through RTAs and the size of the German vehicle fleet, the authors estimate that in the ten-year average life of a car, each car is responsible for 820 hours of lost life and 2800 hours of handicapped life. This compares to the average amount of use of a car in its ten-year life, which is 2400 hours. This produces a very revealing social cost–benefit analysis of the car. The 'price' to be paid for 2400 hours of use of this piece of technology is 820 hours of lost life and 2800 hours of handicapped life. This is a very poor performance.

Structure of the Book

This Earthscan Reader contains 16 articles selected from seven years of publication of the journal *World Transport Policy & Practice*. The articles have been selected for the originality of the approach, the importance of the policy issues, the quality of the insight and the relationship to practice. *World Transport Policy & Practice* has always been about the communication and dissemination of best practice. The objective of the journal is to improve the transport situation globally and to do this on the basis of good science, good people-centred analysis and insight, and a strong sense of ethics, equity and awareness of human rights. In addition, seven chapters were commissioned especially for this Reader from leading transport experts from around the world. Each chapter provides an overview of the transport problems which are of concern in the seven regions covered in this book. The issues covered in the following chapters are wide-ranging, but all relate to particular aspects of the global transport problem. As the nations of the world consider the outcome of the UN World Summit on Sustainable Development in South Africa, it is time to assess the progress that has been made in moving towards a more sustainable transport system and to recognize the enormous challenge that the global transport problem poses to today's society and future generations. It is hoped that the contributions here will demonstrate that there are steps that can be taken to improve transport provision and use, and to reduce the impact on the environment in both the developed and developing world.

Notes

1   $L_{Aeq (8-hour)}$ refers to the equivalent continuous noise level. Due to the fact that noise levels may vary over the period that a noise is measured, this measure provides the sound level of a steady sound having the same energy as a fluctuating sound measured over an eight hour period.

References

Appleyard, D (1981) *Livable Streets*, University of California Press, Berkeley

Boege, S (1995) 'The well travelled yoghurt pot', *World Transport Policy & Practice*, vol 1, no 1, pp7–11

Bosan, A, Zaidi, S H and Nobel, T (1995) 'The problem of noise', *Pakistan Journal of Otolaryngology*, vol 11, pp128–131

Campell, C (1996) *The Twenty First Century, The World's Endowment of Conventional Oil and its Depletion*, http://www.oilcrisis.com/campbell/cen21.htm

EEA (2001) *Are We Moving in the Right Direction? Indicators on Transport and Environment Integration in the EU*, TERM 2001, European Environment Agency, Copenhagen

Hillman, M, Adams, J and Whitelegg, J (1990) *One False Move ... A Study of Children's Independent Mobility*, Policy Studies Institute, London

Hong, Y, Lee, J, Kim, H, Ha, E, Schwartz, J and Christiani, D C (2002) 'Effects of air pollutants on acute stroke mortality', *Environmental Health Perspectives*, vol 110, no 2, pp187–191

IEA (2001) *World Energy Outlook: 2001*, International Energy Agency, Paris, http://www.iea.org

IEO (2001) *International Energy Outlook 2001*, Energy Information Administration, US Department of Energy, Washington, DC, http://www.eia.doe.gov/oiaf/ieo/transportation.html

IIEC (1996) *The World Bank and Transportation*, International Institute for Energy Conservation, Washington, DC

IPCC (2000) *Methodological and Technological Issues in Technology Transfer*, Cambridge University Press, Cambridge

Itrat, J and Zaidi, S H (1999) 'Deafness in Paskistan', *Pakistan Journal of Otolaryngology*, vol 15, p 78–83

Japanese Bank for International Cooperation (2002) 'JBIC loan supports metro developments in Delhi', press release, March, http://www.jbic.go.jp/english/index.php

Leech, G (2001) 'The coming of the oil decline', *Tiempo: Global Warming and the Third World*, vol 42, December, pp7–8, http://www.cru.uea.ac.uk/tiempo/

NAO (2001) *Tackling Obesity in England*, National Audit Office, London

Rank, J, Folke, J and Jesperson, P H (2001) 'Differences in cyclists' and car drivers' exposure to air pollution from traffic in the city of Copenhagen', *The Science of the Total Environment*, vol 279, pp131–136

Satterthwaite, D (1999) *The Earthscan Reader in Sustainable Cities*, Earthscan, London

The Times (2002) 'Prosperous Chinese get off their bikes', Monday 22 April, p20

TRL (2000) *Estimating Global Road Fatalities*, Transport Research Laboratory, Crowthorne, UK, www.trl.co.uk

UNCHS/UNEP (2001) *Urban Air Quality Management Handbook*, United Nations Centre for Humans Settlement/United Nations Environment Programme, Nairobi, Kenya

UNCSD (2001) *Protection of the Atmosphere – Report to the Secretary General*, E/CN.17/2001/2, Commission for Sustainable Development, New York

UNDP (1999) *Human Development Report 1999*, United Nations Development Programme, New York

UNEP (2000) *Global Environmental Outlook 2000*, Earthscan, London

UNEP/WHO (1992) *Urban Air Pollution in Megacities of The World*, Blackwell, London

UNEP/WHO (1996) *Air Quality Management and Assessment Capabilities in 20 Major Cities*, MARC, London

UNESCAP (2000) *State of the Environment in Asia and South Pacific 2000*, United Nations Economic and Social Commission for Asia and the South Pacific, Bangkok

UPI (1995) *Folgen einer globalen Motorisierung*, UPI Bericht, Nr 35, March, Umwelt und Prognose Institut, Heidelberg

UPI (1999) *Oeko-Bilanzen von Fahrzeugen*, UPI Bericht, Nr 25, 6 Auflage, May, Umwelt und Prognose Institut, Heidelberg

US DOT (1997) *Transportation Statistics Annual Report 1997: Mobility and Access*, BTS97-S-01, US Department of Transportation, Bureau of Transportation Statistics, Washington, DC, pp250–261

Walsh, M P (1999) 'Motor vehicle pollution and its control in Asia' in McGranahan, G and Murray, F *Health and Air Pollution in Rapidly Developing Countries*, Stockholm Environment Institute, Sweden

WB/ADB (2001) *Workshop Synthesis and Recommendations of the Regional Workshop on the Reduction of Emissions from 2–3 Wheelers*, 5–7 September, Hanoi, Viet Nam

Worldwatch Institute (2001) *Vital Signs 2001*, Earthscan, London

WBCSD (2001) *Mobility 2001: World Mobility at the End of the Twentieth Century and its Sustainability*, World Business Council for Sustainable Development, Geneva, www.wbcsdmobility.org

WRI (1997) *World Resources 1996–97: The Urban Environment*, World Resources Institute/Oxford University Press, Oxford

WRI (1998) *World Resources 1998–99: A Guide to the Global Environment*, World Resources Institute/Oxford University Press, Oxford

Whitelegg, J (2003) 'Transport in the European Union: time to decide' in Lowe, N P and Gleeson, B J (eds) (2003) *Making Urban Transport Sustainable*, Palgrave–Macmillan, Basingstoke

Whitelegg, J and Williams, N (2000) 'Non-motorised transport and sustainable development: evidence from Calcutta', *Local Environment*, vol 5, no 1, pp7–18

WHO (1993) *Community Noise: Environmental Health Criteria Document*, World Health Organization, WHO European Office, Copenhagen

WHO (1997) *Health and Environment in Sustainable Development: Five Years After the Earth Summit*, World Health Organization, Geneva

WHO (1999a) *Guidelines for Community Noise*, World Health Organization, Geneva

WHO (1999b) *Injury: A Leading Cause of the Global Burden of Disease*, World Health Organization, Geneva

Zaidi, S H (1989) 'Noise level and the sources of noise pollution in Karachi', *Journal of Pakistan Medical Association*, vol 39, pp62–65

Part 2

Transport in Africa

2

Four Decades of Road Transport in Africa

Eddie Akinyemi

One of the dominant sectors in African transport over the past four decades has been road transport. Before and immediately after independence in many African countries, the focus was mainly on the rail sector. The European colonialists constructed over 10,000km of railway lines, mainly to facilitate the transport of goods between the interior, the main ports and neighbouring countries. However, since the 1960s, the road sector has dominated in terms of investments and demand. For example, roads are known to consume 5–10 per cent of recurrent budgets, 10–20 per cent of development budgets and 80–90 per cent of passenger and freight traffic (Heggie, 1995).

The character and performance of road transport on the African continent are as diverse as its people. In addition, published and/or reliable data are scarce and based on many perspectives. Nevertheless, based on available information and personal experiences, there are two distinct eras in road transport in Africa.

The first important era, described as the road and motor vehicle sector boom era, was between the early 1960s and 1980s. The era seemed to coincide with the United Nations Transport and Communications Decade for Africa (1978–1988), whose objectives included the final construction and improvement of the major highways and the development of rural roads as well as domestic vehicle assembly plants. During this period, new road construction and reconstruction consumed, on average, approximately 1.1 per cent of the gross domestic product (GDP) of each country (Mason and Thriscutt, 1989). There were also significant investments by international donor agencies and countries. For example, the European Union (EU) invested over US$3 billion, mostly in road projects between 1970 and 1990. In addition, governments and individuals imported large numbers of private vehicles. Nigeria and Kenya are illustrative examples. In Nigeria, the total paved road density increased from about 17km per $1000km^2$ in 1960 to about 160km per $1000km^2$ in 1979. In addition, in the 1980s a massive rural road construction programme resulted in rural road densities of between 30 and 490km per $1000km^2$ of land in the Nigerian states. At the same time, the total number of registered motor vehicles increased from fewer than 1 per 1000 people in the 1960s to about 22 per 1000 people in 1979 (Akinyemi, 1983). Similarly, in Kenya the network of paved roads increased from about 1000km in 1960 to about 52,000km in 1985. Overall, the classified road density increased from 1.1km per $1000km^2$ to 100km per $1000km^2$, while the rural access road density increased to about 10km per $1000km^2$ in 1985.

Meanwhile, during the same period the economies of many countries started to stagnate or deteriorate and structural adjustment programmes were initiated. The combination of high costs of materials and equipment, inadequate maintenance policies, non-availability or inadequate allocation of funds, and/or low institutional capacities resulted in inadequate levels and quality of road maintenance services in many countries. For example, in Nigeria, despite average maintenance expenditures that were 70–500 per cent higher than the desirable routine maintenance expenditures in developing countries, as well as the adoption of several maintenance approaches, potholes and bumps were ubiquitous on the roads (Akinyemi, 1983). In a west and central African survey carried out in 1981–1982, only 4 per cent of paved roads were either resealed, strengthened or reconstructed each year, while only 3 per cent of gravel roads were either regravelled or rehabilitated (Mason and Thriscutt, 1989). At the end of the period more than 50 per cent of paved roads and 20–30 per cent of unpaved roads needed substantial rehabilitation.

The net outcomes and impacts of the combination of these factors were multi-dimensional. In the rural transport sector there were two major outcomes. First, despite the massive investments, the levels of connectivity and rideability on rural roads were still generally low. Many villages were not connected to the road network and significant proportions of the roads were impassable, especially during the rainy seasons in many countries. Second, there were significant incompatibilities between rural transport supply and demand. While the focus was on intercity highways and inter-village roads, 80 per cent of the time spent on transport, 95 per cent of the total weight of goods carried and 80 per cent of the load-carrying effort was accounted for by transport within and around villages. Also, few people in the rural areas could afford private motorized or non-motorized vehicles (Adebisi, 1985), and there were few vehicles providing commercial transport services. Most of the vehicles providing commercial services were structured for intercity/village transport. The net impacts were a paucity of goods and passenger movement on the rural roads, high freight costs (four to six times those of comparable countries in Asia) and a heavy transport burden for rural dwellers. For example, transport costs accounted for up to 15 per cent of the prices of major export commodities, the levels of access to essential services were poor, and transport activities occupied between 12 and 16 hours per capita per week, and involved carrying loads of 10–50kg for distances of up to 12km. In addition, women carried 80–90 per cent of the overall transport burden (Howe and Bryceson, 1993).

In the urban transport sector, two additional factors contributed to the quality and quantity of services. The first major factor was the magnitude and nature of the growth of the cities. In many urban areas there was a combination of controlled growth with the establishment and expansion of some infrastructure in a few areas, and rapid or uncontrolled growth (10–13 per cent per year) with minimum infrastructure in many areas. The second major factor was the nature of the populations and economies of the cities. The deteriorating national economies and neglect of the agricultural sector led to the inmigration of people from rural areas and contributed to increasing difficulties faced by governments in meeting minimum service provision obligations in many areas. In addition, it led to increasing levels of poverty and the proliferation of slums and squatter settlements. One of the net outcomes was the widening gap between urban transport supply and demand characteristics. On one hand, road supply was relatively small (between 2 and 6km per 10,000 people in many African cities, compared with 40–140km per 10,000 people in many developed cities) and a large proportion was in a poor state. Also, many of the existing roads played multiple roles in terms of traffic, economic survival and social facilities. On the other hand, public transport provision was inadequate, as travel by train or non-motorized vehicles did not feature and the number, condition and carrying capacities of the buses in service were low. In addition, facilities for pedestrians were either non-existent or in a poor state. As a result, unique and sometimes chaotic mixes of motorized vehicles and pedestrians shared the available road space. Thus, there were frequent conflicts between pedestrians and vehicles and between the demands for access and movement. The major consequence of a combination of these factors was that transport conditions in many cities became a combination of the good, the bad and the ugly. The good part was that there were a few areas in each city where the levels of accessibility and mobility for motor vehicles were relatively good. The bad and ugly parts were that, in the majority of the areas where medium and low income people lived, it was difficult for anyone to move around by any mode without being physically, financially and mentally exhausted in the process. Traffic congestion was routine on the major roads while access roads were difficult to use by any mode. Access to any public transport route was only possible after a very long walk through areas where walkways were non-existent or in a bad condition. Furthermore, public transport was expensive and provided by old, air-polluting and noisy vehicles. Bicycles were virtually non-existent and many of the households spent up to 45 per cent of their incomes on transport, and travelled between two and six hours a day to make an average of 1–1.5 return trips.

In the national transport sectors of Africa, one of the major issues was the high rate of traffic accidents, as killer potholes, trucks on the roads, incompatibilities between imported road designs and local traffic characteristics, and inadequate road and traffic management combined to make roads unsafe. Traffic accidents cost 1–3 per cent of gross national product (GNP) as road accident fatalities increased by about 20–30 per cent annually, and caused between 50–200 fatalities per 10,000 vehicles during the period. In addition, 30–60 per cent of the traffic fatalities involved vulnerable road users – pedestrians, cyclists and motorcyclists (TRRL, 1991).

With increased international realization and concern about the problems, the second major era, described as the era of externally initiated and financed transport sector reform programmes, started around the end of the 1980s and early 1990s. One of the well known programmes was the World Bank/Economic Commission for Africa (ECA) Sub-Saharan African Transport Programme (SSATP), which was intended to help improve and sustain transport efficiency through policy reform and institutional improvements. It had different components dealing with road maintenance, urban and rural transport, and railways and waterways. Another major programme was the International Labour Organization's (ILO) African Programme of Advisory, Support, Information Services and Training (ASSIST) for labour-based infrastructure works. The programmes led to recommendations and guidelines for policy reforms relating to road maintenance, rural access and mobility as well as urban mobility. The recommendations and guidelines were later followed by comprehensive road rehabilitation projects funded by donor consortia in some countries. There were also some international and country-specific activities, such as the urban mobility and non-motorized transport pilot project in four East African cities, labour-based road construction and maintenance in Kenya, Botswana and Ghana among other states, the Roads 2000 programme in Kenya, and the Integrated Roads Programme in Tanzania. The urban mobility project showed that the mobility of the urban poor as well as urban traffic safety are likely to be substantially increased by the large-scale application of simple engineering interventions (De Langen, 1998). The activities in Ghana demonstrated that the use of small, locally based contractors is beneficial to the poor, the economy and the condition of the roads. Between 1986 and 1994, 2.6 million person-days of employment were created and 1200km of rural roads were rehabilitated with 40 per cent less cost and 33 per cent less time than equipment-based methods (Stock, 1996). Furthermore, Tanzania's Integrated Roads Programme, which was initiated with approximately US$830 million of donor funds between 1990 and 1995, has been successfully developed using second-generation road maintenance funds. There have been some other projects to facilitate the availability and purchase of low cost, non-motorized vehicles, and, amongst other things, to improve rural footpaths, tracks and footbridges and urban walkways and bike routes.

Undoubtedly, the activities seem to have led to a better understanding by many governments, agencies and people of the nature and causes of the problems and the need for improvements in many areas. Unfortunately, continued deterioration or stagnation of the economies, and an accompanying increase in poverty levels, had continued during this period. For example, in Kenya between 1994 and 1997 there were increases of 20 and 5 per cent in urban and rural poverty levels, respectively (Charles-Harris, 2000). These have resulted in significant reductions in new motor vehicle fleets, movement demands, mobility levels and the number of households that can afford new bicycles or the use of public transport. In addition, there have been significant increases in the use of third-hand motorcycles, cars and buses. One of the consequences is an increase in urban traffic congestion, accidents and traffic-related air pollution. For example, in 1996 the external cost of road transport (ie, congestion, accidents and air pollution costs) in Dakar, Senegal, was between 8.65 and 12.6 per cent of GDP (World Bank, 2000). This value is higher than in many US and European cities. It is also known that in Lagos and Cairo concentrations of carbon monoxide (CO), lead and suspended particulate matter (SPM) currently exceed World Health Organization (WHO) guidelines by at least a factor of two (World Bank, 2000). Furthermore, recent research shows that rural transport services continue to experience major problems (Ellis and Hine, 1998) while road condition surveys conducted in 1995 in more than 30 countries in east and west Africa have revealed severely deteriorated and deteriorating road networks (Sylte, 1996; 1997). The main corollary is that, at the end of the century, the road maintenance, accessibility, mobility and safety problems that started in the first era were still enormous.

At the beginning of the 21st century, the era of externally initiated and financed programmes continues. However, the focus is now on poverty alleviation instead of development. While the long term effects of the current focus are not yet known, it is obvious that there is an urgent need for governments, agencies and researchers to undertake an assessment of past experiences in this sector. Most of the past policies and actions do not seem to be compatible with sustainable development. Thus, what is required is a combination of unique or ingenious policies, strategies and actions that will ensure that the needs of the majority of the people will be met with the resources that are available or can be afforded in each country.

References

ACP (1997) 'Learning the lessons in the transport sector', *The Courier*, no 103, May–June, pp15–16

Adebisi, O (1985) 'Rural transport in northern Nigeria' in Barwell, I J, Edmonds, G A, Howe, J G H and de Veen, J (eds) *Rural Transport in Developing Countries*, International Labour Organization and Intermediate Technology Publications, London

Akinyemi E O (1983) 'Towards a developed national transportation system in Nigeria: technological challenges and mechanisms for progress' in Ibiejugba, J and Adeniyi, J (eds) *Technological Developments and Nigerian Industries*, vol 1, 1983, pp190–210

Akinyemi, E O (1986) 'Contributing road factors in accidents on rural roads in Nigeria' in Ovuworie, G, Onibere, E A and Asalor, J O (eds) *Road Traffic Accidents in Developing Countries*, vol 1, pp278–284

Akinyemi, E O (1998) *Sustainable Urban Transport: Current Problems and Future Challenges for Engineers in Africa*, Proceedings of the International Conference CODATU VIII, Cape Town, South Africa, 21–25 September, pp769–773

Alokan, O (1995) 'The road freight industry in Nigeria: new challenges in an era of structural adjustment', *Transport Reviews*, vol 15, no 1, pp27–41

Bryceson, D and Howe, J (1992) *African Rural Households and Transport: Reducing the Burden of Women*, IHE Working Paper IP-2, Delft, The Netherlands

Charles-Harris, M (2000) *The State of Mobility in African Cities: Implications for Poverty Reduction*, Low Cost Mobility in African Cities, Proceedings of the Expert Group Meeting, Delft, The Netherlands

Cure, C (1992) 'Transport, traffic and mobility in sub-Saharan African cities dossier', *The Courier*, no 131, January–February, pp69–71

DFID (2001) 'Focus on Africa', *DFID Newsletter*, Special Issue, 12 May, Department for International Development, London

De Langen, M (1998) *Urban Mobility and Economic Realities in Sub-Saharan Africa*, IHE Working Paper T&RE-17, Delft, The Netherlands

Ellis, J D and Hine, J C (1998) *The Provision of Rural Transport Services – Approach Paper*, SSATP Working Paper no 37, World Bank, Washington, DC

Fouracre, P, Kwakye, E and Okyere, J (1994) 'Public transport in Ghanaian cities – a case of union power', *Transport Reviews*, vol 14, no 1, pp45–61

Heggie, I (1995) 'Commercialising Africa's roads: transforming the role of the public sector', *Transport Reviews*, vol 15, no 2, pp167–184

Howe, J and Bryceson, D F (1993) 'Rural household transport in Africa: reducing the burden on African women?', *World Development*, vol 21, no 11, pp1715–28

Kaira, C K and Oyeagoro, E A (1989) 'Transport planning in rural areas', *Nigerian Journal for Technological Development*, vol 1, no 2, September, pp31–37

Mason, M and Thriscutt, S (1989) *Road Deterioration in Sub-Saharan Africa*, SSATP Road Maintenance Policy Seminar, Addis Ababa, Ethiopia, May

Riverson, J D and Carapetis, S (1991) *Intermediate Means of Transport in Sub-Saharan Africa*, World Bank Technical Paper 151, Africa Technical Department Series, World Bank, Washington, DC

Stock, E A (1996) *Developing Successful Labour-Based Contractor Programmes: Lessons from Ghana*, Infrastructure Note Number RD-21, World Bank, Washington, DC

Stren, R E and White, R R (1989) *African Cities in Crisis: Managing Rapid Urban Growth*, African Modernization and Development Series, Westview Press, London

Sylte, O K (1996) *Review of the Road Sector in Selected Common Market for Eastern and Southern Africa (COMESA) Countries*, SSATP Working Paper No 23, World Bank and UN Economic Commission for Africa, Washington, DC

Sylte, O K (1997) *The Road Sector in ECOWAS Countries: A Comparative Assessment*, World Bank Seminar on Management and Financing of Roads, Abidjan, 2–6 June

TRRL (1991) *Towards Safer Roads in Developing Countries: A Guide for Planners and Engineers*, Transport and Road Research Laboratory, Overseas Development Administration, London

World Bank (2000) *Cities on the Move: A World Bank Urban Transport Strategy Review*, World Bank Consultant Draft Policy Paper, World Bank, Washington, DC

3

Liveable Streets for Pedestrians in Nairobi: The Challenge of Road Traffic Accidents

Meleckidzedeck Khayesi

Introduction

Pedestrians constitute a most vulnerable group in road traffic accidents (RTAs). Their vulnerability largely results from the neglect of their mobility needs in transport planning. This neglect contrasts sharply with the unrivalled and undue advantages given to the motor vehicle (Whitelegg, 1993; Conservation Law Foundation, 1995; Monheim, 1996).

In Nairobi, the capital city of Kenya, pedestrians constitute the largest single victim group of RTA fatalities and injuries. The lives of pedestrians in Nairobi are therefore at great risk from RTAs. In other words, the streets of Nairobi do not offer a liveable environment to pedestrians. The streets of Nairobi should not just be seen as part of the urban jungle, nor should they be viewed as satisfying mainly the needs of motorized traffic – rather, they should be seen as liveable streets. This means that they should contribute to realizing the economic and social goals of all road users, including pedestrians.

This chapter examines the trend in pedestrian fatalities and injuries in RTAs in Nairobi from 1977 to 1994. It then briefly outlines the transport policy context of pedestrian RTAs. The chapter concludes by suggesting a strategy to improve the safety of pedestrians in Nairobi.[1]

The Reality of Pedestrian Deaths and Injuries in Road Traffic Accidents in Nairobi

The picture that emerges from the data presented in this chapter is one of an increasing loss of life and injuries that accrue to pedestrians in Nairobi. Between 1977 and 1994, Nairobi experienced a rising trend in the number of RTAs (see Figure 3.1). A total of 54,350 RTAs occurred in Nairobi during this period. These accidents resulted in 6005 deaths. Pedestrians constituted the largest number of road traffic fatalities (3929 or 64.5 per cent). The second largest group of victims was passengers (1189 or 19.8 per cent). They were followed in relative importance by drivers (615 or 10.2 per cent),

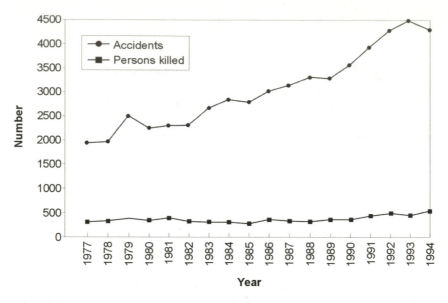

Figure 3.1 *Number of road traffic accidents and persons killed in Nairobi, 1977 to 1994*

cyclists (183 or 3 per cent) and motorcyclists (89 or 1.5 per cent). This aggregate pattern is more or less repeated for the individual years.

A look at the trend in serious injuries reveals that pedestrians also constitute the highest single victim group. Out of a total of 14,826 persons who were seriously injured, 6465 (43.6 per cent) were pedestrians, 4025 (27.1 per cent) were passengers, 2669 (18 per cent) were drivers, 913 (6.2 per cent) were cyclists and 754 (5.1 per cent) were motorcyclists. The pedestrians are also the largest victim group with respect to slight injuries (see Figure 3.2). There were 47,100 slight injuries, of which 19,469 (41.3 per cent) were to pedestrians, 15,049 (32 per cent) were to passengers, 7739 (16.4 per cent) were to drivers, 2946 (6.2 per cent) were to cyclists and 1906 (4 per cent) were to motorcyclists.

The picture that emerges from the data in the diagrams underscores the fact that pedestrians are a premium RTA risk group in Nairobi. The official statistics on which this chapter is based reveal only a small proportion of the threat to pedestrians in Nairobi. The situation may even be worse than portrayed here if all the data on pedestrian accidents were included. There is the universal problem of under-reporting in RTA statistics (Adams, 1986). The question that arises is: What is transport policy doing to improve pedestrian safety in Nairobi?

The Pedestrian in Nairobi: Transport Policy and Practice

Transport policy and practice in Nairobi do not appear to reflect the reality of the trip-making characteristics of the residents. Walking is a dominant mode of transport in

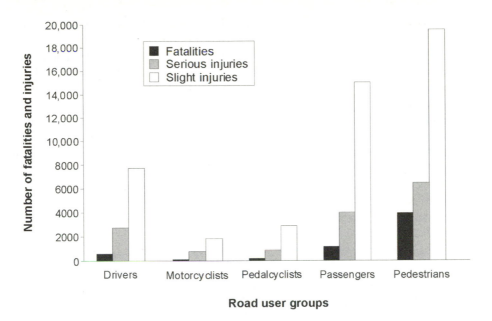

Figure 3.2 *Road traffic accident fatalities and injuries in Nairobi by road user group, 1977 to 1994*

Nairobi. A survey carried out in 1973 revealed that about 44.6 per cent of household trips were made on foot. These trips were for essential purposes such as work, school, personal trips and business (Nairobi Metropolitan Growth Strategy, 1973). A 1994 survey of mode use in 302 households in a low–medium income area in Nairobi revealed that walking is the predominant mode of travel in these households. A modal split for the first four trips in the day combined revealed that walking had a 47 per cent share. It was followed by public transport (41 per cent), private car (7 per cent), bicycle (1 per cent) and others (4 per cent). The importance of walking in these households was further emphasized by the fact that a large proportion of the first trips of the day, and the most important everyday trips, were made on foot. In fact, walking had over 40 per cent of the share of such trips (Omwenga et al, 1994).

Pedestrian trips in Nairobi cover varying distances, within a complex web of origins and destinations. For instance, in the survey by Omwenga et al (1994), the average travel distance among households was estimated at 5–8km. Residents in some new settlement areas were found to cover over 10km. Pedestrian, as well as motorized, mobility arises due to the separation of activities in time and space in Nairobi. This pattern of movement is closely related to residential patterns, locations of workplaces, locations of shopping zones and locations of entertainment places. This is the reason for a web of movement patterns in Nairobi in terms of origins, destinations, purposes, mode uses, directions and volumes. It is in the course of these movements and interactions that pedestrians come into contact with motor vehicles.

This contact should not always lead to a pedestrian RTA. However, due to deficiencies in transport planning, pedestrians often become victims of RTAs. An analysis of the distribution of accident spots in Nairobi reveals that the most dangerous places are those with heavy pedestrian traffic in the central business district (CBD) and along the main primary distributor roads leading to the CBD from low income, high density residential areas (Ogonda, 1976; Maina, 1978; Omwenga et al, 1993). These roads also happen to be those with heavy, fast moving motor vehicle traffic, eg Jogoo Road and 1st Avenue-Eastleigh.

Road transport planning in Nairobi is by and large motor vehicle-oriented (Omwenga et al, 1993). The general policy statement on urban transport in Kenya has tended to ignore non-motorized transport such as walking and cycling. Priority in transport planning has been given to the development of motorized transport (Omwenga et al, 1993). The existing road networks in Kenyan urban areas, including Nairobi, do not meaningfully cater for non-motorized modes. The existing pedestrian infrastructure is inadequate. In brief, there is a general lack of infrastructure for pedestrians and cyclists in the urban transport system in Kenya (Omwenga et al, 1993).

Though pedestrian mobility needs are now receiving some attention in some of the countries of Europe, the USA, Japan and Australia, no meaningful and clear policy shift is evident in Nairobi. The pedestrianization of the transport system is yet to receive the policy and action programmes it deserves. Nairobi has very few and inadequate (in some cases non-existent) pedestrian facilities in terms of footbridges, underground passages, exclusive walking paths, zebra crossings and pedestrian precincts. It is not unusual to find motor vehicles in narrow streets which should ideally be for pedestrians. The situation of pedestrians is worsened by the use of limited walking space on pavements for parking and hawking. Pedestrians have to use this limited space or walk in the road, thus exposing themselves to the likelihood of being hit by motor vehicles.

The pedestrian is often blamed for carelessness as a road user. The roads in Nairobi are used by both motorized and non-motorized traffic. Such a traffic mix creates a high probability of conflict that could easily lead to an RTA. This probability becomes even stronger in a situation where road users do not adhere to the traffic rules, a state of affairs that is prevalent in Nairobi. The pedestrian turns out to be a weak and disadvantaged negotiator when confronted with strong motor traffic.

Many motorists in Nairobi do not give pedestrians the right of way. Pedestrians are even in danger from motorists at zebra crossings. To facilitate pedestrian mobility at zebra crossings, the traffic police often have to stop motorists. Recently, a non-governmental organization (NGO) called Road Safety Network (RSN) was formed. It deploys personnel at peak hours at critical points to control traffic. They even try to stop motorists to make it possible for pedestrians to cross the road. Pedestrians tend to be blamed for crossing the road when conditions are not favourable. They are accused of failure to heed the presence of vehicular traffic. Children are often blamed for playing in the road. A contextual analysis reveals that these actions cannot be wholly blamed on pedestrians. In the absence of adequate pedestrian facilities and in a situation where there is little regard for the pedestrian right of way, pedestrians are obliged to take risky actions to cross the roads. This can easily result in an RTA, for instance, when an oncoming vehicle hits a pedestrian who is halfway across the road.

Reclaiming the Streets of Nairobi for Pedestrians: A Strategy

An issue that is increasingly drawing much attention in transport planning is how to reclaim streets for pedestrians (Conservation Law Foundation, 1995; WALKBoston, 1996). Literature on the liveability of streets indicates that they have an important function to play in the social and economic life of the resident population (Appleyard et al, 1981; Hass-Klau et al, 1999). The liveability of streets has been lost with the passing of time, largely due to increasing motorization, which led to the neglect of pedestrians in transport planning. The threat posed by RTAs to pedestrians is thus a global problem.

For Nairobi, it is necessary to tackle the problem of RTAs, especially with a view to making the streets liveable for pedestrians. The key to tackling this problem lies in effectively and meaningfully addressing the critical issues which have been raised concerning transport planning and the road user system. The strategy to improving pedestrian safety in Nairobi requires intervention at two principal levels: policy framework and practice.

Policy Framework

At the policy level, there is a need for a rethink. In specific terms, there is a need for a comprehensive policy and institutional framework that incorporates the needs of pedestrians and other non-motorized traffic modes. The policy fixation on the needs of mainly motorized transport requires a drastic reversal. What is needed in transport policy is a reorientation from motor vehicle fixation to inter-modal compatibility. In particular, the neglect of pedestrians has to be addressed. The present transport policy in Kenya lacks a clear statement on urban transport in general and non-motorized traffic in particular (Omwenga et al, 1993). Transport policy generally does not fully recognize that 'walking is transport' (Monheim, 1996; Nebe, 1996). At the institutional level, Omwenga et al (1993) observe that there is no strong lead agency empowered to coordinate and implement comprehensive urban transport policy measures in Kenya. An effective institutional framework to consistently plan and manage the urban transport system is lacking. There are several agencies and institutions concerned with various transport matters at mixed levels. A clear policy statement, a coordinated institutional framework and the political commitment to pedestrian needs in Nairobi will constitute significant first steps towards tackling pedestrian accidents.

Transport Practice

Beyond goal and target-setting in transport policy, there is a need to undertake specific action programmes that are aimed at improving pedestrian safety. There are a number of measures that are necessary. Among these are: the pedestrianization of some roads in the CBD, residential traffic calming and the provision of adequate pedestrian facilities (walking lanes, zebra crossings, footbridges, underground passages and ample time for pedestrians at traffic lights). Along with these action programmes, there is a need for effective legal enforcement that incorporates a strong element of road safety education. A city-wide programme of road safety education is needed in Nairobi. Nairobi residents will then become aware of the dangers of RTAs and, even more, of the need to improve their personal behaviour on the road. In other words, road safety in Nairobi needs to be community-oriented, whereby the residents and road users see themselves as part of both the problem of road safety and its solution.

Conclusion

An analysis of RTA statistics for Nairobi for the period 1977–1994 reveals that pedestrians are the largest single victim group of fatalities and injuries. The increasing vulnerability of pedestrians to RTAs is largely due to the neglect of their needs in transport planning in Nairobi. There is a strong orientation towards the needs of motorized traffic at the expense of non-motorized traffic. The key to ensuring pedestrian safety in Nairobi lies in policy re-orientation, which should address the neglect of pedestrians. There is an urgent need for meaningful traffic-calming measures in Nairobi.

Notes

1   This chapter was first published as a paper in *World Transport Policy & Practice*, vol 3, no 1, pp4–7.

References

Adams, J (1986) *Risk Homeostasis and the Purpose of Safety Regulation*, paper presented to the CEC Workshop on Risky Decision-Making in Transport Operations, TNO Institute for Perception, Soesterberg, The Netherlands, 9 November

Appleyard, D, Gerson, M S and Lintell, M (1981) *Livable Streets*, University of California Press, Berkeley

Conservation Law Foundation (1995) *Take Back your Streets: How to Protect Communities from Asphalt and Traffic*, Conservation Law Foundation, Boston

Hass-Klau, C, Crampton, G, Dowland, C and Nold, I (1999) *Streets as Living Space: A Town Centre Study of European Pedestrian Behaviour*, Landor Publishing, London

Maina, B R (1978) *Road Safety in Nairobi: An Analysis of Road Accidents on Nairobi Road Network*, MA thesis, University of Nairobi, Kenya

Monheim, H (1996) *The Triangle of Transport–Economics–Environment in Europe*, paper presented at the Kouvola Conference,

Nairobi Metropolitan Growth Strategy (1973) *Nairobi Metropolitan Growth Strategy* (volume 2), City Council of Nairobi, Nairobi

Nebe, J M (1996) *Feet First: The Debate and Progress Towards More Livable Cities in Germany*, lecture given to WALKBoston Initiative, 10 October

Ogonda, R (1976) *Transportation in the Nairobi Area: A Geographical Analysis*, MA thesis, University of Nairobi, Kenya

Omwenga, M E, Obiero, S and Malombe, J (1993) *Non-motorized Urban Transport Studies, Eastern and Southern Africa*, Preliminary Assessment Report of Issues and Interests, Report No 4A, Africa Technical Department, World Bank, Nairobi

Omwenga, M E, Obiero, S and Malombe, J (1994) 'Nairobi Action Plan for Urban Mobility and Non-motorized Transport', in *Proceedings of the SSATP Seminar on Urban Mobility and Non-motorized Transport in Sub-Saharan Africa*, Africa Technical Department, World Bank, Nairobi, p4

WALKBoston (1996) *Walkable Communities: Five Steps to Making Your Community Safe and Convenient for People on Foot*, WalkBoston, Boston

Whitelegg, J (1993) *Transport for a Sustainable Future: The Case for Europe*, Belhaven Press, London

4

Sustaining Africa's Rural Road Networks: The Asset Management Approach

John Howe

Introduction

Many rural roads in Africa are 'returning to the bush' because of inadequate maintenance. This is not helped by development loans that encourage the construction of new roads and the rehabilitation of existing infrastructure rather than better-value ongoing maintenance. Much of the problem lies in the technical arguments put to decision-makers. In this chapter the argument is put in a way that non-technical people can understand.[1]

Road Conditions

Africa's roads were in poor condition before the El Niño storms in the spring of 1998 added selectively to the damage. Road condition surveys for the World Bank in more than 30 countries in east and west Africa revealed a picture of severely deteriorated – and deteriorating – networks from which not even the main highways have been spared (Sylte, 1996; 1997). A May 1998 journey in Tanzania between its major port and commercial centre, Dar-es-Salaam, and the capital Dodoma showed that the condition of sections of the highway reduced traffic to a crawl while large potholes were negotiated laboriously. Newspaper reports indicated that significant areas of the northwest of the country were not reachable by road other than through Kenya and Uganda, a detour of several hundred kilometres. Off the main roads conditions were far worse, with the majority of tracks in poor condition and a significant proportion unusable by normal vehicles. (Technically, a road is said to be in a poor condition if is not in a maintainable state and requires rehabilitation before maintenance operations can be reinstated.)

Tanzania's situation is particularly revealing because of the relative stability of its political climate over the past four decades, and the substantial donor assistance its road sector has received under the first phase (1990–1995) of the Integrated Road Project – approximately US$830 million – and is due to receive (US$650 million committed to date) under the second phase. The Integrated Road Project is focused on the trunk and regional road network of approximately 25,000km. There are also district and feeder road networks comprising another 26,000 and 22,000km respectively. These are the rural roads that provide local access and are of most concern to the majority of the population. It is with them and their equivalents in other African countries that this chapter is concerned.

The factors underlying the poor condition of Africa's road networks would be less depressing if they were new, but this is not so. The fundamental issues were identified in 1979 (World Bank, 1981). However, despite two decades of effort, until recently progress has been patchy. Since it was initiated in 1989, the World Bank/UN Economic Commission for Africa's Road Maintenance Initiative has made progress in defining a framework for reform that gives primary emphasis to the commercial management and financing of road systems. Commercialization is based on four inter-dependent building blocks of reform:

1 involving road users so that they can take part in decisions on levels of service and charges;
2 stabilizing road financing by a mechanism to ensure an adequate, steady flow of funds;
3 clarifying responsibility in the area of network management; and
4 improving the management and efficiency of the bodies in charge of road maintenance.

These ideas are in various stages of implementation in roughly a dozen countries and the progress made by the best performers gives grounds for guarded optimism. However, the immensity of the reforms is such that for the next decade main roads are likely to be the principal beneficiaries. Rural road networks will receive little benefit because there are political limitations to the rate at which road user charges and fuel prices may be increased without risking civil unrest (which can be extreme). This is more than likely when the populace has become accustomed to very low real costs, a lesson that countries as culturally diverse as Indonesia, Nigeria and Venezuela have learned to their peril. Thus, funding the maintenance, let alone development, of entire road networks out of locally generated funds remains a distant prospect in most countries. The main highways necessarily will come first.

For the rural road networks, there are additional difficulties. First, they are normally managed by local government administrations whose weak financial, institutional and human resource bases render the sustainability of all public investments immensely difficult. Second, local administrations also feel the full effects of a number of fundamental characteristics that inhibit Africa's development. Geography, population dynamics and neglect of the financial realities necessary to sustain road networks stand out as being crucial to its predicament.

Geography and Population Dynamics

The sheer size of Africa has been systematically misrepresented ever since Mercator drew his famous map of the world in the 16th century. Few people realize that Argentina, China, Europe, India, New Zealand and the USA can be placed inside Africa with space to spare. (The total area of these countries amounts to 30,245,000km^2 whereas

Africa's area is estimated at 30,345,000km².) This huge area contains a comparatively small, impoverished population that is, moreover, very unevenly distributed. Thus whilst there are areas where the population is densely concentrated – Rwanda, Burundi and the major volcanic mountains of east Africa are examples – its average density is approximately 20 persons per km² over the continent, compared to six times this figure in most of Asia.

The sparseness and poverty of its population mean that it is inherently difficult to support the maintenance of all types of infrastructure. There are vast distances with very few people to generate the revenues necessary to sustain maintenance. Without maintenance, even bitumen-surfaced roads will become unusable in as short a time as 10–12 years; with gravel roads, it is normally of the order of 6–8 years; and for earth-surfaced roads it is as short as 3–5 years, depending on the climate. Rural road networks are confronted by a special difficulty – many carry very little traffic, although these modest vehicle flows may be vital to sustain local communities.

There seems to have been a reluctance among all concerned to confront the unfortunate issue of the very low demands in many areas. Construction is the easy part, as there is a never-ending stream of donors willing to finance capital investment. But roads incur recurrent costs if their initial effects are to be sustained into the creation of long term impacts, and these are high measured against locally generated budgets.

Financial Realities

The financial realities of sustaining road networks can best be illustrated by some simple calculations, based on realistic estimated values. Under African conditions, 1km of rural road might have an influence area of 10km² (5km either side), or influence a population of 200, some 30 households. Since the annualized cost of maintenance per km is of the order of US$500 for an earth road and US$1500 for a gravel road, the yearly cost per household (US$17–50) is significant. This is because, although the notional gross national product (GNP) per capita per year for sub–Saharan Africa is some US$540, the actual cash income for many rural households living at subsistence level is likely to be of the order of US$100 or less per annum. Even if it were possible to tax such households efficiently, which has defeated generations of administrators and is not even feasible in the much more controlled urban areas, any realistic taxation rate would evidently still not yield sufficient revenue to pay for road maintenance.

The constraint imposed by financial realities is not one which has been heeded by politicians, and the length of road systems has expanded substantially even during the so-called 'lost decade' of the 1980s and the depressed 1990s. Tanzania again provides a reasonably typical example. The aggregate length of its trunk, main and district road categories more than doubled from around 24,000km in 1972 to some 51,000km in 1997. Continentally, the UN Economic Commission for Africa remains committed to the notion of trans-African highway networks, with the southern terminus presumably in Cape Town, although the additional route length does not represent new construction since South Africa already possesses an excellent highway system and, in this respect, is an exception. It has been argued elsewhere that the whole vision of the trans-African highway system needs to be rethought to conform to financial realities (Howe, 1997). Suffice to note here that the continuing calls for its construction are a triumph of notions of status over common sense. A continent with a 1996 external debt of US$305 billion clearly cannot afford such extravagance unless there is compelling evidence that it would provide the catalyst to accelerate economic growth. Unfortunately there is no scientific basis for such a claim; quite the reverse. The consensus of experience supports the view that investment in road infrastructure is a comparatively crude instrument for stimulating economic activity: sometimes it does and sometimes it does not. When it fails, the opportunity costs, in the form of the legacy of debt servicing, can be high, as both Brazil and Nigeria have discovered. Investment has to be carefully targeted and not based on the assumption that economic growth follows automatically.

Too Many Roads?

The scale and intractability of sub-Saharan Africa's road network problem prompt the question: Does it have too many roads? This has already been alleged by the World Bank, but only in a qualitative rather than quantified way: 'while Africa is underequipped in relation to its potential it is overburdened by the little infrastructure it possesses' (Riverson et al, 1991). The 1994 World Development Report offered further quantified support to this notion (World Bank, 1994). It shows a correlation, for all developing countries, between paved roads per million population and notional GNP per capita in purchasing power parity dollars. It is notable that the majority of the African countries are well above the trend line. A similar conclusion can be drawn from the road condition surveys referred to previously, which reveal that most countries are able to finance no more than 25–30 per cent of their nominal maintenance requirements. Even these proportions are over-estimates since much is spent on the wages of overstaffed public works departments rather than productive work.

Lack of finance will result in attrition of the network and has already done so, although not in any strongly rational way since the political instinct is to spread available money as thinly as possible over the entire network in order to benefit the maximum number of people. While this is understandable, it does not necessarily constitute the best use of these resources. In most countries some degree of network reduction is likely to be necessary, although it will be fiercely resisted. It will happen in any event due to attrition: the choice is to manage the process in a rational way or to have it occur haphazardly.

What Needs to be Done?

Recent surveys in four African countries (Ethiopia, Lesotho, Tanzania and Uganda) indicate that – over and above other resource problems – finance is the binding constraint on rural road network sustainability (Howe et al, 1998). However, international experience suggests that the problem lies as much with the misallocation of financial resources as with their absence – specifically a destructive emphasis on construction to the almost complete neglect of maintenance. It is notable that in most of the study countries, road investment has been for rehabilitation rather than the opening up of completely new routes. The very notion of rehabilitation is indicative of a failed maintenance policy – ie, the construction–lack of maintenance–deterioration cycle has been gone through at least once. This raises the question: Why it is so difficult to obtain political and local support for more sensible road investment policies? Part of the explanation may lie in the focus, language and process of communication.

Road network finance is normally discussed as an element of the government budgetary process. There is no concern with the inherent value of the assets that are being created or whether that asset base is increasing, which any meaningful interpretation of the term 'development' would appear to require. The normal dialogue is technocratic and conducted in terms that only the initiated really understand – 'routine', 'recurrent' and 'periodic' maintenance, 'optimal grading', 'regravelling cycles', etc. It usually passes as a plea from the technically literate to those who do not really comprehend these terms to place their faith in the technocrat's proposals. Experience from the Road Maintenance Initiative and elsewhere indicates that for rural road network sustainability to be a realistic prospect, first the operational model needs to be more strongly focused on the conservation of the asset base that is created by progressive investment in a road network, and, second, the language and process of dialogue need to be changed.

Managing Rural Road Networks Using the Asset Value Approach

The previous situation, which is common in many countries, has led to proposals for road network management strategies based on a concept that is readily understandable by a wide range of decision-makers at all levels in the administrative hierarchy – the conservation of the inherent asset value of the network expressed in money terms. (The notion of asset-based management has arisen from the joint work of the World Bank and the German aid agency Gesellschaft für Technische Zusammenarbeit (GTZ) under the Road Maintenance Initiative, and is practised by other utilities such as the water sector and metropolitan boroughs in the UK: see Metschies, 1998; Banyard and Bostock, 1998). The basic idea is very simple:

- The current asset value of any road network can be estimated in monetary terms with reasonable accuracy at a particular point in time, in the same manner as the balance sheet of a company.
- Lack of maintenance will result in the deterioration of the network by physical attrition due to the effects of climate and traffic, which implies a continuous decrease in its asset value. Earth and many lightly gravelled roads will deteriorate to the point at which they are unusable, except with great difficulty, in as short a time as three to five years, depending on location. This is a matter of common experience; therefore it is easy to reach agreement on what sort of interval should be assumed for estimation purposes.

- While investment in the rehabilitation of currently unusable routes or the addition of completely new roads implies an increase in the asset value of the network, this may and indeed is likely to be more than counterbalanced by the losses incurred from the non-maintenance of existing maintainable routes.
- Thus the wisdom of any investment programme and, crucially, the balance between capital and recurrent expenditure can be judged on whether or not it increases the net asset value of the network. Programmes that result in a decrease in the asset value simply cannot be regarded as developmental. Such would be the likely consequence of an over-emphasis on investment in construction relative to that in maintenance.
- Since the calculation of the outcome of various investment options is straight-forward and only in money terms, then these options could be carried out in a participatory manner so that local decision-makers could determine for themselves the financial consequences of their own proposed actions.

In essence, such an approach is likely to require giving first funding priority to the regular routine maintenance of all roads in a maintainable condition, and only under-taking further investment in rehabilitation once this objective has been satisfactorily secured.

The data in Table 4.1 will be used to illustrate the principles of the asset value approach using supplementary data from Kibaale district, Uganda. This is for illustrative purposes only, but does impart a degree of realism to the calculations. The table is a simplified version of an original based on Rwanda, which incorporated the notion of a road fund to determine appropriate fuel taxation levels, and gives figures for an entire national road network. However, the principle can easily be adapted to a typical rural district (Metschies, 1998). In this respect the most important figures are those which indicate asset values and maintenance requirements for gravel and earth roads, in columns 3 and 6 respectively. Asset replacement values are estimated at US$50,000 and US$10,000 per km, and annual maintenance requirements at 3 per cent and 5 per cent of these figures, respectively.

Kibaale District Road Network

Kibaale district is thought to have a nominal feeder road network of about 470km. Allocation into gravel and earth roads is more problematic since, due to the prevailing lack of maintenance and climate-induced deterioration, conditions change substantially within two to three years. Present informed opinion is that some 250km of the network is in a maintainable condition, with the remaining 220km having 'returned to the bush' due to lack of maintenance.

Core assumptions

In the first scenario (Case 1), roads in a maintainable condition will be treated as having an earth surface with an asset value of US$10,000 per km, and annual maintenance will be assumed to be 5 per cent of their asset value. With nil maintenance, it is

Table 4.1 *Financing of rural road maintenance – the Rwandan case*

Road surface	Length		Asset replacement value per km	Total asset replacement value	Total network value		Annual maintenance requirement[1]		$/km pa	Yearly expenditure road maintenance[2]		Rule of thumb for national road maintenance funds
	km	%	$/km	million $		%	% of asset value[3]			million $	%	%
	(1)	(2)	(3)	(4=1*3)	(5)		(6)	(7)		(8=4*7)	(9)	(10)
Asphalt	900	7.3	400,000[4]	360	60		1.5	6000		5.40	36	–
Gravel	2500	20.2	50,000	125	20		3.0	1500		3.75	25	65–70
Earth	8500	68.5[5]	10,000	85	14		5.0[6]	500[6]		4.25	28	20–25
Urban road	500	4.0	80,000	40	6		4.0	3200		1.60	11	10
TOTAL	12,400	100.0	–	610[7]	100		2.5[8]	–		15.00	100	100

Notes:

1 Costs comprise labour-intensive routine recurrent maintenance and periodic maintenance. Maintenance for asphalt roads (resealing) is needed every eight years and for gravel roads (refilling) is needed every five years, as well as spot reconstructions.

2 This table is without backlog requirements of previous years and without new construction or rehabilitation.

3 Empirical assumptions are according to road surface classes.

4 The value of 1km of asphalt road (2cm double surface dressing) is US$400,000.

5 More than two-thirds of the network are rural roads (earth roads).

6 According to the lengthman system: two men for 3km (US$1 per working day + equipment + supervision).

7 The total asset replacement value of US$610 million is equivalent to 41 per cent of the GNP of the country.

8 The total expenditure needs of US$15 million may also be obtained by generally applying 2.5 per cent to the asset value of US$610 million of the total network.

assumed that the roads will deteriorate to 40 per cent of their nominal asset value (ie, to an impassable condition) over a three-year period. The roads that have 'returned to the bush' may be unusable, but they still have a residual asset value since the right-of-way is usually preserved, albeit overgrown, along with some earthworks, drainage and possibly structures. These roads are valued at 40 per cent of their asset value and are assumed to have a zero annual maintenance cost. In Box 4.1, the asset balance after three years as a result of different investment strategies can be examined.

Box 4.1 *Comparing asset values*

Case 1
Nil maintenance: Year 1 asset balance
Asset value of road in maintainable condition 250km @ US$10,000 = US$2,500,000
Asset value of non-maintainable road 220km @ US$10,000 × 0.4 = US$1,000,000
Total asset value = US$3,500,000

Annual maintenance cost for a stable network is @ 5 per cent of the asset value of those in a maintainable condition = US$125,000. If this were spent on maintenance then the network would have the same asset value in Year 3.

Assume that the cost of rehabilitating other roads in a non-maintainable condition is US$6000 per km, based on experience in Kibaale district, and that for three years the nominal maintenance money is spent for this purpose instead of maintenance, then 3 × US$125,000/6000km can be rehabilitated = 62.5km.

The expected asset balance will then be as follows:
Year 3
Reduced asset value due to nil maintenance of roads in a maintainable condition in Year 1 250km @ US$10,000 × 0.4 = US$1,000,000
Asset value of non-maintainable road (220–62.5km) @ US$10,000 × 0.4 = US$630,000
Asset value of 62.5km of rehabilitated road @ 6000 = US$375,000

Total asset value = US$2,005,000
Net asset loss Year 1–3 = US$1,495,000
It would be difficult to argue that such an investment balance is developmental and yet this approximates to what many countries are actually doing.

Case 2
Assume roads are partly gravelled in order that they could justifiably be considered to have a higher asset value of, say, US$30,000 with an annual maintenance esti-mated at 4 per cent of this sum. With nil maintenance it can be assumed that the roads will deteriorate to 40 per cent of their nominal asset value (ie to an impass-able condition) over a five-year period. Using a similar logic as for Case 1, it can be shown that:

net asset loss Years 1–5 = US$4,000,000

Conclusion

These examples are simplistic, but all of the assumptions are close to real values. Moreover, they represent what has actually been happening in many rural areas and illustrate why the three stage cycle of rehabilitate–inadequate maintenance–deteriorate is so economically wasteful; and the assumptions can easily be changed until a consensus is reached that they reflect local experiences and values.

It is then possible to vary the rehabilitation maintenance expenditure ratios over a range of values to reflect various options, and for the decision-makers themselves to determine what happens to the net asset value of the network as a result. Since the calculations are no more than simple arithmetic, non-technical people can readily understand them. It seems likely that most will also agree that investment policy is not really serving a development purpose if, as a result, the asset value is actually decreasing.

Notes

1   This chapter was first published as a paper in *World Transport Policy & Practice*, vol 5, no 1, pp11–16.

References

Banyard, J K and Bostock, J W (1998) 'Asset management – investment planning for utilities' *Proceedings of the Institution of Civil Engineers, Civil Engineering*, vol 126, May, pp65–72

Howe, J (1997) 'Africa's highway network: re-thinking the vision' in Dick, A (ed) *Global Highways in the 21st Century*, Atalink Project, London

Howe, J, Jennings, M and Savage, C (1998) 'Study of Irish aid road projects – Ethiopia, Lesotho, Tanzania, Uganda', *Irish Aid Evaluation Report*, IHE, Delft, The Netherlands, November

Metschies, G (1998) *Financing and Institutional Aspects of Rural Roads*, paper presented at 3rd International Workshop on Secondary Rural Roads, 19–21 May, Josefow, Poland

Riverson, J D N, Gavira, J and Thriscutt, S (1991) *Rural Roads in Sub-Saharan Africa – Lessons from World Bank Experience*, World Bank Technical Paper No 141 Africa, Technical Department Series, World Bank, Washington, DC

Sylte, O K (1996) *Review of the Road Sector in Selected Common Market for Eastern and Southern Africa (COMESA) Countries*, SSATP Working Paper No 23, The World Bank and UN Economic Commission for Africa, Washington, DC

Sylte, O K (1997) *The Road Sector in ECOWAS Countries: A Comparative Assessment*, World Bank Seminar on Management and Financing of Roads, Abidjan, 2–6 June

World Bank (1981) *The Road Maintenance Problem and International Assistance*, World Bank, Washington, DC

World Bank (1994) 'Infrastructure for development', *World Development Report 1994*, World Bank, Washington, DC

Part 3

Transport in Asia

5

Southeast Asian Urban Transport: A Kaleidoscope of Challenges and Choices

Paul Barter

Southeast Asia is a region of remarkable contrasts in urban transport: an interesting laboratory of urban transport practice (and perhaps malpractice). There are wide variations from city to city in the mode of transport that predominates. For example, public transport is very important in large Philippine cities, while the private car has become the primary mode in Malaysian cities and Vietnam's urban areas have for decades been dominated by two-wheel transport – formerly by bicycles and recently by motorcycles. The region also has a colourful array of unusual transport modes, including pedicabs with almost as many names and designs as there are countries, bicycle taxis, motorcycle taxis, a number of variations on the jitney, a type of small bus (including Manila's jeepneys), and Jakarta's *mikrolet*.

There are also huge variations in the degree of success in meeting the various transport challenges. Chapter 6 focuses on Bangkok, a city that has become a symbol of serious urban transport woes. It also mentions the experience of Singapore, whose success story has become an icon and which stands in marked contrast to Bangkok's apparent failure.

This chapter focuses on urban transport and highlights a series of important issues for the region by choosing certain experiences of individual cities as case studies. For a more systematic, data-oriented approach see Barter, Kenworthy and Laube (2001).

Jakarta

Jakarta highlights two important themes, both of which reflect social polarization. Despite a car ownership rate of almost 100 per 1000 persons and a motorcycle ownership rate of almost 170 per 1000 persons, Jakarta nevertheless has rather low rates of motorized travel per person (Kenworthy and Laube, 2001). Walking remains very important for the bulk of the low income population, with approximately 46 per cent or so of all trips being made on foot. The public transport system generally provides a poor service with insufficient capacity throughout the long peak periods. Low fares and grave inefficiencies in the operation and governance of public transport reduce the potential to improve services, especially since the regional financial crisis has raised costs and squeezed revenues further. Large numbers of people cannot afford to use public transport daily even at current fares.

Assault on non-motorized taxis (pedicabs)

Jakarta has seen a concerted assault on the role of pedicabs, known in Indonesia as *becak* (pronounced 'bay-chuck'). This issue highlights official and elite views that mobility in motor vehicles is more important than local access (especially if it is in slow-moving, human-powered vehicles that obstruct 'real' traffic). It also represents a failure to empathize realistically with the poor.

After many years of tightening restrictions, pedicabs were banned in Jakarta in 1988. However, during 1998 as a response to the economic crisis and at the urging of local social activists, Jakarta's Governor Sutiyoso announced the lifting of the ban. However, he did this without first repealing the 1988 law, and soon faced strong criticism from the city council. After only one week the policy was reversed and pedicabs again began to be confiscated. Nevertheless, thousands of pedicab drivers had already flooded into the city from the outlying provinces, where they had never been banned.

Ever since mid-1998 pedicabs have continued to ply the streets and alleys of Jakarta in defiance of the law and have organized themselves into a Pedicab Drivers' Network (which was 3000 strong by late 1998). A large demonstration in October 1998 resulted in the release of all confiscated pedicabs to their owners. Unfortunately, this reprieve ended in November 1999, when President Abdurrahman Wahid defended the ban on pedicabs 'on humanitarian grounds', saying the drivers worked 'like horses' and that they needed to be found other jobs (*Jakarta Post*, 1999a). This prompted Governor Sutiyoso to order the authorities to again 'begin cleansing the city's streets of *becak*' (*Jakarta Post*, 1999b). At the time of writing (September 2001), there is no resolution. The debate remains polarized and the defiance of the pedicab drivers and their supporters continues, as do the efforts of the city authorities to eliminate them. August and September 2001 have seen sometimes violent confiscations of almost 2000 pedicabs as well as some angry and violent retaliations.

Indonesian fuel subsidy blues

A second issue that Jakarta (and Indonesia generally) illustrates clearly is the vexed, even tragic, issue of fuel subsidies and the difficult politics of removing them. Even after some reductions in the subsidy, a large proportion of petrol costs in Indonesia is still subsidized and a government study has shown that a very large percentage of this benefit goes to high income earners who own and drive cars (*Straits Times*, 2001). Since late 1997, the International Monetary Fund (IMF) has been urging the elimination of the subsidy. Ironically, the most violent objections come from forces representing the poor. This is because of fears over the price of kerosene in particular (which is used as a fuel for cooking) and concern over rising prices of other essential goods and public transport. These fears are well founded, since public transport operators and retailers often use fuel price rises as opportunities to increase their prices (despite the fact that fuel is a relatively small percentage of their total costs). The poor are extremely vulnerable to even modest inflation in essential goods. So, tragically, poor people oppose the removal of a subsidy that primarily benefits the very rich!

Recently, the new government of Megawati Sukarnoputri proposed another 30 per cent increase in gasoline prices (*Straits Times*, 2001). This follows a similar increase in June 2001, which coincided with steep rises in food prices, and triggered a round of violent protests in many cities. Such events are extremely alarming for Indonesians, who remember clearly that fuel price rises were the initial trigger for the May 1998 riots which led to the toppling of President Suharto.

A sustainable and equitable approach to this issue demands that fuel subsidies be removed. But the transition pain for the poor certainly needs to be addressed. The government has had great difficulty communicating the rationale for the change to the public and has apparently been unable to develop a convincing package to ease the initial pain of the reform felt by the poor. Societies such as Japan, South Korea and most European countries had rather high fuel prices for most of the decades since World War Two. These high prices probably actually benefited the poor by slowing down motorization (even if only a little) and by helping the alternatives to private vehicles to remain viable even as incomes rose (Barter, 1999).

Bangkok: Traffic Saturated and in Need of Good Governance

With regard to Bangkok, two issues stand out. Firstly, Bangkok, with its extreme levels of traffic congestion and traffic impacts, and public transport speeds of only 10km/h, can be characterized more accurately as private vehicle-saturated rather than automobile dependent. Bangkok has had rapid motorization within its relatively dense urban fabric since the late 1990s, but it has not yet significantly reoriented its urban fabric to accommodate private vehicles. It offers a warning for large, dense cities that traffic saturation can easily emerge quickly with even moderate motorization (Barter, 2000). Secondly, Bangkok shows starkly that a lack of effective urban governance is a huge obstacle to effective policy-making and its implementation (Poboon, 1997). Bangkok's fragmentation of urban transport decision-making is almost legendary, but it is by no means unique in this respect.

Ho Chi Minh: Motorcycle City

The dangers of the 'Bangkok syndrome' loom large for Ho Chi Minh, which has a particularly high urban density (higher than Hong Kong, despite a generally low rise urban fabric) (Kenworthy and Laube, 2001). A highly space-efficient urban transport strategy focused on the most space-efficient modes, walking and public transport, would seem to be imperative here. However, along with other Vietnamese cities, Ho Chi Minh currently has the distinction of having some of the lowest levels of public transport service and usage of any large city, with only 2 per cent of mechanized trips being made on public transport (MVA Consultancy, 1997).

In fact, Vietnamese cities seem to be pioneering a completely new kind of urban transport system, one based almost completely on motorcycles, having recently shifted rapidly from relying on bicycles. A number of other southeast Asian cities (in Cambodia, Thailand, Indonesia and Malaysia) also have quite high rates of motorcycle ownership (and rather poor public transport), but none so high as Vietnam. Ho Chi Minh's motorcycle-dominated situation is unprecedented and it is unclear what policies and trends to expect or recommend. Is a motorcycle-dominated system viable in the long term in a potentially richer Ho Chi Minh, given that even small numbers of cars will quickly lead to gridlock in this very dense city? There are no examples elsewhere to look to for successful transitions from a totally two-wheeler-based transport system towards, for example, a larger role for public transport.

This case highlights the urgent need for a wide-ranging debate on the role of motorcycles, which is of relevance also in China, south Asia and certain African countries (Burkina Faso in particular). Motorcycles are extremely problematic in many ways (especially on safety and environmental grounds, and for the viability of public transport) but they do provide rather affordable mobility. So what is an appropriate, sustainable and equitable policy, taking into account long term synergies with public transport and urban land use patterns?

The Vietnamese experience also highlights the vulnerability and fragility of a prominent role for bicycles. They are especially vulnerable to being displaced by small motorcycles, which nearly match the agility and ease of bicycles in terms of parking, have a wider range and command higher status. Non-motorized transport, particularly bicycle use, is also especially vulnerable and easily discouraged by hostile street conditions.

Manila

Manila is used here to illustrate a potential opportunity offered by the urban structure that has emerged in a number of large southeast Asian cities. Bangkok, Jakarta and Manila all display a pattern of intense commercial development extending in corridors along major thoroughfares throughout the inner areas of the city. This unplanned pattern has some problems but may also offer potential to be later fitted with reasonably effective mass transit. Furthermore, in Manila a polycentric pattern of major sub-centres has emerged in response to the city's radial and circumferential road pattern. Important concentrations of jobs and services have appeared where radial roads intersect with 'EDSA' (the major orbital road, approximately 8km from the centre). The successful privately planned and developed sub-centres of Makati and Cubao, which began to thrive in the 1960s, are examples (Electrowatt Engineering Services and Pak-Poy and Kneebone, 1985). In many ways Makati now rivals the old central business district (CBD). The process of linking these sub-centres with quality, high capacity mass transit has begun: the city's new second mass transit line runs in a circumferential route along EDSA, but it is too soon to judge how successful this will be.

Transport and housing for the urban poor

Another dimension that is well documented for Manila is not so positive. This relates to how transport interacts with the lack of housing rights and tenure security for low income residents (Williams and Barter, 2001). For example, transport projects are unfortunately an important cause of the eviction and resettlement of low income people. In Metro Manila, an unusually close watch is kept on evictions by the non-governmental organization Urban Poor Associates (2000a; 2000b; 2001). Large numbers of people are threatened with eviction by transport projects in the Manila area. The Department of Public Works and Highways (DPWH) estimates that Radial Road 10 (a road expansion project funded by the national government) will require the resettlement of 10,000 families. The Philippine National Railways Road Widening, Skyway and Beautification project (a road and railway project) would displace an estimated 15,000 families. Circumferential Road 5 (C-5) is estimated to threaten more than 10,000 urban poor families. Two major rail projects in and beyond the Manila region threaten about 44,000 families with eviction. These figures emphasize the desirability of minimizing the space consumed by transport infrastructure in dense cities and the importance of establishing fair and consistent procedures for any resettlement that is unavoidable.

Another transport connection with evictions is that, whatever the cause of the eviction, many communities are involuntarily relocated to inaccessible (usually peripheral) locations. For reasons of cost, governments frequently site housing for low income households (including those who have been relocated) in peripheral locations. An example from the Manila area is typical (Urban Poor Associates, 2000b):

> Somewhere in Montalban, Rizal, mountains have been literally moved to pave way for Erap City… Montalban is a great distance from Makati, Manila, Mandaluyong, Pasig, Quezon City – the places Erap City residents were relocated from. Commuting to and from work, therefore, has become more expensive. As a result, some relocatees have resorted to renting rooms near their places of work and go home only on weekends. Others simply try to cope with the drastic increase in expenses. The more unfortunate lost their jobs… Other problems cited include uncooperative local governments, the lack of schools and health centres, the lack of livelihood opportunities, maintenance of peace and order, the possibility of flooding and the lack of financial support from government.

Surabaya: Traffic-free *Kampung* but Hostile Main Roads

Indonesia's second city, Surabaya, with about 4 million people, can be used here to highlight one positive issue and one negative. The positive issue relates to the city's low income vernacular settlements. These areas, known as *kampung*, have now mostly been improved with paved alleyways, drainage, plantings for shade and improved security of tenure under the long-running Kampung Improvement Programme (KIP) (Silas, 1989). They have become surprisingly high quality low cost neighbourhoods. They tend to be traffic-free by virtue of their narrow alleyways and the fact that the residents demand that motorcyclists dismount when they enter. Transport can also play a role in preserving inner-city low income areas from the threat of gentrification. In Surabaya, a conscious decision was taken to avoid providing four-wheeled-vehicle access into *kampung* in the inner city. The policy is said to have been successful in slowing gentrification (Silas, 2000).

The negative issue highlighted by Surabaya is traffic management on the main roads, which is extremely unfriendly to pedestrians and non-motorized vehicles. The swirling one-way traffic systems minimize traffic lights and offer continuous private traffic flows at the expense of public transport convenience, non-motorized vehicles and pedestrian safety. This traffic management philosophy is also marked by increasing numbers of overhead pedestrian bridges, which generally work to speed up traffic rather than benefit pedestrians.

Klang Valley: Kuala Lumpur's Metropolitan Region

Klang Valley in Kuala Lumpur's metropolitan region is used here to illustrate two issues. Firstly, along with Brunei's Bandar Seri Begawan, Malaysian cities are the only Asian urban areas so far to confront the possibility of becoming automobile-dependent, in the sense of building in high car use as a fundamental feature of their urban fabric (Barter, 2001). Malaysian cities have reached a point in their motorization where the challenges associated with transport are beginning to have much in common with those in the wealthy countries of western Europe, North America and Oceania. The Klang Valley is much less dense than Bangkok and most other Asian cities, allowing it to avoid becoming so severely traffic saturated but increasing the danger of car dependence setting in. Malaysian urban areas have not progressed as far along the path of automobile dependence as cities in North America, Australia or New Zealand. Nevertheless, there is considerable evidence of momentum towards more automobile dependence, including increasing signs of car-oriented land use development patterns, continued rapid motorization and continued heavy investment in a dense network of expressways. In addition, since 1990 the role of public transport has dropped to very low levels (less than 10 per cent of motorized trips), which will be difficult to reverse even with the investment in expanding mass transit that is also taking place.

Gender and transport

Transport planning in most places has so far failed to be gender-aware or gender-sensitive (Peters, 1998). An anecdote from the Klang Valley can be used to illustrate some of these issues. Women often face particular transport-related hardships as a result of their multiple duties in households and communities. For example, Eli is a woman in her forties who works as a cleaner. She is wholly dependent on her husband and his motorcycle to take her to her various places of employment as there are no other means of reaching the houses where she works. Cross-suburban travel by public transport is almost impossible for her as it would involve walking long distances from the bus drop-off points, and a very long wait for hourly services that are often late. Her reliance on her husband for transport frustrates her and her husband (even more so when it starts raining!), yet she is left with no choice as her options for employment are restricted and determined not only by the labour market, but by the work she is expected to perform at home (Zaitun and Barter, 2001).

Singapore: Deliberately Slowed Motorization Pays Off

One of the most important lessons from Singapore's experience, along with those of Hong Kong, Japanese cities, Korean cities and many western European cities, is that deliberately slowing down (or delaying) the motorization process is often an important factor in easing the task of creating a balanced and effective transport system (Barter, 1999). Singapore began to restrain motorization in the early 1970s, when car ownership was well below 100 per 1000 persons. This policy helped prevent rapid motorization from undermining the role of public transport and instead allowed the role of public transport to build up gradually in conditions of rising incomes but low vehicle numbers and relatively low pressure to invest heavily in roads. The delay in motorization meant that spending on expensive public transport infrastructure such as mass transit could be delayed until it was affordable and yet still be guaranteed high levels of use when it was finally completed in the late 1980s. This is in contrast to the experiences of Kuala Lumpur and Bangkok, where unrestrained motorization has led to congestion and modal competition, causing bus services and usage to deteriorate, intense pressure to expand roads, and making investments in mass transit less viable.

Conclusion

This brief review of southeast Asian cities is intended to raise a number of the key issues for the region. It also suggests that some key choices and dilemmas are central to urban transport policy in the region. The challenges are great, but it is not all bad news. There has been no attempt at a comprehensive comparative perspective. However, this review hopefully has provided the context for the more detailed discussions provided by the other chapters in this section.

References

Barter, P (1999) *An International Comparative Perspective on Urban Transport and Urban Form in Pacific Asia: The Challenge of Rapid Motorisation in Dense Cities*, unpublished PhD dissertation, Murdoch University, Perth, Western Australia

Barter, P (2000) 'Transport dilemmas in dense urban areas: examples from eastern Asia' in Jenks, M and Burgess, R (eds) *Compact Cities: Sustainable Urban Forms for Developing Countries*, Spon Press, London

Barter, P (2001) *Towards Eastern Asia's First Automobile Dependent City? Transport and Space in the Klang Valley Urban Region*, paper presented to the Third International Malaysian Studies Conference, 6–8 August, Universiti Kebangsaan Malaysia, Bangi, Malaysia

Barter, P, Kenworthy, J and Laube, F (2001) 'Lessons from Asia on sustainable urban transport' in Low, N and Gleeson, B (eds) *Earth on the Move,* Palgrave, Basingstoke

Electrowatt Engineering Services and Pak-Poy and Kneebone (1985) *Metrorail Network Options Feasibility Study* (Volume 1), Ministry of Transportation and Communications, Manila

Jakarta Post (1999a) 'President Abdurrahman defends ban on "becak"', 21 November, p1

Jakarta Post (1999b) 'Sutiyoso firm on "becak" raids', 22 November, p3

Kenworthy, J and Laube, F (2001) *UITP Millennium Cities Database for Sustainable Transport* (CD database), International Union (Association) of Public Transport (UITP), Brussels

MVA Consultancy (1997) *Ho Chi Minh City Transport Study: Diagnostic Report,* Transport and Urban Public Works Service of Ho Chi Minh City, Vietnam

Peters, D (1998) 'Breadwinners, homemakers, beasts of burden: a gender perspective on transport and mobility', *Habitat Debate,* vol 4, no 2, http://www.unchs.org/unchs/english/hdv4n2/forum.htm#5

Poboon, C (1997) *Anatomy of a Traffic Disaster: Towards a Sustainable Solution to Bangkok's Transport Problems,* unpublished PhD Dissertation, Murdoch University, Perth, Western Australia

Silas, J (1983) 'Spatial structure, housing delivery, land tenure and urban poor in Surabaya, Indonesia' in Angel, S, Archer, R W, Tanphiphat, S and Wegelin, E A (eds), *Land for Housing the Poor,* Select Book, Singapore

Silas, J (1989) 'Marginal settlements in Surabaya, Indonesia: problems or potential?', *Environment and Urbanization,* vol 1, October

Silas, J (2000) interview, October

Straits Times (2001) 'Fuel subsidies that benefit mainly the rich are slashed', 8 September

Urban Poor Associates (2000a) *1999 Demolition Monito,* http://www.codewan.com.ph/balay/updates/monitor99_0623.htm, accessed January 2001

Urban Poor Associates (2000b) *Resettling Communities,* http://www.codewan.com.ph/balay/updates/resettling_0727.doc, accessed January 2001

Urban Poor Associates (2001) *Year 2000 Demolition Monitor (Second Quarter Report and End-of-year Report),* http://www.codewan.com.ph/balay/updates/, accessed January 2001

Williams, B and Barter, P (2001) 'Double jeopardy: the link between transport and evictions', *Habitat Debate,* vol 7, no 3, http://www.unchs.org/hd/hdv7n3/9.htm

Zaitun, M K and Barter, P (2001) *Zero Visibility: A Call for More Attention to the Neglected Area of Gender in Transport Planning in Malaysia,* presented at the National Seminar on Sustainable Transport Issues and Challenges in Malaysia, RECSAM, organized by the Consumers Association of Penang and Sahabat Alam Malaysia, 7–11 September, Pulau Pinang

6

Automobile Dependence in Bangkok: An International Comparison with Implications for Planning Policies

Jeff Kenworthy

Introduction

Any discussion of automobile dependence today will usually involve some reference to Los Angeles. As an archetype for cities that have tried to build their transport systems almost totally around freeways – and failed – it is almost unparalleled. However, the Asian region is rapidly developing its own archetype of urban traffic dysfunction: the Bangkok metropolitan region. Interestingly, by a perverse coincidence, the similarities between Los Angeles and Bangkok today also have some deeper historical significance.

In 1781, the Spanish governor of California, Felipe de Neve, established the community that is known today as Los Angeles or the City of Angels. In 1782, in an almost prophetic leap that would seal a strange connection between the two places, King Rama I of Thailand established a new capital for his country, the original name of which translates as the Great City of the Angels.

Whether any more should be read into this coincidence depends a little on one's penchant for intrigue. But for those who once knew Bangkok as the Venice of the East with its serpentine river and network of canals, the unfortunate reality is that it is fast becoming the Los Angeles of the East. Most canals have been paved over with roads (which are now congested). Elevated freeways and spaghetti junctions punctuate the urban landscape. The air is so laden with automotive air and noise emissions that walking outside is an ordeal; and, in true Los Angelino style, there are plans to turn the Chao Phraya River into a floating freeway. Bangkok presently adds approximately about 600 new cars daily to the traffic stream, which equates to an extra 3kms of bumper-to-bumper traffic. At this rate, in less than four years, a sufficient number of cars are added to fill the entire road system with one lane of traffic.

Bangkok's traffic predicament raises some interesting questions about how a city can descend into such chaos and what factors underlie the situation. Importantly, it raises questions about what policies and strategies are best for relieving the situation, irrespective of the present political likelihood of realizing them. An effective way of providing the perspectives needed to answer these questions is to compare Bangkok to other cities around the world, especially other Asian cities in the region.

This chapter provides a detailed comparison of Bangkok's land use and transport system characteristics with cities in North America, Europe and Australia and, in particular, other Asian cities such as Kuala Lumpur, Jakarta, Manila, Seoul, Surabaya, Singapore, Hong Kong and Tokyo.[1] The data on the developing Asian cities (other than Bangkok) are taken from Barter et al (1994); Bangkok data are taken from Poboon et al (1994).[2] On the basis of this investigation, the chapter highlights those areas of planning policy that need attention and suggests a suite of policies that are likely to improve the present transport situation in Bangkok.

Land Use Patterns

One of the most important factors in determining a city's level of car use and the viability of public transport, walking and cycling is urban density (Newman and Kenworthy, 1989). Higher densities, and the mixed land uses that are associated with them, shorten the length of trips by all modes, make walking and cycling possible for more trips and create sufficient concentrations of activities for an effective, frequent public transport service. Figure 6.1 depicts the relationship between urban density, energy use per capita and the percentage of workers using public transport across a global sample of cities. As can be seen from the graph, higher urban densities, particularly those characteristic of Asian cities such as Tokyo, have much lower rates of energy use per capita for transport and much higher rates of use of public transport for work trips.

Figure 6.2 provides average urban densities for selected cities in Asia, Australia, Europe and the USA. Bangkok metropolitan area, with 6 million people living at 162 persons per hectare (ha), is clearly a densely settled city in an international context,

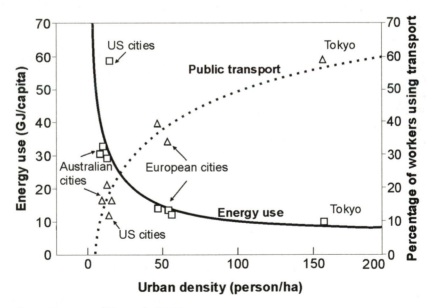

Source: Newman and Kenworthy (1999)

Figure 6.1 *Urban density, energy use and public transport for the journey to work in a global sample of cities*

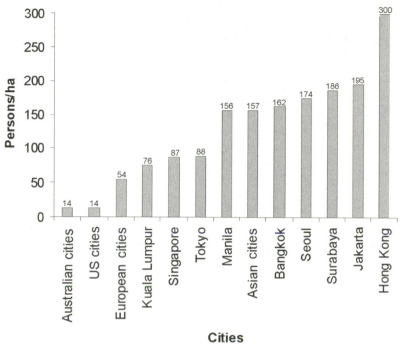

Source: Newman and Kenworthy (1999)

Figure 6.2 *Average urban densities for selected cities in Asia, Australia, Europe and the USA*

being a little above average for an Asian city. By examining densities within Bangkok it is found that the inner zone of 3 million people has a density of 257 persons per ha (virtually the same as Manhattan and central Paris), the middle zone of 2 million people is settled at 138 per ha and the outer zone of 1 million people has 74 persons per ha, which is still some five times denser than the average metropolitan area in the USA and Australia (Poboon et al, 1994). Bangkok therefore fulfils one of the chief criteria for minimizing automobile dependence.

Provision for the Automobile

Another key factor in automobile dependence is how well the automobile is catered for in basic infrastructure. The length of road per person and the amount of parking in the central business district (CBD) are indicative of this factor. Figure 6.3 summarizes the length of road per person in selected cities and shows that the Asian cities are extremely low in this factor when compared with other cities around the world (0.7m per person compared to as high as 8.7m in Australian cities). Bangkok is about average for an Asian city, but this relatively low road provision only partly helps to explain the congested traffic, as shown later. Figure 6.4 provides the number of parking spaces per

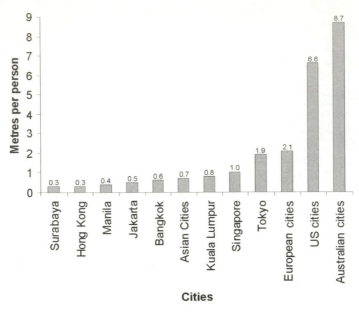

Source: Newman and Kenworthy (1999)

Figure 6.3 *Length of road per person in selected cities in Asia, Australia, Europe and the USA*

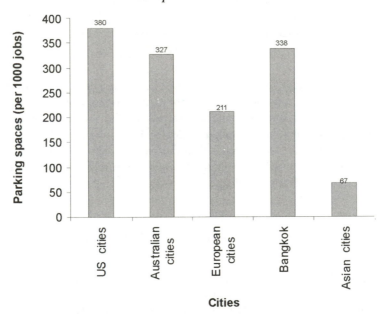

Source: Newman and Kenworthy (1999)

Figure 6.4 *Parking spaces (per 1000 jobs) in the central business district in Bangkok compared with selected cities in Asia (Hong Kong, Tokyo and Singapore), Australia, Europe and the USA*

1000 jobs and shows that Bangkok, with 338, exceeds the average Australian city and is only a little less than the average US city with 380. By contrast, Singapore, Tokyo and Hong Kong average a mere 67 spaces per 1000 CBD jobs.

Vehicle ownership varies considerably in cities around the world as shown in Figure 6.5, which summarizes car and motorcycle ownership. US and Australian cities are clear leaders in car ownership, but they have very low motorcycle ownership (95 per cent of the combined car and motorcycle ownership consists of cars). At the other end of the spectrum, Hong Kong has only 47 vehicles per 1000 people and, again, these are mainly cars (91 per cent). Bangkok is the highest of the Asian cities in total vehicle ownership (296 per 1000 people) and is only a little behind the European average of 341. However, only 56 per cent are cars in Bangkok, unlike in European cities, where 96 per cent are cars. Motorcycles are popular in Bangkok and other Asian cities such as Jakarta and Surabaya, where they dominate vehicle ownership. This is because they are cheaper, smaller and easier to park, and can cut a path through congested streets and negotiate the narrow streets of the urban *kampongs* (informal housing).

Bangkok is very much higher in total vehicle ownership than the average Asian city (296 per 1000 people compared to 167). It has double the level of the much wealthier Singapore, which has only 143 vehicles per 1000, and is even higher than Tokyo with 261 vehicles per 1000 people (although Tokyo's ownership is 86 per cent cars).

Figure 6.6 shows the paradox associated with such high levels of vehicle ownership in Bangkok by comparing national purchasing power per capita in various nations in

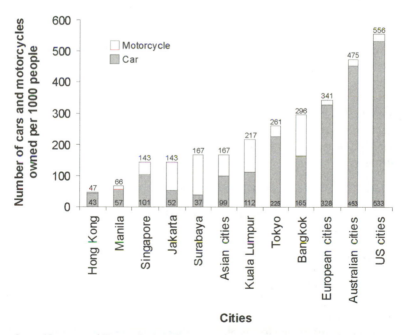

Source: Newman and Kenworthy (1999)

Note: Asian cities' figures are from 1990, the other figures are from 1980

Figure 6.5 *Car and motorcycle ownership (per 1000 people) in selected cities in Asia, Australia, Europe and the USA*

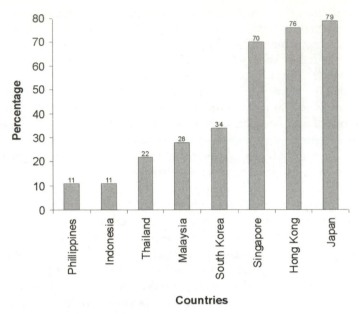

Source: Newman and Kenworthy (1999)

Figure 6.6 *National purchasing power per capita in Asian cities compared to the USA (1990)*

1990 compared to the USA. For example, Thailand had only 28 per cent of the purchasing power of Hong Kong, but Bangkok in 1990 had some six times more vehicles (cars and motorcycles) per capita. Similarly, Bangkok's car ownership is 63 per cent higher than in Singapore, but Thailand's purchasing power is only one-third that of Singapore. Wealth levels alone are clearly not the only determinants of vehicle ownership. This factor is returned to later in the chapter.

What kind of transport patterns are associated with these basic land use and transport features?

Transport Patterns

Private transport

Figure 6.7 provides the total vehicle kilometres of travel per person in the selected cities. As expected, the US and Australian cities are clear leaders (9747 and 7090km respectively), followed by European cities with much lower levels (3959km). Bangkok, however, is heavily motorized for its physical characteristics, being 74 per cent higher in vehicle use than the average Asian city. It has almost the same level of private vehicle use as Tokyo which, based on national figures in 1990, had 3.5 times more purchasing power than Bangkok. Again, there are clearly more factors than wealth at work in urban automobile dependence.

Figure 6.8 shows the modal split to private transport (including motorcycles) for all trips in a variety of Asian cities. Bangkok stands out as a leader in the Asian cities with 51 per cent of all trips by private means, compared with an overall average for these Asian cities of 33 per cent, and Manila as low as 21 per cent.

Public transport

Figure 6.9 shows that the use of public transport, expressed as transit's share of total annual passenger kilometres, is very low in US and Australian cities (4 per cent and 8 per cent respectively), while in Europe it is 25 per cent. The Asian cities in this figure are Singapore, Tokyo and Hong Kong only, which have 64 per cent of all passenger travel by public transport and which, today, are heavily dependent on rail-based transit. By comparison, Bangkok – with its gridlocked bus-only transit system – has only half this level of public transport use. Although this is quite high on an international scale, it is too low for a city such as Bangkok, with its low road provision and a dense urban fabric unsuited to accommodating automobiles. This aspect is also developed further in the chapter.

Figure 6.10 shows public transport's share of all trips for a wider range of Asian cities, and shows that Bangkok does moderately well with its basic bus system and other collective modes (33 per cent compared to an average for Asian cities of 35 per cent). Nevertheless, Manila and Seoul have much higher levels of public transport (49 per

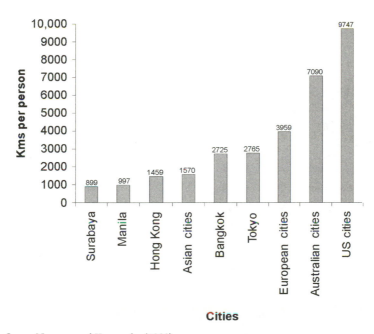

Source: Newman and Kenworthy (1999)

Figure 6.7 *Total private vehicle travel (kms per person) in selected cities in Asia, Australia, Europe and the USA*

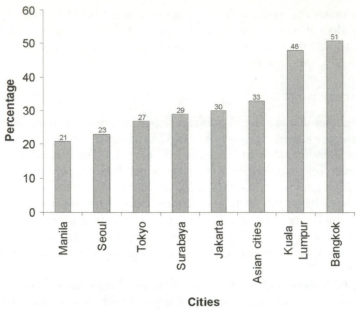

Source: Newman and Kenworthy (1999)

Figure 6.8 *The proportion of all daily trips by private transport in Asian cities*

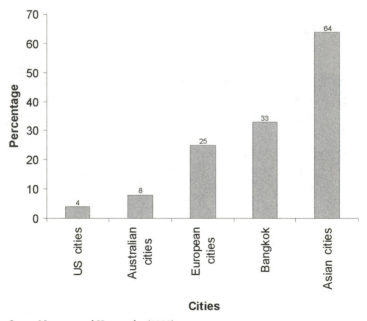

Source: Newman and Kenworthy (1999)

Figure 6.9 *The proportion of total annual passenger travel by public transport in Bangkok compared with proportion for selected cities in Asia (Hong Kong, Tokyo and Singapore) Australia, Europe and the USA*

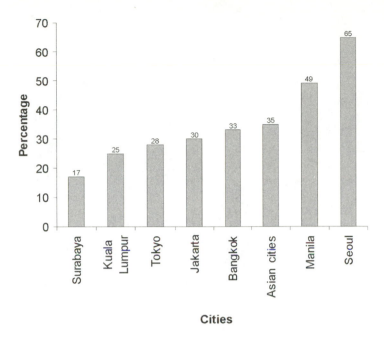

Source: Newman and Kenworthy (1999)

Figure 6.10 *The proportion of daily trips on public transport in Asian cities*

cent and 65 per cent of all trips). Figure 6.11 shows the proportion of motorized work trips on public transport for an even larger sample of cities. This is very revealing, as it shows that Bangkok has rather low use of public transport (only 10 per cent compared with an average for the Asian cities of 25 per cent.

Non-motorized modes

Figure 6.12 shows the use of walking and cycling for the journey to work in cities around the world and reveals that US and Australian cities – with their low densities, heavily-zoned land uses and long trips – have only 5 per cent of workers walking or cycling; European and Asian cities have 21 per cent and 25 per cent respectively; while Bangkok is very low with only 10 per cent. Figure 6.13 shows that, as a percentage of all daily trips, levels of walking and cycling in Bangkok are relatively low for Asian cities (14 per cent, or less than half of the Asian city average of 32 per cent). Tokyo, on the other hand, has a massive 45 per cent of all trips on foot and by bicycle, exceeded in this sample only by Surabaya, with 53 per cent.

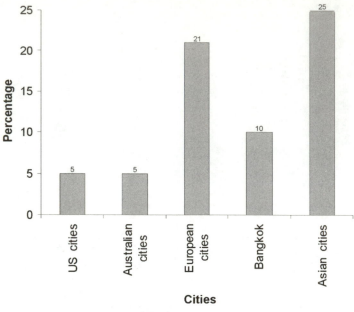

Source: Newman and Kenworthy (1999)

Figure 6.11 *The proportion of motorized work trips on public transport in selected cities in Asia, Australia, Europe and the USA*

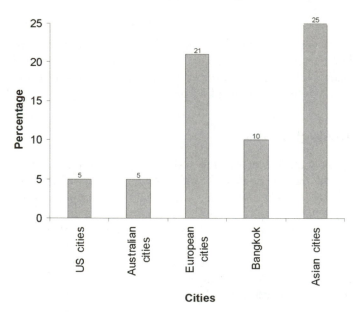

Source: Newman and Kenworthy (1999)

Figure 6.12 *The proportion of workers walking and cycling to work in Bangkok compared with proportions for selected cities in Asia (Hong Kong, Tokyo and Singapore) Australia, Europe and the USA*

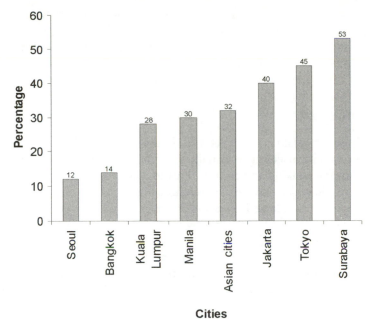

Source: Newman and Kenworthy (1999)

Figure 6.13 *The proportion of daily trips by non-motorized modes in Asian cities*

Implications of the International Comparisons

The above has provided some useful examples of differences in the land use and transport patterns of cities across the globe. What are the implications of these comparisons for Bangkok?

Vehicle ownership

Bangkok clearly has a burgeoning vehicle population, which is higher than is to be expected if wealth were the only factor involved. It can be argued that the absence of a real public transport alternative together with the serious problems associated with walking and cycling are helping to fuel exponential growth in vehicles, particularly since 1980 (Poboon et al, 1994). There is also a lack of government policy that would help to curtail the trend. Close ties with Japanese car and motorcycle manufacturers, financial aid from Japan and other financial institutions for road projects, plus low tariffs and other government charges associated with vehicle ownership, suggest that high vehicle growth will continue (Kenworthy, 1994; Mallet, 1994).

Singapore highlights Bangkok's need to establish some policy constraints on motor vehicles. The suppression of vehicle ownership in Singapore compared with Bangkok can be seen in Figure 6.5. Singapore's strict economic and physical planning disincentives against cars and its excellent public transport explain this picture, especially in the light of the city's economic capacity to purchase cars, as depicted in Figure 6.6 (Kenworthy et al, 1994).

Singapore's policies include the Area Licensing Scheme, which now provides all-day (7.30am–6.30pm) restrictions and high charges for vehicles entering the CBD, and the certificate of entitlement (COE) system, which requires purchase of the right simply to buy a car (costs depend on vehicle size and the time that the vehicle will be operated, but range from S$28,150 for a weekend-only car to S$63,000 for a large car).

Public transport

Bangkok's dense urban fabric, combined with intensively-mixed land uses throughout a major part of the city, makes it potentially an ideal environment for public transport and particularly for walking and cycling. This is especially true because of the linear nature of the city, in which residential areas and commercial and retail strips are densely built up along road corridors. This is well suited to a fixed route, segregated transit system, whereas drivers of buses attempting to ply these corridors find themselves at a standstill with other traffic.

Public transport use in Bangkok is correspondingly low for an Asian city because only occasionally do buses operate on effective bus lanes (in particular contraflow lanes). Moreover, the crowded, mostly non-air conditioned buses are unable to provide an acceptable transport alternative for the growing middle class, who are fuelling the demand for car travel. The Asian cities that *do* have high levels of public transport use are those with effective rail systems that have been able to capture middle class travellers on attractive, air conditioned fast trains (eg Hong Kong and Singapore). The existence of a viable alternative to cars, combined with disincentives to car ownership, has kept car travel and congestion in these cities to a minimum.

An effective rail-based public transport system would appear to be a priority for Bangkok if it is to ever compete with cars.

Walking and cycling

Bangkok's level of walking and cycling is atypically low for an Asian urban environment. This appears to be related to the general hostility of the pedestrian environment and the dangers of riding a bicycle – there are no cycle lanes or other facilities. Most main roads have poor footpaths, and even where they have been widened and perhaps planted with trees – to relieve the hot climate – there is so much noise and so many fumes that walking is an ordeal.

The *sois*, or residential roads, on which most of Bangkok is built are narrow, and those that connect the *sois* with major roads are particularly crowded with traffic and speeding motor bikes. The narrowness of the *sois,* combined with the high walls that surround the houses, create a very unattractive environment for pedestrians and cyclists, and there is almost nowhere to walk or cycle safely. However, in smaller *sois* with lower traffic volumes, it is common to find people walking to street vendors, local businesses and schools. For trips to the shopping areas on main roads or to board buses, many people use hired motorcycles.

It can be concluded that if priority were given to improving pedestrian environments and facilities for walking and creating a shaded cycleway system, people would naturally choose non-motorized modes for short trips because these are the most convenient modes in dense environments with fine-grained, mixed land uses; Tokyo strongly demonstrates this point.

Waterways

Water transport is an attractive, fast way to travel in Bangkok. It provides passengers with relief from the hot climate and separation from the fumes and noise of the roads. However, many canals have been filled in for roads, and even the river is the focus of an attempt to build a floating freeway. Water transport's present contribution to passenger transport is thus very low, but, with more reliable boats, improved jetties and effective feeder services, waterway transport could be further developed.

Paratransit

Bangkok's *tuk-tuks, silor-leks* and hired motorcycles currently fill an important transport niche and offer cheap fares. Their overall contribution to daily trips is very small when compared with buses and other modes, but could be improved by using them as formal feeder services to bus stops, piers and railway stations, and through improved shelters and government regulation to maintain vehicle standards and safety.

Roads

The important issue in Bangkok is roads. The greater part of capital investment in transport goes into large road projects (see Poboon and Kenworthy, 1995) and the dominant perception of the root of Bangkok's traffic problems is simply that there is a shortage of roads. Much is made of the fact that Bangkok has only 11 per cent of its urbanized area devoted to roads, whereas other cities have upwards of 20 per cent (Tanaboriboon, 1993).

As shown in Figure 6.3, however, Bangkok is not atypical of Asian cities in the length of roads it provides per person. Indeed, Jakarta, Manila, Hong Kong and Surabaya provide less. To compare Bangkok's road area with those of other cities is more difficult because of a lack of data. However, it is worth making a comparison because this parameter incorporates road widths. Figure 6.14 draws together data on a number of cities and shows that Bangkok is not so unusually low (eg Paris, Hong Kong and Munich are almost identical to Bangkok in this respect). The crux of the issue is that cities that have a low proportion of urbanized land under roads also have extremely good public transport services – in particular, very good rail systems. They also have high levels of walking and cycling because of the provision of an improved infrastructure and environments more conducive to these modes.

The important conclusion about policy to be drawn from this analysis is that Bangkok is suffering not so much from a lack of road space as from a poorly developed transit system and a very low level of walking and cycling. Bangkok's public transport system and low level of non-motorized mode use do not sufficiently complement its small road provision. In other cities, these factors are better matched and although there is still congestion, there is no traffic crisis.

There is another very important point to stress in relation to Bangkok's tightly-woven urban fabric which, as is the case in many other Asian cities, has not been built

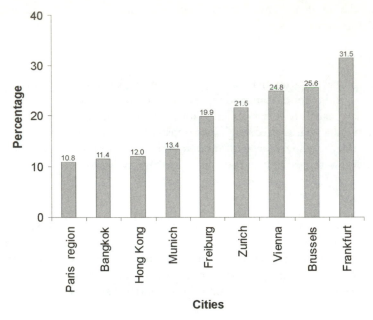

Source: Newman and Kenworthy (1999)

Figure 6.14 *The percentage of urbanized land in Bangkok occupied by roads compared with percentages for a selection of global cities*

for the automobile: non-motorized modes, especially waterway transport, were the basis of Bangkok's early development, followed by trams and buses. It is only since about 1980 that vehicle ownership, and thus congestion, have gone out of control (Poboon et al, 1994). It is certainly possible to try to accommodate Bangkok's growth in vehicles with an aggressive road building programme, but not without tearing apart the urban fabric.

Figure 6.15 estimates the results of trying to expand Bangkok's proportion of urban land devoted to roads from its present 11 per cent up to 20 per cent. Based on present average population and job densities, the new roads would displace the equivalent of a city the size of Chiang Mai. Resettling these people, and the necessary employment enterprises, at densities typical of the outer zone of Bangkok would require new land equivalent to 10 per cent of Bangkok's present urbanized area. Moreover, because they would be in automobile-dependent areas distant from public transport, they would themselves generate huge new volumes of traffic.

Policy Conclusions

Based on the analysis presented here, there appears to be a range of essential policies that Bangkok needs to consider in order to begin resolving its desperate traffic situation. They are summarized briefly in what follows. A more detailed discussion of these

		Equals....
Existing road space	3844 ha	
Extra land needed for roads	2888 ha	Lat Pro district
Displaced residents	469,000	City
Displaced jobs	145,800	of
Total activities displaced	615,100	Chiang Mai
Land required to resettle	14,598 ha	10 per cent BMA

BMA - Bangkok Metropolitan Administration

Source: Newman and Kenworthy (1999)

Figure 6.15 *The implications of increasing the percentage of urbanized land under roads in Bangkok to 20 per cent*

policies can be found in Poboon et al (1994), Poboon and Kenworthy (1995), Kenworthy et al (1994) and Barter et al (1994).

Restraints on cars

This requires an economic approach in the form of increased vehicle taxes, registration duty and fuel tax and perhaps even a Singapore-style COE for car ownership. It also requires physical restraint in the form of an area licensing scheme, which has already been outlined in a major air pollution study (Boontherawara et al, 1994).

The level of CBD parking also needs to be controlled as it is excessively high. Designating particular parts of inner Bangkok as pedestrian and public transport priority zones, and some full scale pedestrianization in central Bangkok, would be appropriate.

Public transport development, especially rail

In order to make restraints on private transport politically feasible, public transport would need to improve greatly.

A first and absolute priority is the establishment of a mass rapid transit system, notwithstanding the enormous technical, institutional and political complexities that currently need to be overcome. Buses need to be given effective, enforceable priority in the traffic system in the form of bus-only lanes and bus-actuated signal priority. Waterway transport and paratransit modes need to be greatly improved.

Walking and cycling environments

In addition to pedestrianization in central locations, there needs to be a comprehensive programme to improve walking and cycling environments at both local and regional levels. Shaded routes, continuous footpaths and cycling routes, separation from dangerous traffic, noise abatement and bicycle facilities at destinations all need to be considered. If Tokyo can achieve 45 per cent of daily trips on foot and bicycle, Bangkok must set its sights on more than its present 14 per cent.

Transit-oriented, mixed use development

Although much of Bangkok is already ideally suited to mass transit, there are an enormous number of high density apartments and dispersed townhouse and condominium developments being built, with huge parking facilities and without any thought for public transport. They are all being built and sold on the assumption of car travel. In Europe and North America, automobile dependence is being reduced through urban village-style developments located around rail stations.

These are high density, mixed land use areas with minimal parking, and have pedestrianized or traffic-calmed environments to encourage walking and cycling for local trips (Newman et al, 1992). Without controls on the form and location of future development in Bangkok and the integration of effective public transport, every improvement through other measures will be eradicated.

Institutional reform

Bangkok's quest to build a rail system has, up to the present, been thwarted by the plethora of agencies responsible for transport planning and implementation, causing overlapping in mandates and many conflicts. There should be a much smaller number of agencies and each should have a clear-cut function. A single committee should have decisive power to oversee and coordinate such agencies, and the authority for recommending decision-making to the government.

A Final Word

Bangkok is increasingly referred to as the 'Los Angeles of the East'. Although its present problems can be analysed and understood in a technical way using the data in this chapter, its problems extend deeper, as do those of Los Angeles itself. In a very real sense, the transport problems in these two cities stem from a lack of effective public planning for the common good over many years. Los Angeles has attempted to function almost totally on automobiles and has been reluctant to develop a public transport system of any significance, or to control land use. The notion has been that if individuals are allowed to maximize their private good, then the sum of these decisions will be a good city. This has not happened, and Los Angeles is now one of the most problematic environments in the Western world.

Bangkok, too, runs the risk of allowing itself to be plundered by private interests associated with road transport systems. Unless public planning for the common good can gain a foothold, as it is beginning to do now in Los Angeles – with the development of an extensive rail system, integration of some development around stations, and land use controls to minimize new travel – there is little hope that any of the policies outlined in this chapter can be implemented.

Notes

1   This chapter was first published as a paper in *World Transport Policy & Practice*, vol 1, no 3, pp31–41.
2   The research by PhD students Chamlong Poboon and Paul Barter in developing the data on Bangkok and Asian cities in newly industrializing countries is gratefully acknowledged. The data in this chapter on the less developed Asian cities are the best available to date from studies and government sources. They may be subject to some revision if better information bases come to light.

References

Barter, P, Kenworthy, J, Poboon, C and Newman, P (1994) *The Challenge of Southeast Asia's Rapid Motorization: Kuala Lumpur, Jakarta, Surabaya and Manila in an International Perspective*, paper presented to the Asian Studies Association of Australia Biennial Conference, Environment State and Society in Asia: the Legacy of the Twentieth Century, 13–16 July, Asia Research Centre, Murdoch University, Perth, Western Australia

Boontherawara, N, Paisarnutpong, O, Panich, S, Phiu-Nual, K and Wangwongwatana, S (1994) 'Traffic crisis and air pollution in Bangkok', *TEI Quarterly Environment Journal*, vol 2, no 3, pp4–37

Kenworthy, J (1994) 'Exit to Eden or highway to hell?', *The Australian*, 5 December, p9

Kenworthy, J, Barter, P, Newman, P and Poboon, C (1994) *Resisting Automobile Dependence in Booming Economies: A Case Study of Singapore, Tokyo and Hong Kong Within a Global Sample of Cities*, paper presented to Asian Studies Association of Australia Biennial Conference, Environment, State and Society in Asia: The Legacy of the Twentieth Century, 13–16 July, Asia Research Centre, Murdoch University, Perth, Western Australia

Mallet, V (1994) 'Thailand in driver's seat of Asia's accelerating car industry', *The Australian*, 10 November, p39

Newman, P and Kenworthy, J (1989) *Cities and Automobile Dependence: An International Sourcebook*, Gower, Aldershot

Newman, P and Kenworthy, J (1999) *Sustainability and Cites: Overcoming Automobile Dependence*, Island Press, Washington, DC

Newman, P, Kenworthy, J and Robinson, L (1992) *Winning Back the Cities*, Australian Consumers Association/Pluto Press, Sydney

Poboon, C, Kenworthy, J, Newman, P and Barter, P (1994) *Bangkok: Anatomy of a Traffic Disaster*, paper presented to Asian Studies Association of Australia Biennial Conference, Environment, State and Society in Asia: the Legacy of the Twentieth Century, 13–16 July, Asia Research Centre, Murdoch University, Perth, Western Australia

Poboon, C and Kenworthy, J (1995) *Bangkok: Towards a Sustainable Traffic Solution*, paper presented to Urban Habitat Conference, 15–17 February, Delft

Tanaboriboon, Y (1993) 'Bangkok traffic', *Journal of International Association of Traffic and Safety Sciences*, vol 17, no 1, pp14–23

7

Kolkata City: An Urban Air Pollution Perspective

Dipankar Chakraborti

Introduction

Kolkata city is a metropolis with a rich cultural heritage and a long, glorious tradition of political and social struggles. Kolkata (formerly known as Calcutta) receives its name from *Kali-ghat* (the steps of the goddess Kali). Kali is the goddess of death and destruction. Located in West Bengal, its influence cuts across the state boundary. In a sense, the entire eastern region of the country, with a population of more than 200 million, constitutes its hinterland. Kolkata is a vast melting pot where people from different cultures, disciplines and heritages meet and work side by side. In the early part of the 20th century it was called City of Palaces, or City of Gardens. However, 50 years later it was called 'the dirtiest city in the world'. With time, the city received all sorts of contempt and ridicule: 'the city of garbage', 'the city of darkness', 'the city of slums'. In 1988, the German writer Günter Grass wrote: 'Calcutta city appears to me as if blood were dropping from Kali's tongue. A city that can swallow the whole country, the whole world'. This chapter describes the range of factors that contribute to the current environmental situation of Kolkata and discusses the contribution of transport to urban air pollution.[1]

Kolkata City

A review of the data in Table 7.1 clearly indicates the population pressure in Kolkata. Almost 9 per cent of West Bengal's population congregate in an area of approximately 100km² during the daytime. This is one of the unique features of Kolkata. Another feature, which is not comparable to other cities throughout the world, is the population density per square kilometre. Out of 100 municipal wards in Core Kolkata, there are four city wards where the population is approximately 100,000 per km², and 20 city wards with a population of approximately 70,000 per km². In the Calcutta Municipal Corporation (CMC) area (1350km²), the population is 11.86 million.

Kolkata was originally built for just 1 million people, but the urban population has grown and the city now accommodates more than 6 million people during the day. This results in constraints in all spheres of life, such as the provision of essential health services and public transport. The population of CMC is estimated to increase to 18 million by 2011, and open space under present land use strategies will be reduced to 300km². If this occurs then it will exacerbate existing pressures on the city.

Table 7.1 *Some characteristic features of Kolkata city and surroundings*

West Bengal area	88,752km^2
Population of West Bengal	68 million
Core Kolkata: CMC area	104km^2
Population of Core Kolkata	Night-time: 3.3 million
	Day-time: 6 million
Total urban area of West Bengal	2600km^2
Total urban population	15 million
Kolkata urban agglomeration area	852km^2
Kolkata urban agglomeration population	9.2 million
Kolkata metropolitan area	1350km^2
Kolkata metropolitan population	11.86 million

Kolkata has grown in an unplanned manner. The alarming condition of Kolkata was a cause for concern over 86 years ago. The Calcutta Improvement Act of 1911, which came into force on 2 January 1912, clearly mentions the necessity of improving the city by opening up congested areas, altering streets and providing open space for the purpose of ventilation. This concern was further expressed in 1935 by the first chief engineer of the Calcutta Improvement Trust. However, 50 years after independence little progress has been made in addressing these issues. In fact, open space has been significantly reduced and construction continues to encroach on many gardens and parks. It seems that the ecology of the city is being ignored by both town planners and engineers.

Kolkata City Dwellers

The vast majority of the people in Kolkata are poor or middle class. Although there are elegant mansions, beautiful monuments and an underground metro system, there is a large number of poor people: beggars with pot bellies and begging bowls, pavement dwellers in huts made of plastic sheets and bamboo sticks, shanty huts, rickshaw pullers carrying other humans on their rickety shoulders, rag pickers with their dirty sacks, and scavengers fighting among themselves for a scrap of metal on a garbage dump. Kolkata can be divided according to the living status of the people as follows (see Table 7.2).

Table 7.2 *From rich to poor*

%	Class
< 1	Elite
8–9	Upper middle class (PCPME over 700 rupees)
40	Lower middle class (PCPME 185–255 rupees)
50	Poor and slum dwellers (PCPME 0–185 rupees)
3	*Lakhs* (people who sleep on footpaths)

Note: PCPME = per capita per month expenditure

Within the inner centre of Kolkata there is not a single ward without a slum. Approximately 50 per cent of city people live in slums and close to 70 per cent of slum dwellers live below the poverty level. Kolkata is often referred to as the slum city of the world, and most probably it is so because of the sub-human living conditions in the slums and on the pavements of the city. In recent years, thousands of pavement dwellers have crowded the city streets, parks and vacant places. Poverty and hunger drove them from the villages and they are using the city pavements and parks as public latrines.

The growth of the slum population is much higher than the overall growth of the country. In the course of time, those people who do not have access to nourishing food and education will form a major part of the population. The urban quality of life is defined in terms of the physical quality of life index (PQLI). The PQLI takes into consideration longevity, child mortality, shelter, sanitation, educational facilities, power, health, etc. The PQLI of Kolkata is one of the lowest, as the majority of people do not have these basic facilities. In West Bengal there are approximately 40,000 villages and nearly 150 towns. All these villages and towns were neglected for over 200 years. Over the last hundred years, thousands of people rushed to Kolkata, and they are still doing so today: it is their only hope of survival. If this trend continues, soon all of Kolkata and its metropolitan area will be one large slum.

Urban Air Pollution in Kolkata

From a health perspective, urban air pollution is regarded as an important factor in Indian cities. It is generally agreed that Kolkata's air is heavy and difficult to breathe. The climate of Kolkata has an important impact on the city's air pollution. During the monsoon season (July–October), the air is comparatively clean due to the heavy rainfall, but the water quality becomes worse. During the summer (April–June), high winds disperse the pollutants, thus reducing the severity of air pollution. Air quality is worst during the winter months (November–February), as inversions occur during these months and the pollutants cannot disperse.

Following his visit to Kolkata in the winter of 1994, Patrice Riemes of the Department of Human Geography at the University of Amsterdam wrote to the director of the School of Environmental Studies at Jadavpur University:

> You may not be surprised to know that six weeks after coming back from Calcutta, I am still spitting black when clearing my throat. For the last two weeks this has become only a few greyish streaks, but before, real chunks of black slime used to come out. Another boost to the Calcutta pollution legend.

Table 7.3 presents data for selected urban air pollutants in Kolkata for the years 1985 and 1994. During this period there has been an increase in the level of urban air pollutants, mainly from vehicle exhaust emissions. Over the same period, the number of motor cars within the city has doubled. Table 7.4 shows the number of cars passing through strategic junctions per minute in the city during 1985 and 1994.

A comparison of data on selected urban air pollutants for Delhi and Kolkata over the period 7 January–7 February 1994 shows that during the winter, Kolkata is more than three times more polluted than Delhi with respect to measured pollutants (see Table 7.5).

Table 7.3 *Selected urban air pollutants in Kolkata for 1985 and 1994*

Year	Nitrogen dioxide	Sulphur dioxide	Suspended particulate matter
1985	$159\mu g/m^3$	$69.3\mu g/m^3$	$757\mu g/m^3$
1994	$182\mu g/m^3$	$110\mu g/m^3$	$1395\mu g/m^3$

Table 7.4 *Cars passing through key junctions*

	Shambazar	Dalhousie	Moulali	Gariahat	Jadavpur
1985	15	41	–	24	12
1994	34	56	60	49	23

Table 7.5 *Selected urban air pollutants in Kolkata and Delhi, winter 1994*

Pollutant	Kolkata	Delhi
Nitrogen dioxide	$183\mu g/m^3$	$49\mu g/m^3$
Sulphur dioxide	$108\mu g/m^3$	$26\mu g/m^3$
Suspended particulate matter	$1352\mu g/m^3$	$421\mu g/m^3$

One of Kolkata's biggest problems is the high concentration of suspended particulate matter (SPM) in the air. The World Health Organization's (WHO) recommended maximum value is $90\mu g/m^3$. In winter, an average value of approximately $1300\mu g/m^3$ has been observed, and it has been as high as $3000\mu g/m^3$. To estimate the impact on city residents, an experiment was undertaken by Jadavpur University. Air was inhaled through a filter at the rate of normal inhalation at rest (7l/minute). The filter turned black after two hours of inhalation due to soot and particulate matter in the air. This is indicative of the high incidence of respiratory problems among Kolkatans during winter. Asthma among children is very common and some school children use air masks in an attempt to improve the quality of the air they breathe.

British researchers (*Guardian*, 17 February 1994) showed that an increase in air pollution is related to a higher incidence of asthma, and in London it has almost doubled in the last ten years. In an editorial, *The Times* (1994) wrote:

> Children are particularly vulnerable. Those under three breathe in twice as much air for each pound of their body weight as adults. Their airways are narrower and their lungs still immature. Pollution can affect them permanently.

Higher benzene soluble organic matter (BSOM) in urban air means that it is polluted. Automobiles and coal burning are the main sources of BSOM. The BSOM concentration in urban air increased by more than 30 per cent over the period 1987–1994 (see Table 7.6).

In BSOM, there is a group of compounds known as polynuclear aromatic hydrocarbons (PAH). Some of these compounds, such as benz(a)pyrene, are considered to be carcinogens. The School of Environmental Studies at Jadavpur University analysed 16 PAHs in the urban air of Kolkata over a four-year period. It calculated the probability of street hawkers developing cancer due to the inhalation of benz(a)pyrene over a period of eight hours sitting near strategic road junctions. This calculation suggests that

Table 7.6 *Benzene soluble organic matter in Kolkata air*

Year	Concentration ($\mu g/m^3$)
1987	82
1992	105
1994	125

street hawkers who sit for eight hours each day for 15 years will have a high risk of developing cancer, whereas the same risk for a London street hawker is approximately 50 years. Evidence from epidemiological studies suggests that an increase of $1\mu g/m^3$ of benz(a)pyrene corresponds to an increase of 5 per cent in the lung cancer death rate.

The concentration of lead in the urban environment is due to the use of tetra-alkyl-lead in petrol. The human health effects of lead are well documented. Children, in particular, are susceptible to lead pollution. Tetra-alkyl-leads are more poisonous than many other lead compounds. The levels of lead and organolead in Kolkata are much higher during the winter compared to other large cities (see Tables 7.7–7.8).

Table 7.7 *A comparison of lead concentrations*

City	Concentration ($\mu g/m^3$)
Kolkata	6.600
Berlin	1.400
Brussels	2.320
Kanpur	5.350
Mumbai	0.463

Table 7.8 *A comparison of organolead concentrations*

City	Year	Concentration (ng/m^3)
Kolkata	1993	443
Frankfurt	1980	45
Belgium	1981	166
London	1980	94
Los Angeles	1977	100

Coal *chulla* and benzene in the air of Kolkata

Benzene, toluene and xylene are three volatile organic compounds (VOCs) present in urban air mainly due to the use of petrol and diesel in automobiles. Benzene is a suspected carcinogen. The limit of benzene in air for health safety should not exceed approximately $10mg/m^3$. The School of Environmental Studies has measured benzene, toluene and xylene in Kolkata city air during the winter for the last three years.

During the winter of 1994–1995, someone breathing Kolkata's air at main street crossings for 12 hours was inhaling the benzene equivalent of smoking at least 100 cigarettes each day. London air, in comparison, is equivalent to 15 cigarettes per day.

Kolkata city is unique from a pollution perspective. While in most Western cities concentrations of benzene in urban air are lower than concentrations of toluene and xylene, in Kolkata city the benzene level is higher than those of toluene and xylene. The main reason for this is the use of a coal *chulla* (a crude coke burning stove). In Kolkata, more than 80 per cent of the families still use coal for energy, which results in high levels of benzene. Most of the Kolkatans awake in the morning after inhaling smoke from the coal *chulla* and in many houses the smoke enters the bedroom from the kitchen. In slum areas during the morning and evening, when the *chulla* are fired, the whole area is covered with smoke. This becomes unbearable during the winter months.

When a coal stove burns, the concentration of benzene may be $5497\mu g/m^3$ (an average of eight results) near the *chulla*. A comparative study of ambient benzene concentrations in a few cities of the world is given below in Table 7.9.

Table 7.9 *Benzene concentrations around the world*

City	Concentration ($\mu g/m^3$)
Kolkata	1500
London	40
Boston	60
Los Angeles	140

Note: Average value during 1994–1995 winter.

Air Pollution from Transport

Transport is a headache for the authorities in Kolkata, and is the biggest inconvenience to the people of the city. The transport system in Kolkata is unique, as it consists of buses, local trains, the metro, trams, taxis, auto-rickshaws, ferry services, bicycle rickshaws and rickshaws pulled by human beings. Despite these varied modes of transport, the entire system is under severe strain. Every day, 6.6 million commuters travel in different vehicles but the capacity of the transport network is just 2.8–3 million. Overloading during peak hours is 250–300 per cent of the capacity of buses, trams and trains.

Present statistics show that approximately 50 per cent of all the passenger cars in India are used in just five cities: Delhi, Mumbai, Kolkata, Bangalore and Madras. Table 7.10 shows that that the city of Delhi registered the greatest number of vehicles in 1991.

Table 7.10 *Car registrations*

City	Number of vehicles
Delhi	1,598,000
Mumbai	576,400
Kolkata (August 1993)	525,482
Madras	415,100
Bangalore	391,500

The total number of vehicles registered in Kolkata municipal city during 1992 was approximately 0.5 million. The rate of growth of the number of registered vehicles was approximately twice that of the total national registered vehicular population during 1983–1993. The growth of vehicles in Kolkata during this period was broken down as follows:

- two-wheelers: 300 per cent;
- four-wheelers: 25 per cent;
- taxis: 200 per cent; and
- goods carriages: 300 per cent.

It is evident that registered two-wheelers constitute approximately 40 per cent of the total registered vehicles in Kolkata, and more than 80 per cent of the cars in West Bengal are in Kolkata. Although the number of cars in Kolkata is much less than in any Western city, the car density (849 vehicles per kilometre of road length in 1989) is much higher than in Delhi and Mumbai.

In a modern city, the expected emission of air pollutants per million inhabitants is approximately 850 tonnes per day. In Kolkata, this value is approximately 1100 tonnes for 3.3 million people (night-time population), of which the auto exhaust contribution is approximately 400 tonnes per day (in 1991). Thus, compared to most cities of the world, Kolkata's emission load is much lower (for example, in New York the total emission was approximately 16,000 tonnes per day in 1970, with a population of 7.5 million and an area of $512km^2$).

From an environment perspective, Kolkata is unique in all spheres, and transport is not an exception. Problems are very much localized in the inner city. Only a few kilometres away from the downtown area, the surrounding area looks like a large village. This concentration of facilities is the main reason why people want to stay as close as possible to the city. Thus, Kolkata city has become a human ocean. The pressure on Kolkata city will not subside until its hinterlands are developed with improved transport infrastructure.

In Kolkata the transportation infrastructure is outdated and in need of repair. The tram tracks and rolling stock are more than a century old. The entire public transport infrastructure is in a poor state of health. The new metro is running at a loss and suffers from many problems.

During the last ten years, two new transportation corridors were developed in Kolkata: the Eastern Metropolitan (EM) bypass and the second Hooghly Bridge. Apart from these new developments, a number of road-widening programmes and flyovers have been completed. Nevertheless, the general feeling of every Kolkatan is one of concern. The reasons are many, and include:

- limited road space (less than 6 per cent of the city area);
- hawkers occupying the footpaths with and without permission;
- increasingly difficult traffic management;
- lack of parking facilities;
- new bus and minibus routes being introduced without proper termini (private bus stops can be anywhere on the road sides);

- very few traffic lights;
- traffic rules that most of the drivers do not obey;
- poor road conditions;
- most vehicles being in various states of disrepair (80 per cent would fail a basic vehicle safety test);
- traffic jams that are a common phenomenon, with thousands of cars remaining gridlocked for hours;
- overloaded goods vehicles operating throughout the city and causing significant traffic problems; and
- almost 90 per cent of the motor cars emitting black smoke.

Industrial Pollution

Within 100km^2 of core Kolkata, there are 11,516 small and large factories registered with the CMC. In addition to these, there are a large number of unregistered factories. There is not one single ward where there are no factories and where people are not complaining about the factories' activities. The problem is even worse on the opposite bank of the Hooghly river in Howrah district. Due to the high concentration of factories, the area is known as the Sheffield of West Bengal. Furthermore, after Western countries decided to reduce smelting operations, the number of lead factories is increasing in the countryside. The problem will be further aggravated if the government of India agrees to accept the industrial wastes of Western countries. The acceptance of battery waste from lead recovery from Australia is not yet decided upon, but if it is agreed the consequence will be serious in terms of pollution and human health.

Of these factories, a few hundred are using or manufacturing toxic chemicals. Due to negligence at these factories, environmental hazards often occur and people are seriously affected. In PN Mitra Lane, Behala, a factory producing Paris Green (copper-aceto-arsenite) discharged untreated arsenic-rich effluent. As a result the aquifer was contaminated with arsenic, which 10,000 people unknowingly continued to drink. Many people in the area are suffering from arsenical skin lesions. A few died from arsenic-related diseases. At present the people have a piped water supply, but due to leaching and the flow of arsenic from the contaminated aquifer, the wells of some nearby areas have become contaminated. Again, in the Picnic Garden area of Kolkata (68 Ward) there are 27 lead factories producing lead ingots and lead alloys.

Approximately 200,000 people live in the surrounding areas. The concentration of lead in the soil, in dust on leaves and in road dust is very high (5000–20,000μg/g). Even on dining tables, the concentration of lead in dust exceeds 5000μg/g. The School of Environmental Studies studied the area and found that lead is not the only contaminant. The area is also highly contaminated with arsenic, nickel, chromium and mercury. In the Tiljala area there are many tanneries that are discharging untreated chromium-rich effluent. Occasionally, high concentrations of chromium from tubewell water are reported in the nearby residential areas. Approximately 250 small acid chemical processing (eg hydrochloric acid, nitric acid and sulphuric acid) units are situated in Ward 14 of the CMC area. The people of the locality have complained many times to local authorities about the acid smell and pungent odours of other gases. The problem becomes acute during the winter when, due to inversion, the acid fumes cannot easily disperse.

Conclusion

With regard to urban air pollution, Kolkata city is different from most other cities around the world. The methods adopted by other countries to reduce urban air pollution, especially from transport, may not work in Kolkata. India's large population (heading towards 1 billion) is the root of a number of major urban environment problems. A simple example clearly demonstrates this point. In one study of benz(a)pyrene (a suspected carcinogen) in Kolkata air and its effect on human health, it was estimated that hawkers selling goods sitting on a footpath for eight hours a day inhaling benz(a)pyrene ($30-120\mu g/m^3$) could develop cancer after approximately 15 years. If the hawkers were informed about this, would they stop selling their goods? It is their livelihood. Hunger in India is more important than cancer. The World Bank states that 'India is among the poorest of poor nations in Asia'. Most of the population live in poverty and suffer grossly from inadequate access to resources, such as transport, health services, education, infrastructure, land and credit. Malnutrition is another problem. At present in India, 63 per cent of children under six years of age are malnourished; this is second only to Bangladesh. Thus, the environment is one of the greatest development challenges in the world today. The reason is not the complexity of the environmental issue but the complex linkages between growth, population, poverty and environment. For environmental development in India, grassroots development is needed. The chances of a cancer patient being cured by applying a superficial ointment are very poor indeed.

Notes

1   This chapter was first published as a paper in *World Transport Policy & Practice*, vol 3, no 2, pp15–23.

References

Chakraborti, D (1990) 'Calcutta's environment' in Chowdhury, S (ed) *Calcutta, The Living City* (volume 2), Oxford University Press, Oxford

Chakraborti, D (1993) 'Calcutta environmental profile: air pollution' in Sivaramakrishnan, K C (ed) *Managing Urban Environment in India: Towards an Agenda for Action Volume 3 – Industry, Energy, Transport and Air*, Times Research Foundation, Kolkata

Chakraborti, D, Ghosh, D and Niyogi, S (1987) 'Calcutta pollutants: part 1 – appraisal of some heavy metals in Calcutta city sewage and sludge in use for fisheries and agriculture', *International Journal of Environmental Analytical Chemistry*, vol 30, pp243–253

Chakraborti, D, Van Vaeek, L and Ven Espen, P (1988) 'Calcutta pollutants: part 2 – polynuclear aromatic hydrocarbon metal concentration on air particulates during winter 1984', *International Journal of Environmental Analytical Chemistry*, vol 32, no 1, pp109–120

Chakraborti, D and Raeymackers, B (1988) 'Calcutta pollutants: part 3 – toxic metals in dust and characterisation of individual aerosol particles', *International Journal of Environmental Analytical Chemistry*, vol 32, no 1, pp121–134

Chakraborti, D, Das, D, Chatterjee, A, Jin, Z and Jiang, S G (1993) 'Calcutta pollution: part 4 – direct determination of some heavy metals in urban air particulates by electrothermal atomic absorption spectrometry using Zeeman background correction after simple acid decomposition: application to Calcutta air particulates', *Environmental Technology*, no 13, pp95–100

Chatterjee, A, Das, D and Chakraborti, D (1993) 'A study of ground water contamination by arsenic in the residential area of Behala, Calcutta due to industrial pollution', *Environmental Pollution*, vol 80, no 1, pp57–65

Chattopadhya, G, Chatterjee, S and Chakraborti, D (1996) 'Determination of benzene, toluene and xylene in ambient air inside three major steel plant airsheds and surrounding residential areas', *Environmental Technology*, vol 17, pp477–488

Das, D, Chatterjee, A, Samanta, G and Chakraborti, D (1993) 'Preliminary estimation of tetraalkyl-lead compounds (TAL) in Calcutta city air', *Chemical Environmental Resources*, vol 1, no 3, pp279–287

Guha Mazumder, D N, Das Gupta, J, Chakraborty, A K, Chatterjee, A, Das, D and Chakraborti, D (1992) 'Chronic arsenicosis in south Calcutta, West Bengal', *Bulletin of World Health Organization*, vol 70, no 4, pp481–485

Samanta, G, Chatterjee, A, Das, D, Chowdhury, P, Chanda, C R and Chakraborti, D (1995) 'Calcutta pollution: part 5 – lead and other heavy metal contamination in residential area from a factory producing lead ingots and lead alloys', *Environmental Technology*, vol 16, pp223–231

The Times (1994) 'No hiding place: dirty air threatens the nation's children', 17 February

8

Road Infrastructure Investment in Bangladesh: Environment under Threat?

John Howe

Introduction

The Bangladesh infrastructure experience has been presented as evidence for the leading catalytic role of roads in inducing development, and thus as a model that should be copied by other similarly poor countries (Ahmed, 1990; Ahmed and Hossain, 1990; World Bank, 1990a; World Bank, 1991a). However, in Bangladesh all new road infrastructure works have environmental disbenefits, the consumption of land being both the most evident and significant in the context of the relationship between landlessness and poverty. These disbenefits have been glossed over by the vigorous promotion of road development.

Few ask whether gross benefits are thought sufficient to compensate for negative environmental effects and still make investment worthwhile.

The fragility of Bangladesh's environment is internationally renowned and is dictated by its physical geography. It is deltaic, annually flooded by numerous major rivers and located in one of the most cyclone-prone parts of the world, making the risk of disaster ever present. Risk reduction is the foundation of the proposed Flood Action Plan, an expensive (US$5–10 billion) and controversial infrastructure investment (World Bank, 1990b). Part of the controversy is whether such massive physical infrastructure changes will affect Bangladesh's sensitive environment. This is acknowledged in the cautious sequencing of further studies, pilot projects and initial investments pending a decision to proceed with the full plan.

Road infrastructure investments in Bangladesh, on the other hand, are not accorded such environmental concern. The piecemeal nature of road projects may well provide the explanation for this anomaly, since few are of such a scale that their individual effects are very significant. However, the cumulative environmental impact of whole programmes conducted over decades is another matter. The consumption of land and the other disbenefits associated with rural road development lead this chapter to challenge the prevailing assumption that more roads enhance rural welfare to such an extent that environmental considerations are not significant.[1]

Roads in Bangladesh

From only a few hundred kilometres at the time of the country's separation from India in 1947, the length of the road network has increased rapidly. In 1970 there were 3200km of main roads, which had increased to 12,300km by 1990. There were also 22,000km of rural/feeder roads and over 90,000km of local earth roads constructed primarily under Food for Work programmes. The main and rural roads represent one of the highest density networks in Asia (World Bank, 1991b) with Bangladesh having a density of 86km of road per 100km² of area, as compared with 50 for Sri Lanka, 45 for India, 18 for Malaysia and 15 for Thailand.

In terms of rural land requirements, it is more meaningful to examine road densities per unit of agricultural land, and in relation to the apparent ability of the country to afford the infrastructure. Table 8.1 shows that of the poor countries with an annual GNP per capita of US$430 or less, only Sri Lanka has a density of roads close to that of Bangladesh.

Table 8.1 *Road density in relation to agricultural land and GNP per capita*

Country	GNP per capita $ (1990)	Road density per 100km² agricultural land	Road density per 100km² agricultural land per US$100 GNP per capita
Nepal	170	9	5.3
Bangladesh	210	118	56.2
China	360	20	5.6
India	360	74	20.6
Sri Lanka	470	139	29.6
Thailand	1420	37	2.6
Malaysia	2320	134	5.8
Korea	5400	230	4.3

Source: World Bank (1991b)

When corrected for GNP, the agricultural road density of Bangladesh is double that of Sri Lanka, three times that of India and approximately 12 times that of China or Nepal. Its pre-eminent position is all the more surprising given the high cost of road construction.

Because of the alluvial soil, the large numbers of rivers which must be bridged or crossed by ferries, and the annual threat of flooding making roads on high (2–3m) embankments essential, road building in Bangladesh is very expensive – 60 per cent higher per km, for example, than in India (Smillie, 1991).

Roads and the Environment

The three most evident environmental effects resulting from rural road development in Bangladesh are: the loss of land; land degradation through inadequate road planning and design; and forest destruction.

Loss of land

A feature of many rural infrastructure investments – embankments, roads, river train-ing works, drainage canals and ditches – is that they involve significant scale earthworks. These consume one of the country's most precious assets: land. For roads, embankments and river training works, an additional and greater need for land results from the structures themselves, in the form of areas or 'borrowpits' from which soil is dug for their construction, since the land is uniformly flat. Such areas are not always recultivated and often remain as flooded ditches or ponds, which serve mainly as water tanks for soaking jute, or fish production.

Land degradation

Roads and embankments often lead to a further loss of land due to waterlogging, which results from poor planning, design and construction of alignments and drainage (KBN Engineering and Applied Science, 1991). Most road structures of this nature are an artificial imposition on natural drainage patterns, which are very finely demarcated on an alluvial flood plain. Unless implemented with great care they obstruct flood disper-sion, leading to waterlogging that will lower yields or, in extreme cases, render land useless for cultivation.

Unfortunately, the necessary care has rarely been taken. An apparent feature of Bangladesh's rural road network is the way roads zig-zag across the flat landscape. Right-angle turns averaging less than 50m apart are common. In other flat deltaic regions, such as Thailand or The Netherlands, this is seldom the case and lines of com-munication, both road and rail, are as direct as the river and canal systems will permit. The curved alignment of roads in Bangladesh is not due to elaborate provision for drainage requirements. The reverse is the case – difficult-to-drain areas are created within the arcs of the many changes in direction of the road alignment.

One explanation given for the zig-zagging roads is that they follow the boundaries of individual land parcels to minimize the loss and inconvenience to any one farm (Associ-ates in Rural Development, 1989). Alternative explanations are that such alignments result from deliberate actions to avoid the large land plots of the relatively wealthy and powerful, and conversely take the small land plots of the poor and uninfluential (Wood, 1988). There is evidence that this is the case, and it is consistent with the mechanisms by which the poor become landless (Hartmann and Boyce, 1983; Jansen, 1987).

Whatever the real explanation, the effect is the same. Such alignments offer no engineering advantages and create environmental and operational problems, including slower and longer journeys. Moreover, in following the alleged path of least social resist-ance, the lengths of road embankments and the number of drainage structures per kilometre are greater than those of straight alignments. This unnecessarily increases the cost of construction and maintenance, and the consumption of land.

Forest destruction

Forest destruction is a direct environmental consequence of road development due to the use of burnt bricks, both as the major road surfacing material and, when broken, as aggregate for the construction of low strength structures such as small bridges and culverts. This technology is common to the plain of the River Ganges in Bangladesh and India because of the absence of any other naturally occurring hard-surfacing material. The plain – 300km wide in places – is composed of materials that can be baked into bricks but otherwise are structurally very weak.

Assumed benefits from investment in roads

The benefits to be expected from the lowest cost investments, ie maintenance benefits, are in theory non-controversial. They comprise reductions in vehicle operating costs and can be estimated relatively easily and accurately if the roads are in a sound condition and carry reasonable volumes of motorized traffic. Techniques for estimating user benefits when existing roads are upgraded are also reasonably well established.

The real uncertainties lie with new roads where the benefits are essentially the economic and social changes that are likely to be induced by the investment. The difficulty that all developing countries face is that, despite considerable research, these changes have defied generalization. Sometimes they are positive, sometimes negative, and occasionally so few in number that it is difficult to discern any at all. Certainly, it has so far not been possible to develop a reliable method for predicting the outcomes of investment either quantitatively or qualitatively (Howe and Richards, 1984).

This uncertainty is clearly not shared by the government of Bangladesh (GOB). Road investment has been, and continues to be, viewed as a key mechanism for engendering positive economic and social change, although this role was emphatically challenged by the foreign contributors to the 1977 Bangladesh Rural Transport Survey (Transport Survey Section et al, 1978). Under the conditions prevailing in Bangladesh, they concluded that by improving rural transport without complementary changes in credit, the provision of agricultural inputs and marketing arrangements would provide benefits only to the large farmers and to the traders.

A further boost to the pro-roads lobby resulted from a joint study by the Bangladesh Institute of Development Studies (BIDS) and International Food Policy Research Institute (IFPRI). Although conducted in 1982, the study has only recently received widespread international publicity, and has been considered by some commentators to hold important investment lessons for other poor countries (Ahmed, 1990; World Bank, 1990a; World Bank, 1991a). However, major issue can be taken with the structure and scope of the BIDS/IFPRI study, and especially with the interpretations that have been placed on its results.[2]

In essence, the BIDS/IFPRI study attempts to isolate the development impact of rural infrastructure, in particular roads, on the rural economy of Bangladesh. The 16 villages in its sample were categorized into two groups – developed and underdeveloped – based on an aggregate infrastructure index reflecting ease of access to various services such as markets, schools and banks. Villages that had better-than-average access were classified as 'developed', and these were found to be significantly better off in a number of areas – including agricultural production, household incomes, wage incomes of landless labourers, health and the participation of women in the economy – than underdeveloped villages. According to the authors, the most important finding is *the profound effect that infrastructure has on the incomes of the poor* (present author's emphasis).

Overall, estimations based on the most and least developed villages indicate that infrastructural endowment causes household income to rise by 33 per cent. Income from agriculture increases by approximately 24 per cent, that from livestock and fisheries by approximately 78 per cent, that from wages almost doubles, but income from business and industries only rises by 17 per cent. Most striking, however, is the distribution of these increases: the functionally landless and small farmers garner a larger share of the increases from crops, wages and livestock and fisheries, while the large landowners capture most of the smaller increases in business and industries.

The study concluded that development of rural infrastructure, with roads explicitly identified as the central component, had to play a key role in any development strategy for Bangladesh (Ahmed and Hossain, 1990); further, that past allocations to infrastructure, based on experience and judgment about current or emerging bottlenecks, should be replaced by the conscious creation of excess capacity that would induce production of agricultural and non-agricultural goods, services and employment (Ahmed, 1990).

It is the advocacy of road investment as a strategic catalyst, or causative factor, of more general development that appears to be fundamentally unsound. The proposition, which adds fuel to Bangladesh's already strong propensity for investment in roads, is open to criticism on a number of grounds:

1   it contradicts the consensus of theoretical argument and empirical evidence;
2   it is based on a short term view of the economic and social changes associated with new roads, which, in Bangladesh, are fundamentally unsustainable owing to the endemic lack of maintenance; and
3   it rests on an appeal to gross rather than net benefits, which leaves the real effect on the poor indeterminate.

Points 1 and 2 above are discussed elsewhere, although it is germane to note that approximately 40 per cent of the present network is functionally ineffective because it is physically incapable of carrying the motorized traffic for which it was designed. The main barrier to use by motorized traffic is the presence of gaps in the embanked roads: sections where major cross-drainage structures – bridges or large culverts – have either collapsed and remain in that state due to lack of maintenance, or were never built with the main earthworks. These obstacles usually mean that four-wheeled vehicles cannot pass, and may be a barrier to all wheeled traffic (Howe, 1994). This chapter limits itself to point 3 (above), since environmental effects are the main disbenefits associated with road investment.

Disbenefits from Investment in Roads

Landlessness and poverty

Poverty is highly correlated with landlessness not only in Bangladesh, but elsewhere in Asia, Africa and South America (World Bank, 1990a). Although there is disagreement about the general strength of the connection, Begum (1986) argues that in Bangladesh landlessness and poverty are closely linked due to the very limited opportunities for non-agricultural employment. Moreover, it has the unenviable distinction of having experienced one of the most dramatic transitions from a predominantly landowning to a landless society of any country in the world. Hartmann and Boyce (1983) have graphically described the relentless process by which ownership of land has become concentrated in a smaller number of hands over the past few decades and the subsequent plight of the landless, for whom life undoubtedly becomes more precarious.

Jansen (1987) has corroborated their findings and argued that through the process of landlessness, Bangladesh is gripped by an almost inexorable impoverishment that threatens catastrophe, which present policies and plans do little to address. More refined assessments of poverty in Bangladesh also confirm that it is generally the rural landless labourers, and their families, who are among the poorest of the poor and the most vulnerable to death from starvation (Ahmed et al, 1991).

In 1978 it was predicted that by the turn of the century the majority of the population in Bangladesh would be functionally landless (USAID Mission to Bangladesh, 1978).[3] Projections made a decade later confirmed that this was likely to be the case, with the proportion of households without land expected to reach 60 per cent by roughly 2010 (World Bank, 1990b).

Land consumption

Given the overwhelming evidence of the negative effects caused by landlessness, then investments that actually require land – not only its transfer but also its sacrifice indefinitely – ought to be subject to rigorous scrutiny. Such programmes should not be entered into without a thorough investigation of the full costs and benefits, including the costs and methods of compensating those made landless. This is difficult for the road sector, since investments take place under different programmes and are supported by a multiplicity of governmental and, especially, foreign agencies, who have both formal and informal investment criteria. Some investments have been the subject of detailed cost–benefit analyses, but not all. It is the lower and most extensive categories of rural roads that have most often been omitted from consideration.

Roads have consumed at least 94,000ha, or 1 per cent of the available cropland. This may seem small, but in a densely populated and overwhelmingly agricultural country it could support more than 1 million people. The land required for a road is approximately 0.75ha per km: one-third right-of-way, two-thirds borrowpits (Merril et al, 1990). However, a consequence of the 1987 and 1988 floods has been to increase the land required in flood-prone areas, since engineers consider embankment heights to be inadequate and the desirable level has been raised from 2m to 3m. Further increases in land-take seem certain, since global warming is now accepted as irreversible and sea levels are expected to rise by between 20–80cm in the next 100 years (European Federation for Transport and Environment, 1995). Thus a further increase in embankment heights and land-take seems inevitable.

Deforestation

Deforestation is particularly significant in Bangladesh because its forests have important functions as wind barriers to limit cyclone damage and as sources of domestic fuel. The main remaining area of forest is the coastal mangrove swamps, or *sunderbans*, which provide protection to inland areas from the endemic cyclones to which they are subject. They are also the last remaining refuge for much of the country's wildlife, including the Bengal tiger.

Bangladesh's forest area is estimated to have declined from 11,000km^2 to 8000km^2 between 1980 and 1990 (World Bank, 1994). The annual rate of deforestation, at 3.9 per cent of total forested area, was second only to Jamaica among the 72 low and lower-middle income countries for which data are available (World Bank, 1995).[4] These figures imply that there will be no significant forested areas within 25 years.

In Bangladesh, bricks for road and other construction purposes are traditionally fired with fuelwood. Each brick needs 0.43kg of wood, enough for two-thirds of a person's daily needs for domestic fuelwood. A typical road in Bangladesh uses 200,000 to 300,000 bricks per km – which means around 100 tonnes of firewood. This could supply the needs of 450 people for a year in a country where there are already desperate shortages of this basic rural resource, shortages which over the past few years have resulted in the price of wood increasing at the rate of at least 25 per cent per year.

The GOB is attempting to switch production of bricks from wood to coal as the main fuel but, given the large number of traditional brick producers and the difficulty of policing production at remote sites, this is bound to take many years. It is also not clear if the country can afford to import all the coal it needs. In the interim, building only the most essential roads, and surfacing them with bricks only when there is no alternative, are sensible ways in which Bangladesh can move towards a more sustainable use of its resources in the road sector.

Conclusions

It is difficult to understand why one of the poorest countries in the world tries to support and relentlessly enhance a road density far in excess of its neighbours when measured against the resources available for the task. This is especially the case when the environmental costs of this policy appear to be so high. The benefits claimed to result from this process can only be sustained by a very short term view. If the demonstrable lack of sustainability of the resulting infrastructure were considered, allowance were made for the permanent loss of land assets that many of the poorest incur due to road construction, and the destruction of the country's remaining forested areas were taken into account, then it seems likely that the conclusions would be substantially different.

Unsustainability, owing to lack of maintenance, makes large scale road investment in many rural areas in Bangladesh a huge waste of resources accompanied by only a few measurable but ephemeral benefits for the asset-rich population, whereas the asset-poor population are bypassed or suffer significant disbenefits.

To an impoverished peasantry that walks, or whose vehicle ownership is confined to boats and bicycles, roads built for use by motor vehicles are almost irrelevant, especially when they have to be purchased at such a high personal cost.

Notes

1   This chapter was first published as a paper in *World Transport Policy & Practice*, vol 2, no 2, pp28–33.
2   It appears that after enthusiastically endorsing the study in 1991, the World Bank has also reassessed the results. In 1994 it commented that: 'It is difficult ... to verify whether the Bangladesh study took into account all possible intervening factors, such as unobserved differences among the communities in natural endowments' (World Bank, 1991a; 1994).
3   Generally considered to be households owning < 0.2ha (0.5 acres) of agricultural land. This provides food for a small household for about two months and makes sharecropping or employment obligatory.
4   Of these countries, 12 achieved either zero loss or a net gain in forest area.

References

Ahmed, A K, Khan, H A and Sampath, R J (1991) 'Poverty in Bangladesh: measurement, decomposition and intertemporal comparison', *Journal of Development Studies*, vol 27, no 4, pp48–63

Ahmed, R (1990) 'Infrastructure and agricultural production', *Technology Policy for Sustainable Agricultural Growth*, IFPRI Policy Briefs 7, presented at a seminar held 2–3 July, the Hague, The Netherlands

Ahmed, R and Hossain, M (1990) 'Development impact of rural infrastructure in Bangladesh', *Research Report 83*, International Food Policy Research Institute in collaboration with Bangladesh Institute of Development Studies, Washington, DC

Associates in Rural Development (1989) *Bangladesh Rural and Feeder Roads Sector Assessment*, USAID, Dhaka

Begum, S (1986) *Poverty in Bangladesh – A Profile*, Intermediate Technology Development Group, School of Arts and Social Studies, University of Sussex, Brighton

European Federation for Transport and Environment (1995) 'A new round of warnings on the threat to the global environment', *Bulletin No 43*, European Federation for Transport and Environment, Brussels, November

Hartmann, B and Boyce, J K (1983) *A Quiet Violence: View from a Bangladesh Village*, Zed Books, London

Howe, J (1994) 'Infrastructure investment in Bangladesh: who really benefits and how?', *IHE Working paper IP–6*, Fourth Workshop of the European Network of Bangladesh Studies, 25–27 August, Driebergen-Zeist, The Netherlands

Howe, J and Richards, P (1984) *Rural Roads and Poverty Alleviation*, Intermediate Technology Publications, London

Jansen, E G (1987) *Rural Bangladesh: Competition for Scarce Resources*, University Press, Dhaka

KBN Engineering and Applied Science and Tropical Research and Development (1991) *Programmatic Environmental Assessment of the USAID/Bangladesh Integrated Food for Development Program*, USAID, Dhaka

Merril, S, Garnett, H, Heinig, S and Battaglia, M (1990) *Bangladesh Road Saturation Study*, CARE – Bangladesh/Integrated Food for Work Program/Abt Associates, Dhaka

Smillie, I (1991) *Mastering the Machine: Poverty, Aid and Technology*, Intermediate Technology Publications, London

Transport Survey Section, Planning Commission, Government of Bangladesh and Overseas Development Group, University of East Anglia (1978) *Bangladesh Rural Transport Study*, Transport Survey Section, Planning Commission, Government of Bangladesh, Dhaka

USAID Mission to Bangladesh (1978) 'ID development strategy for Bangladesh', January, for submission to a meeting in Washington, DC, 6–7 February 1978, quoted in Hartmann, B and Boyce, J K (1983) *A Quiet Violence: View from a Bangladesh Village*, Zed Books, London

Wood, G D (1988) 'Plunder without danger: avoiding responsibility in rural works administration in Bangladesh', *IDS Bulletin*, vol 19, no 4

World Bank (1990a) 'Poverty', *World Bank Development Report 1990*, Oxford University Press, Washington, DC

World Bank (1990b) *Flood Control in Bangladesh: A Plan for Action*, World Bank Technical Paper No 119, Asia Region Technical Department, World Bank, Washington, DC

World Bank (1991a) *Republic of Ghana Rural Road Subsector Strategy Paper*, Infrastructure Operations Division, West Africa Department, Africa Region, World Bank, Washington, DC

World Bank (1991b) *Bangladesh Transport Sector Review*, Report No 9414 – BD, Infrastructure Operations Division, Country Department 1, Asia Regional Office, World Bank, Washington, DC

World Bank (1994) 'Infrastructure for development', *World Bank Development Report 1994*, Oxford University Press, Washington, DC

World Bank (1995) 'Workers in an integrating world', *World Bank Development Report 1995*, Oxford University Press, Washington, DC

Part 4

Transport in Australia

9

Back on Track? Will Australia Return to Rail?

Philip Laird and Peter Newman

Australia has one of the most road-dominated transport systems in the world, though this was not always the case. In the first half of the 20th century, extensive rail systems were developed in all cities and throughout rural areas. The constitution of the new country, formed in 1901, recognized the rail system as the glue joining the states together. However, the federal government never took full responsibility for the system and hence a unique mix of railway gauges and parochial state-based concerns were allowed to override the national interest throughout the 20th century.

By 1950 these rail systems were in decline but, rather than invest in their upgrading, Australia chose the road for its future land transport needs. As the tarmac was rolled out cars, trucks and buses were given priority. Country rail lines were closed, trams were all but scrapped (apart from in Melbourne) and rail in general went into a holding pattern, unable to compete with road transport. In the last quarter of the 20th century the federal government began a massive investment in a national highway system. From 1975 to 1999 the federal government poured Aus$43 billion into roads, a mere Aus$1.2 billion into rail and Aus$1.3 billion into urban public transport (Laird et al, 2001). Little wonder that Australians followed the bitumen trails rather than the rail systems. As seen by the federal Bureau of Transport Economics (BTE, 1999), 'total travel in the urban areas of Australia has grown remarkably – almost nine-fold over 50 years. Almost all of that growth came from cars and "other" road vehicles ...'

International comparisons show that by the 1990s, Australian cities such as Canberra and Perth were almost as car dependent as cities such as Detroit and Houston in the USA (Newman and Kenworthy, 1999). Only in Sydney and to some extent in Melbourne is there a level of public transport that is anything like the major cities in Europe or even Canada. In all cases, the cities and parts of cities with some reasonable alternative to the car are those where there is a rail alternative. However, outside these rail corridors the car dominates.

Non-urban passengers also have moved away from rail to road transport. In 1952 non-urban rail passenger kilometres (pkms) were overtaken by car pkms. Non-urban rail pkms were displaced by air pkms in 1973 and then by bus pkms in 1975. However, Queensland's new passenger tilt trains, operating over upgraded mainline tracks since 1998 with a resulting large boost to patronage, have demonstrated a clear potential for intercity rail in Australia when improved services are offered.

Rail was able to maintain dominance in land freight until about 1983, when the road freight task measured in tonne-kilometres overtook the rail freight task. However, by then, much of the rail freight task was for the movement of coal in New South Wales and Queensland, and the very efficient movement of iron ore in the Pilbara region of Western Australia. The loss of general freight by rail was severe, including a great deal of long distance intercity freight. One relevant factor was a 1954 decision by the Privy Council in London, on appeal from Australia's High Court, that effectively deregulated inter-state trucking. Ongoing freight deregulation and problems in the different rail systems, along with improvement in articulated truck technology, have also helped to boost the road freight task. By the mid-1990s, Australia's road freight activity was the highest per capita in the world (Austroads, 1997).

It is now possible to gain estimates of the total costs of this complete changeover to road transport. In 1997–1998, the net cost of road accidents was Aus$7 billion (being the overall cost of Aus$15 billion (BTE, 2000) less Aus$8 billion insurance per annum), road system costs Aus$7 billion, net tax refunds for motor vehicle expenses were about Aus$3 billion, with estimated environmental costs of some Aus$3 billion. That fiscal year, specific road user charges and taxes were about Aus$12 billion. As a result, there was a hidden road deficit in 1997–1998 of approximately Aus$8 billion. This road deficit does not include road congestion costs estimated at Aus$12 billion per annum (BTE, 1999). These Australian hidden costs compare with an estimated UK£30 billion in the UK, including congestion (Maddison et al, 1996).

The operation of articulated trucks in Australia is found to incur hidden subsidies of about Aus$2 billion a year. These subsidies comprise unrecovered road system costs of about Aus$1.24 billion, road accident involvement costs of some Aus$450 million and at least Aus$280 million in environmental costs. The hidden road freight subsidies contrast with the aggregate rail freight profits following rail freight reforms throughout the 1990s (see, for example, Laird, 1998) resulting in the elimination of aggregate rail freight deficits. Yet popular understanding would still suggest that rail systems are in deficit while trucks are only good for the economy.

The high costs of road transport, with its severe environmental and social impacts, and an under-performing rail system, have given rise to many federal government inquiries since 1990. These studies include:

- Inter-state Commission (1990);
- Ecologically Sustainable Development Working Group on Transport (1991);
- Industry Commission (1991, rail transport);
- National Transport Planning Taskforce (1994);
- Industry Commission (1994, urban public transport);
- Bureau of Transport Economics (1996, transport and greenhouse emissions);
- House of Representatives Standing Committee on Communications, Transport and Microeconomic Reform (roads, 1997, and then rail, 1998, 2001);
- Prime Minister's Rail Projects Task Force (1999); and
- Productivity Commission's inquiry into progress in rail reform (1999).

These major studies may have been reasonably expected to lead to action by the federal government. However, apart from a rail reform agenda limited to downsizing, increased productivity, corporatization and privatization of most rail systems, application of national competition policy, and limited road reform, the 1990s was basically a decade of policy paralysis in land transport reform. Indeed, with the abolition of some road tolls, reduction of some fuel excise, and introduction of uniform annual charges for heavy vehicles with neither mass nor distance differentiation for the various classes of heavy trucks, road reform arguably went backwards.

A major reason for this policy paralysis in land transport on both sides of federal politics has been the influence of Australia's powerful and diverse road lobby groups. In fact, there are no fewer than 60 road lobby groups operating at national, state or regional levels, with three major well resourced groups (the Motor Trades Association of Australia, the Australian Automobile Association and the Australian Trucking Association) operating in the federal capital city of Canberra. These three major groups interact with three government-based groups – Austroads representing the state road authorities, the National Road Transport Commission regulating road transport, and the Australian Local Government Association. The net result is ever more government land transport funds being allocated to roads at the expense of rail, and a trucking culture that ensures trucks are lightly regulated and in receipt of growing hidden subsidies.

By way of contrast, a relatively weak rail and urban public transport lobby could only watch as the federal government put more funds into roads and, throughout the 1990s, cut back funds to rail and public transport capital works. However unbalanced federal transport allocations were in the 1980s, the trend during the 1990s was even more disturbing. Specific federal funds for urban public transport funds ceased in 1993, and in the years from 1989–1990 to 2000 (in 1999 dollars) the roads allocation was Aus$17.6 billion, rail capital works were less than Aus$600 million and urban public transport funds were less than Aus$300 million.

Australia's cutback of federal funding for rail and public transport is in contrast with the USA. Under the 1991 Intermodal Surface Transportation Efficiency Act and the 1998 Transportation Equity Act in the USA, about 20 per cent of federal land transport funds were being applied by 2000 to mass transit.

One major reason for reducing automobile and truck dependence is their high liquid fuel consumption. Although some cars have increased their fuel efficiency, the uptake of larger cars and sports utility vehicles (SUVs, otherwise known as four-wheel drives) has resulted in Australia's passenger vehicle fleet retaining an average fuel consumption of 10 to 12 litres per 100 km between 1966 and 1999 (Mees, 2000). Rail, on the other hand, is three times more energy efficient than cars in Australian cities.

Most liquid fuel in Australia is used in its major cities. Thus, a modest modal shift from cars to public transport in major cities would result in liquid fuel savings, less air pollution and cleaner air, and would be a clear 'no regrets' measure for reducing greenhouse gas (GHG) emissions (BTE, 1996).

Whilst articulated trucks have increased their average energy efficiency from about 0.55 net tonne km (tkm) per megajoule (MJ) in 1976 (where 1 litre of diesel equates to 38.6MJ) to about 0.83tkm/MJ in 1995, average rail freight energy efficiency is much higher and has increased during this time from about 1.6tkm/MJ in 1976 to about 2.7tkm/MJ in 1995. This rail freight average excludes the iron ore trains in the Pilbara, which by 1980 were the most efficient in the world and whose energy efficiency now exceeds 10tkm/MJ. Shifting long distance road freight to rail is a further 'no regrets' measure to reduce GHGs as well as oil imports (BTE, 1996).

As well as mainline inter-state track upgrades that are necessary to improve rail freight efficiency and competitiveness, there is a case for improved road pricing for heavy trucks. This includes a move within southeast Australia's populous zone towards mass-distance charges. Such charges have been in successful use in New Zealand since 1978.

Transport funding in Australia has become dysfunctional. As well as major urban and intercity highways, mostly without tolls, receiving generous funding for substantial upgrades, secondary roads are also favoured. Intercity mainline rail tracks have been starved of funds, and Australia has substandard national track. Within most states, considerable investment has again begun to be made in rail, but little comes from the federal government. States often have to raise their funds for rail from loans. Many of the above cited inquiries have recommended a more balanced approach between road and rail funding. There is now a strong case for government road funds to be abolished and replaced by transport funds.

Australia is poised for a rail revival. Truck capacity has been reached on major highways and the freight rail systems are now fairly competitive. As found by a recent major rail track audit (Australian Rail Track Corporation, 2001), a major part of the future growth in land freight can be absorbed by rail with a track upgrade at a modest cost of Aus$507 million. In the cities an even more obvious transition is underway. Urban freeways are hopelessly congested and the costs and politics of building more are increasingly high. The sheer capacity of rail (carrying 50,000 people per hour as against 2500 per hour on a freeway lane) means that urban rail is back in favour. Sydney's system was able to provide for the 2000 Olympic Games with minimal private car use, Melbourne is expanding its rail system again with fast trains to its regional towns, and Perth's new rail system has had remarkable growth with bipartisan support for a Aus$1 billion extension.

Australians have shown they will use rail systems when they are provided; all they need is a transport decision-making system that can begin to shift the balance towards them.

A ten-point plan to bring Australian land transport 'back on track' is suggested (Laird et al, 2001):

1   Road safety measures such as those in the National Road Safety Strategy 2001– 2010 for Australia need to be implemented, with stronger provisions to further reduce the loss of life and injury on the roads. Shifting passengers to all other non-car modes whilst reducing the need to travel, along with shifting freight to rail, should be seen as part of road safety.

2   Vehicle technology needs to be regulated to world best practice for new vehicles, with high standards for maintenance of the existing fleet through vehicle inspections. Standards need to include reducing transport GHG emissions by 2010 to their 1990 levels.

3   All 'road funds' should be replaced by 'transport funds' and Australia should instigate a more democratic funding-allocation process, similar to the USA's process of

regional transport plans involving all local stakeholders linked to broad national goals.

4   All cities need to levy a central business district (CBD) parking fee with proceeds used to improve urban public transport facilities.

5   All states need to ensure that their capital cities use congestion tolling on at least one major urban arterial road, and part of the national highway system linking the city to an outlying urban area as part of a process of educating motorists of the real costs of transport.

6   All states, territories and the Commonwealth need to increase the aggregate level of road cost recovery from heavy vehicles to at least 25 per cent of road system costs, with development of New Zealand-style mass distance charges in the populous zone of Australia.

7   The problems of continuing oil vulnerability and the full costs of transport fuel use need to be explained to the Australian and New Zealand public. Fuel excise needs to be progressively increased in order to recover all external costs of road vehicle usage and to allow for a reduction of annual charges for small energy efficient cars, along with the improvement of urban public transport and rail freight.

8   Agreed world best practice standards need to be set for the delivery and coordination of urban public transport in major urban areas including high service delivery, the integration of land use, the development of public–private joint projects and fully integrated ticketing.

9   Federal taxation benefits need to be reduced for motor vehicle ownership and use, and improved for urban public transport use.

10 A National Bureau of Transportation Statistics should be formed to provide the publication of accurate, comprehensive and up-to-date information on all modes of transport, including energy use and GHG emissions.

This ten-point plan has much in common with 22 recommendations made by the Senate Environment, Communications, Information Technology and the Arts Reference Committee (2000). Of the 106 recommendations made by the majority of this committee, no fewer than 21 addressed transport GHG emissions and solutions. However, only four of these 21 transport recommendations received the full support of the federal government (Australian Greenhouse Office, 2001), with a further 11 recommendations being considered to have already been supported or addressed through existing measures. The remaining six recommendations, coupled with a minority party recommendation to replace road funds by transport funds, were not supported by the government.

It requires a new approach to address the heavy bias towards oil-based road transport in Australia. A whole new programme is also required to move passengers from road to rail in Australia's cities and regions, and to shift freight from road to rail. The authors suggest that government at a federal and state level will need to assist Australia to adjust to a regime of higher international oil prices in a manner that encourages improved energy efficiency in transport. This would also reduce transport GHG emissions.

References

Australian Greenhouse Office (2001) *Government Response to the Report 'The Heat Is On: Australia's Greenhouse Future'*, Australian Greenhouse Office, Canberra

Australian Rail Track Corporation (2001) *Interstate Rail Network Audit*, Australian Rail Track Corporation, South End, South Australia

Austroads (1997) *Australia at the Crossroads: Summary Report*, Austroads, Sydney

BTE (1996) *Transport and Greenhouse: Costs and Options for Reducing Emissions*, Bureau of Transport (and Communications) Economics, AGPS, Canberra

BTE (1999) *Urban Transport: Looking Ahead*, Bureau of Transport (and Communications) Economics, AGPS, Canberra

BTE (2000) *Road Crash Costs in Australia*, Bureau of Transport (and Communications) Economics, AGPS, Canberra

House of Representatives Standing Committee on Communications, Transport and Arts (formerly Microeconomic Reform) (1997) *Planning not Patching*, Parliament of the Commonwealth of Australia, Canberra

House of Representatives Standing Committee on Communications, Transport and Arts (formerly Microeconomic Reform) (1998) *Tracking Australia*, Parliament of the Commonwealth of Australia, Canberra

House of Representatives Standing Committee on Communications, Transport and Arts (formerly Microeconomic Reform) (2001) *Back on Track*, Parliament of the Commonwealth of Australia, Canberra

Industry Commission (1991) *Rail Transport* (final report), Australian Government Publishing Service, Canberra

Industry Commission (1994) *Urban Transport* (final report), Australian Government Publishing Service, Canberra

Inter-state Commission (1990) *Road Use Charges and Vehicle Registration: A National Scheme*, AGPS, Canberra

Laird, P G (1998) 'Rail freight efficiency and competitiveness in Australia', *Transport Reviews*, vol 18, no 3, pp241–256

Laird, P G, Newman, P W G, Bachels, M A and Kenworthy, J R (2001) *Back on Track: Rethinking Australian and New Zealand Transport*, UNSW Press, Sydney

Maddison, D, Pearce, D, Johansson, O, Calthrop, E, Litman, T and Verhoef, E (1996) *The True Costs of Road Transport*, Earthscan, London

Mees, P (2000) *A Very Public Solution: Transport in the Dispersed City*, Melbourne University Press, Melbourne

Newman, P W G and Kenworthy, J R (1999) *Sustainability and Cities: Overcoming Automobile Dependence*, Island Press, Washington, DC

Prime Minister's Rail Projects Task Force (1999) *Revitalising Rail: The Private Sector Solution*, Australian Government, Canberra

Productivity Commission (1999) *Progress in Rail Reform*, Report No 6, Australian Government Publishing Service, Canberra

Senate Environment, Communications, Information Technology and the Arts Reference Committee (2000) *The Heat Is On: Australia's Greenhouse Future*, Australian Government, Canberra

10

A Wish Called Wander: Reclaiming Automobility from the Motor Car[1]

Ian Ker and Paul Tranter

Introduction

In transport economics textbooks it is always argued that the demand for travel is a derived demand: that is, travel is not sought for itself but for what it enables people to do. If that is so, then why are ever greater amounts of time devoted to it rather than to trying to minimize the travel undertaken? Although those economics texts recognize tourist and certain types of leisure travel as exceptions, most urban travel is for utilitarian purposes. According to the theory, we should aim to minimize, rather than increase, our consumption of travel. Yet, when faced with an increase in the speed of travel (for example, by the construction of a new rapid transit system), there tends to be a reduction in the gains in terms of longer journeys, thus maintaining the same travel times.

Collectively, transport planners then treat this additional travel as a benefit, on the basis that it reflects an increase in the range of choice available to everyone. One might well question the utility of additional choices when most people are already suffering from information and option overload (Keyes, 1991). Might it also not be possible that the additional choices made available through time savings are less of a benefit than they seem at first sight? Has the stage been reached where more time is spent choosing, thereby resulting in a real disbenefit through continually wondering whether the right choice has been made?

It is increasingly being recognized that in making private choices, unforeseen costs are often imposed on others. This chapter shows that the pursuit of a specific kind of automobility has led unwittingly to a reduction in the independent mobility of many people in the community, including the elderly, the disabled, women and children. As a result of this, access to opportunities such as employment, education, recreation and social interaction has been reduced. In the particular case of children, their development of independence has been inhibited, with far-reaching and long term consequences.

Yet it is not only the transport disadvantaged whose freedom is curtailed by the motor car. Motorists themselves have also been misled by the myth of cars as freedom machines: the myth that car-based mobility directly complements autonomy or self-directedness. Consequently, motorists become more dependent on others (including car manufacturers and repairers) rather than gaining autonomy.

In this chapter, the following questions are addressed:

- Is 'automobility 'bad language'?
- Who has access to car-based mobility?
- Are children and women marginalized by an increased reliance on car-based mobility?
- Is it a myth that cars provide freedom?
- What are the dangers of a high-tech vision for automobility?

Is 'Automobility' Bad Language?

In the study of transport (or any other social issue), the subtle effects of language on the acceptance of dominant ideologies are often overlooked. Modern English-speaking societies have uncritically accepted the use of the word 'automobile' to mean the private car, and hence 'automobility' to mean private car use. However, an examination of the meanings behind this term suggests that such usage is based on false assumptions. Dictionaries give the following definitions: *auto-* (in combination): self, own, of or by oneself (Greek *autos*); *mobile*: shifting position readily, not fixed.

It needs only a little reflection to realize the absurdity of equating *shifting position readily by oneself* with the private motor car, in many of the major cities of the world. Not all cities are as congested as Bangkok, where traffic moves at not much more than walking pace, but all cities have times and places where the car is not a very mobile piece of equipment. Jokes about freeways (roads with restricted access) being very expensive linear car parks are too often not far from the truth.

But even when it is mobile, the motor car does not provide 'automobility' to people. Simply to keep oneself mobile in a car requires large vehicle manufacture enterprises, service and repair industries, the road building industry, an international oil industry and, of course, an external source of energy.

Therefore a paradox is in operation. The motor car appears to provide its owners with the independence to travel when and where they choose. Yet there is a fundamental dependency on the goods and services provided by a multitude of others. The apparent independence provided by the car is quite illusory.

The only true automobility is achieved by walking, but cycling comes pretty close since most people can effect the necessary maintenance and repairs to keep a bicycle in running order, and the rider provides his or her own energy to achieve the mobility.

The consequences of this are not trivial. Alternatives to the use of the private car must be sought. However, this suggestion can be interpreted as advocating a reduction in the ability of individuals to be independently mobile, and is in conflict with modern concepts of individuality and encounters strong opposition. Yet much of this opposition may be based on a misunderstanding of 'automobility' and of the supposed freedoms provided by the motor car.

Automobility for Whom?

Automobility, in its current (mis)usage as car-based transport, applies only to a minority of the population at any one time. Even in Western societies, almost half the population does not have independent access to a car.

Using data from Western Australia, the transport disadvantaged are disproportionately the young (100 per cent of those younger than 17), the aged (43 per cent of those over 60 do not have a driver's licence) and women (25 per cent of women over 17, and 60 per cent of those aged 60 and over, do not have a licence to drive).

Australian cities are among the most car-dependent cities in the world. Yet despite the dominance of the car in Australian cities, 45 per cent of people do not have a driver's licence, either because they are too young to drive (26 per cent) or because of disability, the cost of owning a car or historical circumstances (particularly amongst the elderly). There are also a significant number who have a licence to drive, but do not have access to a car.

So far, the most common approach to the mobility disadvantages of such groups as children, women, the elderly or the disabled has been to attempt to provide more car-based mobility for them, usually as passengers. While this may seem an appropriate choice in some circumstances, in doing so, we have, often unknowingly, contributed to the lack of true automobility (ie independent mobility) for the rest of the population. Ironically, one of the most hazardous tasks for any pedestrian (especially children, the elderly or those with disabilities) is trying to negotiate the traffic jams around schools at the end of a school day – traffic jams caused by parents trying to compensate for their children's lack of genuine automobility.

Automobility for Those too Young to Drive

Children represent an obvious group that has not been a major beneficiary of developments in mobility via the car. Although they can travel as car passengers, children aged from 7 to 12 years old in many Western countries now have much less freedom than in previous generations to travel around their own neighbourhood or city without an adult (Hillman et al, 1990; Tranter and Whitelegg, 1994; Tranter, 1994).

The reduction of children's true automobility can be related to the growth in reliance on the motor car, either directly through its effect on traffic danger, or indirectly through its effect on the location of activities, and the reduction in local, neighbourhood-based communities.

It could be argued that the loss of this independent mobility has been compensated for by extra car trips as passengers. As car passengers, children can travel to more (and more distant) locations than they could otherwise. However, there are considerable costs involved in depriving children of their freedom, not only for the children themselves, but also for their parents, the wider environment and for the whole community (Moore, 1986; Tranter, 1994; 1995; van Vliet, 1983; Kegerreis, 1993). The independent mobility of children is something that may not be compensated for by the increased mobility of children in cars.

The most significant costs of the lost freedom relate to the children themselves. Children's own personal, intellectual and psychological development may be impaired when their independent mobility is restricted (van Vliet, 1983; Kegerreis, 1993; Moore, 1986). In order for children to be able to become familiar with their own neighbourhoods and communities, they need to have active exploration. This is not provided when children are passengers in cars: children may see more, but they learn less. Without true automobility, children are unlikely to experience a strong sense of local community, nor are they likely to feel as though they are an important part of that community.

The importance of independent mobility for children is expressed very powerfully by Engwicht (1992):

> ... freedom to explore the local neighbourhood ... gives [children] an opportunity to develop a relationship with the placeness of their physical environment. Robbing children of a sense of place robs them of the very essence of life.

Another consideration is that if children are constantly driven to school and to other places, they lose one regular way of maintaining their physical fitness. The effect of this lack of fitness on self-esteem and obesity has been noted by an Australian paediatrician, Dr Simon Clarke:

> ... their parents bring them to see me because they are overweight and have self-esteem problems. Of course they are overweight. They are all ferried about by car to organized sport and organized music (Donaghy, 1994).

While it is important that children are able to reach local play areas by themselves, walking or cycling journeys to school and to other destinations also provide genuine play activities in themselves (de Monchaux, 1981). Research in the UK (Keynes, 1995) found that the majority of primary schoolchildren would rather walk or cycle to school than be taken by car.

Not only is the automobility of children decreased by excessive reliance on the motor car, but the automobility of their parents is also decreased when parents are forced to spend more time acting as conscript chauffeurs, and hence have less time available for walking or cycling. Children in car-dominated environments are much more likely to be driven to school, to sport, to entertainment and even to their own friends' homes. Those who are most likely to be the chauffeurs are the mothers of these children.

Women and Automobility

There are some important gender implications of the increased dominance of the motor car. Although some women may appear to have been advantaged through increasing car ownership, in general, women have benefited much less than men. Women generally have less access to private motor vehicles (Pickup, 1988). However, many women feel forced into purchasing a motor vehicle because of fears for their personal safety as pedestrians, as cyclists or on public transport (Hamilton and Gregory, 1989; Wekerle, 1984). Thus women may feel deprived of the freedom *not* to own a car.

Despite recent changes in the rates of women in the workforce, research in Australia, the UK and the USA demonstrates that 'outside the home, women are still primarily responsible for domestic-related travel purposes; for example, shopping and school escort journeys' (Pickup, 1988). As Tivers (1988) argues, 'this is clearly the result of gender role differentiation of activities'. Women's traditional childcare roles now include the responsibility to keep children safe when moving from one private space to another, safe from traffic dangers for example. Thus women not only have less access to cars, but they are more likely to have to use them for purposes that are nothing to do with autonomy or self-directedness, but more to do with perceived constraints or obligations.

Automobility for Motorists? Mobility, Freedom and Unfreedom

The emphasis on private motorized mobility systematically discriminates against substantial sections of the community in terms of access to the facilities, services and opportunities most people take for granted. Yet even those who still have car-based transport are being deceived by the apparent advantages of the motor car.

Residents of modern cities have collectively constructed a myth concerning the freedom provided by the car. As argued above, the mobility provided by the car is contingent on the support provided by a plethora of goods and service providers. The myth that the car provides people with freedom is also based on the false premise that mobility facilitates freedom. This idea is related to the mechanistic model of the world that still pervades Western society (Capra, 1982). In this worldview, objects (including people and machines) are not seen as productive unless they are doing things or moving. Unfortunately, so much emphasis is placed on moving that we have forgotten what movement can destroy. As Engwicht (1992) explains, 'for many people, movement can be an expression of tyranny, a loss of freedom'. For example, people may be forced to drive children to organized sport simply because they feel it is too dangerous to let them play locally. Engwicht suggests that 'true freedom lies in having access to the interaction (exchange) that we need for personal and community wellbeing'.

Motorists themselves often do not have the freedom *not* to own a car. As Catton (1993) argues: 'freedom involves the ability to act in ways that are consonant with one's values'. Growing numbers of people now value:

* a safe and liveable urban environment, protected from dangers such as traffic, pollution and the risk of assault;
* strong neighbourhood-based communities, which allow people to feel as though they are an important part of a meaningful community;
* equity; and
* physical, psychological and spiritual wellbeing.

When people use their cars, collectively they are behaving in ways that are not consistent with this set of values. If people feel forced into car ownership, then this means that they have relinquished the freedom to behave according to their values.

But even if it is accepted that speed of movement can be equated with freedom, the motor car has let us down. During peak hour traffic, average speeds in Australian cities are often less than the speed of a bicycle. Also, when the time devoted to earning money for the purchase, maintenance, insurance and so on of cars is taken into account (as well as the external costs of cars), the social speed of driving is less than that of a cyclist.[2] 'In the final analysis, the car wastes more time than it saves and creates more distance than it overcomes' (Gorz, 1973).

Despite the current emphasis on speed and convenience, the value of wandering around is still recognized in our society, sometimes in seemingly unlikely contexts. For example, even within the US Air Force it is realized that the best leaders adopt the 'LBWA' strategy: 'lead by wandering (walking) around' (Lester, 1995). This allows leaders to stay in touch with people and with their working environment.

In the same way, urban residents need time to wander around their neighbourhood to give themselves a sense of place and a sense of community. When people walk (or cycle), this is not merely transport as 'a means of getting to a place, it can be an experience of place in itself' (Engwicht, 1992; see also Ohlenschlager, 1990).

Dangers of a High-tech Vision for Automobility

As motorists travel at speed, vision is restricted to a narrow band, approximately the width of the road. Similarly, transport planners can easily be narrowly focused on technological solutions to the problems of the motor car. A current example of this is the technological view of automobility as 'cars that drive themselves'. This new development in transport policy may make it even harder to reclaim automobility from the car. Zygmont (1993) suggests that in 'traffic-choked regions such as the Los Angeles basin, automatic driving will first appear around 2010'. This would be facilitated by 'intelligent vehicle highway systems', which may eventually facilitate cars driving in 'platoons' at speed on freeways, steering themselves by following a guidance system transmitted from sensors in the cars. Such a system is claimed to increase freeway capacity by up to 300 per cent. This approach supposedly solves the problems of cars by making cars better!

One of the many problems which such a technological approach is that even if it works on the freeways, it will simply mean that there will be more cars coming off the freeways into urban areas at either end, where the cars will disrupt communities, kill people and make streets even more unliveable. It will also further encourage the trend towards the dispersal of land uses, because when people save time on transport they use it to buy more distance. Consequently, life will be even harder for pedestrians and cyclists.

By adopting a more logical definition of automobility, different directions for our cities and their transport can be envisioned. In a city in which people are genuinely automobile:

• walking and cycling are the primary modes of transport; motorized transport (public and private) is used only where non-motorized transport is unsuitable.

- Streets are places for people, rather than simply movement corridors for motor cars (Tranter and Doyle, 1996). Adults as well as children use the streets as places to socialize and wander.
- Most of the present road space and car parking space is used primarily for non-motoring uses including recreation, work activities and food production.
- Significant car-free areas are provided (Reutter and Reutter, 1996).
- Public transport operates in ways that promote ease of independent use by all people, without itself creating barriers for those who wish to wander.

Such a city is one where people of all ages, abilities and incomes are more free to wander, explore, interact, play and socialize. Such a city is ultimately more equitable, because the ability to access opportunities becomes less dependent upon being able to command the substantial resources necessary for private motorized travel.

Conclusion

People may well have an innate 'wish to wander'. When they rush from one activity to another, when they treat themselves as machines, trying to be as productive as possible, they are depriving themselves of important experiences. They lose their sense of place and history. They lose the opportunity for the sense of belonging that comes from keeping in touch with their communities.

Activists for more liveable cities are constantly searching for new ways to reduce the dominance of the motor car. Already there are numerous in-action models throughout the world showing how to move towards this goal, eg traffic-calming, reclaiming streets for people and charging the full costs of cars (Hass-Klau, 1990, 1992; Hawley, 1993; CART, 1989). The difficulty arises in being able to engender widespread enthusiasm for the necessary changes. An attitudinal change in society is needed; dominant social values need to be challenged.

This chapter has identified one important way to help produce such an attitudinal change: raising an awareness of the misuse of language. The widespread misuse of 'automobility' is not just bad language: it also helps to repress challenges to the myth of cars as freedom machines. If a sufficient number of people can understand the basis of this myth, if the link between cars and 'unfreedom' and the value of wandering can be understood, then perhaps automobility can be truly reclaimed from the motor car.

Notes

1 This chapter was first published as a paper in *World Transport Policy & Practice* (1997), vol 3, no 2, pp10–16.
2 'Social speed' is a new definition of car speed that explicitly takes into account the amount of time we need to work in order to earn the money to pay for a car. Put simply, if we need to work for 200 hours each year to earn the money to pay for the

car that we then drive for 10,000km, then we must add the 200 hours to our estimate of the time that it takes to cover that distance by car; this reduces the
measured speed. Social speed is lower than measured speed because it takes a wider
view of the time associated with driving. That is: the total time associated with
driving equals the actual time plus the time taken to earn the money to pay for
both the vehicle and the fuel.

References

Capra, F (1982) *The Turning Point: Science, Society and the Rising Culture,* Fontana, London
CART (1989) *Traffic Calming: A Solution to Route Twenty and a Vision for Brisbane*, Citizens
Advocating Responsible Transport, Queensland
Catton, P (1993) 'Freedom machines myth', unpublished discussion paper, Department of
Philosophy and Religious Studies, University of Canterbury, Christchurch
de Monchaux, S (1981) *Planning with Children in Mind: A Notebook for Local Planners and
Policy Makers on Children in the City Environment,* NSW Department of Environment and
Planning, Sydney
Donaghy, B (1994) 'Busy children, exhausted parents', *Sydney Morning Herald,* Tuesday 5 July,
p15
Engwicht, D (1992) *Towards an Eco-City: Calming the Traffic,* Envirobook, Sydney
Gorz, A (1973) 'The social ideology of the motor car', *Le Sauvage,* September–October, http://
www.hrc.wmin.ac.uk/campaigns/SocId1.html
Hamilton, K and Gregory, A (1989) 'Women, transport and health', *Autodestruction* (special
issue of *Radical Community Medicine*), vol 38, pp10–13
Hass-Klau, C (1990) *The Pedestrian and City Traffic,* Belhaven Press, London
Hass-Klau, C (1992) *Civilised Streets: A Guide to Traffic Calming,* Environmental and Transport
Planning, Brighton
Hawley, L (1993) *Towards Traffic Calming: A Practitioners' Manual of Implemented Local Area
Traffic Management and Blackspot Devices,* Federal Office of Road Safety, Canberra
Hillman, M, Adams, J and Whitelegg, J (1990) *One False Move: A Study of Children's Independent
Mobility,* Policy Studies Institute, London
Kegerreis, S (1993) 'Independent mobility and children's mental and emotional development' in
Hillman, M (ed) *Children, Transport and the Quality of Life,* Policy Studies Institute, London
Keyes, R (1991) *Timelock: How Life Got So Hectic and What You Can Do About It,* Harper
Collins, New York
Keynes, P (1995) *School Travel: Health and the Environment,* Cleary Hughes Associates,
Nottingham
Lester, R (1995) 'Leadership, management and command', seminar at Australian Defence Force
Academy, 30 November
Moore, R C (1986) *Childhood's Domain: Play and Place in Child Development,* Croom Helm,
London
Ohlenschlager, S (1990) 'Women also travel' in Trench, S and Oc, T (eds) *Current Issues in Plan-
ning,* Gower, Aldershot
Pickup, L (1988) 'Hard to get around: a study of women's travel mobility' in Little, J, Peake, L
and Richardson, P (eds) *Women in Cities: Gender and the Urban Environment,* New York
University Press, New York
Reutter, U and Reutter, O (1996) 'Car-free households: who lives without an automobile today?'
World Transport Policy & Practice, vol 2, no 4, pp32–37

Tivers, J (1988) 'Women with young children: constraints on activities in the urban environment' in Little, J, Peake, L and Richardson, P (eds) *Women in Cities: Gender and the Urban Environment*, New York University Press, New York

Tranter, P (1994) 'A child-friendly focus for transport reform: children's travel freedoms and urban form', *Nineteenth Australasian Transport Research Forum*, Australian Transport Research Forum, Melbourne, pp517–538

Tranter, P (1995) 'Behind closed doors: women, girls and mobility' in TransAdelaide (ed) *On the Move: Debating the Issues that Affect Women and Public Transport*, Conference Proceedings, TransAdelaide, Adelaide

Tranter, P and Doyle, J (1996) 'Reclaiming the residential street as play space', *International Play Journal*, vol 4, pp81–97

Tranter, P and Whitelegg, J (1994) 'Children's travel behaviours in Canberra: car-dependent lifestyles in a low density city', *Journal of Transport Geography*, vol 2, no 4, pp265–273

van Vliet, W (1983) 'Children's travel behaviour', *Ekistics*, vol 298, pp61–65

Wekerle, G (1984) 'A woman's place is in the city', *Antipode*, vol 16, no 3, pp11–19

Zygmont, J (1993) 'Automobility: cars that drive themselves', *Omni*, vol 15, p38

11

Urban Transport Policy Paradoxes in Australia

Paul Mees

Introduction

Melbourne's extensive heavy and light rail networks are suffering from a decline in usage as the city becomes increasingly car-dominated. This chapter discusses reasons for this trend and contrasts Melbourne with Canadian cities and with Perth, Western Australia.[1] The popular explanation for Melbourne's problems – the low density nature of post-war suburban development – is held to be a rationalization, rather than an explanation. The real cause is government transport policies that reduce the attractiveness of public transport while expanding road capacity.

Summer of Discontent

April 1994 brought an Indian summer to Melbourne, a fortnight of unseasonably fine autumn weather. What should have been an occasion for enjoyment soon turned sour, as the build-up of car exhausts produced the city's worst ever bout of photochemical smog. Instead of sunning themselves, the 3 million residents of the city designated the 'world's most liveable' by the Washington Research Institute were coping with irritations to the eyes and respiratory system.

The smog episode refocused concern on the poor state of Melbourne's public transport. Despite possessing the English-speaking world's largest tram/light rail network, and an electrified urban rail system the size of the London Underground with a fleet of modern trains (none more than 20 years old), Melbourne has lost public transport passengers at a world-beating rate since wartime petrol rationing was lifted in February 1950. The Labour government that held office from 1982 to 1992 and was committed to reversing decades of neglect of public transport could do no more than slow the rate of decline: current modal share is about 8 per cent of total travel and 15 per cent of work trips (Moriarty and Beed, 1992). The rail system operates at only a fraction of capacity, even in peak periods (Mees, 1993), and occupancies are now so low that rail transport actually produces similar greenhouse gas (GHG) emissions per pkm to the car (Richardson, 1993).

The Conservative Victorian state government, elected in November 1992, is responding with a reform programme comprising service reductions, fare increases, productivity improvements and privatization (urban transport is a state responsibility).[2]

The government has also announced an accelerated urban freeway programme called 'Linking Melbourne' (VicRoads, 1994). These policies have the support of most transport academics and other experts, although some believe the government should go further. Their reasoning is:

- Urban public transport requires a large public subsidy, but returns little benefit, because so few people use it.
- Little can be done to improve patronage, sadly, because social change and post-war development have made the radial rail and tram systems, and even conventional route bus services, irrelevant to most people's travel needs.
- The only logical response is to cut costs ruthlessly and bring the subsidy to an acceptable level, and to privatize and deregulate as much of the system as possible.
- Since most travel is going to be by road, an expanded freeway network is needed.

But transport policy is not just about moving people and goods around. Transport is one of the major influences on the form of cities. Los Angeles and Barcelona both did most of their growing in the last 120 years. They look very different largely because of differing transport histories. If Melbourne is to be surrendered entirely to the car, the consequence will be a city more like Detroit, Dallas or Los Angeles, with more smog epidemics. If, as 'Linking Melbourne' proposes, a ring-freeway is built, the expectation will be a shapeless sprawl of drive-in shopping centres and office parks around the interchanges, uncontrollable suburban traffic congestion and pollution, as can be seen around most US cities and along London's M25 orbital freeway.

Few planners – even those who support ring-freeways or public transport cuts – want this future for Melbourne, but the policies they advocate amount to a return to the 1960s and 1970s, when Thomson noted that Melbourne was 'gradually being transformed from a strong-centre to a weak-centre structure' (Thomson, 1977).

The Dispersed City

The argument that low-density, decentralized post-war development makes conventional public transport non-viable is not new. As early as 1960, the authors of the Chicago Area Transportation Study confidently claimed:

> The conditions of land use and density ... are the major determinants of the travel market. If demand is constrained by these factors, it is unlikely that changes in supply will have any great impact on the number of users (CATS, 1960).

The argument was presented more thoroughly in Meyer et al (1965) and has not been improved on since.

A 1985 study for the European Conference of Ministers of Transport noted extremely low levels of public transport use in Australia (as well as in New Zealand and the USA), which was attributed to 'high levels of car ownership ... and extensive low density suburbs, which are difficult to serve adequately by public transport' (Webster et al, 1985).

This is the conventional explanation for the decline of public transport in Melbourne and in other Australian cities. A local road engineering text observes:

> Although every effort should be made to encourage the efficient use of public transport ... current land use trends in Australian cities are towards continued low density development that cannot be effectively or economically served by public transport (Underwood, 1990).

Underwood discusses a series of flexible and demand-responsive alternatives, such as shared taxis and neighbourhood car cooperatives. This is also a common theme: in a dispersed, low density city, innovative, flexible, car-like (and consequently, highly polluting) forms of public transport are the only viable options. Traditional modes such as rail have a declining role, and public transport is for niche markets such as schoolchildren and other people without cars (Hensher, 1994).

An additional form of dispersion is movement of employment, retailing and other activity from the central business district (CBD) to the suburbs, a result of the flexibility created by the car and the truck and of technological change, particularly electronic communications. This process, noted in the USA by Meyer et al (1965), has produced a diffuse pattern of trip-making, which Hall (1990) describes as a general feature of Western cities:

> The traditional downtown is now only the leading commercial centre among a number of others, some of which may compete strongly with it. Thus the traditional pattern of movement – radially inward during the morning peak, outward during the late afternoon – has increasingly been overlain by other movements, both reverse commuting and criss-cross commuting ... [like] a box of matches thrown almost randomly onto a table.

This dispersed journey pattern does not produce the concentrated flows of passengers required to support public transport. Much of the new suburban travel is cross-suburban, and cannot be conveniently served by the radial fixed-rail system. Even where suburban jobs are concentrated in centres, these are too small, and attract trips from too many directions, to support much in the way of public transport. Hall, however, is less eager to write off public transport: 'in metro areas where suburban jobs are clustered around transit interchanges, for instance, it may not be true at all' (Hall, 1990).

Canadian Contrasts

The 1985 study for the European Conference of Ministers of Transport (ECMT) (Webster et al, 1985) noted that Canadian cities have been much more successful than their Australian and US counterparts at retaining public transport patronage:

> The situation in Canada is particularly interesting, since suburban development ... is very much in the North American, car-oriented pattern, yet public transport use is at European levels, and the trend is strongly upwards.

The report suggests that this may be due to government policies that have concentrated employment and other trip destinations in CBDs. Newman and Kenworthy (1999) have sparked controversy in Australian transport planning circles by presenting Toronto as an example of the successful integration of transport and land use planning, emphasizing the siting of high density housing near rapid transit stations.

Critics of this approach argue that large increases in density are neither feasible nor desirable (eg Hensher, 1994). Public transport will continue to decline or at best play a minor role, because densities cannot or should not be increased substantially nor jobs recentralized. This again echoes the reasoning of the Chicago Area Transportation Study (eg CATS, 1960). But some planners argue that the environmental damage created by over-reliance on the car makes increased densities imperative. They point to successful examples – 'urban villages' – of residents of affluent cities happily accepting high density lifestyles. Even the proponents of increased densities, however, are generally at a loss to deal with employment decentralization, except to argue that existing levels of centralization should be protected.

> Looked at in very simplistic terms, the solution to the public transport dilemma is to alter the way in which Melbourne is developing, to induce a form and density that create favourable conditions for public transport to operate under (Kohut, 1991).

There are, however, other explanations for the apparent success of Canadian urban transit. Vuchic (1981) also regards Toronto as a model, but not primarily of land use planning:

> Another interesting comparison is between several US cities and Toronto. In 1950 Toronto had a similar transit service to that in US cities; it had a simultaneous increase in auto ownership, it experienced urban sprawl (it has even fewer space limitations), and it constructed some of the widest freeways in the world. The drastic difference is that, unlike most US cities, Toronto made a serious commitment to continuous improvement of transit. It constructed a rapid transit system and introduced numerous operational innovations. The consequences of this policy are clear: between 1961 and 1976 transit ridership in Toronto increased by 46 per cent. During the same period ridership in most US cities ... continued to decline (Vuchic, 1981).

Cervero (1986), comparing Canadian and US public transport, concludes:

> the overriding factor behind transit's success in Canada is, plainly and simply, the superior levels of service, combined with the careful integration of transit and land use planning.

Another possible explanation for Melbourne's public transport decline thus emerges. Melbourne, similarly to Canadian cities, had a choice about the type of transport system it was to have; policy-makers chose the path of declining public transport and car dominance. This contrasts with the urban form explanation, which is more deterministic, portraying transport changes as the outcome of natural processes of city growth and technological change.

Toronto stands out even in Canada as having achieved the apparently impossible task of providing high quality, cost-effective public transport in a sprawling city. The secret of success is service and integration. Trains are fast, safe and clean, running every few minutes until 1.30am. Buses and trams operate as feeders to the rail system, with frequent services and 24-hour coverage on trunk routes, and changing modes is easy. The excellence of the rail system draws passengers to the feeder buses, which also serve local and cross-suburban travel. The buses generate patrons for the rail system, completing the virtuous circle. Public transport has been supported by a two-decade moratorium on freeway construction except in outer areas, limits on downtown car parking and supportive land use policies (although the latter may have been honoured more in the breach than the observance: Frisken, 1990).

Canada should be able to provide lessons for Australia, particularly since the two nations share many features that distinguish them from the USA, such as the absence of urban race tensions. In many respects, the Australian situation is actually more favourable to public transport: Toronto opened its first rail line in 1954, and must build each addition to its small network underground, while the Melbourne rail and tram systems have been in place for over a century, shaping the city's development. Less than 10 per cent of Melbourne's population lives more than 5km from a rapid transit station, compared with 60 per cent in Toronto; 17 of the 25 largest suburban shopping centres (ABS, 1986) are adjacent to rail stations, compared with only five in Toronto (Metropolitan Toronto Planning Department, 1992).

However, public transport service in Melbourne has been deteriorating for decades. Frequencies have been cut, reliability is poor and trains are no faster now than when the first electric services commenced in the 1920s (see Table 11.1). New trams and buses have hardly affected operating speeds, which are determined mainly by traffic conditions. Buses are not timetabled to connect with trains or trams, despite scheduling having been under the control of a single authority between 1982 and 1999. Nothing has changed since 1953 when Melbourne's planning authority lamented:

A few … buses run to and from the city, but in most cases they act as feeders to the rail and tram services… On account of infrequent service and poor coordination … there are relatively few who can save much time by using these services (MMBW, 1953).

Table 11.1 *Decline in train service on Melbourne's Sandringham line*

	Service frequency (min)	
	1929	*1994*
Peak	3–4	15
Shoulder	7–8	15
Interpeak	15	15
Evening and Saturdays	15	20
Sundays	15	40
Fastest service (min)	26	27
Line length (km)	18	
Number of stations	14	14
Population in line's catchment area	80,000	120,000

Toronto's approach to service has received little attention from transport planners in Melbourne, as both sides of the local transport debate accept the urban form explanation for the decline of public transport. Little attention has been paid to learning what makes public transport successful, because the conventional explanation for its decline has acted as a self-denying ordinance closing off debate.

Developments in the West

Meanwhile, on the West Coast of Australia, a new approach has emerged. Perth, a sprawling, car-dominated city, compared with which Melbourne seems almost European, is following the Canadian model. Newman (1991) comments that other Australians view Perth's rail revival with 'some amazement': the reactions of conventional transport planners on the East Coast could be more appropriately described as hostility (eg Industry Commission, 1993).

Perth spent heavily on rail upgrading over the last decade. The line to Fremantle, closed in 1979, was reopened in 1983 by a new State government and the rail system was electrified and modernized. The effect on performance was dramatic. Trains are faster, more frequent and cheaper to run; many bus routes now act as rail feeders, giving a more reliable service at lower cost. Cost-recovery is improving as patronage grows, with the new Northern suburbs line, built along a freeway median, recovering 49 per cent of operating costs from the farebox (Ministry of Transport, Western Australia, 1994).

Newman (1991) claims Perth's improvements were fought at every turn by the transport bureaucracy and other experts, a claim corroborated by the views of unnamed officials cited approvingly by a more orthodox author:

> Railway officials commented somewhat ruefully after this episode [the reopening of the Fremantle line] that the [previous] government should have waited a little longer, ended freight and passenger service simultaneously, and torn up the line so that the restoration of passenger trains would have been impossible (Stevenson, 1987).

Their thinking was trapped in paradigms from the 1960s: public transport can never compete with cars in a low-density city, so there is little point improving it (eg Director-General of Transport, WA, 1982). The government used Newman (1991) and Vuchic (1981) as consultants to break the impasse.

In Melbourne, the old thinking dominated decision-making. The transport bureaucracy advised the incoming Labour Transport Minister that only minor increases in patronage could be achieved, and even this would create a deficit blowout (Ministry of Transport, Victoria, 1982). When Labour insisted on spending money on public transport, the experts responded with a programme of indiscriminate modernization, rather than a strategy for expanding, coordinating and improving service. Meanwhile, the construction of freeways continued.

From the mid-1980s the Victorian government's attention returned to cost-cutting. Rail stations were de-staffed at night just as a series of films about New York subway graffiti hit the cinemas: the resulting outbreak of vandalism afflicts the system to this day. The government met its nemesis in a 1990 industrial dispute sparked by a proposal to eliminate tram conductors. Lines of trams were parked in city streets for weeks, and the lottery-style self-scratch tickets introduced to save the cost of vending machines were ridiculed by the public and media. The government backed down.

The conservative State government elected in 1992 returned to the remedies of previous decades: service cuts, fare rises and new technology for public transport, coupled with an accelerated programme of freeway construction. The reform programme received the full support of mainstream transport planners and Thatcherite economists (eg Hensher, 1993; Industry Commission, 1993), despite having produced a 10 per cent fall in patronage in only 18 months. The magic wand of competition will create the flexibility needed for public transport to serve marginal niche markets in a car-dominated city. Bus deregulation in the UK is cited glowingly as a success story, a fact which may surprise British readers.

Conclusion

Melbourne's land-use planners continue their four-decade struggle to preserve the public transport-oriented land-use pattern inherited from the pre-war city. The Melbourne and Metropolitan Board of Works' 1954 metropolitan plan emphasized containment of urban sprawl and the creation of rail-based suburban district business centres. The most recent update (Ministry of Planning, Victoria, 1987) continues the tradition, prescribing rail-based development corridors and district centres, and urban consolidation (redevelopment of established areas at higher densities). Melbourne has recently emerged as a world leader in traditional neighbourhood design. It has been argued by the author elsewhere (Mees, 1994) that the land-use planners have been largely successful.

Meanwhile, transport planners continue their long-established approach of discouraging public transport use through declining service quality and expanding the road network, paradoxically claiming that they have no choice but to do so because Melbourne's urban form is so car-oriented. Unfortunately, they have also been successful.

Urban form is not Melbourne's major transport problem; rather it is an excuse used to perpetuate the real malaise, which is a refusal by transport planners to treat seriously transport modes other than the car (Mees, 2000).

Notes

1   This chapter was first published as a paper in *World Transport Policy & Practice* (1995), vol 1, no 1, pp20–24
2   Since the original version of this article was published, the Victorian government has privatized the train and tram networks, relying on the British model. Shortly after the completion of privatization in 1999 the conservatives were unexpectedly

defeated at a State election. However, the succeeding Labour administration has largely continued its predecessor's transport policies.

References

ABS (1986) *Retail Census, Small Area Statistics*, Victoria, Australian Bureau of Statistics, Canberra

Cervero, R (1986) 'Urban transit in Canada: integration and innovation at its best', *Transportation Quarterly*, vol 40, no 3, pp293–316

CATS (1960) *Chicago Area Transportation Study 1956: Volume 2 – Data Analysis*, State of Illinois, Chicago, IL

Director-General of Transport, Western Australia (1982) *Transport 2000: A Perth Study*, WA Government Printer, Perth

Frisken, F (1990) 'Planning and servicing the greater Toronto area: the interplay of provincial and municipal interests', *Urban Studies Working Paper No 12*, York University, Toronto

Hall, P (1990) 'Managing growth in the world's cities', *Planning the Toronto Region: Lessons from Other Places*, Canadian Urban Institute, Toronto

Hensher, D A (1993) 'The transportation sector in Australia: economic issues and challenges', *Transport Policy*, vol 1, no 1, pp49–67

Hensher, D A (1994) 'Technology, pricing and management systems futures for urban public transport', *Urban Public Transport Futures*, Australian Urban and Regional Development Review, Canberra

Industry Commission (1993) *Urban Transport – Draft Report*, Australian Government Printer, Canberra

Kohut, R (1991) *Shaping Public Transport's Future*, Public Transport Corporation, Melbourne

Mees, P (1993) 'The capacity of the Melbourne rail system', *Road and Transport Research*, vol 2, no 2, pp105–107

Mees, P (1994), 'Continuity and change in marvellous Melbourne', *Urban Futures*, vol 4, no 1, pp1–11.

Mees, P (2000) *A Very Public Solution: Transport in the Dispersed City*, Melbourne University Press, Melbourne

MMBW (1953) *Melbourne Metropolitan Planning Scheme 1954: Surveys and Analysis*, Melbourne and Metropolitan Board of Works, Victorian Government Printer, Melbourne

Metropolitan Toronto Planning Department (1992) *Retail Floor Space and Employment Characteristics in the Greater Toronto Area*, Municipality of Metropolitan Toronto, Toronto

Meyer, J, Kain, J and Wohl, M (1965) *The Urban Transportation Problem*, Harvard University Press, Cambridge, MA

Ministry of Planning, Victoria (1987) *Shaping Melbourne's Future: The Government's Metropolitan Policy*, Ministry of Planning, Melbourne.

Ministry of Transport, Victoria (1982) *Future Context for Transport: Metropolitan Transit Authority*, (unpub), Melbourne

Ministry of Transport, Western Australia (1994) 'Data on Northern Suburbs Transit System', (unpub), Western Australia

Moriarty, P and Beed, C (1992) 'Explanation of personal travel increases in Australian cities', *Papers of Australasian Transport Research Forum*, vol 17, part 2, Canberra, pp259–70

Newman, P (1991) 'The rebirth of the Perth suburban railways: a personal and policy perspective', *Institute for Science and Technology Policy Working Paper 4/91*, Murdoch University, Perth

Newman, P and Kenworthy, J (1999) *Sustainability and Cities: Overcoming Automobile Dependence*, Island Press, Washington, DC

Richardson, A J (1993) *Environmental Impacts of Urban Villages*, Transport Research Centre, University of Melbourne

Stevenson, G (1987) 'Rail Transport and Australian Federalism', *Research Monograph 48*, Centre for Research on Federal Financial Relations, Australian National University, Canberra

Thomson, J M (1977) *Great Cities and Their Traffic*, Victor Gollancz, London

Underwood, R T (1990) *Traffic Management: An Introduction*, Hargreen Publishing, Melbourne

VicRoads (1994) 'Linking Melbourne: A Strategy for Managing Melbourne's Traffic', *VicRoads Special Report 93–1*, Melbourne

Vuchic, V R (1981) *Urban Public Transportation: Systems and Technology*, Prentice-Hall, Englewood Cliffs, NJ

Webster, F V, Bly, P H, Johnston, R H, Paulley, N and Dasgupta, M (1985) *Changing Patterns of Urban Travel*, European Conference of Ministers of Transport, OECD Publications Office, Paris

Part 5

Transport in Europe

12

European Regional Transport Issues

Frazer Goodwin

From the remoteness of the northern forests of Scandinavia through thriving urban centres to the near deserts of southern Andalusia, conditions and means of transport in Europe change dramatically. Moreover, the transport needs and conditions of daily life also change across the continent. From the stress of the daily business commute in western Europe to the eastern European farmer trying to get to market, daily experiences of transport vary enormously. Thus the transport problems that European citizens face are more a reflection of the place in which they live and the lifestyle they lead than of a particularly European character.

Nevertheless, there is one thing that does bind together the continent – an ever-increasing mobility and an ever-larger scale of the problems of transport. Before considering what problems Europeans face as a result of transport, it is instructive to examine past trends in some detail.

Given the large increase in mobility of both goods and people over the last two decades there are some rather surprising statistics. For freight transport, the amount of tonne kilometres (tkm) has increased dramatically, as has the value of goods transported. These trends are clear in Figure 12.1 and Table 12.1. But the total tonnage of goods transported is approximately the same now as it was in 1970. There are two reasons for these apparently contradictory trends.

Firstly, trade has expanded further afield than in the past. The result of increased trade in the European Union (EU) following completion of the single market alongside the effect of a liberalized global trade regime has meant more freight transport. The goods in Europe are smaller, have greater value and in general travel further than previously. Indeed many of the production process innovations that have emerged over the last two decades have been based on an abundant supply of cheap transport. Just-in-time delivery systems, for example, have transferred holdings of stock from warehouses to roads. Outsourcing the elements of the production process has also resulted in an increase in the number of firms required to produce even the simplest product, thereby increasing the distances each product has travelled in its production.

Secondly, a great deal of the heavy industrial and manufacturing activities of Europe has moved to other world regions. The majority of the transport for much of this heavy industry and manufacturing is therefore undertaken by international shipping, the tkms of which do not feature in aggregate data for Europe on its own. Another facet of this change in the character of goods transported is the mode of

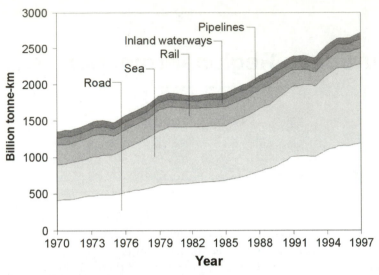

Source: EEA (2001)

Figure 12.1 *Rise in freight transport by mode*

Table 12.1 *Growth in freight transport demand in EU Member States in tonne-kilometres (tkm)*

Country	1970	1980	1990	1992	1993	1994	1995	1996	1997
Austria	21.7	29.8	32.6	33.7	33.7	36.1	36.9	38.0	40.0
Belgium	50.0	69.2	94.2	99.8	97.3	106.9	109.1	104.2	105.9
Denmark	22.3	27.3	32.6	36.6	35.3	38.7	39.9	41.0	41.4
Finland	77.5	99.8	118.6	120.9	123.1	130.1	134.5	137.6	139.9
France	213.0	293.1	355.1	368.9	354.6	379.6	401.3	397.8	410.6
Germany	316.4	400.5	420.6	467.6	463.4	501.4	513.7	509.8	535.4
Greece	17.7	56.9	68.0	71.4	65.6	68.6	78.2	78.9	79.5
Ireland	15.6	12.0	14.6	15.1	15.6	16.8	17.6	17.8	17.8
Italy	169.8	278.5	360.8	374.9	364.4	381.7	397.2	402.9	414.4
Luxembourg	1.3	1.6	2.2	2.6	2.7	2.6	2.7	2.7	2.8
Netherlands	88.6	132.6	155.8	165.5	158.8	169.3	175.2	177.5	184.5
Portugal	13.6	29.1	36.9	38.5	36.4	41.1	43.5	40.9	41.6
Spain	78.2	134.2	186.7	198.1	194.0	206.3	224.6	218.8	224.4
Sweden	47.7	59.3	69.5	69.2	70.8	75.0	78.3	80.2	82.4
United Kingdom	203.4	266.9	339.6	335.5	346.0	369.4	381.9	389.7	393.5
EU15	1336.8	1890.9	2287.8	2398.3	2361.7	2523.6	2634.6	2637.9	2714.0

Note: 'EU15' stands for the 15 Member States of the European Union
Source: EEA (2001)

transport favoured for their carriage. Bulky and heavy goods that have traditionally been transported by rail have been supplanted by lighter, higher value goods that use road transport. The growth in the amount of freight moved has occurred at a time when the amount of rail freight has been stable or even declined for some areas.

The result has been a large and noticeable growth in the number of lorries on Europe's roads, accompanied by an increase in the impacts and problems they bring. Recently there has also been a trend for the dependency on road haulage to be used by the industry to extract political favours from Europe's leaders.

This growth in lorry traffic has been most noticeable in those locations where there is no other option for lorries other than to travel through residential areas. Small villages have therefore campaigned for their own bypasses, and Alpine regions have seen resident groups campaign to shift the transit freight traffic off the roads completely. The resulting increase in road infrastructure capacity is a marked contrast to the stable or declining rail infrastructure capacity illustrated in Figure 12.2.

It is in the Alpine regions that the problems caused by growing road freight have been most acute. Squeezed into the same narrow passes as villages and sensitive environments, the increases in lorry numbers and size have caused numerous problems and confrontations. The impacts of lorry traffic are felt severely here not only because of the vulnerability of the Alpine ecosystems, but also because of the cultural significance these ecosystems have to Alpine nations.

A result of the long discord created by such transit traffic in Switzerland has been a multi-decade programme to eventually switch all transit traffic from the roads to railways. The Swiss have a participatory democracy, and this policy has been the outcome of five referenda. The policy has thus been incorporated into the Swiss national constitution.

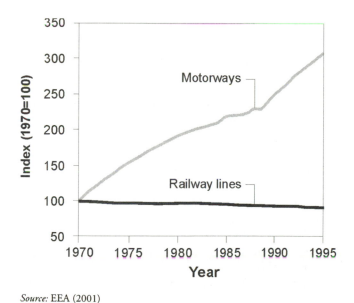

Source: EEA (2001)

Figure 12.2 *Transport infrastructure capacity in the EU*

The Swiss are constructing rail infrastructure that will take the additional freight traffic from roads, and two new, large rail tunnels are being constructed through the Alps. Additionally, the programme will upgrade much of the existing rail infrastructure. It is funded by a mixture of state-guaranteed loans and earmarked taxes or charges. The largest revenue source is income from a new electronic kilometre charge on all lorry traffic in Switzerland. Heavy goods vehicles are charged electronically for every kilometre travelled. The fee is comprised of distance, the emissions class of the vehicle (the dirtier the vehicle, the higher the fee) and the gross unladen weight (so a full lorry pays the same as one that is empty). This means there is a direct economic incentive for trucks to travel as little as possible, for them to be as modern and clean as possible, to be as small as possible, and to be as fully loaded as possible. The use to which the revenues from this new charge are being put means that investments in rail solutions to Switzerland's Alpine lorry traffic problems are largely being financed by the origin of the problem – road freight itself.

In contrast to Switzerland, other regions of Europe seem intent on generating additional transit traffic on their roads. Across the countries of central and eastern Europe (CEE), governments are planning and starting the construction of grand road projects that will complete the trans-European network. For many of these countries, the car and road transport symbolize freedom and a high level of wealth in a consumer society. The transport problem perceived to be the priority here is the construction of the infrastructure deemed necessary to fit into the road-dominated pattern of western European transport.

However, the results for ordinary people are mixed. With the sums being spent on the construction of new links, no money is left to finance the upgrade and maintenance of existing roads (see Figure 12.3). Those who live in remote rural areas are as isolated by this free market road culture as they were by its communist predecessor.

In addition, the move to the free market has marked a sharp decline across the CEE region in the support given to public transport in all its guises. This is particularly so for trolley-bus, tram and conventional bus services but also applies to rail services across the region. Despite the large sums being found for investment in road construction, there is no public money available for the modernization of the vehicle fleet for many public transport authorities. The crisis is so severe that some public transport authorities are importing western European cast-off vehicles donated by western European authorities that are renewing their own vehicle fleets. Ordinary CEE citizens, once used to reliable, cheap and efficient public transport, now find themselves confronted with an under-funded, unreliable service with over-crowded and outdated dirty vehicles.

Much was made of how the old communist system was so systematically destructive to the environment and, as a result, to people's health. Yet, although the end-of-pipe technology once so lacking has now been imported from the West, it has been accompanied by the systematic environmental problems that plague the West – particularly in transport. This car culture also has its health impacts, in terms of air pollution and accidents, especially as it is the older, more polluting vehicles that are finding their way to CEE countries. This is in part an explanation for the large increases in asthma and certain cancer rates in some EU accession countries since the fall of the Berlin wall (see Figure 12.4).

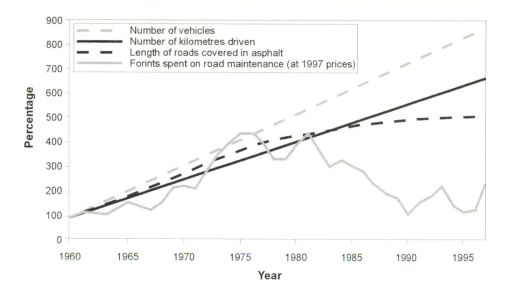

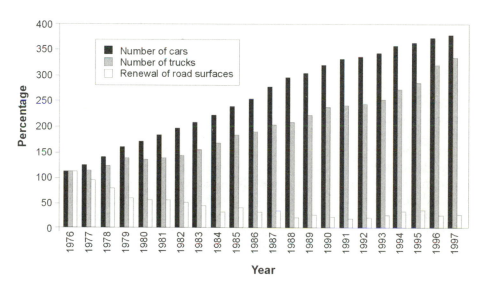

Source: Lukács (2001)
Notes: 1960 = 100%; 1976 = 100%

Figure 12.3 *Hungarian road programme and decline of road network*

Moreover, large parts of the border regions of CEE countries now act as a honey pot for Western shoppers searching out low price bargains or even casual sex. As a result, long stretches of roads have become red light pick-up posts, not the type of transport and freedom of movement originally envisaged by those who promote transit traffic road schemes in CEE countries.

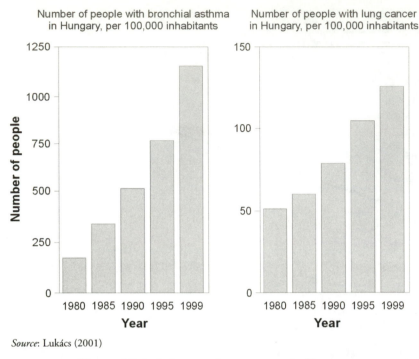

Number of people with bronchial asthma in Hungary, per 100,000 inhabitants

Number of people with lung cancer in Hungary, per 100,000 inhabitants

Source: Lukács (2001)

Figure 12.4 *Asthma and cancer rates in Hungary*

Another result of the rapid rise in road transport in the CEE region has been large increases in road traffic accident rates. Of all the transport problems faced by Europeans, road safety is arguably the one that has the most severe impact. With more than 40,000 deaths in the EU alone, road accidents are the largest single cause of death for those under 45 years of age (see Figure 12.5). Yet accident rates vary enormously across the continent (see Figure 12.6), with the UK and Sweden standing out as most successful in reducing accident rates, whilst the countries of the Mediterranean and CEE region suffer high accident rates. Those in the latter region are continuing to rise.

The largest contributors to this litany of disaster are excessive speed, alcohol and/or drug use. Therefore, although these deaths are usually described as accidents, they are frequently the result of individual actions outside the law rather than anything that may genuinely be described as accidental. It is certainly true that the road sector is relatively unregulated for safety considerations when compared to other transport modes such as rail or air.

Yet despite the fact that the death rate from road accidents is so high, there may actually be more lives lost as a result of air pollution caused by traffic. This certainly is the view of the World Health Organization's (WHO) report to the Third Ministerial Conference on Health and the Environment, which took place in London in 1999.

Air pollution from traffic is continuing to prove damaging to health despite the technical improvements to both vehicles and fuels – a trend that is set to continue. This is because the increase in traffic offsets the gains made on the emission levels from individual vehicles (see Table 12.2 and Figure 12.7).

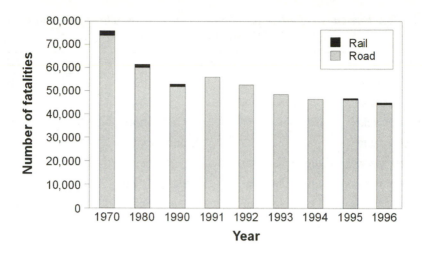

Source: EEA (2001)

Figure 12.5 *Fatalities from road and rail transport in the EU*

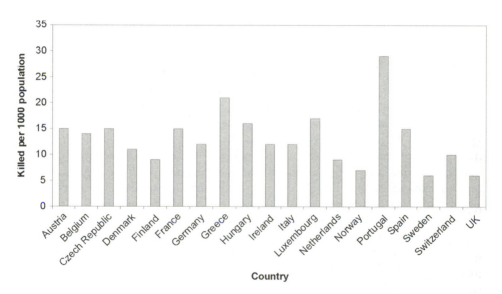

Source: OECD (2001)

Figure 12.6 *Road accident rates across Europe*

Yet the more pervasive impact that motorization has had on Europeans' health may be the higher rates of heart conditions and other illnesses associated with the sedentary lifestyle motorization promotes.

A further result of the high accident rate of motor traffic is an increase in the number of disabled people. However, it is not only road traffic accidents (RTAs) that are causing increases in the number of people with mobility impairments. There is an

Table 12.2 *Percentage of urban population living in cities where pollution levels are higher than EU limit values*

Pollutant	Averaging period	1995[a] %	2010[b] %
Sulphur dioxide	1 hour	23	2; **3–6**
Sulphur dioxide	24 hours	25	7; **9–11**
Nitrogen dioxide	1 hour	5	5; **0**
Nitrogen dioxide	Calendar year	65	5; **20**
Particulate matter (<10μm in diameter)	24 hours	89	62; **73**
Particulate matter (<10μm in diameter)	Calendar year	87	62; **52**
Carbon monoxide	8 hours	14	0.5–1.5
Ozone	Daily 8 hour max	48	6
Benzene	Calendar year	50	**13**
Lead	Calendar year	23	**0**

Notes: a: Fraction estimated from urban air quality assessment model (UAQAM) and ozone fine structure (OFIS) model calculations.
b: Fraction estimated from UAQAM and OFIS model calculators; results obtained by UAQAM are in bold.
Source: CEC (2000)

ageing of society as the continent's demographics are changing, and older people have far higher rates of mobility impairments.

In the USA it is illegal to discriminate against people because of a disability, and therefore transport services have been designed for all. For example, buses have been fitted with lifts for wheelchair users. However, people with disabilities in Europe still face considerable barriers to many of their transport needs. Public transport in particular has been slow in Europe to serve the needs of the disabled, with costs being cited by public transport operators as the main problem. Yet the number of passengers who could be described as having a mobility impairment is extremely high. Regie Autonome des Transportes Parisiens (RATP), the main public transport operator for Paris and its suburbs, has estimated that as many as 40 per cent of their passengers have an impairment to mobility that would, for example, make stairs difficult. These passengers include not only a small fraction who are wheelchair users or those who need an aid to walk, but also parents with small children or infants, travellers with suitcases, or passengers carrying other large items.

Moreover, as Europe's population ages there will be an increase in the number of those in the community who are disabled. Removing the transport barriers that disabled people face and ensuring access to wheelchair users would therefore serve huge sections of the travelling public and make possible many more journeys by public transport.

The severity of the problem disabled people face in Europe means that for many the only option viable to them for transport is adapted private cars. Of course, for some – those with epilepsy, blindness etc – this option too is unavailable, and the failure of public transport to cater for all effectively excludes them from a society that is increasingly dependent on motorization.

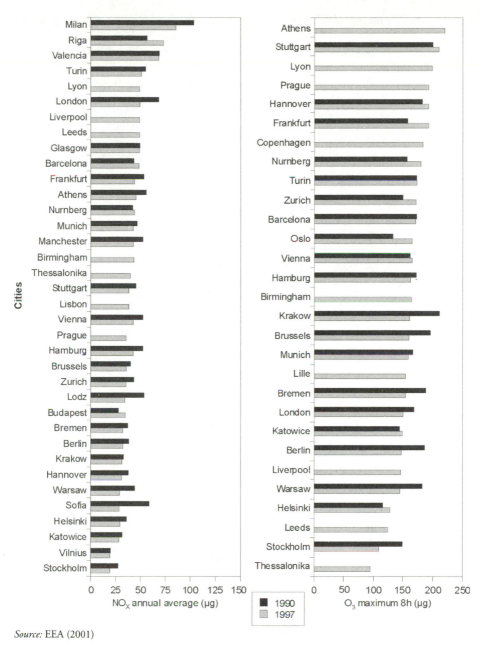

Source: EEA (2001)

Figure 12.7 *Pollution levels in various European cities*

In fact, motorization is so pervasive, particularly in western Europe, that it has shaped not only travel and transport but also much of daily life. The character of towns and cities has developed and changed to accommodate the car. Car parking areas and large arterial roads have altered the character of ancient urban centres and cleaved communities. The effect has been an increase in the size of stores alongside a decrease in their number, and an increased reliance on car transport for food shopping (see Figures 12.8 and 12.9).

Another unanticipated impact has been the emergence of 'food deserts' as retailing becomes more and more reliant upon car-borne shoppers for profitability. These areas lie in impoverished urban areas where residents, particularly women with small children, have no access to a car. Yet many of the local food retailers have been forced out

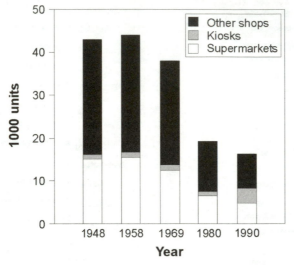

Source: EEA (2001)

Figure 12.8 *Convenience stores in Denmark*

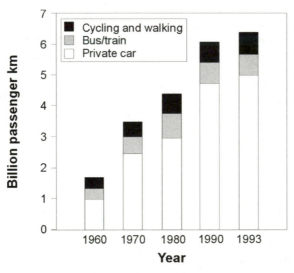

Source: EEA (2001)

Figure 12.9 *Transport to convenience stores by mode in Denmark*

of business by large out-of-town shopping complexes that are relatively close yet inaccessible for non-car owners.

This is not the only downside of motorization for the poorer sections of society. Car dependency frequently means that those at the lower end of the pay scale are required to choose between spending large portions of their income on a car to get to work, or not working, as without a car employment is inaccessible. For such people, the car is not a liberating symbol of freedom.

In rural areas, the situation may be even worse as public transport alternatives to the car are even more limited. The fact that the rural poor may have to travel long distances in order to access basic services exacerbates the high travel costs of a car and its use.

This is compounded by the fact that governments have not devised systems to charge the true external costs of car usage, and instead mainly apply the blunt instrument of fuel taxes to raise revenue (see Figure 12.10). Although a trip to the doctor by rural dwellers in northern Sweden may cause very little environmental damage by car, they are charged the same tax as wealthy Stockholm residents who use similar vehicles to cross the centre of the city at rush hour to visit the gym, and in so doing cause urban air and noise pollution as well as adding to congestion.

It has not only been the poor or socially excluded who have felt the inequity of this. Many sections of commercial transport have firstly argued and then taken direct action against rising fuel price levels. Indeed, the road haulage industry has found that members of society have become so dependent not only on oil but on road transport that they now have a great ability to hold governments to ransom, a power they used to great effect across Europe in the autumn of 2000.

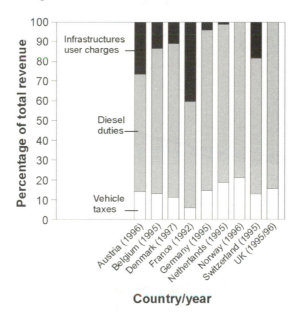

Source: EEA (2001)

Figure 12.10 *Government transport revenue by type from the freight sector*

Yet transport prices still do not reflect the enormous amount of environmental damage that transport causes (see Figure 12.11). Moreover, the prices charged for private car use have been relatively unchanged in real terms, whilst those for public transport have risen (see Figure 12.12).

The problem is that some basic principles have been ignored in the way that transport prices have been arranged. Firstly, the 'polluter pays' principle would mean that car drivers would have to pay for the pollution they cause. Secondly, the 'user pays' princi-

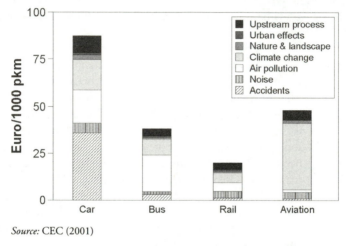

Source: CEC (2001)

Figure 12.11 *External costs of passenger transport*

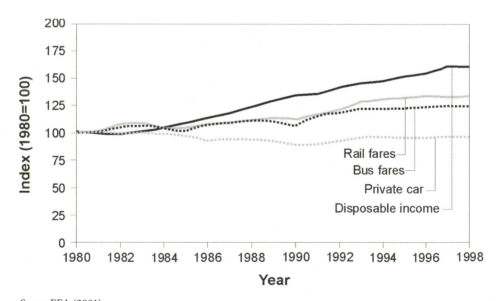

Source: EEA (2001)

Figure 12.12 *Evolution of (real) transport prices*

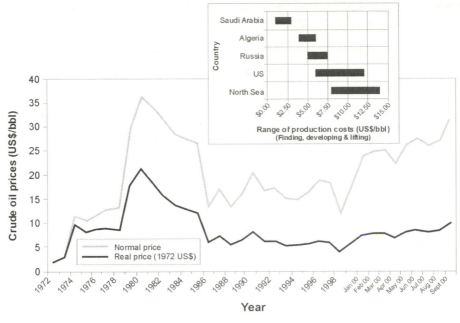

Source: IEA (2000)

Figure 12.13 *Crude oil price evolution*

ple means that transport users should pay as they go far more than they do currently; large parts of the costs for car drivers are made up of ownership costs (purchase price, car tax, insurance etc) rather than use costs (fuel). Moreover, governments have long used fuel tax as a means to raise general revenue. Whilst this use of revenue from excise taxes is legitimate, despite the transport industry's claim that the revenues raised somehow 'belong' to transport, it has meant that transport prices are rather distorted. This reliance on applying excise taxes to transport also means that people believe transport costs to be high even if, in real terms, fuel prices at the height of the fuel price protests were only 10 per cent above those before the first oil crisis of the 1970s (see Figure 12.13).

Reconciling this particularly thorny problem of pricing will require not only a different approach to pricing transport, but also a genuine public debate about the way government revenues are raised and spent. It is indeed notable that the country that has undertaken the largest public debate on road pricing has been the first to implement a large scale scheme and the first to dedicate the revenues to finding alternative solutions to road transport – Switzerland. Its system for pricing goods transport reflects environmental costs and applies the 'user pays' principle.

There is no reason why this pricing system could not be applied to all vehicles across Europe, including time elements that consider congestion and peak time usage. As well as being economically more efficient, such a pricing scheme would have the advantage of being a fairer system. It would also finally send the right price signals to Europe's economy. This would mean that transport would begin to serve Europe's needs more economically and effectively, rather than Europe continuing to serve the ever increasing need for transport to grow.

References

CEC (2000) *The Auto-oil Programme – A Report from the Services of the European Commission*, Commission of the European Communities, Brussels

CEC (2001) *White Paper on European Transport Policy For 2010: Time To Decide*, COM 2001 (370), 12 September, Commission of the European Communities, Brussels

EEA (2001) *TERM2001: Indicators Tracking Transport and Environment Integration in the European Union*, European Environment Agency, Copenhagen, http://www.eea.eu.int

IEA (2000) *Oil Prices and Taxes in the Year 2000: An IEA Statistical Factsheet*, International Energy Agency, Paris, http://www.iea.org

Lukács, A (2001) 'The EU enlargement process and transport – the case of Hungary', Clean Air Action Group, Budapest, http://www.levego.hu/english/euept/euept.htm

OECD (2001) *Transport Statistics*, Organisation for Cooperation and Economic Development, Paris, http://www.oecd.org/dsti/sti/transpor/road/stats/index.htm

13

The Future of Public Transport: The Dangers of Viewing Policy through Rose-tinted Spectacles

Mayer Hillman

Introduction

Improved public transport services are generally viewed as the most effective means of encouraging transfer from the car, especially on urban journeys. Accordingly, substantial public funds are being invested to this end. This chapter demonstrates that such an approach achieves little of this transfer.[1] By comparing patterns of travel in the UK and The Netherlands it shows that the prioritizing of walking and cycling is not only far more effective and cost effective in achieving transfer, but is more likely to deliver a wider range of social, health and environmental objectives of public transfer additional to those related to transport (Hillman, 1992a). There must therefore be a presumption in favour of investing in networks of walking and cycling and in other measures enabling journeys to be made by these non-motorized modes well in advance of investment in public transport.

The Conventional View

It is the conventional view that the key element of a package to deal with the adverse effects of the growth in car-based, geographically-dispersed patterns of activity is much improved bus and rail services in order to provide equivalent levels of convenience, speed and comfort to the car. In this way, car users can be encouraged more easily to transfer back to public transport.

These judgements about public transport – as by far the most important substitute for the car – are apparent in documents produced by the European Commission, notably in its Citizens Network, professional papers by academics and from transport institutions and transport-related commercial bodies, in party political agenda-setting statements, local and central government reports, in most spheres of information gathering and dissemination, and in the media. They are also reflected in attitudinal surveys revealing that the public, including most motorists, agree.

One of the primary explanations for this outcome, additional to the obvious one of the relative power and influence of both the private and public motor lobbies, is the fact that published statistics on patterns of travel are focused on a modal split that usually excludes journeys over short distances and by non-motorized means, thereby resulting in an exaggeration of the significance of longer journeys and of the importance of public transport. This then encourages solutions to be seen to lie in the area of investment in transport infrastructure – road building, rail electrification and other improvements in public transport services to reduce travel times on these journeys.

So influential has been the support for substantial investment in public transport that it is rarely questioned, with the sole problem lying with budgetary limitations. Many cities have invested in, or are proposing, new high quality systems in spite of their capital costs per kilometre being not dissimilar to those for road building, largely because of the expensive rolling stock and, in some instances, tunnelling.

Current Patterns of Travel

Any examination of the current role of public transport must differentiate between bus and rail. Their characteristics vary significantly in terms of meeting the demand for travel over shorter and longer distances. Table 13.1 shows that in the UK the near-exclusive use of buses at present is for journeys of between one and ten miles, but accounts for only one in ten within this distance band, though for eight times as many as by rail. Indeed, only 1.6 per cent of journeys of any length are made by rail, which is rarely used to travel less than ten miles (16 kilometres) – 86 per cent of all journeys. Rail comes into its own on longer journeys over ten miles in length, but caters for only one in 15 of them. However, it can be seen that most journeys are still sufficiently short that they can be made by non-motorized means. A third of all journeys are made within one mile, a distance fairly well suited to walking. A further third are made over distances of between one and four miles, which would involve a cycle ride of between 5 and 20 minutes. The fact that few of these journeys are made by bicycle in the UK may be explained by the lack of provision of safe bicycle networks, rather than the unsuitability of the bicycle for journeys within this distance band.

The last two lines of Table 13.1 show the ratio of walking and cycling journeys to those by bus, and the ratio of car journeys to those by rail, both ratios being recorded within each distance band. It can be seen that walking and cycling cater for five times as many journeys as do buses – in urban areas the proportion is still higher – and 35 times as many journeys are made by car as by rail. Although it is clear that many issues other than travel time influence personal decisions on modal choice, even on journeys of up to two miles, journeys on foot do not take much longer than journeys involving use of a bus. Cycling is almost twice as fast: on journeys of up to ten miles, it takes less time than bus or rail. On longer journeys, that is over 25 miles – accounting for only 4 per cent of all journeys – the car is used seven times more than rail.

On work journeys in the UK, where public transport comes into its own – albeit largely owing to parking control, road congestion and other deterrents to car use – the number of journeys on foot is similar to that by all public transport modes combined; the number by cycle is similar to that by rail in spite of the very limited provision for cyclists. In general, buses are rarely used for most types of journey. In the case of shopping, walking accounts for nearly four times the number made by bus – a similar ratio

Table 13.1 *Modal split of journeys in the UK by distance band*

Mode	Distance band in miles							
	<1	1<2	2<5	5<10	10<25	25+	All	Trips per week
Walk	236	45	10	–	–	–	292	5.9
Cycle	5	6	5	1	–	–	18	0.4
Public transport	5	14	33	17	8	4	79	1.6
Bus[a]	5	14	30	12	3	–	63	1.2
Rail[b]	–	–	3	4	5	4	16	0.3
Other	3	9	16	10	8	7	51	1.0
Total	290	173	254	143	100	40	1000	20.3
Walk and cycle: bus	51	3.6	0.5	0.1	–	–	4.9	
Car: rail			63.0	28.0	16.0	7.0	35.0	

Notes: base = 1000
a: London Transport bus and other stage bus
b: British Rail and London Underground
Source: Department of Transport (1994a)

to that for school journeys and for most leisure journeys. Bus and rail are rarely used for day trips or holidays.

It would seem that the prospect of buses playing a significantly larger role for most types of journey under four miles currently made by car is small. For journeys of four miles or more, the prospect of much substitution of journeys from car to coach or rail without considerable limitations on car use is also small. Neither improvements in urban services, recently introduced or under consideration (such as light rail, more comprehensive networks of bus lanes, computer-controlled traffic lights favouring buses, electronic indicators showing expected time of arrival or even lower fares), welcome though these are or would be for bus users, nor improvements for longer intercity journeys (such as faster trains, seat-back videos and concessionary fares) bring about more than a modest transfer of people with the choice of travelling by these services rather than by car.

Indeed, in the UK, for every passenger kilometre (pkm) 'lost' to bus travel, 13 car pkms have been added over the 30-year period to 1993 (Department of Transport, 1994b). Growth in car use has not come about from transfer from public transport but from walking and cycling – in the UK in 1949, cycle mileage exceeded car mileage, whereas it is now exceeded by a factor of 75! It has stemmed from more journeys newly generated by the ownership of a car; and increasingly from travel to and from more distant destinations in new developments of low density – housing, shopping, commerce and leisure centres, convenient access to which is realistically only possible by car. In general, door-to-door travel time by car is far lower than by bus or rail, from which it can again be observed that it is wholly unrealistic to anticipate that improving public transport could result in it competing with the car on journeys up to 50 miles, accounting for over 98 per cent of all journeys. The expectation that, given sufficient improvement in public transport, especially rail, people will return to it from the car, overlooks the fact that, in the main, these journeys were neither previously made by public transport nor do they lend themselves to being matched by it.

Lessons from The Netherlands

The use of the bicycle as a far more appropriate substitute for many car journeys (as has been seen, over half of these journeys even today are over distances of less than four miles) is apparent by comparing patterns of travel in the UK and The Netherlands. The travel surveys for the two countries reveal similar levels of household car ownership, and a considerable degree of congruence within each distance band both in the overall distribution of journeys and in car use. However, one particular difference stands out, namely the much higher proportion of journeys made by cycle, a lower proportion on foot, and a lower proportion by public transport. In The Netherlands, over a quarter of all journeys are made by cycle – including over half of school journeys (only 1 per cent in the UK) – and journeys by cycle and on foot exceed those by public transport by a factor of ten (CBS, 1994). The ratio of car journeys to cycle journeys is about 2 to 1, whereas in the UK the ratio is 32 to 1. Moreover, the number of cycle journeys in The Netherlands easily outstrips those made by public transport on journeys in all distance bands up to 15km.

Given the fact that most urban settlements in Europe are topographically not cycle-unfriendly, it is clear that the explanation for the high level of cycle use in The Netherlands has much to do with its transport policy over the last 25 years, which has led to the bicycle playing such a significant role in spite of a continuing rise in car ownership. Nor can the relatively low use of public transport in The Netherlands, much lower than in the UK, be explained by a poorer service, for the reverse is true: 12 times as much money is spent on that mode as on cycling. Indeed, higher densities of population, which in turn promote public transport use, are more commonplace in The Netherlands. This again points to the limited role of public transport in attracting people who currently use cars.

Investment Decisions in Transport

Repeated calls are made in transport circles for a level playing field in road and rail investment. Balance, least-cost planning and an integrated approach in policy decisions are recommended. All travel methods are claimed to incur environmental costs. That is true for motorized travel: like private transport, all forms of public transport are the source of noise, pollution, danger to other road users, severance, etc. It is untrue for walking and cycling.

What sort of sensible balance, however, can be struck when the transport modes incurring high economic, social and environmental costs are given preferential treatment to those incurring low costs; when investment in all the modes is not evaluated according to common criteria; and when the benign non-motorized modes are largely left out of consideration other than in the context of road safety?

Even when significant investment has been made in high quality public services, the outcome has been disappointing. On average, the best new public transport systems cost far more than budgeted and then carry far fewer passengers than predicted. In spite of their high capital costs, rapid transit systems add no more than a few per cent to public transport patronage for a whole city and have relatively little effect in terms of the objective of relieving road congestion by attracting car users; the benefit of the small transfer to public transport tends to be overtaken within a year or two by the continuing rise in the use of the car.

Even discounting criteria other than direct economic considerations, a comparison between investment in walking and cycling networks and public transport points overwhelmingly to one decision based on achieving the best rate of return: the capital costs per kilometre for the new type of public transport systems currently under construction or being reviewed are hundreds of times higher than those for cycling provision, and are likely to be much less effective in meeting travel demand. Indeed, the total 2000km cycle network for London would cost the equivalent of 2km of the Leeds Supertram system, or 0.4km of the Jubilee Line extension!

Discussion

At this juncture, it must be acknowledged that, of course, public transport does have an important role to play. First, it is needed to cater for journeys by people without access to a car, and for those who, for whatever reason, prefer to travel by it rather than use their cars on particular journeys. Second, it is required for commuting, where it may be especially necessary to oblige motorists to use public transport owing to the shortage of parking space and problems of congestion in central urban areas – thereby rendering its services extremely uneconomic, as vehicle occupancy, and therefore revenue, are low outside the rush hour. Its third role is for long distance intercity travel but, as has been seen, door-to-door travel time and convenience – and overall cost where several people are travelling together – can easily tip the balance in favour of the car, even when rail journeys are on fast electrified routes or coach journeys are largely on motorways. Unless the real and perceived costs of car travel are dramatically increased, holding down fares is likely to have only a minor effect on this particular modal choice.

At the heart of the debate concerning the future role of public transport lie three questionable and dubious, albeit unspoken, assumptions. The first is that people's appetite for travel – 'further and faster' – is insatiable and that longer journeys at higher speeds are somehow more significant. This is certainly true as far as environmental impacts and other costs are concerned! The second is that current and future demand must be met, although perhaps in less environmentally-damaging ways, because people have an inalienable right to have their wish to travel met, if not by car, then by some alternative form of motorized transport to which they can be won over because it largely matches the car's attractions. The third, and perhaps most worrying, is that the accumulation of greenhouse gases (GHGs) from all sectors of the economy, especially transport, can continue to rise without putting at risk the ecological balance of the planet.

It may be through response to the urgent need to curtail dramatically the use of fossil fuels that the inappropriateness of bus and rail as substitutes for car and air travel will be recognized. Not only do all these modes rely completely on the use of fossil fuels but, taking account of typical vehicle occupancies, public transport's fuel consumption per pkm is only a third to a half lower than that of the car, whereas for walking and cycling no fuel is required.

The Intergovernmental Panel on Climate Change (IPCC) has called for a global 60–80 per cent fall in carbon dioxide emissions to stabilize the world's climate (IPCC, 1990 and 1992). With the moral imperative as stewards of the planet to modify people's lifestyles to meet this objective, and political realism to reflect the fact that developing countries cannot realistically be called on at this stage in their development to reduce their low levels of fuel consumption, the author of this chapter has calculated that for western European countries, the reduction determined on an equitable per capita basis is over 90 per cent. Without action to this end, the overriding message of the Brundtland Report, the 1992 Rio Conference and European Union states' response to it – a commitment to sustainable development, that an environment no worse and preferably better than the one we inherited must be handed on to future generations – will prove to be only pious and unfulfilled expressions of intent.

Conclusions

A consensus is being reached that, in the light of all its adverse consequences, demand for car travel must be reduced. Restrictions will have to be progressively but speedily phased in during the next two decades – for instance, through private and public parking control, much lower and properly enforced speed limits, traffic calming, much heavier taxation of fuel and possibly fuel rationing. However, while investment in public transport is justified for the motorized travel of all adults without access to a car or who prefer not to use a car, and of course for all children who can be allowed to travel on their own, buses are generally a far less satisfactory alternative to the car than the door-to-door convenience of walking on short journeys or the door-to-door convenience of cycling on journeys up to four to five miles in length – in combination, representing close on two in three of all current journeys. While rail can be a more convenient alternative to the car on long journeys, in practice these represent only a very small proportion of all journeys and opportunities for transfer from car to rail are limited.

Thus, to meet the objective of providing a realistic substitute for the car, an investment strategy would be more appropriately directed to provision: first, for safe and convenient pedestrian networks for short journeys; second, for safe and attractive cycle networks for other urban journeys; and third, for the non-motorized modes in combination with public transport for longer journeys (Hillman, 1992b). Any evaluation of the costs and benefits of each form of transport, taking account of social, health, economic and local and global environmental criteria, is likely to reveal that the non-motorized modes are by far the most cost effective. Such a strategy must take precedence over one aimed at encouraging significant transfer from the car to public transport, for that is an ephemeral goal.

Notes

1   This chapter was first published as a paper in *World Transport Policy & Practice*, vol 2, no 3, pp24–27.

References

CBS (1994) *Netherlands National Travel Survey 1993*, Centraal Bureau voor de Statistiek, Vooerburg, Heerlen

Department of Transport (1994a) *National Travel Survey: 1991/93*, HMSO, London

Department of Transport (1994b) *Transport Statistics Great Britain 1994*, HMSO, London

Hillman, M (1992a) 'Reconciling transport and environmental policy objectives: the way ahead at the end of the road', *Public Administration*, vol 70, no 2, pp225–34

Hillman, M (1992b) 'The role of walking and cycling in public policy', *Consumer Policy Review*, vol 2, no 2, pp81–9

IPCC (1990 and 1992) *Report of Working Group 3*, Inter-Governmental Panel on Climate Change, UN Environment Programme and World Meteorological Organisation, Cambridge University Press

Walmsley, D and Gardner, G (1993) *The Economic Effects of Public Transport*, paper for the International Workshop on Environment, Traffic and Planning, June, Delft

14

New Roads Generate New Traffic

Rudolf Pfleiderer and Martin Dietrich

Introduction

Traffic planners and policy-makers argue that new roads are required to meet an increasing demand for transportation. It is claimed that the improvement of road infrastructure contributes to economic progress, helps the environment by relieving congestion-related air pollution and improves living conditions in residential areas. In addition it is frequently argued that an updated rail and bus infrastructure will further contribute to the relief from environmental pollution as motorists are provided with a fast and thus attractive alternative to using the car.

A simple and fundamental principle of economics is that consumption increases as goods become more attractive to the consumer. If transportation is viewed as a consumable good, then transportation infrastructure will partly determine its attractiveness to the potential user. Improving the overall attractiveness of a transportation system will increase traffic and therefore ultimately lead to more traffic-related pollution.

Apparently, one of the most important features determining attractiveness, and thereby controlling the demand for transportation, is the speed of travelling. Faster transportation systems allow for longer distances to be covered and thus for more or more distant destinations to be reached, while the time spent in traffic remains constant. This simple fact is bluntly ignored by most traffic planners and politicians. Rather, the standard paradigm of traffic planning presumes that speed influences the choice between different modes of transportation, but has no effect on the choice of the destinations and the total distances covered by individual travellers.

This chapter examines the widespread ignorance concerning the generation of additional traffic.[1]

New Roads Generate New Traffic

New roads are frequently built on the grounds of shifting traffic from congested arterials to areas where pollution and noise affect less people. Such new roads accelerate the traffic and the motorists save time. The question then arises of how the motorists spend the time saved. The answer to this question is surprisingly simple but is key to understanding the increase in traffic: the time saved is used to generate more traffic. This traffic is ignored by conservative traffic experts, although – apart from the direct impacts on the landscape – it is the most important impact of a new road on the environment. There is a technical term for this kind of traffic: induced or generated traffic.

The phenomenon that people tend to spend a fixed amount of their time travelling is known as the law of the constant travel time budget. The travel time budget is the average time a person spends in traffic each day. The law of the constant travel time budget is well established (John Allard and Frank Graham and Partners, 1987; Herz, 1985) but is rarely, if at all, applied in the context of transportation planning and impact assessment.

The travel time budget depends on demographic and sociological parameters. For example, it has been found that employees have a greater travel time budget than housewives or pensioners (Herz, 1985). Progress in transportation, for example the invention of the bicycle or the motorized vehicle, has not changed travel time budgets considerably, although nowadays there is a tendency to spend more time in traffic as a result of increased leisure time and reduced working hours.

It is not known whether the law of the constant travel time budget also applies to the transportation of goods. However, there is a close connection between the improvement of transportation infrastructure and economic globalization (Norberg-Hodge, 1994). Thus, it appears that as infrastructure is improved, goods are being shipped over longer distances. This is particularly true if companies are allowed to externalize most of their transportation costs owing to massive direct and indirect transportation subsidies.

The acceleration of public transportation also induces traffic. Interestingly, while the induction of motor car traffic through improved infrastructure is consistently ignored, the increase of ridership in systems of mass transportation as a result of improved services is widely praised as a means of protecting the environment. It is usually implied that one traveller more on the bus or on the train corresponds to one motorist less. Because of this widespread superstition, an alleged reduction in motor car traffic resulting from the improvement of public transportation is often simply stated without being backed by appropriate survey data.

Few studies have been published on the interdependence between the improvement of public transport systems and the amount of motor car traffic. In Stuttgart, Germany, a new light rail line (S-Bahn) opened in 1985. The new rail allowed for faster commuting, and a survey was conducted to demonstrate the expected effects of the new rail on road traffic. The following quotation, which summarizes the result of the investigation, is taken from Younes (1990):

> The Stuttgart case study of a new S-Bahn linking the city of Stuttgart with the industrialized region of Böblingen has some surprising findings. Based on in-depth surveys and studies carried out by both the city and the local public transport authority, it is clearly shown that the growth in motor vehicle traffic along the corridor of the new S-Bahn has increased substantially since it was opened and that this increase was significantly more than the increase in traffic for all roads in the city.

The Basis of Cost–Benefit Calculations is Nonsense

In Germany, road projects are evaluated according to standardized cost–benefit procedures. In the course of the cost–benefit analysis a monetary value is attributed to the following potential benefits of a road:

- improved accessibility;
- reduced operating costs of vehicles (reduced fuel consumption);
- improved safety; and
- environmental benefits.

Time savings for road users are evaluated within the improved accessibility criterion. Typically, this criterion contributes significantly to the alleged benefit of a new road. It is worthwhile to note in this context that new roads tend to be designed for high speeds in order to claim high accessibility benefits. However, since travel time budgets are constant there are no overall time savings and thus there should be no benefits with respect to time budgets alone.

The most drastic error of the cost–benefit analysis is made when fuel savings and the reduction of other vehicular operating costs are calculated. In Stuttgart, 2km of a four-lane urban highway are projected to relieve a bottle neck. Motor car traffic on the new road is predicted to be about 80,000 vehicles per day. Allegedly the project will result in a daily fuel conservation of about 8 tons (Stadt Stuttgart, 1987). Calculations of reduction in fuel consumption were based on the assumptions that traffic from other routes will be concentrated on the new highway and that motor vehicles, driven at a speed of 50–100km/h, will consume less fuel per distance than vehicles in congestion. Not surprisingly, the rule of the constant travel time budget was ignored in the calculations. The calculations are therefore wrong. Similarly, calculations concerning traffic accidents and air pollution are also wrong, because induced traffic generally is ignored.

Past cost–benefit calculations in the German Federal Transportation Plan entirely neglect induced traffic. According to these cost–benefit estimates, new roads generally yield substantial economic and environmental benefits. Benefits supposedly result from time savings and associated fuel conservation translating into reduced carbon dioxide emissions.

Recently, a new method for cost–benefit estimation has been introduced for calculations relating to future transportation plans. Approximately 7.7 per cent of the induced traffic is taken into account by this method. As a result, calculated benefit for selected road projects typically decreased by about 10 per cent (Ministry of Transport, Building and Housing, 2000). Thus, it can be concluded that the calculated benefit of a new road commonly would be negative if 100 per cent of the induced traffic were taken into account.

Road Construction Contributes Significantly to Traffic Increase

According to the German Ministry of Transportation and the private institutes largely funded by it, traffic demand does not increase with improved road infrastructure. Rather it is claimed that improved road infrastructure and the promotion of public transport systems both reduce fuel consumption, thereby contributing to environmental protection. This is similar to the idea of a corpulent person eating more food in order to slim down.

No attempt has been made as yet to calculate the amount of traffic induced by the construction of new roads in Germany. However, based on the law of the constant travel time budget, a coarse quantitative estimate of induced traffic can easily be obtained.

For the four-lane highway projected in Stuttgart, an overall time saving of 5 million hours/year was calculated (Stadt Stuttgart, 1987). Altogether, motorists spend 93 million hours/year on Stuttgart's roads, and car traffic in Stuttgart consumes 302,500 tonnes of fuel each year (Ministry of Nutrition, Agriculture, Environment and Forestry of Baden-Württemberg, 1986). The highway project therefore would boost road traffic with respect to the overall traffic in Stuttgart by as much as approximately 5 per cent. Fuel consumption would increase by roughly 44 tonnes per day.

Since it can be assumed that official calculations over-estimated actual time savings within the framework of the cost–benefit analysis, the actual increase in traffic and fuel consumption is probably less than 44 tonnes per day. However, without any doubt, fuel consumption is going to increase as a result of the new highway. The decrease in fuel consumption claimed in the cost–benefit analysis is nonsense.

Extrapolating from this one road project in Stuttgart to all road projects under consideration nationally, it is estimated that annual traffic growth induced by road construction presently is approximately one-third of the total growth in traffic in Germany. Improvement of the road infrastructure is thus one of the major causes of traffic increase in general.

Conclusion

Based on the law of the constant travel time budget, we argue that the improvement of infrastructure contributes significantly to the general increase in traffic as it allows for faster transportation. Standard cost–benefit analyses neglect traffic induced by improved infrastructure and therefore are faulty. Traffic induced by improvements in infrastructure can easily be estimated from the time savings for motorists as a result of a construction project.

Any measure that makes road traffic faster induces new traffic. Any measure that makes road traffic slower reduces traffic. Therefore, the most important objective of environmentally-oriented traffic policy must be the de-acceleration of road traffic.

Systems of mass transportation can contribute to environmental protection only if improvements in public transport are paralleled by measures to de-accelerate motorized traffic, thus allowing for changes in the modal split without increasing overall traffic.

Notes

1   This chapter was first published as a paper in *World Transport Policy & Practice*, vol 1, no 1, pp29–31.

References

Herz, R (1985) *Verkehrsverhalten im zeitlichen und räumlichen Vergleich. Befunde aus KONTIV 76 und 82 (Behaviour of Travellers in Temporal and Spatial Comparison: Findings from a Continuous Survey of Behaviour of Travellers in 1976 and 1982)*, Schriftenreihe der Deutschen Verkehrswissenschaflitchen Gesellschaft e V Reihe B 85 (German Association of Traffic Science, Series B85), Berlin, pp238–72

John Allard and Frank Graham and Partners (1987) *A Review of the Traffic Generation Effect of Road Improvements*, PTRC Europe, Road Improvements, Transport and Planning, 15th Summer Annual Meeting, Highway Appraisal and Design, Proceedings of Seminar E, September, pp 57–75

Ministry of Transport, Building and Housing (2000) 'Induced traffic – adjustment of methods, case examples and modifying factors' (Induzierter Verkehr Verfahrensanpassung, Anwendungsfälle und Zuschlagfaktoren) Bundesministerium für Verkehr, Bau und Wohnungswesen, Berlin

Ministry of Nutrition, Agriculture, Environment and Forestry of Baden-Württemberg (1986) *Emissionskataster Stuttgart, Quellengruppe Verkehr (Assessment of Air Pollution in Stuttgart, Traffic-related Sources)*, Ministerium für Ernährung, Landwirtschaft, Umwelt und Forsten des Landes Baden-Württemberg (Ministry of Nutrition, Agriculture, Environment and Forestry of Baden-Württemberg), Stuttgart

Norberg-Hodge, H (1994) 'Building the case against globalization and for community-based economics', *Newsletter International Society for Ecological Economics*, vol 5, no 2, pp3–4

Stadt Stuttgart (1987) *Variantenuntersuchung Pragsattel, Wirkungsanalyse zum Neu-/Ausbau der B 10/B 27 in Stuttgart zwischen Friedrichswahl und Pragsattel (Survey of Road Construction Variants 'Pragsattel', Efficiency Analysis for the Construction of the B 10/B 27 between 'Friedrichswahl' and 'Pragsattel')*, Stadt Stuttgart (City of Stuttgart), Stuttgart

Younes, B M (1990) *The Effectiveness of New Road Schemes in Urban Areas*, thesis submitted to the Department of Civil Engineering, Imperial College of Science, Technology and Medicine, University of London, London

15

Car-free Households: Who Lives without an Automobile Today?

Ulrike Reutter and Oscar Reutter

Introduction

Many people have come to recognize private motor vehicle traffic as being one of the major driving forces behind declining environmental and residential qualities in cities. High numbers of motor vehicles and increases in the mileage covered by privately owned vehicles bring with them growing accident risk, land-take, soil contamination, overall resource depletion and energy use with the concomitant carbon dioxide problems, wastes in the manufacture and disposal of automobiles, and noise and air pollution. The countenance of the city and the quality of life in cities both suffer.

Conventional strategies for solving such problems, including widespread traffic calming or optimizing motor vehicle technology, are approaching the limits of their efficacy. Although such strategies reduce the stress on the environment, the gains achieved are more than offset by increasing loads emanating from an unbroken rise in the number of vehicles and volume of travel. Planning concepts aimed at reducing the number of automobiles need to adopted. In this effort, regional, urban and traffic planning should provide incentives to encourage households to do without a car.

Car-free neighbourhoods within towns would make it possible for people to experience, both individually and collectively, the benefits that liberation from the private car offers. All the residents, children as well as adults, could then move freely within the public roadway area, not endangered by vehicle traffic, and be able to cycle, play or simply sit and relax in this newly reclaimed space – without automobile exhausts and noise.

The data presented in this chapter are derived from broad-based German statistics and from a telephone survey covering 146 car-free households selected at random in Dortmund; the authors conducted this survey in November 1992 (Reutter and Reutter, 1995).[1] Here, a car-free household is defined as one that has not owned a vehicle for at least six months and does not have access to either a company car or a motorcycle. The empirical results are representative of the car-free households in Dortmund.

How Many Car-free Households are There?

In 1998, Germany was home to a total of 82 million people; at the same time 43 million passenger cars were registered (Deutsche Institut Wirtschaftforschung, 2000). In the period since the first Einkommens und Verbrauchsstichprobe (income and consumption sampling) (EVS), which was conducted in 1962, the number of non-motorized households has fallen continuously as a result of ongoing mass motorization, down from the original 73 per cent of all households (see Figure 15.1). The EVS conducted in January 1998 revealed that of the 38 million households in Germany, approximately 10 million (26 per cent) did not have a car, while 28 million (74 per cent) owned at least one vehicle. Approximately 16 per cent of the total German population lives in car-free households; expressed in figures, that comes to 13.1 million of the 82 million people in Germany (Statistisches Bundesamt, 1999).[2] Nationally, on average at least one household in four does not own a vehicle. It is thus not possible to speak of full motorization in Germany. In Dortmund, approximately 81,000 (32 per cent) of the total of 255,000 households do not own a vehicle. Figure 15.2 clearly shows that there is a considerable demand or market potential for planning and setting up car-free zones due to the large number of people who currently do without a car.

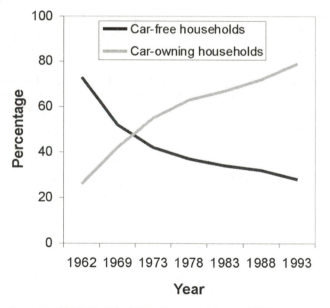

Source: Pöschl (1993), Euler (1989), Reutter and Reutter (1995)

Figure 15.1 *Car-free households in western Germany*

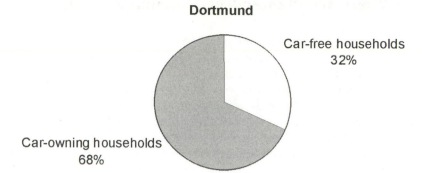

Dortmund

Car-free households
32%

Car-owning households
68%

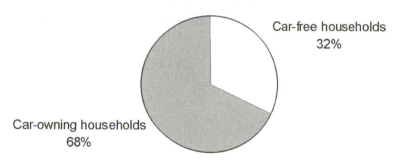

Cities with 100,000–500,000 residents

Car-free households
32%

Car-owning households
68%

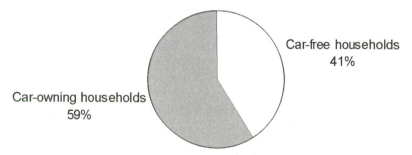

Cities with more than 500,000 residents

Car-free households
41%

Car-owning households
59%

Source: Statistisches Bundesamt (1999), Reutter and Reutter (1995)

Figure 15.2 *Share of car-free households in Dortmund
and in large western German cities*

Where are the Car-free Households Located?

The more urban the surroundings, the greater the number of car-free households. The proportion of non-motorized households rises with the size of the town or city. Taking the average of all cities and communities in Germany, the share of car-free households lies at 28 per cent; in the larger towns with 100,000 residents or more, this proportion is considerably higher. In fact, in the major cities with populations exceeding 500,000, car-free households now account for more than 40 per cent of the total.

Within these large cities, the percentage of car-free households in inner city and mixed use areas is especially high. In areas of this type within the city of Dortmund, almost half of all the households are without a car (46.4 per cent); only slightly more than half of all households there have one or more vehicles at their disposal (53.6 per cent) (see Figure 15.3).

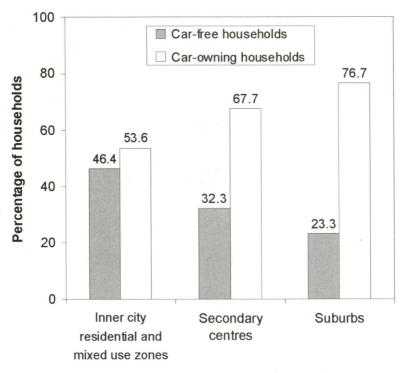

Source: Reutter and Reutter (1995)

Figure 15.3 *Car-free households according to the structure of the respective residential area in Dortmund, November 1992*

These findings clearly indicate that the large cities particularly lend themselves to the planning of car-free zones, and within a city the inner city residential and mixed use areas are especially suitable for car-free zoning. The factors are summarized below:

- almost half of the households in the inner city residential areas in the large cities in western Germany already live without a car;
- these areas are characterized by a comparatively large number, variety and density of activities that represent destinations for individual journeys, including residential areas, workplaces, shopping facilities and cultural and recreational facilities; and
- these destinations can easily be reached using the so-called green modes – namely on foot, by bicycle and with public transport.

The logical conclusion is that the future focus should be on identifying such quarters, capitalizing on the favourable existing situation there, in addition to pursuing city-wide planning projects to promote car-free living.

Car-free city zones in inner city residential and mixed use areas should be set up both within existing urban structures and in newly redeveloped areas – including those built on rehabilitated inner city land such as abandoned commercial properties, evacuated barracks and other military facilities or former railway freight yards. Conversion and redevelopment projects in existing residential areas over longer periods of time are so decisive because, in comparison to the volume of new construction, the bulk of available housing is to be found there. In addition, a large number of non-motorized households are located in such areas today; if they wanted to enjoy the collective advantages of car-free living they would first have to relocate. Older citizens in particular, no longer wanting or able to move house, would have little prospect of enjoying the benefits of a car-free neighbourhood unless projects were carried out in existing residential areas.

Who Currently Lives without a Car?

In addition to the role played by the character of the neighbourhood itself, the socio-demographic household type to which a given unit belongs correlates to a large degree with its daily internal organization with regard to time and distances. If, for example, many people live in a single dwelling, their activities have to be jointly arranged. If there are children in the home, their activities have to be coordinated with those of the parents – and more often than not, of the mother alone. The daily routines of older people are quite different from those of young people; if members of the household are gainfully employed, then they face very specific constraints in terms of time and space.

Mobility research efforts and particularly action radius studies (time and space) show three significant socio-demographic characteristics:

1   the ages of the adult members of the household;
2   their participation in the working world; and
3   the presence of children in the household.

These can be used to describe quite accurately the situation within which a household operates, ie the family's rhythms form the basis for specific time-and-space constraints

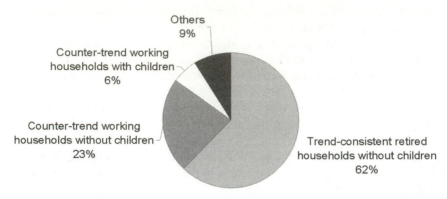

Source: Reutter and Reutter (1995)

Figure 15.4 *Situation homogenous types of car-free households in Dortmund, November 1992*

(see Holzapfel, 1980; Holz-Rau, 1990; Kreibich et al, 1989; Mentz, 1984; Neuwerth, 1987; Reutter et al, 1991).

Applied to the non-motorized households in Dortmund, three homogeneous types of car-free households emerge:

1   retired households – aligning with the trend;
2   working households without children – countering the trend; and
3   working households with children – also counter to the trend.

Taken together, these three types describe 93 per cent of all car-free households in Dortmund (see Figure 15.4).

The retired households in line with the trend include:

- those made up of older and elderly persons, where the individual responding to the survey was 55 years of age or more;
- those in which there are no working adults;
- those in which there are no children under 18; and
- those in which the adults are retired, have taken early retirement or are housewives.

The members of these households have to consider only relatively minor outside constraints in terms of space and time since none of them is involved in gainful employment. They must cover the distances and routes required for personal business (eg shopping, errands, banking, medical appointments) and for leisure activities. Among those older households in Dortmund, where the person responding to the survey was 65 years of age or more, approximately three-quarters were single-person households, comprised almost exclusively of women living alone; approximately one-quarter were two-person households where the only constraints arise from the need for coordination between the two adults. Four out of ten retired households in line with the trend could, in their own estimation, afford a car. In Dortmund, retired households account for almost two-thirds of the non-motorized households; they are estimated to number approximately 54,500.

The structure of the retired households corresponds precisely to the trend that can be read from the data for western Germany (Reutter and Reutter, 1994), the proportion of car-free households being relatively high in households:

- that are made up of older or elderly respondents;
- where the respondents are not employed;
- that are without children; and
- that are smaller, particularly one-person units.

Included in those 'working households without children' which run counter to the trend are:

- young and middle aged households where the person responding was in the employable age bracket, from 18 to a maximum of 55 years;
- households in which at least one adult is gainfully employed; and
- households in which there are no children under 18 years of age.

The working members of the household must deal with major limitations in terms of time and distance, since they must pursue the mandatory activity of working at fixed workplaces and during fixed working hours. Also affected by these constraints are the other activities of these particular household members, such as taking care of personal business and pursuing leisure activities; the other adult members of the household are also affected even if they are not working. When the members of the household want to spend free time together, for instance, they are restricted to the early mornings, late afternoons and evenings and weekends, all times at which public transit services are considerably sparser than during normal working hours.

In Dortmund, at least half of these households are single person households. Approximately four out of ten households are two person households and only approximately 5 per cent include three or more persons, in which the need to orchestrate activities among the adult members of the household is particularly evident. Two-thirds of the counter-trend working households without children could, in their own opinion, afford to keep a vehicle. In Dortmund this type of household structure, estimated to number 19,700, accounts for almost a quarter of the car-free households. When it manages without a vehicle, the working household without children behaves exactly contrary to the trend that can be gleaned from the data for western Germany (Reutter and Reutter, 1994), the proportion of car-free households being relatively low among those households with:

- younger or middle aged respondents;
- gainfully employed respondents; and
- higher net household incomes.

Among the working households with children that operate contrary to the trend are households with:

- young and middle aged occupants, where the person replying was of employment age, from 18 to 55 years;
- at least one adult gainfully employed; and
- at least one child under 18 years of age.

In these households – almost 90 per cent of which include three or more persons in Dortmund – the activities and associated journeys taken by the adults and the children must be particularly carefully coordinated and – especially where smaller children are present – closely synchronized. The organizational effort in this type of household is enormous. Family members have high mobility requirements to cope with the need to coordinate time and the journeys resulting from the variety of activities to be carried out: travel to and from work at regular times and fixed locations, tending to personal business, leisure-time journeys and the various trips occasioned by the children all have to be harmonized. This is aggravated by the increased amount of transportation capacity required not only for the foods and beverages needed daily but also for the equipment used on family excursions and holidays. In their own estimation, two-thirds of these households could, without qualification, afford a vehicle. In Dortmund this group accounts for 6 per cent or approximately 5500 of the car-free households.

Where the working household without children does not own a car, it also contradicts the trend seen in the data for western Germany (Reutter and Reutter, 1994), the proportion of car-free households being relatively low among those household groups:

- with younger or middle aged respondents;
- with gainfully employed respondents;
- with at least one child;
- made up of three or more persons; and
- with higher net combined income.

On the basis of the typology elucidated in this chapter, urban planning and traffic planning should, in the authors' opinion, support the everyday organization of time and space requirements specific to those people now living in car-free households so that individuals who today do without a motor car will not need to purchase one in the future to cope with living in cities.

People who live without a car in the trend-consistent retired households are particularly dependent on an intact infrastructure close to their homes to take care of personal business and to pursue leisure activities – particularly daily walks in the nearby neighbourhood. This is because older people often suffer from motor and sensory limitations relevant to negotiating traffic, complicated by physical frailty; as a consequence they are particularly sensitive to distances and are at high accident risk. Older and elderly people who organize their day-to-day living without a car require services that are easily reached and universally accessible (including safe walking and cycling paths) in the transportation options offered by the green modes so that they are not limited in their mobility.

For people who live without a vehicle in counter-trend working households without children, efforts designed specifically to promote this target group would concentrate particularly on the evenings and weekends, namely when they are pursuing activities which are not work-related – such as shopping, running errands and enjoying leisure activities – making the organization of daily living both simple and efficient. This is particularly important for people in car-free households with several employed individuals who can spend only a relatively small part of their time together in leisure activities. Simple and efficient day-to-day organization for people in car-free households means in particular an arrangement of activity destinations, such as workplaces, shopping facilities, leisure and recreational facilities, which adheres to the principle of keeping distances short. Also essential are adequate transit services within the green modes, particularly in the evening and at the weekend.

For those living in counter-trend working households with children, support efforts targeted specifically at this group would also mean – over and above the measures initiated for the counter-trend working households without children – that the children's infrastructure facilities such as kindergartens and daycare centres, school or recreational facilities be located near the home, where they may be easily and safely reached with green modes. It should be possible for children to play in the immediate vicinity of their homes safely and without hazard, these being the most accessible play areas for children and young people. In addition, improved delivery services could ease the increased transportation requirements for the groceries required daily. The greater amount of transportation capacity needed to carry luggage and equipment when travelling with children should be met with carefully considered improvements in public transport services, particularly on weekends.

Conclusion

The demand for car-free city neighbourhoods is evident. All that needs to be done is to implement car-free zones in the cities when planning new areas and within existing residential structures.

Notes

1 This chapter was first published as a paper in *World Transport Policy & Practice*, vol 2, no 4, pp32–37.
2 See Reutter and Reutter (1995, pp19–42) for detailed information on the socio-demographic structure of car-free households.

References

Deutsche Institut Wirtschaftforschung (eds) (2000) *Verkehr in Zahlen 2000* (Traffic in Figures 2000), Federal Ministry of Traffic and Transportation, Bonn/Berlin
Euler, M (1989) 'Austattung privater Haushalte mit ausgewählen langlebigen Gebrauchsgütern im Januar 1989', *Wirtschaft und Statistik*, no 5, pp307–15

Holzapfel, H (1980) *Verkehrsbeziehungen in Städten* (Traffic Interrelationships in Cities), Dissertation Technische Universität, Berlin

Holz-Rau, H C (1990) *Bestimmungsgrössen des verkehrsverhaltens – analyse bundesweiter haushaltsbefragungen und modellierende Hochrechnung* (Determining Factors in Traffic Behaviour – Analysis of National Surveys of Households and Model Extrapolation), Dissertation Technische Universität, Berlin

Kreibich, B, Kreibich, V and Ruhl, G (1989) 'Vom funktionsraum zum aktionsraum: wissenschaftliche grundlagen für eine modernisierung der infrastruktur- und regional-planung' (Scientific principles for modernization of infrastructure and regional planning), *Informationen zur Raumentwicklung*, vol 1, pp51–71

Mentz, H J (1984) *Analyse von Verkehrsverhalten im Haushaltskontext* (Analyses of Traffic Behaviour in the Context of the Private Household), Dissertation Technische Universität, Berlin

Neuwerth, K W (1987) *Abhangigkeit des Verkehrsverhaltens vom raumstrukturellen Angebot* (Dependency of Traffic Behaviour on Spatial Structure), Braunschweig

Pöschl, H (1993) 'Ausstatting privater Hauschalte mit lanlebigen, Gebrauchsgütern im Januar 1993', *Wirtschaft und Statistik*, no 12, pp924–928

Reutter, O and Reutter, U (1994) 'Autofreie Haushalte, Daten zur Sozialstruktur einer unterschätzten Bevölkerungsgruppe' (Car-free households: data on the social structure of an underestimated population group), *RaumPlanung*, vol 65, pp112–118

Reutter, O and Reutter, U (1995) *Autofreies leben in der stadt: eine beschreibung des autofreien lebens in westdeutschen Grossstädten am ende des 20. Jahrhunderts und vorschläge die stadt- und verkehrsplanung zur förderung des autofreien lebens in der stadt, insbesondere durch die einrichtung autofreier stadtquartiere in bestehenden innerstädtischen wohngebieten* (Car-free Living in the City: A Description of Car-free Living in Western German Cities at the Close of the 20th Century and Suggestions for Urban and Traffic Planning to Promote Car-free Living in the City, in Particular Through the Establishment of Car-free Zones Within Existing Inner-city Neighbourhoods), dissertation, Urban and Regional Planning Department, University of Dortmund, Dortmund

Reutter, O, Schütte, F-P and Kreibich, V (1991) *Reisezeitverkürzung im ÖPNV* (Reducing Travel Times in Local Public Transit), ILS-Schriften 55, Dortmund

Statistisches Bundesamt (German Federal Statistics Office) (1999) *Einkommens und Verbrauchsstichprobe (EVS) 1998*, (Income and Consumption Sampling 1998), Wirtschaft und Statistik, Statistisches Bundesamt, Wiesbaden, Germany

Part 6

Transport in Latin America

16

Urban Transport in Latin America

Eduardo Vasconcellos

Introduction

Latin America is comprised of 17 countries with populations varying from 2.5 million (Panama) to 168 million (Brazil) and land areas stretching from 21,400km^2 (El Salvador) to 8.5 million km^2 (Brazil). Total population is approximately 450 million.

While Brazil was colonized by the Portuguese, all the other countries were colonized by the Spanish, yielding two different languages and cultures, although similar in several aspects in the face of their common Latin origin. Large distances, high mountains, desert areas and immense forests create further obstacles to permanent integration between the Latin American Spanish-speaking countries and Brazil.

Most countries may be classified as poor (or very poor), with a regional average gross domestic product (GDP) per person in 1992 of approximately US$2200, varying from US$512 (Nicaragua) to US$4327 (Argentina). Large income disparities among social groups is the rule. Motorization levels may be classified as low – around 70 vehicles per thousand people (as compared to 560 in the USA). The region has about 7 per cent of global vehicle population and contributes a proportionally small share of global air pollution.

Most states in Latin America are weakly institutionalized, with powerful small groups controlling public policy decisions. There are also states with higher average incomes, but with large social differences within society and a powerful, often well educated elite working closely with 'modernity-seeking' bureaucracies such as in Argentina, Brazil, Chile and México. Some important political and social aspects may be summarized as follows:

- Most political systems are fragile, subject to external and internal destabilization pressures, leading to constant threats of disruption; educational and economic disparities among social groups are enormous; the power to influence decisions is unevenly distributed; citizenship, as political consciousness of right and duties, is weakly developed, which is worsened by the deep social and political differences among social groups and classes.
- In the face of large areas and/or poor economic development, most countries developed poor regional transport systems. Both railways and highways are limited in coverage and quality. Rural communities are poorly connected to each other and people still rely on precarious transport means such as ox carts, tractors and adapted trucks to gain access to distant places. Urban transport systems, which are

much more developed, face several deficiencies, especially poor public transport supply, accidents, congestion and pollution.
- Adequate public agencies either do not exist or are badly coordinated. They lack proper human and technical resources to perform their tasks.

This chapter will focus mainly on urban transport problems due to the fast urbanization process in Latin America.

Economic Development and Transport

Most countries in the region had their railway systems developed in the late 19th and early 20th centuries. These systems were progressively abandoned after World War Two and were replaced by extensive highway systems that defined a new pattern of supply: trucks and buses became the most important means of transport. The largest countries – Brazil, Argentina and México – had, in 1992, respectively 30,000, 34,000 and 26,000km of railways (Wright, 1996), as compared to vast highway systems (approximately 150,000km in the case of Brazil). As a consequence, in Brazil, highway transport in 1998 was already responsible for 62.6 per cent of tonnes per kilometre (tkm), as compared to 18.9 per cent on railways (GEIPOT, 1999). Waterways are rare, except in the case of México (especially for trade with the USA) and Brazil, where they already carry 17.5 per cent of tkm.

Such a transport system generated four main consequences: first, a large dependence on fossil fuels and especially diesel oil used by trucks; second, large social and environmental impacts, related to new roads crossing forest areas or urban and indigenous people's communities; third, very high traffic accident rates on highways; and finally, the burden on public resources to sustain dilapidated railways operating under unfavourable conditions.

On the urban side, transport became increasingly important. Between 1950 and 1990 the urban population as part of total population increased from 41.6 to 71.4 per cent in the region, and industry and commercial activities were progressively concentrated in cities. Severe problems of lack of adequate housing, infrastructure and transport, over-crowding and serious environmental degradation followed. Three particular features of such development must be emphasized. First, large income and cultural differences led to the physical separation of wealthy groups, the middle classes and the poor, although mixed land use patterns may also exist. Second, public investments driven by the uneven distribution of political power generated sharp differences in the availability of public infrastructure and services such as schools, hospitals, roads and public transport. Finally, the built environment was produced and modified by a myriad of micro-powers which escape state control, and is thus associated with two pervasive actions: that of poor or low middle class people occupying the peripheral or depressed areas of the city, and that of irregular or illegal land use by the elite and the middle classes to support business and leisure activities. The latter process has dramatic effects on the environment as well as on the demand for infrastructure and public services, while the former generates a high demand for private transport and aggravates externalities. Cities can therefore be said to have two built environments, one organized by urban planning interventions and the other independent of them, the latter often being larger than the former.

Urban Transport

Since the beginning of the century, foreign railroad and streetcar companies had permission to provide public transport services. After World War Two, competition from buses and adapted trucks rendered it impossible for these companies to provide competitive services in the newly urbanized areas. Subsequently, all were progressively dismantled and replaced with bus operators. Few efforts were made to provide large scale mass transport systems and all major cities (except México City and Buenos Aires) evolved with public transport systems highly dependent on bus operators but with poor rail systems. Not until the 1970s did São Paulo and Santiago inaugurate new, high standard metro systems capturing only a small part of the demand. Currently, most motorized trips are made by public transport, although in some cases (such as São Paulo and Caracas) cars are being used for a large part of daily trips (see Table 16.1).

Table 16.1 *Modal split of daily motorized trips (percentage) in selected Latin American cities*

| City | Motorized trips (per cent) | | |
| | Public | | |
	Bus[1]	Rail[2]	Private (cars)
Rio, Brazil, 1994	78	7	15
Santiago, Chile, 1991	69	9	22
México City, México, 1994	60	12	28
Buenos Aires, Argentina, 1992	59	12	29
Caracas, Venezuela,1991	41	19	40
São Paulo, Brazil, 1997	41	11	48

Notes: 1: Includes mini-buses and shared taxis; 2: railways and metros
Source: Vasconcellos (2001)

Buses became the dominant form of transport, and two different patterns of supply emerged. In all countries except Brazil, the most common pattern is private supply through cooperatives of operators, picking up individuals in bus corridors with little or no public control over routes, fares and service quality: Lima, Santiago, Bogotá, Caracas and México City each have from 30,000 to 60,000 vehicles in operation. Conversely, in Brazil, bus services are regulated and provided by medium and large enterprises, with fixed routes and fares, and enjoy monopoly services once contracted by the government. In urban areas there are nearly 100,000 large diesel buses responsible for approximately 95 per cent of public transport.

Both models were unable to provide convenient public transport to the users. In the less regulated markets current conditions are very poor, with most users subject to unreliability, discomfort and danger with old badly maintained vehicles. Some systems experience an increase in service provision but at the expense of higher fares, congestion and pollution; moreover, they can be driven to an 'elitization' of supply and to the organization of local private monopolies, sustained by violent forms of control. In the more regulated Brazilian market, vehicle and service conditions are generally better; however, the relative contractual stability generates pressures for cost increases, disregard for some users' needs and localized inefficiencies. The system prevailed all over the country until 1995, when it began to be severely challenged by illegal transport providers; it now faces a threat of disruption, having already lost approximately 25 per cent of its patronage.

With private transport, the increasing support devoted to it has been reshaping cities, with profound environmental and equity consequences. Of particular interest is the position of the middle classes and the technocracy in designing policies to support the use of the car. Caracas is remarkably selective from a spatial point of view, with hills occupied by poor people and valleys occupied by the middle class. Initial road plans were developed in the 1940s, with the resulting freeway network working to rearrange space according to the new consumption needs, dependent on automobile availability (Marcano, 1981). Recently, Buenos Aires has been enlarging its expressway network through privatization, with adjacent land use changed to accommodate large apartment, commercial and office complexes, physically segregated and directed to middle and upper classes, also dependent on automobile availability (Vera, 1999). In São Paulo, the reshaping of the road system in the 1970s corresponded to the needs of the lifestyle of the new middle classes generated by the income concentration process, whose daily activity network incorporated new trips, primarily related to private services, and which could not be performed using the low quality bus system. Consequent to the increase in auto ownership, a higher portion of daily trips was made by car. In São Paulo, auto trips as part of motorized trips increased from 26 per cent in 1967 to 47 per cent in 1997 (CMSP, 1998). Between 1986 and 1990 auto trips increased from 17–34 per cent in Buenos Aires and from 18–21 per cent in Santiago (Figueroa, 1999).

Therefore, urban transport policies crystallized inequalities: bus systems remained immersed in permanent crisis, and automobiles occupied increased portions of available space, creating sharp differences in transport and accessibility between those with and those without access to private transport. Needless to say, non-motorized transport has been neglected, although walking and cycling still play a major role in the urban transport system.

Institutional issues

In most large cities, planning is complicated by the fragmentation of agencies and institutional overlap. In México City there are four levels of government dealing with the issue, from local to federal authorities (Molinero, 1991). Federally controlled subway lines are operated in a deregulated local bus environment, comprising approximately 60,000 private operators, with little control from public authorities. In São Paulo there has been an historic disconnection between metropolitan-scale transport problems and local transport policies, and conflicts abound when trying to create regional transport infrastructure or services that interfere in local matters. In Buenos

Aires the historical difficulties in coordinating actions by federal, provincial and local authorities were recently aggravated by the privatization of the metro and railway systems, which introduced new actors in the policy arena. The most noticeable exception is Curitiba, where a network of structural bus corridors was implemented along with changes in land use, which allowed for denser occupation, backed by a strong regional agency – the Curitiba Institute for Urban Planning and Research (IPPUC). However, three particular historical features must be emphasized: the intense economic growth of the state of Paraná, the overwhelming power of public agencies in the authoritarian regime, and the political linkages between the local elite and the federal military regime during the 1970s, which combined to ensure economic resources to improve infrastructure in the state. As important as it may be as an example, the Curitiba case implies a frustration: such historical conditions make the Curitiba experience so unique that it would be difficult for it to be transposed to any other large city in the country.

Urban Development, Space and Environment

From an environmental point of view, both air pollution and traffic accidents are worrisome. In México and São Paulo, yearly production of pollutants is, respectively, 2.3 and 1.6 million tonnes of carbon monoxide (CO), 555,000 and 368,000 tonnes of hydrocarbons (HCs) and 18,800 and 48,600 tonnes of suspended particulate matter (SPM). Most CO and HC production comes from transport operations, while SPM also comes from industrial activities (Benitez and Roldán, 1999; ANTP/IPEA, 1998). Most of the pollution is produced by motor vehicles, especially private transport (see Table 16.2).

Table 16.2 *Contribution of motor vehicles to pollutant emissions in selected Latin American cities*

City	Pollutant emitted by motor vehicles (percentage)				
	Carbon monoxide	Hydrocarbons	Nitrogen oxides	Sulphur dioxide	Suspended particulate matter
México, 1994	99	54	71	27	4
Santiago, 1993	95	69	85	14	11
São Paulo, 1990	94	89	92	64	39

Source: Vasconcellos (2001)

Congestion and inefficient operation severely impact on bus reliability and speed, which are well below the desirable level of 25km/h for regular operation (see Table 16.3). In São Paulo and Rio de Janeiro, severe congestion imposes on bus passengers, respectively, 118 million and 80 million additional hours per year (representing, on average, approximately 15 minutes in peak hour). Extra costs imposed on bus operations are 16 per cent and 10 per cent respectively, and annual extra costs charged to users may be estimated, respectively, as US$125 million and US$30 million (ANTP/IPEA, 1998).

Table 16.3 *Average speed of buses, peak hours, several cities*

City (country)	Bus speed (km/h)
Caracas (Venezuela)	16.3
La Habana (Cuba)	18.0
Santa Cruz de la Sierra (Bolivia)	15.7
São Paulo (Brazil)	14.5

Source: Vasconcellos (2001)

With accidents, average rates are much higher than those found in developed countries. The rate of fatalities per 100,000 people in major towns is very high: 16.8 in São Paulo and 20.3 in Bogotá (with, respectively, 1700 and 1300 deaths per year) (CET, 1999; UNCHS, 1996). On average, 28 per cent of deaths attributed to injury in the region are due to vehicle accidents (Roberts, 1997). It is estimated that 100,000 people die in traffic accidents (IDB, 1998) and 1000 million are injured per year in the region; in the five larger countries (Argentina, Brazil, Chile, Colombia and México), 60,000 die while 600,000 are injured. Social and medical costs are high: in São Paulo, for every person killed in 1997 in traffic accidents, there were 22 injured, corresponding to about 50,000 injured people per year; among them, 6000 suffered permanent disabilities (CET, 1997).

Perspectives

Current urban transport conditions in Latin America result from a large set of social, economic and political factors. Improvements in such conditions also depend on several changes, both outside and inside the limits of urban and transport policies. Due to the large differences within the countries' past and current characteristics, perspectives are diversified.

The profound economic and social changes fuelled by the globalization process tend to affect urban transport conditions, especially in the face of the reorganization of production processes and intervention to deregulate markets. The fiscal crisis of the state and the threat of economic disruption – as happened recently with Ecuador, México and Argentina – will bring more pressure on public investments and increase reactions to subsidies, further restraining the implementation of equitable urban transport policies.

The dependence on motorized transport will increase in medium sized and large urban areas and accessibility inequities will worsen, in face also of continuing social segregation. The deficiencies of the political systems and the strong linkages among the elite, the middle classes and the state technocracy make it difficult to have a true democratic representation of the conflicting interests. However, the strengthening of citizenship brought by inherent economic conflicts and the experience with poverty and deprivation may counteract such tendencies to some extent.

Problems and inequities concerning transport and traffic conditions in Latin America can be attributed to structural, social and economic factors and also to two historical processes, translated into clear policies: the dominance of private transport over non-motorized means, and the submission of public transport to a market approach. The dominance of private transport lies behind safety, environmental and space inequities. The market approach to public transport precludes a social approach and translates into deficient accessibility and quality.

Transport is not an end in itself. The 'end' has to be the equitable appropriation of space and the corresponding access to social and economic life. There is no reason to believe that the private sector alone will be able – or interested enough – to provide transport services that fit the needs of the majority of the population, if equity does not belong on the agenda of economic modernization. Structural changes depend on factors beyond the direct influence of urban and transport polices and require enhanced democracy and citizenship, extensive access to education and health, increased wealth for the poor and better income distribution.

But current conditions may be improved also with the adoption of specific actions and policies, as follows:

- the technical and political strengthening of public agencies in charge of transport and traffic policies, along with the creation of open linkages for community participation and social control;
- the redirection of the planning process towards the use of techniques adapted to local realities, along with the avoidance of traditional conservative approaches;
- effective support to non-motorized means, through the building and improvement of sidewalks, pedestrian areas and bicycle facilities, along with the adoption of permanent programmes to improve traffic safety;
- the development of a public transport system based on the assumption of public transport as an essential public service, implying public planning surveillance and control; this requires changing the deregulated environment prevailing in all countries (except Brazil) towards the Brazilian regulated model, together with improving such models in order to make them more cost effective, flexible and adapted to users' needs; and
- the adoption of restrictive measures on the inadequate and undesirable use of automobiles, along with the recapturing of roads for the use of the majority in the roles of pedestrian and public transport users; a particular action refers to priority schemes for public transport, where the extensive Brazilian experience with bus corridors – already being used in other countries – may serve as a guide.

Practical changes will have to be pursued inside a highly conflicting political arena and within an economic globalization process whose impacts will be extensive and severe. Poverty and deprivation will continue in several parts of the region as part of an income concentration process and strict economic adjustment plans. Such powerful transformations will have profound impacts on demographic and social conditions, limiting mobility and accessibility. Income concentration will generate additional middle class segments, which will continue to have privileged access to policy decisions to ensure their social and economic reproduction. Consequently, as long as private motorized transport continues to be seen as vital for such reproduction, the construction of automobile-based spaces will continue to be fostered, although environmental concerns will play a vital role in limiting policy choices. A higher portion of daily trips using cars may be expected in most countries, leading to more serious safety and environmental problems. Increased congestion will foster a reaction from automobile users, and they will continue to exert pressures on traffic authorities to improve conditions for the use of cars. The attempt to improve bus speeds will face opposition in most places since it requires reclaiming scarce road space for buses in the face of automobile-based interests.

A particularly positive aspect is that the feasibility of new solutions may benefit also from the emergence of the environmental movement – and its impact on the way urban transport is seen – and from the urban transport crisis itself. Increasing equity concerns may help to oppose current negative effects.

References

ANTP/IPEA (1998) *Redução das deseconomias urbanas com a melhoria do transporte público* (relatório final), Assoçiacão National de Transportes Públicos/Instituto de Pesquisa Econômica Aplicada, Brasília

Benitez, B N and Roldán, S L B (1999) 'Transporte y medio-ambiente: la experiencia de la ciudad de México', Proceedings of the X Congreso Latinamericano de Transporte Público y Urbano (Clatpu), Caracas, Venezuela, December, pp227–233

CET (1997) *Corredores de ônibus, volumes e velocidades médias 1995* (internal report), Cia de Engenharia de Tráfego, São Paulo

CET (1999) *Acidentes de trânsito, estatística preliminar*, Cia de Engenharia de Tráfego, São Paulo

CMSP (1998) *Pesquisa Origem-destino 1987*, Cia do Metropolitano de São Paulo, São Paulo

Figueroa, Oscar (1999) *Politicas nacionales de desarollo y politicas secoriales de transporte urbano. Coherencias y contradicciones*, Clatpu Caracas meeting, December, Caracas

GEIPOT (1999) *Anuário Estatístico dos Transportes*, GEIPOT, Brasília

IDB (1998) *Seguriad vial en America Latina y el Caribe*, Banco Interamericano de Desarrollo, Washington

Marcano, E E (1981) 'Caracas: producción del espacio urbano para el consumo del automóvil', *Revista Urbana* 3, pp139–156

Molinero, A (1991) 'Mexico City metropolitan area case study', *Built Environment*, vol 17, no 2, pp122–137

Roberts, D (1997) *Mortality from Unintentional Injury and Violence in the Americas: A Source Book*, Pan American Health Organisation, Washington, DC

UNCHS (1996) *An Urbanising World, Global Report on Human Settlements*, United Nations Centre for Human Settlements, Oxford University Press

Vasconcellos, E (2001) *Urban Transport, Environment and Equity: The Case for Developing Countries*, Earthscan, London

Vera, A G (1999) 'De la ciudad del automovil a la ciudad congestionada,' Proceedings of the X Congreso Latinamericano de Transporte Público y Urbano (Clatpu), Caracas, Venezuela, pp15–24

Wright, C (1996) *Latin American Railroads: Myths and Realities*, Technical Notes RE1-96-001, Inter-American Development Bank, Washington, DC

17

Car-sharing in Latin America: Examining Prospects in Santiago

Chris Zegras and Ralph Gakenheimer

Introduction

Urban transport in Latin America, as in most other developing regions of the world, is currently undergoing dynamic changes due to massive and rapid motorization.[1] While public transportation still continues to dominate the urban transportation markets of most of the region, private motor vehicles, particularly the automobile, are quickly eating into this traditional dominance. With per capita private motor vehicle fleet growth approaching 10 per cent per year, trip rates rising, trip distances growing and mode shifts occurring, many of the region's cities are approaching a crisis point. For example, in Santiago, Chile, from 1977 to 1991, while the per capital motor vehicle fleet increased by 3.5 per cent per year, motorized trips per capita increased by nearly 6 per cent per year, auto mode share increased by 4.3 per cent per year, and bus mode share decreased by 2 per cent per year (SECTRA, 1991). These trends have most likely further intensified with the near 8 per cent per capita fleet growth averaged since 1991.

Motorization trends being experienced in varying degrees across much of the region's cities have brought several, now well known, adverse side effects including congestion, air pollution, noise pollution and traffic accidents (see, for example, WRI, 1996; Onursal and Gautum, 1997). The challenge rests in ensuring enhanced mobility/accessibility for residents of the region's growing metropolises within the environmental, social and financial constraints brought on by massive motorization. While the specific tactics to confront this challenge will inevitably vary from place to place, these tactics should fall into an overall strategic framework of (see, for example, Malbrán, 1997):

- prioritizing public transport;
- inducing forms of urban growth that can improve access; and
- promoting the 'rational' use of the private automobile.

There are Latin American cities that already boast a variety of initiatives along these lines, though rarely combining the three strategic components. Perhaps the best known example is Curitiba, Brazil, with its integration of land use with public transportation investments and a network of exclusive bus-ways. Bogotá has also made extensive use of exclusive bus-ways. Other examples of recent innovation include the implementation in Quito, Ecuador of a spinal electric trolley-bus line, running on an exclusive right-of-way, and Santiago's innovative route licensing scheme for its privately owned and operated bus companies, integrating environmental and service improvement incentives into the bidding process. Subways and suburban rail service provide important transport services in México City, Caracas, Santiago, Buenos Aires, São Paulo and Rio de Janeiro.

Perhaps the least pursued aspect of the strategic framework outlined above has been the third: promoting the 'rational' use of the automobile. This strategy aims to internalize the external costs (ie, congestion, air pollution) that auto use can impose on others and to thereby promote more efficient behaviour from an economic perspective. While road/congestion pricing is the most effective tool along these lines, it has proved politically difficult to implement in most places to date.[2] Other cruder forms of internalizing congestion costs include restricting parking (or raising parking costs) in areas of high congestion or outright bans on driving.[3]

How Might Car-sharing Fit In?

The concept of car-sharing potentially fits into the strategic area mentioned above of rationalizing the use of the private automobile. Car-sharing can serve as a method to rationalize the use of the automobile by attempting to match the individual need and/ or desire for automobile travel with the societal need to reduce the costs (congestion, air pollution, etc) that auto travel can impose on all others. Car-sharing can potentially reduce both individual *and* social costs by changing the cost structure confronted by the typical car owner. When a person owns a car, up to 60 per cent of its annual costs are the fixed costs associated with vehicle ownership (vehicle financing or the opportunity cost of capital, registration, insurance, vehicle storage) – these costs are virtually the same whether the car is used once a week or once an hour. The variable costs of car use, on the other hand, are comparatively low. As a result, the owner/operator is essentially encouraged to increase automobile usage to reduce the average ownership costs per km travelled. The owner basically views the fixed vehicle ownership costs as 'sunk' costs; for the owner these sunk costs increase the opportunity cost of using other modes and create the perverse incentive to maximize driving to get his/her money's worth (Steininger et al, 1996; Litman, 1995).

Car-sharing helps to remove these unfortunate inducements by effectively transforming the fixed vehicle ownership costs into variable costs, so that all costs are directly linked to actual vehicle usage. This sends more clear and precise cost signals to users and puts auto usage fees on a more level field of comparison with other transportation modes, in particular public transport and taxis.

By confronting the full personal costs of vehicle ownership/usage with each use, individuals will be able to compare more accurately private cars with the broad range of travel options appropriate for the need. As has been seen in industrialized country experiences, former car owners tend to reduce their overall level of auto usage, while non-car owners will increase their auto usage after joining a car-sharing organization (CSO). On balance, there may be a slightly increased total amount of automobile use, although this use will likely be during non-peak traffic hours. Importantly, car-sharing can serve an important niche market, raising mobility levels at critical moments.

Potential for Application in a Latin American City

Today's CSOs started in the highly industrialized countries of western Europe, particularly Switzerland and Germany, with motorization rates well above those of Latin America. These are economies with a large middle class, contrasting significantly with the countries of the developing world. In addition, western European countries are typically comprised of many relatively small urban areas, most often lacking the single major metropolitan area which often characterizes the urban make-up of a large portion of Latin America (Santiago, Chile; Lima, Peru; Buenos Aires, Argentina; etc).[4] Despite these differences, there is one interesting transport characteristic that both areas do share – similar modal splits in terms of usage of public transport, the automobile and non-motorized modes. The one significant difference in these modal splits might be in their underlying causes. In many respects Latin America's non-motorized and public transport users are a captive market; they have no other choice. The same could probably not be said for the majority of the western European non-motorized transport and public transport users.

Some of the successful industrialized country experiences with CSOs suggest that environmental concerns have played a role in the formation of CSOs and in individuals' propensity to become members (see Shaheen et al, 1998, Steininger et al, 1996).[5] In Latin America and other developing regions of the world, environmental concerns might sometimes fall behind the more immediate daily needs of large segments of the population to satisfy basic requirements such as food and housing. Nonetheless, environmental issues are growing in importance among a spectrum of income groups, particularly in Latin America's most notoriously polluted cities (see, for example, CEDRM/ACPMA, 1994). In such cases, CSOs might take hold as a tool to help mitigate transportation's negative environmental effects. However, even in the absence of serious environmental problems or a strong environmental 'consciousness', the potential for CSO formation should not be discounted. For example, recent research in Switzerland indicates that, while in the early years of CSO existence in that country (prior to 1994) environmental reasons were important for members joining CSOs, in more recent years environmental rationales have declined (Muheim, 1998).[6] A 1994 survey in Germany on the motivations of car-share users identified the most important reasons for CSO use as: convenient location (71 per cent); high probability of an available vehicle (45 per cent); low tariffs (30 per cent); and the availability of a safe/reliable vehicle (23 per cent) (Shaheen et al, 1998).

There may be some inclination to dismiss CSOs as a luxury mobility tool, appropriate only for the highly mobilized and wealthy markets of the industrialized world, but this argument is not at all self-evident. In Latin American cities there are sizeable populations of people with modest but regular family incomes. They are junior accountants, store clerks, restaurant personnel, government clerical workers, tradesmen etc. Their priorities are a higher standard of education for their children than they enjoyed themselves, a better living environment for their families, saving for their retirement and attaining an improved capability to take care of their older relatives. Since they live in localities with reasonably complete transit networks, they may not even aspire to own cars. Car ownership may be among their fantasies, but it is not high among their active priorities. Yet there are special occasions when the use of a car would be very much valued and would be affordable. Note that this is a profile that scarcely exists in the northern countries, where car ownership is relatively cheaper and more indispensable because of the lack of good public transit coverage. Furthermore, many of these families live in localities where garaging would be impossible and protection of a car from theft and vandalism would be very difficult (in many cities of Latin America people never leave cars parked on the street overnight). As a result, car ownership for these families would mean moving to a higher income, lower density part of town. Car ownership, then, comes only as part of an expensive package of change.

As part of an initial attempt to gauge the feasibility of car-sharing in the Latin American context, Gakenheimer (1998) engaged 35 advanced engineering students from various cities in Colombia. The exercise asked the students to portray the accessibility requirements of families known to them, identifying trip requirements that would be a good fit for car-sharing at prices somewhat higher than taxi fares. The results reveal a large number of potential uses for car-sharing:

- Shopping trips: at distant locations where the prices are cheaper (discount stores and supermarkets are in high income areas); at various locations in sequence where transit connections would be too complicated and the multiple taxi fares excessive; and the need to carry awkwardly heavy or large purchases.
- Occupational uses, including the multiple employment of many middle income Latin Americans: off-hours micro-enterprise activities (such as the assembly of joinery for construction projects that have to be delivered during weekends or after hours); sales activities (such as women who sell cosmetics to acquaintances); architects and engineers who need to visit construction sites, or university faculty members who do occasional home tutoring.
- Group or family travel: children's athletic events, picnics, trips to agricultural settlements in nearby countryside.
- Transport for the elderly: providing mobility for elderly people unable to cope with public transport, with the car-share driving done by relatives or friends.
- Privacy: allowing users to conduct the occasional private or intimate social activity, such as dating.
- Security: when a late return is anticipated or in any general situation where there are concerns about personal security.
- Prestige: providing the non-car owner with the status or even respect that sometimes is conveyed by automobility.

In short, there are many candidate trips for car-share. These trips would significantly improve the mobility of urban residents, but on the basis of serving a few high priority trips, not a large number of trips. It seems likely that the vast majority of these trips would not occur at peak hours.

Car-sharing: A Potential Market in Santiago?

Together with considering the potential demand for car-sharing in the Latin American context comes the task of estimating supply. How might car-sharing compare with competing modes in terms of the cost of providing mobility? It is relatively easy to imagine that car-sharing might function in a place such as Singapore, where car owner-ship costs are among the highest in the world, but what about in Latin America? To answer this question, the authors present the following rough financial analysis of car ownership and operating costs for Santiago (all in 1994 prices), derive some initial cost estimates for a CSO and finally compare estimated CSO costs with competing trans-port modes. In Santiago (Chile), similar to other cities, car owners confront the following costs (see Table 17.1):

Table 17.1 *Costs to car owners*

Fixed costs	Variable costs
Depreciation	Fuel
Financing	Maintenance
Insurance	Tyre wear
Registration	Tolls
Parking (at home)	Hourly or daily paid parking

Source: MIDEPLAN (1992)

For the purposes of evaluating the possibilities for car-sharing, the above categorization between users' fixed and variable costs is important because, as discussed above, once owners have paid the fixed costs of vehicle ownership they are encouraged to increase auto use to get their money's worth.

Fixed ownership costs

The principal fixed cost for an automobile is the purchase and/or financing cost. In Santiago purchase price varies widely, depending on make, model, accessories and government-imposed fees. For estimating approximate vehicle ownership costs, the average cost of a 2000cc automobile is used, as summarized in Table 17.2.

Table 17.2 *Typical automobile purchase costs (US$, 1994)*

Engine capacity:	1500cc	2000cc	5000cc
Value at import	6500	9785	45,000
11 per cent tariff	715	1076	4950
18 per cent sales tax	1298	1955	8991
Cylinder tax	0	587	2935
Luxury tax	0	0	29,932
Total	**8513**	**13,403**	**91,808**
Annualized capital cost[a]	1371	2175	14,792

Source: MIDEPLAN (1992)

Note: a: assuming straight line depreciation at 11 per cent interest over estimated vehicle lifespan of 11 years

Additional annual ownership costs in Santiago include:

- *Annual registration fees (permiso de circulación):* the *permiso de circulación* is an annual fee collected by the individual municipalities, and essentially serves as a general revenue generator and an income redistribution mechanism. This fee ranges from 1 per cent of assessed value for vehicles worth less than US$2700 up to 4.5 per cent of assessed value for vehicles worth more than US$18,000, and averages about US$121 annually.
- *Insurance:* vehicle owners are required to purchase liability insurance costing approximately US$20 per year. Approximately 80 per cent of drivers carry only this insurance. Vehicle owners who purchase comprehensive liability and collision insurance typically pay about US$1200 per year.
- *Safety and emission equipment inspections:* inspections at government authorized centres ensure the effective operation of vehicle emission control and safety equipment, including lights, brakes and safety belts. Non-catalytic automobiles are inspected annually, at a cost of approximately US$6 per inspection, while vehicles with catalytic converters only require inspections every two years.
- *Parking costs:* the annual parking cost that is paid as a fixed cost by users is essentially the cost of vehicle storage (ie, parking at home). In the case of homeowners or renters, this cost is almost always the opportunity cost of the occupied land and rarely results in a financial payment (although there may be occasional maintenance costs). In many cases, particularly in suburban neighbourhoods, vehicles park on the street or on open spaces and sidewalks (in which case the parking cost is externalized). In the case of apartment dwellers, the majority with automobiles pay for garage space in the building, either as part of the purchase cost of the apartment, or included in the monthly apartment rental payment. In this case, the cost of parking is more directly felt by the vehicle owner and the possibility to reduce the opportunity cost (ie, via renting the space out to another) is great. This cost varies significantly according to type of parking facility and location in the city; an average annual city-wide estimate is approximately US$270 (Zegras, 1998).[7]

Variable operating costs

Variable operating costs are estimated in Table 17.3.

Table 17.3 *Vehicle operating costs used for planning (US$/km)[a]*

Item	Light vehicles
Repairs	0.025
Lubricants	0.002
Tyres	0.011
Labour	0.013
Fuel	0.042
Total	0.093

Source: MIDEPLAN (1992)

Note: a: figures were converted to US$ 1994 based on an average annual inflation rate of 17.34 per cent and an average exchange rate in 1994 of US$1 = Ch$420

Based on the cost estimates described above, the authors estimate average automobile fixed costs (annual capital costs, registration, insurance, parking and inspections) to average approximately US$2400 per year. For a vehicle driven 15,000km a year, this averages about US$0.16 per km. Variable automobile costs average about US$0.092 per km, or about another US$1380 per year.

For private vehicles (automobiles and light trucks), about 50 per cent of ownership and usage costs are annualized capital costs of vehicle ownership; 6 per cent are estimated fixed parking costs; other fixed ownership costs (insurance, registration, inspections) combined make up about 3 per cent of costs. For a vehicle driven an average 15,000km per year, fuel costs comprise about 17 per cent of total costs and operating and maintenance costs comprise another 17 per cent of costs. The remaining 6 per cent of costs are estimated variable parking costs. In summary, about 60 per cent of user costs are fixed costs; the remaining 40 per cent are operating costs.

Can Car-sharing be Competitive?

To determine whether a CSO could be competitive in the Santiago context, the authors have developed a hypothetical example of a CSO. Per vehicle fixed and operating costs are first estimated. These are summarized in Table 17.4.[8]

Instead of estimating financing charges for the vehicles, an annual vehicle capital cost is estimated, based on an average lifetime of 150,000kms (after which the vehicles would be sold and new vehicles purchased, under the assumption that members would expect access to relatively modern vehicles). Since vehicle resale value depends on annual usage rates (the vehicles are depreciated at US$0.06/km), the lower the usage of the vehicle, the lower the annual capital costs.

Table 17.4 *Estimated fixed and operating costs per CSO vehicle in Santiago (US$)*

	Capital cost	Other vehicle fixed cost[a]	Management and administration[b]	Variable costs[c]	Total costs
15,000km/year	2090	1662	5194	1442	10,387
25,000km/year	2698	1662	6685	2325	13,370
35,000km/year	3357	1662	8262	3255	16,525
45,000km/year	4023	1662	9858	4185	19,716
55,000km/year	4692	1662	11,457	5115	22,914

Source: MIDEPLAN (1992)

Notes: a: other fixed costs including parking, cleaning, insurance, registration and inspections; b: management and administrative costs estimated as 50 per cent of total costs; c: variable costs include repairs, lubricants, tyres, labour and fuel

The calculations are based on very rough estimates of administrative and management costs due to difficulties in calculating these costs for a hypothetical company in Santiago. At this point the authors simply calculated the broad range of management and administrative costs – member credit and driver history screening, corporate insurance, business licences, manager salaries, legal assistance, office rents, furnishing, billing services, communications etc – based on the business plan developed for the recently launched CSO in Portland, Oregon (USA). For Portland, management and administrative costs were projected to average 50 per cent of total costs over the first four years of operation (this includes US$50,000 annually for a company manager) (EcoPlan International, 1998). This same average percentage was applied by the authors to their per vehicle calculations, as summarized in Table 17.4.

Estimating management and administrative costs in this manner is admittedly rough. Furthermore, since the approach to estimating scheme costs is on a per vehicle basis, the possibility is lost to see the potential scale economies that schemes may well experience up to a certain size. Even at a pilot scale, there are indications that a CSO would experience revenue increases greater than expenses. The Portland business plan, for example, projects revenue growth to increase 50 per cent faster than expenses during the first four years of scaling up. The scheme also anticipates a tripling in membership and a 140 per cent increase in fleet size, which translate into an increase from 7.5 members per vehicle during year one to 12.5 in year four of operations.

Without specifically projecting potential business growth and possible economies of scale of a CSO application in Santiago, the authors use the estimated costs from Table 17.4 to flesh out various scenarios of membership ratios, average usage rates and cost structures. These calculations would not be applicable for a small scheme of, for example, fewer than ten cars. The basis of the usage fee ranges presented is 'break even' rates; in other words, fees that would need to be levied, at a minimum, to cover the annual vehicle capital and operating costs, management and administration costs and other associated costs listed in Table 17.4. While clearly not a precise depiction, these calculations offer a useful glimpse into the potential cost-competitiveness of car-sharing in Santiago, as well as an idea of the various trade-offs and implications of various pricing structures.

The results of the authors' calculations are presented in Table 17.5. As would be expected, there is considerable variability in potential cost structures based on the assumptions used regarding vehicle-to-member ratios and average estimated usage per vehicle. The total effective cost per km ranges from US$0.42 for the scheme with the highest number of members per car and the most intensively used vehicles, to US$0.68 for the scheme with a low number of members per vehicle and relatively low annual vehicle usage.[9] The results in Table 17.5 give an indication of how the various CSO charges can be manipulated to maintain financial viability.

The most attractive schemes from a user perspective would apparently be those with relatively high usage rates per vehicle. This can be achieved with a relatively large number of vehicles per user and high usage rates per member, or with a lower number of vehicles per user and low usage rates per member. Which alternative would be successful depends on the overall scale of the scheme as well as on the temporal and distance characteristics of the demand (when the majority of trips are demanded, how long sessions last for and the typical trip distances).

With any given vehicle-to-member ratio and vehicle usage rate, a CSO has great flexibility in establishing charges. For example, with a 1:15 vehicle-to-member ratio and a vehicle usage rate of 35,000kms (2333km/member), financial viability could be achieved with:

- a US$110 annual membership fee and usage rates of US$1.25/hour and US$0.26/km; or
- a US$65 annual membership fee and usage rates of US$1.25/hour and US$0.28/km.

Table 17.5 *Potential cost structures for a CSO[a]*

Car to member ratio	Annual usage per vehicle (km/year)	km/member	Annual member fee	Hourly rate	km charge	Variable $/km	Total $/km[b]	Vehicle revenue	Vehicle cost
1:9	15,500	1722	250	1.50	0.33	0.53	0.68	10,465	10,387
	25,000	2778	155	1.50	0.28	0.48	0.54	13,395	13,370
	35,000	3889	100	1.25	0.28	0.45	0.47	16,533	16,525
	45,000	5000	110	1.25	0.25	0.42	0.44	19,740	19,716
	55,000	6111	65	1.25	0.24	0.41	0.42	22,952	22,914
1:15	15,500	1033	255	1.25	0.26	0.43	0.67	10,438	10,387
	25,000	1667	130	1.25	0.29	0.46	0.53	13,367	13,370
	35,000	2333	65	1.25	0.28	0.45	0.47	16,608	16,525
	45,000	3000	65	1.25	0.25	0.42	0.44	19,725	19,716
	55,000	3667	40	1.25	0.24	0.41	0.42	22,967	22,914

Source: MIDEPLAN (1992)

Notes: a: assumes average time usage rate of 8 minutes per km (based on Portland example), including time not in vehicle; b: total US$/km includes the annual member fee attributed to average annual usage per member

The ultimate rate structure chosen, regardless of the characteristics of the CSO, depends on the goals of the scheme and the socio-economic characteristics of the market. In this regard it is likely that attempts should be made to target the lowest possible annual membership fee. Such an approach would help address the fact that many possible potential members have a high discount rate (thus, unwillingness to pay a large up-front membership cost).[10] Such an approach would also serve as a disincentive for users to maximize their up-front investment (high annual membership charge) through intensive use.[11] A CSO's overall objectives are considered to be:

- from society's perspective, to satisfy highly valued, select mobility while creating overall incentives to rationalize the use of the automobile; and
- from the enterprise perspective, to cover all costs of running the scheme.

In Table 17.5 it can be seen that the optimum CSO structure has:

- a low vehicle-to-member ratio (1:15);
- moderate usage per member (in the range of 3000–4000kms per year); and
- high usage per vehicle (35,000–55,000kms per year).[12]

Based on the rate structures in Table 17.5, it is possible to draw a rough comparison of how car-sharing might compete with relatively comparable modes in Santiago. The results from such a comparison are presented in Table 17.6. It must be emphasized that these are relatively rough comparisons and that it is somewhat difficult to compare, on a level playing field, CSO usage with the private automobile. Among the most important points to keep in mind when making this comparison include the difficulty in valuing the typical capital cost of a private automobile (which depends on the vehicle value, age and usage rates) and in attributing this capital cost to usage, particularly in the single trip case. For the single trip case (town errands) and the weekend trip case, it is assumed that the vehicle owner uses the vehicle a total of 13,750km per year (comparable to the annual total of 550 trips per year from the last column). With capital and other fixed costs attributed across this usage rate, the private vehicle owner is better off with her/his own car than with a CSO membership (again, showing how the private vehicle owner has incentives to maximize use to reduce average costs). This holds true until annual usage rates decline by 50 per cent to 60 per cent of the assumed: in the optimistic CSO scenario (vehicle-to-member ratio of 1:15 and 55,000km/vehicle/year), car-sharing becomes competitive at or below 8250kms per year of usage; in the pessimistic scenario, the CSO becomes competitive at or below 6600kms per year of vehicle usage. In comparison, Shaheen et al (1999) report the following estimated maximum distances for which car-sharing is cost effective: 6875kms per year (average German case); 9064kms per year (Swiss); and 18,306kms per year (Berlin).

Another important point to keep in mind in the trip comparison presented in Table 17.6 is that in the case of the CSO the vehicles are covered by comprehensive automobile insurance, while for the privately owned automobile minimum third party (mandatory) coverage is assumed, with an annual cost of only US$20 per year.[13] By using a CSO vehicle, then, the trip-maker is internalizing a larger share of the costs of motor vehicle use, which is an important additional potential benefit of a CSO in the Chilean context.[14] If the CSO vehicle was competing against a comparably insured private vehicle, then CSO use becomes significantly more competitive across a broader spectrum of total vehicle usage. For example, if the private vehicle owner confronts the same comprehensive insurance cost as the CSO vehicle, then the private vehicle cost for town errands increases from US$7.13 in Table 17.6 to US$9.28. In other words, car-sharing would be competitive with private vehicle ownership for any CSO scheme with km/vehicle/year levels greater than 45,000 (last four rows in Table 17.6). With full insurance costs, any of the CSO schemes in Table 17.6 are competitive for user annual usage rates at or below 12,375kms per year. With private users paying full insurance costs, the most optimistic CSO scenario (last row of Table 17.6) remains competitive with the private car until 16,225kms per year of individual use.

In terms of competing with the taxi or with rental cars, the CSO does surprisingly well. In the case of the taxi, for the town errand hypothesized use in Table 17.6, the car-share trip-maker pays almost half. Indeed, at the relatively long distance (which penalizes the competitiveness of the taxi) assumed in the town errand use, the car-share trip is competitive until eight to nine hours of use (depending on the CSO scenario considered).[16] The taxi is, of course, more competitive for shorter trips of relatively long duration (ie, with a long meeting, meal, movie or other activity at the trip end). For example, for a one-hour trip, the taxi is competitive up until 4kms; for a two-hour trip, the taxi is competitive up until 7kms; for a five-hour trip, the taxi would be competitive up until 16kms (see Table 17.7). In other words, for a trip consisting of a movie and dinner (approximately four hours), the trip-maker would be better off from a purely financial perspective taking a taxi if the total travel distance is less than 13kms.

In comparison to public transport modes in Santiago, the car-share would be much more expensive, since bus and metro fares currently range from US$0.36 to US$0.44

Table 17.6 *Modal competitiveness by example trip types (US$)*[15]

Mode	Use				
	Town errand	**Weekend trip**	**Annual use**	**Annual use**	**Annual use**
	2 hours, 25km	*36 hours, 300km*	*125 trips per year*[a]	*250 trips per year*[a]	*550 trips per year*[a]
Private auto[b]	7.13[c]	85[c]	2936	3226	3924
Rental car[d]	100	200	na	na	na
Taxi	17.10	na	na	na	na
Car-share (35Kkm/car/year) 1:9 ratio	9.50	129	1293	2480	5330
Car-share (35Kkm/car/year) 1:15 ratio	9.50	129	1253	2440	5290
Car-share (45Kkm/car/year) 1:9 ratio	8.75	120	1159	2253	4878
Car-share (45Kkm/car/year) 1:15 ratio	8.75	120	1159	2252	4878
Car-share (55Kkm/car/year) 1:9 ratio	8.50	117	1128	2190	4740
Car-share (55Kkm/car/year) 1:15 ratio	8.50	117	1103	2165	4715

Source: MIDEPLAN (1992)

Notes: a: assumes average trip of two hours, 25kms; b: assumes a new moderately priced car with an annualized capital value of US$2175 (based on a straight line depreciation); c: fixed costs attributed assuming 13,750kms of annual usage; d: based on Hertz rental rates in Santiago (above average rates) of US$127 per day (unlimited kms) or US$80 + $0.75/km

Table 17.7 *Taxi versus CSO in several distance–time dimensions*[17]

Trip time (hours)	Distance (km)	Taxi (US$)	Car-share (US$)
1	4	2.40	2.37
2	7	4.50	4.46
3	10	6.60	6.55
4	13	8.70	8.64
5	16	10.80	10.73

Source: MIDEPLAN (1992)

(peak). Of course, the CSO is not meant to replace these modes, rather to complement them, expanding the potential mobility options available to the trip-maker while making her/him more fully aware of the full costs implied by each modal choice.

Barriers to and Potential Drawbacks of a Car-sharing Organization in Santiago

Despite the apparent financial attractiveness of a CSO in the Santiago context, there are several imaginable barriers to implementation. Perhaps the single largest barrier is that posed by the culture of motorization in Chile (and elsewhere in Latin America). The status and prestige conveyed by automobile ownership is a powerful social force throughout the region, which may actually undermine the potential for CSOs in Latin America or other parts of the developing world. Automobile ownership represents as much a sign of arrival in a certain socio-economic class as a mode of transportation. Real market penetration of a CSO would have to compete against this well ingrained, inertial social and economic force.

Another important barrier arises from the fact that a large number of owners probably are not aware of, or are unable to estimate, the actual ownership and operating costs of their vehicles. For many owners, fuel costs might be the only relevant cost considered in deciding on a trip (in reality, the only immediate costs that might affect most users' decisions for short trips are travel time and parking costs/hassle). Under such conditions, car-sharing would not appear financially competitive.

Some evidence suggests that the potential for car-sharing in Santiago might be limited by the relatively intensive use of vehicles, particularly new ones, in the city. While data are not widely available, according to one estimate the average use of a one-year-old vehicle in Santiago is 23,184kms per year (Lepeley and Cifuentes, 1997). At this rate of usage, the CSO option is priced out of competitiveness (see the previous section). It is important also to consider that a large portion of these kms are likely to be accumulated by out-of-town trips:[18] weekend beach trips or trips to the countryside or mountains. Vacation trips are also typical automobile uses for the Chilean. CSO vehicles are not particularly competitive for these trip types (see Table 17.6), unless special pricing structures are implemented.

An additional potential barrier to CSO feasibility (and related to the culture of motorization mentioned above) is the apparent growing disdain for public transport – particularly the bus system – in Santiago, despite notable and considerable improvements over the past seven years. For a CSO to function effectively, users must be willing to forego the automobile for the majority of trips; of those who already have access to an automobile and its daily convenience, many seem unwilling to revert back to the bus. For example, a study carried out for the Chilean Ministry of Transport in 1995 identified particular characteristics of public transport use that were considered to be 'reductions in personal liberty', including having to accept the driver's decisions in terms of speed and route and having to endure the presence of odours, sounds and other factors (MINTRATEL, 1995). These negatives were contrasted with the 'expansion in personal liberty' that participants associated with the auto.

Of course, it may well be likely that an initial CSO initiative in a place such as Santiago would not target the current car owner but rather the non-owner, for whom certain high valued trips CSO use would be competitive and the only real alternative to not making the trip. In this case the CSO could certainly function in its role as a complementary mode within the suite of transport options available. A potential challenge to this niche role may arise from the fact that many of these potential users may not be licensed drivers.

Furthermore, there is the potential that such an approach to CSO implementation might actually exacerbate the current situation, accelerating motorization rates by accelerating the rate of access (and conditioning) of the population to motor vehicles and their use and drastically increasing vehicle kms travelled (vkt). The European experiences with CSOs suggest that previously carless households' vkt increases by 42 per cent to 118 per cent. Of course, the overall magnitude of the increase depends on the starting point.

For households with little previous auto vkt, a large percentage increase may mean very little in overall urban vkt. Furthermore, the impacts of this increase depends on the ultimate use: the effects on personal mobility may be great (ie, facilitating access to a hospital for an emergency) and the impacts on overall urban mobility and air quality may be small (ie, if the trip occurs during off peak, low pollution times).

There is the additional possibility that CSO use could also significantly eat into trips by competing modes, such as the bus, further eroding the long term viability of this important transport mode.

There are further potential difficulties for CSOs in Latin American cities. For example, accident rates are much higher and the robbery of parts from parked cars is more widespread, which might pose problems with vehicle availability and reliability. Some suggest that the widespread success of CSOs in the northern European context is due in part to the cultural characteristics of the region – promptness and adherence to schedules – which might pose important barriers to the successful application of the CSO concept. These are lessons that would have to be learned through pilot projects.

Potential Benefits

Many of the above-mentioned potential drawbacks have an equally plausible positive side. For example, instead of reinforcing the culture of motorization, the CSO concept might moderate and rationalize it, introducing the concept of transportation variable and fixed costs, opportunity costs etc[19] to the often emotionally and socially charged decision to purchase and use an automobile. In addition, instead of undermining the long term viability of competing modes (particularly the bus system), a CSO might actually work in reverse. If car-sharing penetrates the currently car-owning households, then public transport use in these households would likely increase for many daily trips (particularly the commute trip). For the previously carless household, future bus use may be maintained since these households may forego future car ownership and thus have more modally diverse future travel patterns. An important, but not often considered, medium to long term impact of widespread CSO implementation would be the decrease of total parking/vehicle storage spaces and the freeing up of such space for other uses.

Another potential benefit of CSO use in Santiago relates to a possible improvement in the quality of vehicles on the city's streets. Here there are two different effects. First, there is the possibility that CSO vehicles could replace the older, polluting and inefficient vehicles that many lower income households currently own and use for occasional non-routine use. Instead of owning or purchasing a cheap used auto, a household can buy into an annual CSO membership and have access to a cleaner-burning, new vehicle.[20] The second related effect comes from the likelihood that CSO vehicles will be better maintained than almost all privately owned vehicles on the streets of Santiago. With revenues being collected constantly for maintenance expenses and the CSO owner ostensibly concerned with depreciation of the capital stock, it is expected that CSO vehicles will be consistently well maintained and better performing from an emissions and energy use perspective.[21]

Another related potential benefit is the role that a CSO might play in facilitating the penetration of alternative fuels into the Chilean market.[22] There have been, for example, proposals to convert the taxi fleet in Santiago to natural gas, since fleet conversion to alternative fuels is typically easier than individual vehicle conversion (due to the potential to centralize fuelling stations and capitalize on economies of scale in conversions/purchases and maintenance).[23] While such an option is possible, however, it is not clear whether it is advisable, particularly for a pilot-scale project where the feasibility of the CSO itself is uncertain.

There are several additional potential user benefits. Beyond having access to a relatively new and well maintained vehicle, the user avoids the hassles that accompany vehicle ownership: cleaning, maintenance, inspections, registrations etc (EcoPlan International, 1998). At the same time, as Bealtaine et al (1998) note:

> the habitualized fixation on the car cannot be (re-) established. Before making a trip by car, car-sharers are forced to consciously decide about which means of transport to take ... users learn about the strengths and weaknesses of each means of transport and use the car only in cases where public transport does not hold anymore.

They further highlight the fact that 'car-sharers do not feel restricted in their mobility. Instead, they report an increase in life quality ...' with 'unnecessary' automobile trips 'sometimes accompanied by a reorientation on local offers (shopping, leisure time activities).'

Ultimately, relatively widespread CSO implementation could reduce overall long term vehicle ownership levels. For example, a German survey of CSO users revealed that 48 per cent of users would never buy a car, 21 per cent sell their car to join a CSO, 9 per cent use the CSO instead of owning a second car, while 22 per cent would still buy or would consider buying their own car when the opportunity arises (Harms and Truffer, 1998).

Possible Steps Forward

The potential drawbacks and benefits mentioned above are largely conjectural; clearly more analysis of the market is needed before drawing firm conclusions regarding the potentials, drawbacks and benefits of a CSO scheme in the developing world. While the authors have developed a preliminary analysis in this chapter, they must emphasize that it is preliminary. To give just one example, the estimated administration and management costs were based on a simple straight line percentage of vehicle costs – this likely over-estimates the CSO costs presented here, in part because scale economies are not considered.

Nearly all experiences to date have benefited from initial government start-up funding; it is difficult to imagine this occurring in Santiago in the short term. If a pilot project were to move forward, alternative financing options would have to be found. In this regard it would be worthwhile to explore funding mechanisms linked with global climate change mitigation efforts. For example, the Clean Development Mechanism (CDM)[24] – approved during the Kyoto rounds of the climate change negotiations – offers a tool whereby private sector enterprises from developing and industrialized countries can collaborate on greenhouse gas (GHG) reduction projects for reduction credits. In theory, the CDM provides an opportunity for a successful northern CSO company, such as Mobility Car-sharing (Switzerland), to match up with a local Latin American entrepreneur to show that the concept is feasible and can achieve positive effects. This would, of course, pose the challenge so common to transportation projects within the GHG mitigation realm – how to measure, monitor and ensure that emissions are being reduced.

Conclusion

For reasons of pollution, congestion and limited investment resources, Latin American cities are actively searching for innovative transportation solutions. Can a concept such as car-sharing find currency in this specific context? The authors think that car-sharing can help to rationalize the use of the automobile in Latin America, enhancing high value mobility for urban residents while reducing excessive automobile use. They also feel that this chapter shows, albeit tentatively, that the demand for car-sharing-type services potentially exists in Latin America. Finally, the chapter suggests – but cannot confirm – that this demand can be met, at least in the specific case of Santiago, in a cost-competitive way for a range of trip types.

With this chapter the authors have at least challenged two simplistic beliefs. One is that 'since Latin American car owners will never give up their cars, and taxis are relatively cheap, there is no role for car-sharing in Latin America.' The value of this position is by no means obvious. The other belief that they have challenged is that 'in an environment of rapid motorization, car-sharing might give rise to significantly higher auto use that would badly impact the environment as an unavoidable concomitant to raising mobility.' While it is obviously difficult to predict these effects, the authors think that since car-share trips will likely be short, off-peak and relatively expensive, this fear is not entirely grounded.

Despite these initial positive indications, the chapter probably raises more questions than it answers. Many of these questions can only be addressed through either pilot programmes or more detailed research and market demand surveys. For example, without a pilot programme or a stated preference survey it is almost impossible to gauge the potential attractiveness to users of car-sharing, beyond the potential for financial savings shown here. For non-car owners just below car-owning incomes, it is hard to believe that a conveniently located CSO would fail to attract customers. Nonetheless, the possibly even more problematic economics of car-share use in this category also need demonstration.

Probably even more uncertain are the potential long term implications of car-sharing for motorization rates, pollution, congestion etc. Perhaps a certain number of people will give up car ownership because it is a financial burden they can avoid through the occasional car-share. It might be hard to imagine that many people who can comfortably afford car ownership will give it up, but this is entirely plausible in the medium to long term. The balance is hard to foresee.

Notes

1 This chapter was first published as a paper in *World Transport Policy & Practice*, vol 5, no 3, pp156–175.
2 In Chile, for example, congestion pricing legislation has been languishing in the Senate since 1991.
3 México City, São Paulo and Santiago have each implemented some variation of restricted driving days as a pollution control measure. However, opinions range widely on their success.
4 Brazil, Colombia and even Ecuador might be exceptions to this generalization.
5 According to survey results from Switzerland and Germany, males (25–40 years old) are the typical participants with above average education, below average income (likely due, in part, to age distortion) and sensitive to traffic and environmental issues (Shaheen et al, 1998).
6 Before 1994, more than 25 per cent of members acknowledged the environment as a reason for joining; this declined to 7 per cent in 1997.
7 Clearly there is wide range in this value.
8 Assuming a moderately priced mid-size sedan (2000cc vehicle).
9 Here, effective cost per km is defined as being the total US$/km, including the annual member fee averaged over the annual usage per member.
10 An instalment plan for the annual membership fee would also achieve this goal.
11 Similar to the incentive that car owners have to maximize their use.
12 For comparison, Shaheen et al (1999) report that StattAuto Berlin vehicles average 34,213km per year.
13 Information on vehicle coverage (ie, how many owners have comprehensive versus mandatory insurance policies) is not available. Conversations with vehicle owners suggest the large majority of car owners (particularly of moderately priced vehicles) do not have comprehensive insurance.
14 In Santiago in 1994, automobiles accounted for US$140 million in accident costs, over half of which were external costs (see Zegras, 1997).
15 Modelled on Portland case study in EcoPlan International (1998).
16 The taxi's competitiveness relative to the car-share trip is the fact that the taxi user does not directly pay for the idle time of the vehicle.

17 The comparative car-share in this table is the 'worst case' scenario from Table 17.6 (35,000km/vehicle/year and 1:9 vehicles per member). Taxi travel assumes no time charge in effect (see Table 17.7).

18 These seem to be the case since government authorities estimate an average of 15,000km per private car in the metropolitan region (CONAMA-RM, 1997). If these two numbers are relatively accurate then 65 per cent of Santiago private car use is urban.

19 It would likely be useful to match a car-sharing initiative with an overall public programme to educate users on the full costs and benefits of each mode (see, for example, Zegras, 1998).

20 In Santiago, the incentive might be particularly strong during the nine months of 'La Restricción,' a daily rotating restriction on use of vehicles not equipped with catalytic converters.

21 However, there is the risk that the CSO owner could be revenue-strapped and could choose not to invest in timely maintenance.

22 It has been suggested that the mid-range trips associated with shared vehicle systems are conducive to the use of electric vehicles. Electric vehicles are well suited to shared vehicle systems since they can take advantage of opportunity charging when idle at their holding locations (ie, stations).

23 There is already a pilot natural-gas bus programme operating in the city. In addition, as part of a proposed pollution-offset programme due to the expansion of a electricity generating (natural gas-powered) plant in Santiago, the generating company has proposed purchasing a number of taxis and replacing them with natural gas vehicles.

24 Other potential climate-related sources of funding include the Global Environmental Facility (GEF) and the Interamerican Development Bank's 'Sustainable Markets for Sustainable Energy' programme.

References

Bealtaine Ltd (Taylor Lightfoot Transport Consultants), International Ecotechnology Research Centre, Cranfield University and Verkeersadviesburo Diepens en Okkema (1998) *Pay as You Drive Carsharing: Final Report*, EU Save contract no 4.1031/Z/95–025, European Commission, Brussels

CEDRM/ACPMA (1994) *Estudio sobre actitudes y conductas relativas al medio ambiente*, Comisión Especial de Descontaminación de le Región Metropolitana y Acción Ciudadana por el Medio Ambiente, Santiago

CONAMA-RM (1997) *Inventario de Emisiones Atmosféricas de la Región Metropolitana para 1997 y Proyecciones al 2005*, Comisión Nacional para el Medio Ambiente-Region Metropolitana, Santiago

Departamento de Estudios Económicos (1993) *Memorandum: Costo Social por Congestión de Tránsito en el Gran Santiago*, Cámara Chilena de la Construcción, Santiago

EcoPlan International (1998) *CarSharing '98: Present Status, Future Prospects: A Casebook of Useful Sources*, EcoPlan International, Paris

Gakenheimer, R (1998) *Results from an Investigation of Car-sharing Potential Conducted with Students of the Department of Civil Engineering*, Universidad de Los Andes, Bogota

Harms, S and Truffer, B (1998) *The Emergence of a Nation-wide Carsharing Co-operative in Switzerland* (report from the Strategic Niche Management as a Tool for Transition to a Sustainable Transportation System project supported by the European Commission, DG XII, within Human Dimensions of Environmental Change, RTD Programme Environment and Climate), European Commission, Brussels

Lepeley, F and Cifuentes, L (1997) 'Emisiones de los vehículos livianos a gasolina en Santiago' in Galvéz, T and Munizaga, M (eds) *Actas del Octavo Congreso Chileno de Ingeniería de Transporte*, Congresso Chileno de Ingeniería de Transporte, Santiago

Litman, T (1995) *Transportation Cost Analysis: Techniques, Estimates, and Implications,* Victoria Transport Policy Institute, Victoria, British Columbia

Malbrán, H (1997) *Análisis de los Requerimientos Técnicos del Desarrollo y la Gestión del Sistema de Transporte Urbano de Lima-Callao*, International Institute for Energy Conservation, Santiago

MIDEPLAN (1992) *Inversión Pœblica, Eficiencia y Equidad* (second edition), Ministerio de Planificación y Cooperación, Departamento de Inversiones, Santiago

MINTRATEL (1995) *Actitudes y Motivaciones Ligadas al Uso de Automóvil Particular v/s Transporte Público: Estudio Cualitativo*, Ministry of Transportation and Telecommunications, Santiago

Muheim, P (1998) *Mobility at Your Convenience: CarSharing – The Key to Combined Mobility,* Transport Section, Energie 2000, Berne, Switzerland

Onursal, B and Gautum, S (1997) *Vehicular Air Pollution: Experiences from Seven Latin American Urban Centers,* World Bank Technical Paper no 373, World Bank, Washington, DC

SECTRA (1991) *Encuesta Origen Destino de Viajes del Gran Santiago 1991*, Comisión de Planificación de Inversiones en Infraestructura de Transporte, Santiago

Shaheen, S, Sperling, D and Wagner, C (1998) 'Carsharing in Europe and North America: past, present, and future', *Transportation Quarterly,* vol 52, no 3, pp35–52

Shaheen, S, Sperling, D and Wagner, C (1999) *Carsharing and Partnership Management: An International Perspective*, paper presented at 78th Annual Meeting of the Transportation Research Board, January, Washington, DC

Steininger, K, Vogl, C and Zettl, R (1996) 'Car-sharing organizations – the size of the market segment and revealed change in mobility behaviour', *Transport Policy,* vol 3, no 4, pp177–85

WRI (1996) *World Resources 1996–1997: The Urban Environment,* World Resources Institute/ Oxford University Press, New York

Zegras, C (1997) 'Los costos estimados de accidentes de tránsito en Santiago de Chile, 1994' in Galvéz, T and Munizaga, M (eds) *Actas del Octavo Congreso Chileno de Ingeniería de Transporte*, Santiago

Zegras, C (1998) 'The costs of transportation in Santiago de Chile: analysis and policy implications', *Transport Policy,* vol 5, pp9–21

18

The Urban Transportation Crisis in Developing Countries: Alternative Policies for an Equitable Space

Eduardo Vasconcellos

Introduction

Transport infrastructure and services in developing countries have been provided with the support of methodologies and assumptions that originated in industrializing countries in the 1950s. These methodologies are used to propose transport solutions for hypothetical future conditions, based on forecast social and economic variables. In addition, they adopt market and efficiency paradigms and target mobility as a prime objective.

The actual results of these modelling procedures and their assumptions in the developing world have been widely disappointing. Used as supposedly neutral techniques, they have served as instruments of power for technocrats working mostly within weakly democratized environments. Resources have been abundantly used to create large transportation infrastructures with poor results, often supporting automobile use by a minority while neglecting the transportation needs of the majority. Local transportation technologies and all kinds of non-motorized transportation means have been permanently neglected or rejected (Banjo and Dimitriou, 1990).

Traditional approaches have been criticized as adequate tools to be used in developing countries by several independent researchers (Dimitriou, 1992). The World Bank, which played an essential role in exporting the traditional methodologies to the developing world, has also put forward alternative approaches (World Bank, 1986 and 1996). The continued use of traditional techniques is therefore inadequate; new approaches and methods are needed to overcome present drawbacks and ensure more equitable, socially and environmentally sound transportation policies. Technical drawbacks of the modelling procedures are extensively treated in the literature (Dimitriou, 1992), and will not be repeated in this chapter.[1] The intention is to discuss instead how traditional procedures and assumptions have shaped inadequate transportation and traffic systems in the developing world, and how alternative approaches could replace or complement conventional ones.

The Urban Transportation Crisis in Developing Countries

The urban transportation crisis can be identified first by the urban development process and the increasing commodification of social relations. While pre-automotive cities allowed unlimited consumption of space by any person, modern cities began to spread and occupy larger areas, requiring motorized transportation to be physically accessible and economically affordable. In addition, as in the Brazilian case, changes in the nature of social relations have increased the share of commodified activities, especially for higher income groups (eg, private education, private medical care and leisure). Thus activities once located within walking distances from the household (neighbourhood drugstores, soccer fields) are now located at a considerable distance (regional supermarkets, sport clubs), and dependence on motorized transport is inevitable. Consequently, the deep economic and social differences that are constantly being generated translate into deep differences with respect to access to transportation and activities in urban spaces, and it remains to be asked whether there is any possibility of restoring equity (Hägerstrand, 1987). In addition, in developing countries unemployment levels can be high and the informal employment market can play a major role, posing two burdens on transportation policies. First, there is a wide variation in the origin–destination pattern, as people are constantly finding, losing and changing work activities. Second, programmes designed to meet the needs only of formal employees can end up excluding a large part of the population, as with the Brazilian *vale-transporte* (transport bonus).

The main transportation and traffic problems faced by developing countries can be related to several categories of issues. All relate to each other in some way but analysing them separately can permit a clearer understanding of the problems in question (see Table 18.1).

Table 18.1 *Issues in the developing countries' urban transport crisis*

Issue	Content
Political	Highly centralized states; fragile democracies; uneven distribution of power; coalition between technocracy and middle classes; uneven right to use road space
Institutional	Lack of coordination between agencies and of proper human and technical resources
Social	Unequal accessibility; comfort inequity; activity inequity
Technical	Use of techniques borrowed from developed countries; irresponsible forecasting exercises; conservative planning in support of private transport
Technological	Commitment to automotive transport; neglect of non-motorized means
Economic	Fiscal crisis of the state hindering social policies; persistent poverty; negligent operation of public transportation; over-investment in roads for private transport
Operational	Irregular provision of public transportation; poor traffic conditions; priority to private automobiles in traffic management
Environmental	High traffic accident rates; increasing pollution; disruption of residential areas

Political

The political issue derives from the failure of the political system, which does not ensure democratic representation of the conflicting interests of social groups and classes in the formulation and implementation of transportation and traffic policies. Besides having highly centralized states where decisions are taken by a limited elite, most developing countries continue to suffer from a lack of adequate means of political representation. They are not institutionalized democracies but fragile democracies, with a deep bias in their decision-making processes (O'Donnell, 1988). As in the Brazilian case, besides being controlled by economic and political elites, the decision-making process favours the middle classes, who have direct and indirect means of influencing policy outcomes. The main channel for this influence is provided by the technocracy and the bureaucracy, who are the middle class in power. The working class in general and public transportation users in particular are often kept out of the decision-making process. With traffic, the political issue derives from the peculiar nature of traffic conflicts in the face of different needs and interests, and the social and political characteristics of developing countries. A large mix of non-motorized and motorized modes, coupled with the use of available space by street vendors and leisure activities, renders traffic conflicts unusually critical. As traffic roles and their associated needs change in time and space, demands placed on traffic authorities concerning accessibility, fluidity, safety and environmental quality vary considerably. It is therefore impossible for the state to resolve all conflicting demands simultaneously and planners have to define priorities. Social and political conditions further complicate the issue. Deep class divisions, translated into social, cultural, economic and political differences among people, have profound consequences for the access to transportation modes and for the use of the street. Citizenship, as political consciousness about collective behaviour, is weakly developed: there is a loose apprehension of rights and duties, which is weakened still further by the bias of formal justice in societies characterized by deep class differences: those committing grave traffic offences are seldom punished. Drivers and pedestrians often develop informal ways of dividing space, which either ignore or interpret differently formal traffic laws. In addition, class differences translate into assumed differences in the right to occupy space. While people in the role of drivers actually think that they have priority access to space, people in the role of pedestrians or public transportation passengers actually think that they do not have the same rights (Vasconcellos, 1996). In developing countries, pedestrians are second class citizens. This has an important social meaning, for most walking trips are made by low income people, as independent or combined trips. Another important issue is that since roles, needs and interests change in time and space, no single issue can be called upon to influence traffic policies, and there are no strong, permanent and explicit social movements mobilized around traffic. Thus congestion, as the most visible traffic problem, appears as the dominant problem, further supporting automobile-oriented policies.

Institutional

Institutional issues relate to the power to command and control transportation and traffic policies, and to the level of decentralization that would ensure the best results. In addition to the lack of proper agencies, technical personnel are rare and poorly trained.

Agencies overlap in their jurisdiction, and conflicts over mutual problems are frequent. The problem is especially serious in metropolitan areas (Barat, 1985), where coordinated efforts are essential to ensure the implementation of large scale transportation systems. Excessive centralization at national or regional levels also prevents local authorities from having the required autonomy to formulate and implement transportation policies.

Social

Social issues relate to several inequities in transportation and traffic conditions. The first kind of inequity is unequal accessibility to transportation. This inequity can be broken down into several components: access time to transit (including waiting and transfer times), in-vehicle time and access to the final destination. For all components, public transportation users face worse conditions than car users. The second inequity relates to comfort. Internal conditions in public transportation vehicles are usually inadequate, and average passenger density is sufficiently high to cause discomfort and tension. The third major inequity relates to activity. With longer distances to be travelled and poor transportation services, most of the population have to increase their time and space budgets to cope with essential trips. Thus, in addition to the physical and psychological burdens, low income individuals suffer a reduction in their social lives, since most travel is confined to work-related and basic educational purposes.

Most inequity problems derive from different approaches to the supply of both transportation infrastructure and means. While on the one hand the state provides infrastructure (streets and highways) with public resources, on the other hand the provision of motorized means of circulation is often left to the market: the middle income and upper income strata purchase automobiles while lower income citizens have to rely on the private bus supply. Thus, while middle and upper income groups can consume street systems efficiently (from their own point of view) with their automobiles, most people cannot do so unless affordable and convenient public transportation is provided, along with preferential traffic management measures. In other words, the assumption that streets are a means for collective consumption and should be paid for by everybody is a myth. Similarly, criticisms of public transportation subsidies are therefore unjustified in view of externalities caused by private transportation and the large subsidies provided to ensure its efficient use.

Technical

Technical issues relate to the commitment to applying traditional techniques borrowed from developed countries without proper adjustment to developing world conditions (Willumsen, 1990), and to the myth of traffic management as a neutral technique. The rationale of the transportation planning process is conservative in that it is used to propose ways of accommodating present trends in the future without questioning the forces that shape them. The lack of reliable data, coupled with high rates of demographic, social and economic changes, leads to forecasting activities that generate absurd results (May, 1991). Moreover, it is virtually impossible to verify forecasting exercises and it is always possible to explain any deviation from forecast figures by recourse to a set of 'unexpected' social and economic changes. Thus, the use of these models characterized 'black box' ethics, where only a few experts could decide which data to include and how to handle them. It has served to generate (and propagate) an unequal and unfair distribution of accessibility, further enhancing automobile dominance. This kind of procedure is possible owing both to the image of technology as a symbol of modernity and to the close nature of the political system, which keeps outside interference at very low levels. In addition, traffic management entails the use of technical tools that avoid social and political considerations, and the pursuit of a form of distribution of the circulation space that supposedly benefits everybody. It ends up providing a circulation space where the needs of the weakest (pedestrians, cyclists, bus passengers) are severely impaired to allow efficient conditions for automobile use.

Technological

Technological issues relate to the commitment to an automotive development model that militates against non-motorized and public transportation systems. Traditional transportation means have been constantly neglected and even banned (Banjo and Dimitriou, 1990) and railroads have been dismantled (Barat, 1985). This commitment has strategic reasons (development policies), economic reasons (relevance of the automotive industry) and sociological reasons. In the latter case it relates to the political and economic importance of middle classes for capitalist modernization. As the main fuel for modernization is social mobility, the middle classes, who have the best historical conditions to benefit from the process, pursue this mobility fiercely. Considering prevailing transportation supply and urban patterns they see the automobile as one of the main tools for their efficient social reproduction, and the result is a symbiosis between the middle class and the automobile (Vasconcellos, 1997a; 1997b). Thus automobile-oriented transportation and traffic policies are generated and space is adapted to cope with the increasing use of cars in a way that neglects the basic needs of pedestrians and public transportation users.

Economic

Economic issues relate first to the fiscal crisis of the state, which hinders support for efficient public transportation systems and distributive social policies. Large transportation infrastructures, which rely on public investments, are becoming less feasible and subsidies to special groups are subjected to mounting opposition. Second, this same crisis helps keep most of the population in poverty, which prevents people from having access to convenient public transportation. Third, inefficient and negligent operation of public transportation services – especially by large public operators subject to weak public controls – generate persistent economic deficits.

Operational

Operational issues relate both to the irregular provision of transportation services and to the erratic quality of traffic conditions. Private provision of public transportation is permanently subject to instability, owing both to a market-driven approach to the business and to a never-ending conflict between fare levels and expected revenues (Figueroa, 1991). Public supply is also irregular in the face of continuing economic deficits, operational deficiencies and increasing demand, especially by low income sectors. Traffic management is highly skewed towards automobile traffic fluidity, with the result that scant attention is paid to the circulation needs of pedestrian and transit users, who require specific priority treatment.

Finally, environmental issues concern the steady degradation of the quality of urban life represented by high traffic accident rates, increasingly intolerable air pollution (Faiz, 1993) and disruption of residential and living spaces by undue motorized traffic. All effects are related to the adaptation of space for the automobile within a context of deep social, political and economic differences among social classes and groups. The most striking proof of this irresponsible adaptation is the increase in the number of traffic accidents and the nature of the accidents themselves. In developing countries, accident rates are several times higher than those found in developed countries (TRRL, 1991) and pedestrians are the most jeopardized (Hill and Jacobs, 1981; Guitink and Flora, 1995). Thus safety problems derive primarily from the organization of a new unsafe built environment rather than from particular causes such as individual behaviour.

Alternative Assumptions

Alternative assumptions underlying transportation and traffic policies in developing countries may now be proposed (see Table 18.2).

First, *accountability* refers to the right to participate in policy decisions and to evaluate the results. Planners are political beings, committed to perceptions of reality and political beliefs, however naive the idea of neutrality that prevails in their discourse. Transportation and traffic policies are not an isolated field of technical expertise divested of political interests and influences and therefore capable of promoting neutral solutions for the general wellbeing. The object of policy is not the 'community', perceived as a set of equal people seeking the same collective wellbeing, but social classes and groups with specific needs and interests, often conflicting and sometimes contradictory. Hence, transportation and traffic policies are intervention techniques of both a technical and political nature, which must use technical tools to negotiate politically the distribution of accessibility among these classes and groups. Neutrality is therefore a myth and solutions will always entail judgements and preferences through involving distribution of benefits and handicaps. As stressed by Healey (1977), 'high energy methodologies', of which transportation models are a prime example, are antithetical to participatory processes and should be put under public control. Those who have the power over the information surrounding the decision process should be accountable. Thus, accountability requires an ethical and formal obligation to open up the decision-making process to society. This does not mean a trend towards 'assemblyism', but refers instead to the organization of open and fluid channels for communication and control, operated by democratically selected groups and agents, such as labour unions or neighbourhood and professional organizations. It also entails the proper decentralization of tasks to ensure policies are formulated as close as possible to their targeted groups. Moreover, an open decision-making process does not mean that technical skills and

Table 18.2 *Alternative assumptions and questions*

Objective	Content	Current question	Proposed questions
Accountability	Ensuring the right to participate in policy decisions and to evaluate results	What are the most adequate instruments to support transport and traffic policies?	What are the most democratic ways of using the most adequate instruments to support transport and traffic policies?
Social responsiveness	Identifying and filling existing accessibility gaps	How may current transport demand tendencies be accommodated in the future?	How is the built environment organized? Who can use it and under which conditions? What are the main differences in access to transport and space? How can we eliminate or minimize these differences?
Equity	Targeting of policies to ensure equitable accessibility, safety and environmental conditions	What is the most efficient way of providing the higher mobility?	What is the most efficient way of ensuring the most equitable appropriation of space?
Sustainability	Reorganizing space and transport technology	What are the technological alternatives to ensure the highest mobility?	What are the most efficient, environmentally friendly and sustainable means of ensuring the equitable appropriation of space?

knowledge are useless and that politicians should take care of everything. The political nature of policies does not diminish the importance of planners and their technical skills and it should not be used as an excuse for not doing the job, or insisting on looking for an idealized neutral participation. In fact, this political dimension enhances the importance of transportation-related policies, especially in highly stratified societies such as developing countries. The broadening of social analysis in transportation 'renders indefensible the confusion of technical and political processes' (Healey, 1977). Transportation and traffic planners have to be able to work with both fields of knowledge, enhancing the need for an alternative, diversified university training.

The second assumption is *social progressiveness*. It proposes that the central task is to detect and fill existing accessibility and equity gaps (Moseley et al, 1977) rather than adapting space to accommodate present tendencies in the future. This argues for an alternative strategy of priority financing of improvements in transportation (and living) conditions for low income groups rather than middle classes. Thus the assumption argues against the possibility and convenience of accurate forecasting of the relationships among land use, social and economic conditions and transport demand as a support to conservative proposals. Forecasting techniques are not assumed to be conclusive instruments used to justify vital decisions. Instead, the new assumption requires planners to be more modest and to use short term forecasting simply as a way of identifying approximate trends and ceilings to the amplitude of the analysis. It also requires the use of simplified models adapted to local conditions (Willumsen, 1990). The new assumption also questions strict use of the words 'transport planning' as representing a willingness to control the future, focusing instead on defining transportation policies (Proud'homme, 1990). In short, forecasting exercises are to be replaced by detection of inequalities and inefficiencies in present transportation and traffic systems, and designing solutions to decrease or eliminate them in the present rather than generate proposals for the hypothetical future.

Thus, instead of asking how present trends can be accommodated in the future, the planner should concentrate on some fundamental initial questions: How was the present built environment organized? Who can use it and under what conditions? The answers to these questions have to rely on the analysis of household travel patterns as a complement to individual ones. Mobility in developing countries cannot be reduced to isolated statistics about individual trips, but should instead consider a 'household survival strategy' (Henry and Figueroa, 1985). Social reproduction, and the related transport needs, are defined in the household context, besides being constrained by exogenous factors such as transportation supply and the location of activities. Thus travel and distance budgets (Goodwin, 1981; Hägerstrand, 1987) are essential for both understanding social reproduction in the light of prevailing conditions and identifying constraints on the equitable appropriation of space.

Equity relates to the targeting of transportation and traffic policies to ensure an equitable appropriation of space from the standpoint of accessibility, safety and environmental protection. This involves submitting the prevailing efficiency paradigm to equity requirements (Healey, 1977). Such submission does not mean neglecting efficiency but considering it differently: instead of asking what is the most efficient way of ensuring the highest mobility, the question is what is the most efficient way of ensuring the equitable appropriation of space. The first concern – equitable access – relates to the collective nature of the street system and to the provision of public transportation services. With the former, the challenge is to make streets a public asset. On the one hand, the myth of streets as a means for collective consumption has to be challenged by submitting all investments in transportation infrastructure to equity evaluations. On the other hand, the use of the streets should be reorganized according to priorities given to the most numerous and vulnerable roles, which in developing countries are indisputably the pedestrian, the cyclist and the public transportation passenger. This need not entail eliminating private transportation, but will require submitting it to others' needs and interests. With the latter, the right to public transportation should be seen as the right to participate in the social, economic, political and cultural activities that are essential to living. Thus the prevailing market paradigm must be replaced by a social paradigm, in which transportation is an essential tool for ensuring the right to access and the achievement of broader social goals. This may entail the subsidization of public transportation services whenever necessary to ensure equitable access, provided they reach the targeted groups and are not used to support inefficiency.

The second equity concern relates to safe circulation as a right. As automobile-adapted built environments in developing countries are natural producers of accidents, the crude views of accidents as 'fatalities' or 'inevitable costs of development' must be firmly rejected. The same rejection applies to the blind importing of such assumptions from industrialized countries as the over-weighting of human factors as causes of accidents. Thus the central task is to reorganize the built environment to ensure a safe traffic for the most numerous and vulnerable roles. Finally, the right to environmental quality may also be pursued according to the same objectives, to ensure acceptable levels of noise and air pollution and controlled urban changes. This implies that efficiency must be subjected to safety and environmental needs.

This leads to the fourth assumption, *sustainability*, as the only assumption focused on the future. In practical terms, it means that instead of searching for the modes of highest efficiency regardless of their environmental impacts, it is necessary to ask what is the most environmentally sound and sustainable way of ensuring an equitable appropriation of space. This assumption does not neglect efficiency: instead of dealing with limited technical efficiency, it embodies the broader notion of social efficiency, by representing the levels of technical efficiency within which broad social and democratically determined objectives are being achieved. Central to this objective is the change in urban development patterns to reduce both average distances and dependence on motorized transportation, coupled with the adoption of effective measures to ensure priority circulation and efficient operation to both public and non-motorized transportation.

The equity and sustainability assumptions can then be translated into a final single question: What are the most efficient, environmentally sound and sustainable ways of ensuring an equitable appropriation of space? This question implicitly carries a positive answer to Hägerstrand's (1987) question about the possibility of restoring equality, and represents the main challenge for transportation and traffic planners in developing countries.

Answering this basic question has a very important political meaning in the developing world. It indicates that it is not sufficient to search for efficient, environmentally sound and sustainable means of transportation if equity is not achieved. It is preferable to have an equitable and environmentally unfriendly space than an environmentally friendly but inequitable space. While the former can in the short term lead to a change of course to ensure sustainability – as political power is more democratically distributed – the latter can be frozen in an unequal situation with few opportunities for change. This is the current situation in some developing countries that have been pursuing automobile emission controls as a priority, while keeping most of the people subject to poor transportation conditions. Planners in developing countries should be aware of not falling into the traps laid by biased approaches, and should instead promote policies inside a broader equity framework.

Conclusions

The results of traditional transportation planning techniques in developing countries have been widely disappointing. Used according to black box ethics within weakly democratized environments, and supported by unreliable forecasting techniques, they have been generating transportation systems that propagate an unfair distribution of accessibility. Private transportation has often benefited from this state of affairs, while public transportation means have been neglected and subject to permanent crisis. Economic restructuring and the fiscal crisis of the state have prevented still further the organization of an adequate supply of public transportation for most of the population.

The urban transportation crisis in developing countries requires a radical change in the transportation planning process. The assumptions that have supported traditional procedures have to be replaced by others that are capable of supporting new, socially and environmentally sound transportation policies. Recent trends toward privatization and deregulation further stress the need to clarify assumptions. Thus, the transportation decision-making process has to be accountable and decentralized as close as possible to the targeted users. Planners and engineers have to be able to work with both the technical and political aspects of transportation and traffic policies, instead of looking for an idealized neutral participation. Conservative proposals based on unreliable forecasting exercises have to be replaced by the targeting of immediate measures to fill equity gaps. Central to the objective is the analysis of household time and space budgets to identify constraints on the equitable appropriation of space. The myth of roads as a means for collective consumption has to be challenged by submitting investments to equity evaluations, and by redefining the use of streets in favour of the most numerous and vulnerable roles. Traffic safety and environmental quality have to be seen as rights, and the prevailing automobile-adapted built environment has to be profoundly modified. Finally, urban development patterns have to be gradually changed to decrease both average distances and dependence on motorized transportation.

Notes

1   This chapter was first published as a paper in *World Transport Policy & Practice*, vol 3, no 3, pp4–10.

References

Banjo, G A and Dimitriou, H T (eds) (1990) *Transport Planning for Third World Cities*, Routledge, London

Barat, J (1985) 'Integrated metropolitan transport – reconciling efficiency, equity and environmental improvement', *Third World Planning Review*, vol 7, no 3, pp242–261

Dimitriou, H T (1992) *Urban Transport Planning – A Developmental Approach*, Routledge, London

Faiz, A (1993) 'Automotive emission in developing countries – relative implication for global warming, acidification and urban air quality', *Transportation Research A,* vol 27, no 3, pp167–186

Figueroa, O (1991) 'La crise de court terme des transports en commun: l'experience de San Jose du Costa Rica', *Recherche Transports Securite,* vol 31, pp47–56

Goodwin, P B (1981) 'The usefulness of travel budgets', *Transportation Research A,* vol 15, pp97–106

Guitink, P and Flora, J (1995) *Non-motorized Transportation in Transportation Systems: Back to the Future?,* TRB 74th annual meeting, January, Washington

Hägerstrand, T (1987) 'Human interaction and spatial mobility: retrospect and prospect' in Nijkamp, P and Reichman, S (eds), *Transportation Planning in a Changing World,* GOWER/European Science Foundation, London

Healey, P (1977) 'The sociology of urban transport planning – a socio-political perspective' in Hensher, D (ed) *Urban Transport Economics,* Cambridge University Press, Cambridge, pp199–227

Henry, E and Figueroa, O (eds) (1985) *Transporte y servicios urbanos en America Latina,* INRETS/CIUDAD, Quito

Hill, B L and Jacobs, G D (1981) 'The application of road safety countermeasures in developing countries', *Traffic Engineering and Control,* vol 22, no 8/9, pp464–468

May, A D (1991) 'Integrated transport strategies: a new approach to urban transport policy in the UK', *Transport Reviews,* vol 11, no 3, pp213–247

Moseley, M J, Harman, R G, Coles, O B and Spencer, M B (1977) *Rural Transport and Accessibility,* University of East Anglia, Norwich

O'Donnell, G (1988) 'Democracia delegativa?', *Novos Estudos CEBRAP,* vol 31, pp25–40

Proud'homme, R (1990) 'Urban transport in developing countries: new perspectives and new policies' in Proud'homme, R (ed) *Transport urbains dans le pays en developpement, nouvelles perspectives, nouvelles politiques,* Paradigme, Paris, pp13–28

TRRL (1991) *Towards Safer Roads in Developing Countries,* Transport and Road Research Laboratory, Crowthorne

Vasconcellos, E A (1996) 'Reassessing traffic accidents in developing countries', *Transport Policy,* vol 2, no 4, pp263–269

Vasconcellos, E A (1997a) 'The demand for cars in developing countries', *Transportation Research A,* vol 31, no 3, pp245–258

Vasconcellos, E A (1997b) 'The making of the middle class city: transportation policy in Sao Paulo', *Environment and Planning A,* vol 29, pp293–310

Willumsen, L G (1990) 'Urban traffic modelling with limited data' in Banjo, G A and Dimitriou, H (eds) *Transport Planning for Third World Cities,* Routledge, London

World Bank (1986) *Urban Transport – A World Bank Policy Study,* World Bank, Washington, DC

World Bank (1996) *Sustainable Transport – Priorities for Policy Reform,* World Bank, Washington, DC

Part 7

Transport in North America

19

Regional Transport Issues in North America

Todd Litman

Introduction

North American (USA and Canada) ideology celebrates individualism, freedom and consumption. Unrestricted mobility is important to many North Americans' identity. This emphasis on mobility is more than symbolic. The region has high rates of per capita vehicle ownership, vehicle travel and air travel compared to other developed countries (see Figures 19.1, 19.2 and 19.3).

Most North American communities are highly automobile-dependent. Without a private automobile it is difficult to participate in common economic and social activities in such areas. People are identified by their car; non-drivers are socially inferior. North American vehicles tend to be large, with most motorists driving sport utility vehicles (SUVs), vans, trucks or luxury cars. Middle-class residents seldom walk, bicycle or use public transport and so perceive little reason to support these modes. Roadway

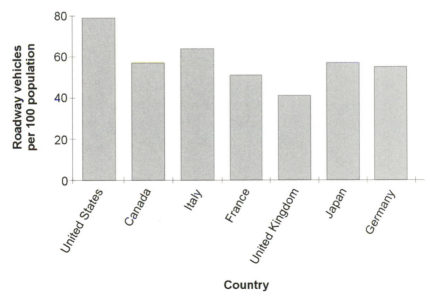

Source: BTS (1999)

Figure 19.1 *Per capita vehicle ownership in selected countries*

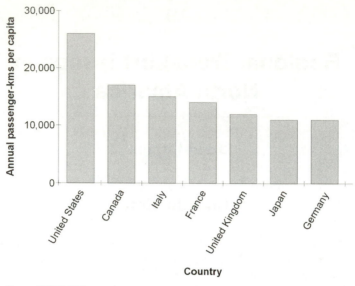

Source: BTS (1999)

Figure 19.2 *Per capita vehicle travel in selected countries*

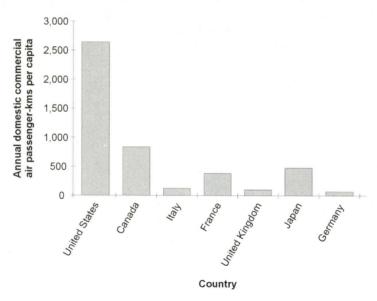

Source: BTS (1999)

Figure 19.3 *Per capita domestic air travel in selected countries*

capacity, parking convenience and the windshield view of the streetscape become dominant factors in how residents perceive their communities.

These patterns are generally considered socially desirable on the grounds that they represent consumer preferences and contribute to economic growth. Many North

Americans assume that efforts to reduce automobile use are harmful to people and business. Transportation policies reflect these assumptions, with an emphasis on accommodating ever-more mobility.

These attributes are not unique to North America. Throughout the world there are people who love their cars, and the independence and prestige they get from driving. Many countries have policies that support automobile industries and roadway development. But North America's wealth and size, and the fact that many North American communities have developed during the last few decades, exacerbate this infatuation with automobiles. More people in North America lead an automobile-dependent lifestyle than anywhere else in the world.

Public Policies that Encourage Mobility

This high degree of mobility results, in part, from public policies.

- *Low fuel prices.* The USA, and Canada to a somewhat lesser degree, have much lower fuel taxes and retail prices than other developed countries (although higher than in some lower income, petroleum-producing countries).
- *Dedicated funding.* In many jurisdictions fuel taxes are dedicated to highway investments. These funds are offered as matching grants to local governments, which 'leverages' additional roadway funding and encourages local officials to define their transportation problems as roadway problems, since other solutions do not qualify for such grants. In addition, various public subsidies support the development of airports.
- *Generous parking and road capacity.* Zoning codes and development policies require generous amounts of parking at most destinations. As a result, parking is usually abundant and free, and buildings and streets are designed primarily for convenient automobile access.
- *Limited travel choices.* In many North American communities there is little effort to accommodate transit, walking and cycling transportation. Transit service quality is inferior, and non-motorized travel is inconvenient and dangerous.
- *Automobile-oriented land use patterns.* Zoning codes and development practices favour low density, segregated land use patterns, with commercial activities scattered along major arterials and highway intersections, and large areas of residential development at the urban fringe. This facilitates automobile access and reduces the access by other modes.

These policies result, in part, from the political power of the automobile and petroleum industries. Efforts to increase vehicle user charges and taxes, reduce funding for transport facilities, restrict automobile access or strongly encourage alternative modes face organized opposition from a wide range of industries and organizations that perceive direct benefits from inexpensive automobile use. But it would be wrong to describe this high degree of automobile dependency as simply the result of industrial manipulation. Policies that favour and subsidize automobile travel receive broad popular support.

Many North Americans have never experienced an effective, multi-modal transportation system. They associate automobile dependency with success, efficiency and prestige, and alternative modes with poverty, inefficiency and sacrifice. In addition, North America also has a long tradition of anti-urbanism. Many North Americans consider cities dangerous, dirty and inefficient. An automobile-dependent, suburban lifestyle is often portrayed as the US ideal.

North American transportation professionals tend to focus on mobility (physical movement) and often treat it as an end in itself. Many do not understand the broader concept of *accessibility* (the ability to reach goods, services and activities) or recognize how increased automobile dependency can reduce accessibility by creating less accessible land use patterns and reducing transportation choices.

It is important to note that these travel patterns vary significantly from one area and individual to another. Newer suburbs tend to be more automobile-dependent than cities and smaller towns. Some North American communities have a relatively balanced transport system, with walkable older neighbourhoods, good bicycle facilities and adequate transit service. Many low income people, students and elderly people often rely significantly on alternative modes. Public officials and citizens in many communities increasingly recognize the value of having a more balanced and efficient transportation.

Saturation?

North America may be reaching its apogee of automobile dependency. Vehicle ownership is near saturation in the USA. More than 90 per cent of households own at least one motor vehicle, and there are now more vehicles than people with driving licences (see Figure 19.4). Some of the factors that contributed to growing per capita vehicle ownership and use have peaked, including growth in employment rates (particularly

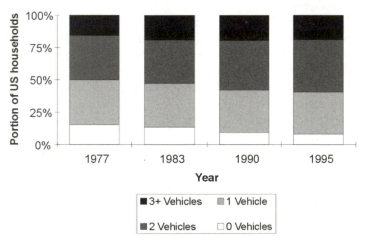

Source: NPTS (1995)

Figure 19.4 *Household vehicle ownership*

the portion of women who work), declining real fuel prices and urban dispersion. In addition, the novelty of automobile dependency may have worn off for many consumers. There is growing scepticism that increasing roadway capacity is a cost-effective way to reduce traffic congestion or address other transportation problems.

Although it is unlikely that North Americans will significantly reduce their vehicle ownership and use in the foreseeable future, at the margin (ie, relative to current travel patterns) many would probably prefer to live somewhat less automobile-dependent lifestyles. For the last five years transit use has grown at a faster rate than automobile travel. The North American real estate industry has discovered demand for housing in more accessible urban neighbourhoods, indicating that many consumers value having better transport choices and more integrated communities, provided that they have security, public services and prestige comparable in quality to that in suburbs. This demand for transport and housing choice is likely to increase in the future as real fuel prices increase, baby boomers age and roadways become even more congested.

Transportation Problems

North America's transportation system can be considered very effective from some perspectives. Motorists can travel nearly anywhere with reasonable convenience, comfort and safety except under urban peak conditions. Fuel prices are low, allowing even lower income people to drive. Parking is generally abundant and free. Vehicles can be rented at airports and other major transportation terminals, creating an efficient transportation network for those who can drive and have enough money.

From this perspective, the greatest transportation problems are constraints on mobility: traffic congestion, inconvenient parking and unaffordable vehicle expenses for low income consumers. This suggests that the solutions that have been used in the past are effective and simply need further implementation: build more road and parking capacity, reduce vehicle user costs, and improve vehicle and road designs to address safety and environmental problems.

However, from other perspectives, the North American transportation system has serious problems that require fundamental changes. Some of these problems are described below.

Traffic congestion

Many North Americans experience daily frustration from traffic congestion, and would name it as their community's single greatest transportation problem. Yet there is no agreement on how to address this problem. There is only modest support for congestion pricing, major transit investments, comprehensive transportation demand-management programmes or major urban highway capacity expansion. It would cost hundreds of dollars annually per capita in new roadway funding to add the required capacity to reduce congestion even modestly, at a time when much smaller tax increases are considered politically unacceptable. The result is a political impasse.

In response, urban residents have learned to live with traffic congestion. They avoid peak-period driving, and incorporate an increasing array of comfort and convenience features into their vehicles. Travel surveys indicate that commute travel times do not necessarily increase with congestion, even in automobile-dependent cities such as Los Angeles. This suggests that congestion tends to maintain a self-limiting equilibrium, which residents endure to the degree they can tolerate.

Facility costs

Fuel taxes and vehicle registration fees are generally considered road user charges in North America, and in many jurisdictions they are dedicated by law to transportation expenditures. Yet despite this guaranteed flow of money many governments find they have inadequate transportation funding. Motorists often assume that the vehicle taxes they pay fully cover roadway costs, but they actually fall short. Local roads are mostly funded through general taxes. User charges would need to increase by more than 40 per cent if vehicle user fees were to cover all roadway costs.

Despite these funding constraints, a significant portion of available funding is spent on highway capacity expansion. Some transportation advocates recommend a 'fix it first' policy, meaning that roadway capacity expansion projects should not be implemented until basic facility repairs and maintenance are fully funded.

Road traffic accidents

Traffic accidents are a major transportation problem, particularly in the USA. Figure 19.5 illustrates US traffic fatality rates between 1960 and 2000. These data can be interpreted in two ways, giving two very different conclusions concerning the magnitude of transportation risks and the solutions to this problem.

Transportation professionals usually measure road risk based on accident and fatality rates per unit of vehicle travel (eg per 100 million vehicle miles or kilometres). Viewed in this way, traffic safety programmes are a huge success, accident rates having declined by more than two-thirds over the four decades. But another perspective tells a

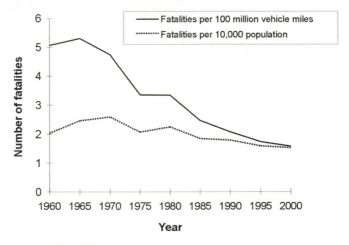

Source: OECD (2001)

Figure 19.5 *US traffic fatalities over four decades*

rather different story. When accidents and fatalities are measured per capita, as with other health risks, there has been surprisingly little improvement over this period despite massive investments in safer roads and vehicles, tremendous increases in the use of seatbelts and other safety devices, reductions in drunk driving and improvements in emergency response and trauma care. Traffic accidents continue to be the greatest single cause of deaths and disabilities for people in the prime of life. US per capita traffic fatalities are fairly high compared with other countries, as illustrated in Figure 19.6. From this perspective, traffic safety continues to be a major problem, current safety efforts have failed and new approaches are needed to really improve road safety.

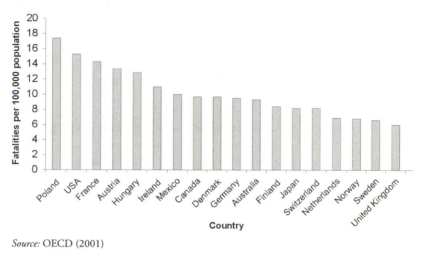

Source: OECD (2001)

Figure 19.6 *International traffic fatality rates (per capita)*

Mobility for the transportation-disadvantaged

Although the North American transportation system provides a relatively high level of service for motorists, people who for any reason cannot drive an automobile often face severe mobility problems. Many communities lack basic infrastructure for non-motorized travel. Dispersed destinations, wide roadways and heavy traffic make it difficult to cross a street and access common destinations.

Inferior transportation compounds the problems facing people who are economically or physically disadvantaged, limiting their opportunity for education, employment and social activities.

Consumer costs

Transportation expenditures represent 15–20 per cent of average household expenditures, and even more if costs for roads and parking that are borne indirectly in housing expenses, taxes and other consumer expenditures are also included. This represents the second largest category of total consumer expenditures, and is particularly high for lower income households as illustrated in Figure 19.7.

These costs are not a significant problem for middle and upper income households, who spend large amounts of money on optional transportation expenditures such as

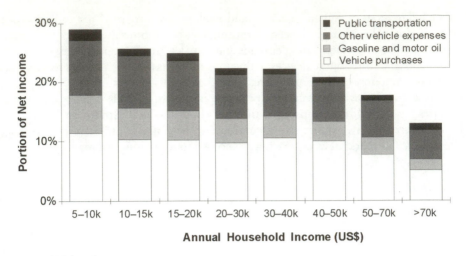

Source: BLS (1997)

Figure 19.7 *Household transportation expenditures (US$)*

luxury vehicles and recreational travel. But it can be a major burden to lower income households. Low income households tend to drive unreliable vehicles, and often lack mandatory liability insurance, imposing additional stresses and risks.

Environmental impacts

Although the USA and Canada have some of the most well established and stringent vehicle emission reduction programmes, vehicle emissions are a major contributor toward air pollution problems in many urban areas.

North American transportation activity is one of the largest single sources of greenhouse gas emissions. The USA refuses to sign the Kyoto Protocol or implement other major emission reduction programmes, partly on the grounds that doing so would reduce consumer and economic benefits.

Inactivity

People throughout the world increasingly face health problems associated with inadequate physical activity, including obesity, cardiovascular diseases and diabetes. Automobile-oriented transportation systems, with limited potential for walking and cycling, can be a major contributor to these problems.

Policy Responses

Although overall transportation policies continue to be highly automobile oriented, there are also some signs of change. Below are examples:

- There is increasing flexibility in federal transportation planning. Some budget categories allow funds to be moved from highway to transit accounts, or even to 'enhancement' programmes that fund pedestrian, bicycle and land use improvements. Some state and provincial transportation programmes are also becoming more flexible.

- At the regional and local level there is increasing appreciation of the need to integrate transportation and land use planning. Some urban governments are implementing 'smart growth' land use policy reforms to help create more accessible, multi-modal communities.
- Some downtown, traditional neighbourhoods and resort communities are being redeveloped as enjoyable pedestrian environments. These demonstrate that even people who normally rely on automobile transportation value being able to walk, and the community interactions that can result.
- Local governments and transportation professionals are learning ways to improve pedestrian and cycling conditions.
- Some innovative transportation management programmes are being implemented, including commuter choice programmes and higher occupancy vehicle (HOV) priority to encourage use of alternative commute modes.

Innovation

Americans tend to believe that 'Yankee ingenuity' can solve any problem, and delight in simple inventions. The USA and Canada have been leaders in many innovations:

- Performance-based vehicle pollution control regulations and corporate average fuel efficiency (CAFE) standards. Although the automobile industry initially opposed these requirements, claiming that they were unnecessary and excessively expensive, they spurred manufacturers to improve engines and develop effective emission control systems.
- Government funding of transportation technological development. Federal programmes have helped to develop and implement various intelligent transportation systems, and alternative fuelled vehicles and transit design innovations. There are also experiments with road pricing and other management innovations.
- Universal design requirements, such as the US Federal Americans With Disabilities legislation, and related policies at the state and local level help create transportation facilities that accommodate people with special needs.
- Development of BMX and mountain bikes. Young men on the west coast who enjoyed riding old bicycles on trails and mountain roads began producing special components and bikes. Eventually, major bicycle manufactures copied these designs and now sell them worldwide, helping to create bicycles that are suitable for transportation in US cities as well as rural Africa.

Conclusion

North America is a highly mobile and automobile-dependent society. With a few exceptions, most North American adults own a personal automobile and use it for most travel. This dependency on motor vehicle travel permeates all facets of society, including land use patterns, economic activity and people's personal identity.

Most North Americans have never experienced any alternative. They assume that reduced automobile ownership and use requires severe reduction in their economic and social opportunities, and their quality of their life. As a result, current public policies tend to support and encourage automobile dependency and it can be difficult to implement changes that cause even modest constraints on vehicle ownership and use.

These patterns are not fundamentally different from what occurs in other parts of the world. Many people and communities have various degrees of automobile dependency, and continue on a trajectory toward what occurs in North America, but nowhere else have these patterns occurred on such a large scale.

There are, however, some signs of change. Planning professionals and citizens increasingly realize that past solutions based on continued expansion of the roadway network are often not cost effective or socially acceptable. There are modest but growing efforts to try new ideas. Although these generally emphasize technological solutions, there are some modest experiments with land use policies and management strategies to create more accessible and efficient transportation systems.

References

BLS (1997) *Consumer Expenditure Survey*, Bureau of Labor Statistics, www.bls.gov

BTS (1999) *G-7 Transportation Highlights*, US Bureau of Transportation Statistics, www.bts.gov/itt/G7HighlightsNov99/G-7book.pdf

NPTS (1995) *Nationwide Personal Transportation Survey*, US Bureau of Transportation Statistics, www.bts.gov/nhts

OECD (2001) *International Road Traffic and Accident Database*, Organization for Economic Co-operation and Development, Paris, www.bast.de/htdocs/fachthemen/irtad//english/we2.html

VTPI (2001) *Online TDM Encyclopedia*, Victoria Transport Policy Institute, www.vtpi.org

20

The North American Growth Fixation and the Inner City: Roads of Excess

Christopher Leo

The road of excess leads to the palace of wisdom
(William Blake, *The Marriage of Heaven and Hell*)

Introduction

'It's the economy, stupid.' Economic growth is the yardstick by which so many governments believe they will be judged, and moderate growth is often considered insufficient. As a result, many slowly growing cities unthinkingly extend their infrastructure on the assumption of rapid growth that does not materialize. Winnipeg has followed such policies, and the results illustrate their weaknesses. The suburbs sprawl while the inner city decays and its infrastructure deteriorates. Plans for a rapid transit line that could both relieve congestion and promote more compact development are postponed year after year while new roads and bridges are extended into sparsely populated fringe areas.[1]

Growth Fixation

In North America, growth has long been the Holy Grail of city politics for reasons that are not entirely frivolous. Since it is of the essence of city life, even more than of life generally, that change is constant, some growth is necessary to avoid decline. As some people or activities vacate a city, or part of a city, either something else must take their place or decay sets in. A certain amount of growth, therefore, is essential to a city's wellbeing.

But, carried to excess, the desire to promote growth can be damaging and it is the author's argument that in many North American cities it is leading people astray. Deference to the god of rapid growth has become a virtual given in North American society, a fixation. Virtually everyone is in some way caught up in the belief that the big apple – New York, Toronto, Los Angeles or the nearest metropolitan centre, wherever one happens to be – is deserving of obsessive attention.

The attention is not all favourable. Those who make their lives outside the realm of such metropolises often feel resentful of them, decrying them as breeders of crime and false values, or maintaining that their administrations and residents are the favourites of the national or regional government, while perhaps simultaneously nurturing a sense of inferiority. But whether the attention is favourable or unfavourable, it bespeaks an obsession with growth, a sense that it represents power, importance, legitimacy.

This obsession has many consequences (Leo et al, 1998), but in this chapter the author focuses on the way growth fixation influences decisions on the development and maintenance of city streets. His argument is that people's common obsession with rapid growth leads to the over-building of roads in anticipation of future growth that may or may not materialize. Such policies are followed indiscriminately in both rapidly growing and slowly growing cities, but are especially damaging to the health of the latter, where the future growth needed to justify current expenditures virtually never materializes. Unlike Blake's road of excess, these roads do not lead to the palace of wisdom.

In making his case for this contention, the author draws extensively on the example of Winnipeg in Canada, a city that takes in most of a metropolitan area with a population of approximately 700,000. Many other examples would have done as well, and the data would have produced similar conclusions, because Winnipeg is a typical example of a slowly growing North American city whose growth, according to the author, has been flagrantly mismanaged thanks to the unthinking pursuit of fast growth policies.

It has become a local cliché that Winnipeg is a city in decline. In this respect as well, Winnipeg's situation is probably more the rule than the exception in North America. Edmonton is sometimes sarcastically referred to as 'Deadmonton'. The inner city of Hamilton, Ontario is decaying, and the city is widely considered to be in decline; St John, New Brunswick has been struggling with decline for decades, indeed, for more than a century. More examples could easily be cited. In the USA, examples are even easier to find: Detroit, Duluth, Omaha, Des Moines, Camden – the list goes on.

Without trying to generalize about all these examples – and referring now to Winnipeg – it is the author's contention that the decline, which is apparent enough, has nothing to do with any failure of needed growth. It is true that Winnipeg is becoming a less important centre in Canada because a number of other cities are growing faster, but to say that adds up to decline is to be hooked on growth. Over the years metropolitan Winnipeg's population has been growing at about 1 per cent per annum. For example, from 1986 to 1991, the population of the Winnipeg census metropolitan area (CMA) grew from 625,304 to 652,354, a percentage change of 4.3 per cent, less than 1 per cent per year, while the economy has been growing at a rate of perhaps 2 or 3 per cent. For those who are not hooked on growth, that is not decline: it is a description of a metropolitan area that is steadily becoming wealthier, in the aggregate.

In what sense then is the decline real? It is the city of Winnipeg, and especially Winnipeg's inner city, that is in decline, not the CMA. Population growth within the city limits crawls along at less than 1 per cent a year, while municipalities bordering the city are growing at rates in excess of 10 per cent, and in some instances more than 20 per cent. Until recently new housing developments within the city were about half of those in the CMA, despite the fact that much new municipal infrastructure remains under-utilized, and older infrastructure is deteriorating at a frightening rate. Some of the most alarming deterioration becomes visible only when an automobile or truck plunges through a hole that suddenly opens up in the street. This has occurred several times in recent years because of deteriorating sewer lines.

The visible inner city is deteriorating less spectacularly, but possibly even faster. Despite heroic efforts on the part of all three levels of government and the local business community, once-bustling inner city streets are becoming ominously quiet, while unoccupied retail premises and boarded-up residences are becoming a common sight. Much of the inner city has been red-lined by insurance companies, with the result that homeowners applying for insurance may be refused, or may be required to pay more than the standard premium. All of these changes are typical features of slowly growing cities across North America. Indeed, Winnipeg is far from the worst case.

It is the author's argument that the glaring disparity between the health of the metropolitan area as a whole and that of the inner city is a result of a set of growth policies based inappropriately on the premise of rapid growth – a result of the fact that people's growth fixation makes it difficult to think about city development in any other terms. The author prescribes the acceptance of slow growth as a reality and the rethinking of policies accordingly. In this chapter, he examines how this argument applies to the extension of the road system.

Civil Engineering Norms and Development Conventions

The ideas about road systems that are being applied in Canadian cities, whether rapidly or slowly growing, have two sources that are important as an illustration: developer proposals and the traditional norms and conventions of civil engineering. The contribution of developers is that they decide on the parcels of land that they think will be suitable for profitable development and present development proposals to the city. In Winnipeg and many other cities they have good reason to expect a sympathetic hearing from local government and, as part of the cost of development, they accept the obligation of building, or paying for, the necessary road connections.

It then becomes the obligation of the city to work out the development of the rest of the city's transportation system to accommodate recent and expected future development. For example, a burgeoning of new sub-divisions at Winnipeg's southern edge in South St Vital and South St Boniface contributed to a city decision to build an expressway serving that part of the city – Bishop Grandin Boulevard – and occasioned the opening up of an under-used and heavily subsidized bus line into Island Lakes, one of the new sub-divisions. It also eventually stimulated the replacement of the Norwood and Main Street bridges with a massive new eight-lane structure. These bridges, located downtown, are part of the road system leading to the newer southern sub-divisions.

While money was readily available for these extensions of the transportation infrastructure, as well as a long list of other similar extensions in all directions from the centre of the city, funds for the maintenance of existing infrastructure dwindled. A meticulous 1998 survey of the state of Winnipeg's infrastructure found a massive disparity between the amount needed to maintain existing infrastructure and the amount actually being spent. Regional streets, for example, were found to be Can$10.2m per year short of the required amount.[2] Even more drastic was the situation of residential streets, which were found to have benefited from an average annual budgeted expenditure of Can$2.5m, compared with a requirement of Can$30m, a disparity of Can$27.5m (City of Winnipeg, 1998).

In all of these respects Winnipeg was following the conventions of modern North American city building: developers decide where they want to locate new development and pay for some of the services immediately required by the new sub-divisions. The city ensures that they become connected into the city-wide service network, and that the city-wide network is expanded as necessary to accommodate them. It is in deciding on the character of this expansion that long established norms of the engineering profession take over.

Most engineering designers and managers now at the peak of the profession were educated in engineering faculties where the dominant tendency was to think of road building as a technical matter, in which road design involved the projection of traffic demands and the efficient accommodation of that traffic at a manageable cost. In that climate of thought the suggestion that there is a social and an environmental dimension to road building was not taken seriously and, when such suggestions came from politicians or members of the public, they were resented as political interference and as an assault on engineers' professional integrity. This belief system is still very much in evidence, especially among the decision-makers in municipal public works departments.

It is important to emphasize that the author is pointing to a belief system, not some special penchant for the pursuit of narrow self-interest. Indeed, engineers are probably less vulnerable to the charge of feathering their own nests at public expense than many other professionals. The Association of Professional Engineers of Manitoba, a typical case, is self-consciously protective of the public interest and shows no reluctance to let colleagues whose professional standards are found wanting feel the full weight of the Association's censure. The problem is not self-aggrandizement, but a predisposition to assume and promote rapid growth, to favour roads over alternative forms of transportation, and sometimes to go to questionable lengths in promoting them.

Easy Decisions

Many examples could be found (Leo, 1977), but a recent case in point was that of the Norwood Bridge, the inner city–suburban link already mentioned. When the plans for the Norwood Bridge reconstruction were being mooted, city officials presented four alternatives, including the following two: it would cost Can$78m for a six-lane divided bridge that was pictured as providing a fair level of safety, and poor traffic capacity, accommodation for transit and accommodation of traffic during construction; by contrast, an eight-lane divided bridge that was rated good in all four categories would cost only Can$80m (City of Winnipeg, 1992) That was an easy decision: only Can$2m extra for a vastly superior bridge. Such easy decisions are standard items in the arsenal of public servants who have made up their minds about which course they wish their political masters and the public to pursue.

Council chose an eight-lane bridge, and it soon became obvious – as it often does in such cases – that the easy choice was not so easy after all. By 1998 the cost of the new bridge had escalated to Can$102m (City of Winnipeg, 1998), and with only one of the two spans built – still less than the six-lane alternative that was portrayed as inadequate – traffic line-ups at rush hour had greatly eased. Given the bias, or lack of reliability, that is apparent from this course of events, it might well be asked whether the officials' advice is deserving of any trust at all. Was a new bridge necessary in the first place? On the face of it, it is not obvious why Canadian bridges are routinely declared to have out-lived their usefulness in decades, while European bridges are functional for centuries.

Over-building of bridges and roads exacerbates the difficulties Winnipeg will face in future. Increased road and bridge capacity has two consequences: first, an improved route draws traffic as it becomes the route of choice for drivers who previously favoured other routes. Sooner or later, this increases pressure on the city council for further road-works. For example, traffic line-ups at a bridge entrance may be replaced by line-ups of vehicles on the bridge waiting to exit onto a narrower road. Such consequences are not unanticipated by engineering staff, and resulting public demands for widening of the road leading away from the bridge may be seen by them as long overdue recognition of necessities they understood from the start.

A second consequence of increased bridge and road capacity is reduced travel time to the urban fringe, which leads to an increase in the economic viability of sprawl and leapfrog development. The upshot is intensified political pressure from developers for the approval of sub-divisions that will be costly to serve – pressure the councils of slowly growing cities have frequently shown themselves unable to resist, precisely because they are predisposed to see rapid growth as a self-evident virtue. Once the new, typically low density, auto-dependent sub-divisions are built, they provide a fresh supply of citizens who have no convenient means of travelling other than by private automobile. It is a vicious cycle, in which each new attempt to solve the problem of allegedly inadequate road capacity has the ultimate effect of exacerbating it (Downs, 1992; 1994).

The high priority accorded to road projects tends to crowd out alternatives. In Winnipeg, City Council has readily agreed to one road project after another, heedless of the fact that each one exacerbates the sprawl dilemma. Meanwhile, transit facilities that could contribute to the amelioration of sprawl are postponed indefinitely. Since the mid-1970s plans have been underway for the construction of the Southwest Transit Corridor, a rapid transit line consisting of cost-effective diesel buses running on a con-crete strip dedicated exclusively to transit.

The Southwest Transit Corridor is considered viable because it connects two popu-lation concentrations – downtown and the University of Manitoba – along the relatively heavily-populated Pembina Highway corridor. It would ameliorate traffic congestion along Pembina Highway – the artery connecting the University of Mani-toba with the inner city – and encourage cost-effective compact development along the route, in contrast to road and bridge projects which would encourage sprawl. Esti-mated total cost for the entire facility would be Can$70m (City of Winnipeg, 1997) – less than the lower cost alternative for the Norwood Bridge, which was deemed inade-quate. However, the estimated cost is a moot point, because postponement of the project has been a routine feature of City Council's annual budget deliberations for at least two decades.

Alternatives

Councils need to reconsider their indiscriminate compliance with road proposals, to the neglect of alternatives. Politicians need not accept the norms of traditionally-minded engineering designers and managers as the major determinant for the extension of transportation infrastructure. In addition, instead of (in effect) delegating to developers the right to decide where the city will expand, cities could exercise their authority to determine the location, development mix and densities of new sub-divisions.

In theory, that power is being exercised now by city councils through their planning departments, but in practice the main influence over those decisions rests with developers. Alternative models are available, both for the planning of roads and transit, and for more compact forms of development. Ironically, they are beginning to be applied in rapidly growing cities (City of Calgary, nd; Oregon Department of Transportation, 1995; 1000 Friends of Oregon, 1997) while many slow-growth centres such as Winnipeg continue to ape what they imagine to be the winning ways of rapid growth.

To stay with the main example, Winnipeg could have developed very differently. It seems very likely that the Norwood Bridge project could reasonably have been much more modest than it was, if it was necessary at all. With a less auto-dependent, more compact form of development, the suburban road system – of which Bishop Grandin is only one example – could have been less extensive, and the transit system less of a drain on the treasury. In their development of roads, as well as the full range of other municipal services, governments are allowing their cities to expand rapidly, at ever lower densities, primarily in response to developers' calculations about where the profit picture looks favourable for them, without serious consideration of how all of these developments will be tied together with infrastructure and services.

When a proposal for a new sub-division is brought to Winnipeg city planners, three cost factors are taken into consideration: roads, underground municipal services (sewer and water services) and parks. If the sub-division proposal incurs extra costs in any of these areas, the developer is responsible. When negotiations are complete, and the sub-division proposal comes before City Council, the typical reaction is delight over the fact that a sizeable chunk of new tax assessment will be added to the city's coffers with the developer covering all the costs.

Forgotten is the fact that the transportation pattern has a large influence on the full range of municipal services. Once the new, allegedly no-cost, sub-division is in place, the new residents rightly argue that, as residents and taxpayers of Winnipeg, they deserve services comparable to those that other residents enjoy. City politicians have no valid answer when they ask: Why is there no conveniently located library branch and community centre? Why are police and fire response times here slower than in other sub-divisions? Why do we not have a neighbourhood school? City council and school boards have no politically realistic alternative but to spend money to meet the demands.

It is easy to see, therefore, why – with Winnipeg expanding at ever lower densities – residential property taxes have reached tax-revolt levels while downtown infrastructure deteriorates. Indeed, the problem is now largely out of the hands of City Council. For some time, residents of the metropolitan area have been voting with their feet, and accepting the property tax reductions they can achieve by moving beyond the boundaries of the city. Businesses are beginning to follow. With ex-urban migration underway, City Council has lost much of the control it once might have exercised over new development. Developers now have alternatives: if the city is not sufficiently generous in dealing with residential sub-division proposals or commercial developments, it is becoming increasingly easy for them to find a parcel of land for a similar development in an adjacent municipality.

Unsustainable Development

Recent studies suggest that these patterns of development are, in the long run, unsustainable or at least dangerously cost-ineffective in any urban area (Blais, 1995; CUPR, 1996; Greater Toronto Area Task Force, 1996). Even the wealthiest and fastest growing metropolitan areas have experienced inner city deterioration in the face of uncontrolled suburban and ex-urban development. The South Bronx was turned first into a jungle and then into something resembling a post-war saturation bombing victim as Queens and Long Island expanded. Most of downtown Detroit became an unoccupied wasteland ringed by older neighbourhoods and prosperous suburbs.

Such decay is a complex phenomenon, and some of its causes can be sought in such disparate phenomena as family breakdown, crime, welfare dependency, inadequate education and de-industrialization. However, there is no doubt that untrammelled suburban expansion and the flight of the middle class from the inner city is a major cause. In the long run, therefore, the typical North American metropolitan development pattern seems likely to be sustainable only at the expense of inner city deterioration, usually followed by deterioration of the first ring of suburbs.

That is bad enough, but the problem is even more acute for slowly growing cities. A rapidly growing city can mask the costliness of sprawl development, at least for a while: a leapfrog sub-division approval may not incur an immediate financial penalty if growth potential is strong enough to assure, within the foreseeable future, that infill development will help to pay for the needed infrastructure. Downtown decay may not occasion immediate alarm when there are proposals for commercial developments to replace decaying downtown residential districts, although it is unlikely that, in the longer run, simply filling empty spaces with office towers will suffice as a strategy for the prevention of decay.

Whatever the situation in a fast growing centre, the piper demands immediate payment when the city council of a slowly growing city calls the low density tune. Here there are no heavy pressures for new development, and assurances of growing tax revenues, to cover up mistakes. Politicians in cities such as Winnipeg and provinces such as Manitoba – in cities such as Des Moines and Omaha and states such as Iowa and Nebraska – need to understand that their mistakes will catch up with them, possibly within their current term of office.

For them, it is important, not only as a substantive matter, but also from the viewpoint of *realpolitik*, to be conservative in their approvals of sub-divisions and new roads, to support infill development and more compact forms of development, to seek out viable alternatives to private automobile trips and to instruct their officials accordingly. In not doing so, many slow growth cities have passed up their chance to remain viable and attractive places to live.

Conclusion

It is possible, however, to end this bleak discussion on a positive note. There are signs (see Leo et al, 1998) that local authorities are moving beyond the narrow, new-roads-to-new-sub-divisions approach to urban expansion and taking instead a regional approach that considers the implications of development decisions for the inner city, for the environment and for the region as a whole.

There is also a different wind blowing in the engineering profession. Many younger engineers are sensitive to the environmental and social dimensions of transportation design and are more oriented to collaborative decision-making processes than the traditionally-minded members of the profession. In future, these younger engineering designers and managers in growing numbers are likely to offer constructive technical advice to politicians and citizens interested in promoting an approach to urban growth that takes the wellbeing of the entire urban region into consideration.

Regionally-focused approaches to urban development, known by various names including Regional Growth Management and Smart Growth, are already fairly well established in a number of jurisdictions, including Oregon, Florida, New Jersey and Washington state, and are drawing influential support in many jurisdictions throughout North America (see Leo and Brown, 2000; Leo et al, 1998). Much of this remains little more than ambitious talk, but if in the end it produces action in a significant number of jurisdictions, the roads of excess may yet lead to the palace of wisdom.

Notes

1   This chapter was first published as a paper in *World Transport Policy & Practice*, vol 4, no 4, pp24–29.
2   The currency used is the Canadian dollar: Can$1 = UK£0.41 = US$0.63.

References

1000 Friends of Oregon (1997) 'Making the connections: a summary of the LUTRAQ project', 1000 Friends of Oregon, Portland
Blais, P (1995) *The Economics of Urban Form*, Greater Toronto Area Task Force, Toronto
City of Calgary (nd) 'Sustainable suburbs study' http://www.gov.calgary.ab.ca/71/71sss/71sss1.html (accessed 17 February 1997)
City of Winnipeg (1992) *Main Street and Norwood Bridges: What do You Think?*, City Council of Winnipeg, Winnipeg

City of Winnipeg (1997) 'Other opportunities and challenges: Southwest Transit Corridor', http://www.city.winnipeg.mb.ca/city/html/govern/oppchal/othsouth.htm (accessed 7 May 1997)

City of Winnipeg (1998) *Strategic Infrastructure Reinvestment Policy: Report and Recommendations*, City Council of Winnipeg, Winnipeg

CUPR (1996) *The Costs of Sprawl: Does Growth Management Pay?*, Center for Urban Policy Research, New Brunswick, NJ, vol 7, no 3 http://policy.rutgers.edu/cupr/cuprreport/cuprreport.htm

Downs, A (1992) *Stuck in Traffic: Coping with Peak-hour Traffic Congestion*, Brookings Institution, Washington, DC

Downs, A (1994) *New Visions for Metropolitan America*, Brookings Institution, Washington, DC

Greater Toronto Area Task Force (1996) *Report*, Queen's Printer for Ontario, Toronto

Jacobs, J (1984) *Cities and the Wealth of Nations: Principles of Economic Life*, Vintage, New York

Leo, C (1977) *The Politics of Urban Development: Canadian Urban Expressway Disputes*, Institute of Public Administration of Canada, Toronto

Leo, C, Beavis, M A, Carver, A and Turner, R (1998) 'Is urban sprawl back on the political agenda? local growth control, regional growth management, and politics', *Urban Affairs Review*, vol 34, no 2

Leo, C and Brown, W (2000) 'Slow growth and urban development policy', *Journal of Urban Affairs*, vol 22, no 2, pp193–213

Oregon Department of Transportation (1995) *Western Bypass Study: Alternatives Analysis*, DoT, Portland

21

Prospects for Sustainable Transportation in the Pacific Northwest: A Comparison of Vancouver, Seattle and Portland

Preston Schiller and Jeff Kenworthy

Introduction

In recent years there has been heightened concern among transportation researchers, policy analysts and environmentalists over the issue of sustainable transportation. In many respects this discussion has flowed from an earlier interest in assessing the environmental problems of transportation and their relation to urban form, especially the burdens created by an excessive dependence upon automobiles for personal transport (Gakenheimer, 1978; Stringer and Wenzel, 1976; Newman and Kenworthy, 1989). As with many other facets of sustainability discussions, sustainable transportation appears to be easier to describe than to define. Common threads in this discussion emphasize that sustainable transportation, in regard to passenger transport, should:

- meet basic access and mobility needs in ways that do not degrade the environment;
- not deplete the resource base upon which it is dependent;
- serve multiple economic and environmental goals;
- maximize efficiency in overall resource utilization;
- improve or maintain access to employment, goods and services while shortening trip lengths and/or reducing the need to travel; and
- enhance the liveability and human qualities of urban regions.

Discussants describe sustainable transportation in terms of decreasing dependency upon cars and fossil fuels and increasing the share of transport undertaken by train, bus, bicycle and foot and integrating transportation and land use planning in order to diminish the need for travel (Replogle, 1995; Spaethling, 1995). Others point to political, economic and behavioural changes or policy confusions that must be addressed in order to advance a sustainable transport agenda (Centre for Sustainable Transportation, 1998; OECD, nd; Wixey and Lake, 1998).

An examination of the prospects for developing sustainable transportation is especially appropriate for the area of western North America increasingly referred to as 'Cascadia' after an ecological utopian novel (Callenbach, 1975). Cascadia comprises the westerly portions of lower British Columbia and Washington and Oregon states. It is a region that shares many common geographical, historical, political and social characteristics.

Its Pacific coastal regions nurture temperate rainforests, its great rivers have been dammed for hydroelectricity, a long and narrow plain from Vancouver to southern Oregon allows for easy rail and road transport north and south, while the volcano-laced peaks of the Cascade Mountains present barriers to east–west travel and development. Peoples indigenous to this area still maintain several linkages to their past – an economy still somewhat focused on fish and forests and a keen maintenance of traditional art forms, as well as a culture substantially different from other North American areas. Cascadia shares a common history of exploration that was carried out under several flags, and frontier settlement and development dependent upon the exploitation of furs, fish and forests. The border has been peaceful since the commencement of settlement; its only disruption is strife among motorists increasingly frustrated by long queues at crossings.

Within Cascadia the cities and metropolitan regions of Vancouver (British Columbia), Seattle (Washington) and Portland (Oregon) invite comparison. Each city has approximately the same number of inhabitants. Each region has been experiencing population growth at approximately 2 per cent per year for the past ten to fifteen years. Most of the population growth has taken place outside the core cities and has generally been in the form of dispersion or 'sprawl'. Each region is experiencing concomitant traffic growth disproportionately greater than its population growth. Each region also enjoys a beautiful setting astride or adjacent to significant bodies of water with spectacular mountain ranges within easy access. Immigration histories and demographics also are more similar than different. Each serves as an important freight rail centre and each has a busy seaport. Each is within a state or province where production and service industries are growing into dominant employment and economic areas, while resource extraction and exploitation (forestry, fishing and mining) are shrinking. Each of the three cities lies at the core of its respective metropolitan region, and each of the three metropolitan areas has developed an ambitious plan for managing and directing growth into urban and suburban centres for the coming decades.

Each region has influential portions of its population active in environmental concerns. Each city is attempting to increase the number of residents living close to the downtown area or near other commercial nodes. Each region appears to be lessening the severity of air pollution in core locales, although the area over which a smog blanket rests appears to be broadening. Each area is growing in terms of automobile ownership, total driving and the emission of greenhouse gases (GHGs). The major road corridors throughout the region are experiencing congestion due to insufficient development of public transportation – local and intercity – and an over-reliance on trucks for freight movement. The region's airports are also suffering inefficiencies due to over-use by commuter or short-haul carriers, which could be replaced by improved intercity passenger rail. In recent years there has been an attempt to unite the three cities with a high speed passenger rail system, to decrease border delays for passengers and freight, to increase economic cooperation and to increase the ratio of freight carried on rail (Discovery Institute, nd). There are also, however, many traditional and contemporary differences among the three cities and regions, which become clear upon examination of data from the three regions.[1]

Comparison of Data for the Three Cities and Regions

The data for this chapter for Vancouver and Portland have mostly come from Kenworthy et al (1999), with some updating to more recent years through direct contact with authorities in each city. Seattle data have been collected as a separate exercise from authorities in the region in order to complete the picture for the Cascadia area.[2]

Population

Table 21.1 sets out data on population for the three cities and region from 1970 to 1990. Each city, which forms the core part of its respective region, has a population of approximately 500,000. Each suffered a marginal decline in population due to demographic changes and suburban exodus in the 1960s and 1970s. Unlike Vancouver or Portland, Seattle has not yet returned to its 1970 population level. Because of its vast area it should be noted that the population of the non-urbanized and undeveloped portion of the Seattle region is considerably larger than in the other metropolitan regions.

Table 21.1 *Population in the three cities and regions, 1970 to the mid-1990s*

Cities	1970	1980	1990	Mid-1990s
City of Portland	379,967	366, 383	437,319	497,600
City of Seattle	551,339	493,846	516,259	532,900
City of Vancouver	429,795	417,955	478,052	508,814
Whole regions				
Portland region	878,676	1,050,367	1,174,291	1,341,700
Seattle region	1,934,500	2,240,400	2,748,900	3,101,100
Vancouver region	1,082,187	1,268,183	1,610,899	1,831,665
Developed areas				
Portland urbanized area	824,926	1,026,144	1,172,158	1,193,500
Seattle urbanized area	1,238,107	1,391,535	1,744,086	1,933,300
Vancouver urbanized area	1,028,320	1,170,015	1,542,933	1,815,317

Source: Kenworthy et al (1999)
Note: mid–1990s data all refer to 1997 except for Vancouver region, which is 1996 (census data for CMA); cities of Portland and Seattle, which are 1995; and city of Vancouver, which is 1994. Decennial Vancouver data are for 1971, 1981 and 1991

Area and population density

In terms of area and population density the three cities are slightly more difficult to compare. While the city of Portland is considerably larger in area than the others, it also has one of the highest ratios of parks and public lands within its limits in western North America. It has also annexed some relatively low density areas in recent years, which are steadily increasing. The boundaries of the city of Seattle and city of Vancouver have remained unchanged for decades. The gross density and urban density of the city of Vancouver are considerably higher than those of the other two cities, which helps to account for some of the transportation differences discussed later in this chapter. Reasons for this difference will also become apparent.

The three regions are slightly more difficult to compare. Portland defines itself quite tightly as the tri-county area of Multnomah, Washington and Clackamas counties (some definitions also include Clark County in Washington State), Vancouver's region (the Greater Vancouver Regional District) contains significant agricultural land reserve tracts, and Seattle's four-county region of King, Snohomish, Pierce and Kitsap contains many areas of agriculture and forestry and settlement remote to its urban and suburban centres. Because such metropolitan region boundaries are set quite arbitrarily, the only way to compare them accurately is on the basis of their urbanized land areas. Table 21.2 contains these data for 1990. One is immediately struck by the density of development in the Vancouver region, which is almost double that of Seattle and Portland.

Table 21.2 *Area and density data for the three cities in 1990*

	Total area (km²)	Gross population density	Urban area (per km²)	Urban density (per km²)
Cities:				
City of Portland	370	1345	131	2370
City of Seattle	217	2376	185	2874
City of Vancouver	131	3649	106	4150
Regions:				
Portland region	7958	168	1005	1170
Seattle region	16,292	190	1523	1145
Vancouver region	2905	555	741	2082

Source: Kenworthy et al (1999)

Note: The urban area and urban density data for the city of Portland and city of Vancouver refer to the inner area of the regions, which in the case of Vancouver corresponds closely to the city of Vancouver, and in the case of Portland incorporates a significant portion of the urbanized part of the city of Portland (for precise definition see Kenworthy et al, 1999)

Housing

Multi-family housing, whether in the form of townhouses, apartments or condominium units, represents a more efficient use of urban space than does single-family detached housing. The Portland and Seattle regions maintain a pattern of having one-third or less of housing as multi-family units (attached wall, townhomes, apartments, condominiums, etc). The Vancouver region has decreased significantly its ratio of single- to multi-family units from 56 per cent in 1980 to 45 per cent in recent years, with the result that higher density housing now dominates the housing stock in the region. By contrast (Table 21.3), Seattle and Portland have essentially maintained the same high ratio of single- to multi-family housing. Much of the increase in multi-family housing has been in the city of Vancouver where some very large redevelopments such as at False Creek have occurred, as well as extensive re-urbanization throughout the city, discussed later in this chapter.

Employment

Each region and each city has been experiencing significant, if not dramatic, increases in employment. While each region has been experiencing employment growth at about the same rate of population growth, the cities and the central business districts (CBDs)

Table 21.3 *Patterns of single and multiple-family housing in the three metropolitan regions in 1980 and 1997*

Region	1980 (thousands)				1997 (thousands)			
	Single	Multiple	Total	Ratio	Single	Multiple	Total	Ratio
Portland region	265	132	397	0.67	394	165	559	0.70
Seattle region	643	252	895	0.72	893	405	1298	0.69
Vancouver region	244	192	436	0.56	316	393	709	0.45

Source: Kenworthy et al (1999)
Note: data for Vancouver are for 1981, not 1980

have not been gaining employment as at rapid a pace as their surrounding regions (Table 21.4).

However, as can be seen from the data, the inner areas of each region continue to grow in absolute terms and contain significant proportions of metropolitan jobs. In 1990 the city of Portland contained 55 per cent of jobs (this had dropped to 46 per cent by 1997), Seattle 33 per cent and Vancouver 41 per cent of jobs. This concentration and growth of work and population (see Table 21.1) in more traditional transit and walking-based parts of the regions remain important in shaping transportation patterns in favour of transit and non-motorized modes. Indeed, globalization appears to be strengthening the growth in higher paid jobs linked to the global economy in favour of more vital and interactive locations such as traditional inner and central areas of cities, while lower paid employment such as in service industries is tending to locate in more auto-oriented outer areas. The renewed popularity of central and inner areas as residential locations seems at least in part to be linked to globalization processes (Newman, Kenworthy and Laube, 1997; Newman and Kenworthy, 1998).

Central business district

Each city has a compact, well defined CBD. Table 21.5 shows that each has a relatively small and moderately rising resident population within the CBD, except for Vancouver whose residential character shows through with a much larger population contained in its West End area, which merges with the core CBD. The CBDs of Portland and Vancouver each contain about 15 per cent of the region's jobs. The Seattle CBD accounts for only 8 per cent of its region's employment. Each is trying to increase residents in, or adjacent to, the CBD. Vancouver's West End development, a highly mixed use part of its central area, comprises some 40,000 residents. It is the most successful of these efforts, along with the very densely populated False Creek redevelopment area, directly opposite, but not in the CBD, which houses over 10,000 people.

Parking supply and pricing are two of the most prominent factors affecting the choice of mode for the journey to work. While all three cities have been increasing the absolute supply of downtown parking, Seattle displays the greatest rate of increase and the highest ratio relative to employment, though parking supply relative to jobs dropped from 1970 to 1980 and remained stable from 1980 to 1990. Seattle's overall downtown strategy, however, appears to be inviting more automobile traffic through increased parking availability. Portland, on the other hand, has diminished its supply of CBD parking per 1000 jobs over the 20-year period from 1970 to 1990 (571 to 403

Table 21.4 *Patterns of employment distribution in the three regions, 1970 to the mid-1990s*

	1970	1980	1990	Mid-1990s
Portland jobs				
Portland CBD	59,039	88,917	100,872	103,000
City of Portland		372,000	417,000	430,000
Portland region	392,628	599,885	750,779	943,978
Seattle jobs				
Seattle CBD	73,161	84,651	117,252	
City of Seattle	310,286	386,684	469,802	
Seattle region	740,927	1,033,407	1,445,243	1,761,900
Vancouver jobs				
Vancouver CBD	94,758	124,239	116,800	
City of Vancouver	232,238	292,907	321,450	
Vancouver region	394,204	632,191	792,485	950,000

Source: Kenworthy et al (1999)
Note: CBD and city data for Portland in the last column refer to 1994. All other data in this column refer to 1997. The Vancouver CBD includes the West End

Table 21.5 *Characteristics of the CBD in each of the three regions, 1970 to 1990*

CBD characteristic	1970	1980	1990
Area of the CBD (ha)			
Portland	280	280	280
Seattle	196	196	196
Vancouver	531	531	531
Population of the CBD			
Portland	8234	8219	9528
Seattle	5630	6045	6785
Vancouver	44,100	43,210	45,825
Off-street and on-street parking spaces in the CBD			
Portland	38,803	37,644	41,861
Seattle	41,500	41,000	56,863
Vancouver	28,819	37,755	46,053
Parking spaces per 1000 CBD jobs			
Portland	571	423	403
Seattle	560	480	480
Vancouver	341	342	443
Transit use to CBD jobs			
Portland			40.5%
Seattle			38.0%
Vancouver			37.0%

Source: Kenworthy et al (1999)

per 1000 jobs) in line with its cap on CBD parking supply, while jobs in the CBD have almost doubled. Vancouver's CBD parking per 1000 jobs rose more sharply from 1980 to 1990 due to a combination of extra parking supply and an apparent (and probably temporary) loss of jobs from this area.

Each CBD enjoys approximately the same ratio of transit ridership for the commuter. However, Vancouver is reaping the benefits of downtown residential development through a rate of non-motorized commuting to the CBD more than double that of either Seattle or Portland (10.3 per cent compared with around 5 per cent).

Motorization

The differences between Vancouver city and region and the neighbouring US cities and regions emerge dramatically in regard to motor vehicle ownership and driving (Table 21.6). The US regions have rates of vehicle ownership and driving fully one-third higher than that of the Canadian region. In comparing the cities of Portland and Seattle, there is a slightly greater amount of driving within Seattle than within Portland, and residents of these two cities own and drive cars at approximately double the rate of the Vancouver dwellers. While the paradox of higher vehicle ownership and driving rates for city dwellers in Portland and Seattle may be partially explained by demographic factors, such as the larger household size in the suburbs, it is noteworthy that the data on vehicle ownership and driving are in the expected direction when comparing city and suburb dwellers in the Vancouver region: city dwellers own fewer cars and drive considerably less than their suburban counterparts. Stated in another way, US cities may be more like suburbs than 'real' cities, while Canadian cities are more like traditional cities in their transportation behaviour. Raad and Kenworthy (1998) have discussed some fundamental physical differences between US and Canadian cities in more detail, as well as the underlying planning and political reasons behind them.

Table 21.6 *Vehicle ownership and car use in the three regions, 1990 and 1997*

Transportation characteristic	1990	1997
Total motor vehicles per 1000 people		
City of Portland	1040	
City of Seattle	1040	
City of Vancouver	560	
Portland region	849	770
Seattle region	790	790
Vancouver region	694	570
Annual total private vehicle travel per capita (vehicle km)		
City of Portland	11,498	
City of Seattle	12,556	
City of Vancouver	5950	
Portland region	11,238	12,673
Seattle region	11,918	14,448
Vancouver region	8750	9110

Source: Kenworthy et al (1999)

The other crucial point to note from the data in Table 21.6 is the rate of growth in driving in US cities between 1990 and 1997. This has clearly continued apace in the US cities, with Seattle growing by 2530km per capita in only 7 years (a 21 per cent increase) while Portland's growth was less at 1435km or 13 per cent, in response to its more positive land use and transit developments through the 1990s (see policy discussion). By contrast, however, total travel per capita only rose by 360km per capita in Vancouver (4 per cent), which reinforces the even more positive land use and transportation evolution of the Vancouver region.

Transit

The differences between the three regions and their cities also emerge dramatically in regard to transit ridership. Portland's total transit ridership is growing, especially since the introduction of the MAX light rail line, while Seattle's transit ridership is stagnant. Vancouver's total transit ridership grew significantly following the opening of its Skytrain service and has stabilized in recent years. Citizens in the Vancouver region take twice as many transit trips per year as those in the Portland region and three times as many as those in the Seattle region.

Table 21.7 *Transit characteristics in each of the three regions, 1980 and 1990*

Transit characteristic	1980	1990	Mid-1990s
Passenger boardings (millions)			
Portland region	48.5	54.2	69.0
Seattle region	87.4	103.9	118.8
Vancouver region	133.2	180.8	226.0
Transit trips per capita per year			
Portland region	46	46	52
Seattle region	39	38	38
Vancouver region	114	117	119
Proportion of all commuters using transit (%)			
Portland region	8.6	5.8	
Seattle region	7.9	6.0	
Vancouver region		12.4	
City of Portland	16.0	11.5	
City of Seattle	19.7	15.9	
City of Vancouver		24.0	
Farebox recovery of operating costs			
Portland region		23%	
Seattle region		22%	
Vancouver region		52%	

Notes: 1: Seattle region 1980, 1990 and 1996 transit use and cost is based on Washington State Department of Transport Public Transport Rail Division reports including walk-on ferry passengers. 1980 walk-ons were estimated at 4,000,000. 2: Vancouver region 1980 data are for 1981, 1990 are for 1991, and mid-1990s are for financial year 1998. 3: Portland region mid-1990s data are for financial year 1998

For the journey to work, commuters in the Vancouver region are twice as likely to choose transit than those in the Portland or Seattle regions. Vancouver city residents are also one-and-a-half to two times as likely to commute by transit as Seattleites or Portlanders. The greater use of transit by Vancouverites also leads to lower net transit costs; Vancouver transit recovers more than half of its operating expenses at the farebox, while Seattle and Portland each recover slightly less than one-quarter.

Non-motorized transport

In North America, where the car is king and queen (Schiller and Bruun, 1995), data on non-motorized travel are very difficult to obtain. Nevertheless, data in this chapter appear to indicate that a small though significant number of persons in each region commute by a non-motorized mode. In the three regions in 1990, between 3.9 per cent and 5.7 per cent of commuters walked or cycled to work (Table 21.8). The city of Seattle (10 per cent) has a very progressive programme to encourage walking, bicycling and transit for commuters to its large urban university (college students are counted as commuters in US transportation statistics), and it leads Vancouver (8.5 per cent) and Portland (7 per cent), although trend data (not shown here) indicate that the ratio of commuters who put feet first is falling in the Seattle region and only remaining flat in the city of Seattle itself. As indicated previously, the ratio of commuters walking to CBD employment in Vancouver is approximately double that of either Seattle or Portland – an important indicator of the success of Vancouver's programme to encourage residential development nearby.

Table 21.8 *Non-motorized mode use for the journey to work in the three regions, 1990*

Proportion of work commutes on foot and bike (%)	1990
City of Portland	7.0
City of Seattle	10.0
City of Vancouver	8.5
Portland region	3.9
Seattle region	5.5
Vancouver region	5.7

Note: City of Vancouver data are 1992 and the Vancouver region 1991

Discussion: Policy Climate

Portland

Portland demonstrates many of the conflicts that have beset US cities in the post-World War Two era: dispersed low density development with separation of residential and other uses, an excessive emphasis on single-family dwellings, and road expansion and travel patterns that are difficult to address with public transport. But Portland has benefited from a long tradition of civic engagement shared among business leaders, elected officials and residents organized in dozens of neighbourhood associations, which shape planning and policy reactively and pro-actively. Portland also benefits from the state of Oregon's progressive land use policies, which have fostered the creation of urban growth boundaries separating rural and urban areas. This policy, together with pro-residential development policies, a long standing cap on growth in CBD parking, priority to public transport access and a fine urban design programme, has promoted the vitality of Portland's CBD. The urban growth boundaries have limited some of the destructiveness of urban sprawl.

Like most other US cities, Portland engaged in a freeway building binge in the 1950s and 1960s. Portlanders in the 1970s reacted by cancelling plans to expand freeways. Rather than build a freeway extension to a suburb (the Mount Hood Freeway to Gresham, which would have destroyed 3000 homes), they used the money to build a light rail line (MAX). Along with the other innovations mentioned above, they created a transit mall and light rail loop in the heart of downtown and replaced a downtown freeway segment with a waterfront park (naming it in honour of the Republican governor, Tom McCall, who had led Oregon into urban growth boundaries).

Portland's previously lacklustre bus system was reorganized during the planning of its first light rail line and its performance has improved since light rail has been implemented. This included creation of generous bus-only lanes in the downtown area, together with greatly improved bus stops in the central city. City government has recently completed a low and modest income housing project downtown without parking spaces – virtually unheard of in US housing planning. Portlanders, originally rather cautious about light rail transit, voted for a major extension, the Westside Line, which opened in September 1998, and this has been attracting 23,000 daily riders in its first few months of operation. Portland has recently completed a new indoor sports arena adjacent to an existing one that will be kept in operation. No new parking has been added since both are adjacent to an expanding light rail line.

While there appears to be considerable consensus among regional leaders that transit (especially light rail), non-motorized mode improvements and land use design that supports these should guide local and regional planning, public support has become more divided, especially in the suburbs in the past two years. Urban growth boundaries have weathered several challenges but – unfortunately – two recent votes, one statewide and the other regional, have resulted in narrow defeats for a proposed north–south light rail extension. It appears that an inflammatory pro-highway/anti-transit minority has combined with well funded pro-sprawl and anti-tax interests in these instances. Shortly after the defeat of the November 1998 rail extension initiative was announced, one of its major opponents circulated a message condemning light rail supporters as 'dark siders' and 'the forces of evil', and boasting how their anti-rail advertisements had successfully linked MAX with the Monica Lewinsky matter: 'One of our best radio spots was a Bill Clinton impersonator saying "You think we tell whoppers in Washington [DC]. You should hear the whoppers those light rail people are saying in Portland, Oregon"' (Zucker, 1998). The Portland 'whoppers' referred to are statements in support of the light rail project's benefits. These same 'forces of good and light' (but not 'light' rail) are curiously silent when asked to specify their own transportation improvement plan – perhaps because it is more highways and more traffic. Whether or not a more informed discussion will take place in the near future before another vote is not clear at this moment.

In recent years Portland has enjoyed acclaim from US planners and environmentalists engaged in growth management and transportation efforts as a model to emulate. As the regional data compiled for this chapter indicate, while there are a few positive trends in Portland some of its acclaim may not be fully warranted. Most of its positive image seems to stem from its revitalized downtown area. Over some 20 years it has been transformed into a transit-oriented, human scale, green and attractive environment, which presently accounts for some 30 per cent of metropolitan retail turnover, up from 5 per cent in the 1970s. The way in which considerable new development has focused on the light rail line is also a strong feature of Portland's reputation. Most other US cities can only boast freeway-led development. Nevertheless, the region as a whole has some way to go before it begins to claw back its high automobile dependence and comparatively low transit use per capita.

One problem frustrating transportation planning in Portland is the extent to which Clark County, immediately to its north on the Washington State side of the Columbia River, is acting as a 'sprawl relief valve' for Portland. Washington State has only recently instituted growth management legislation and it will probably be years, if not decades, before its effects are felt. Homeowners in search of cul-de-sac ranchettes and three-car garages have been drawn there. Although a large percentage of Clark County commuters clog two bridges to Portland, in 1996 they rejected substantially a very reasonable plan to link Clark County to Portland with a new light rail line.

Seattle

An adage oft-heard around Seattle is that 'while Los Angeles developed and perfected the freeway, Seattle developed and perfected the shopping mall!' Neither assertion is completely accurate, yet there is more than a grain of truth in Seattle's attachment to sprawled development, of which the shopping mall is the centrepiece. Like Portland, Seattle once had ambitious plans to cover its city and area with freeways and bypasses. Like Portland, Seattle's citizens arose in anger after experiencing the first fruits of freewaydom, and forced local officials to curtail future freeways and limit expansions of existing ones. But Seattle was not able to cross the threshold as was Portland; it was not able to substitute a rail transit improvement for its last significant freeway expansion.

Seattle made great strides in the 1970s-era reorganization and rationalization of its bus transit system. It expanded its use of electrified buses in the city at the same time as sending buses out over a vast suburban area. It succeeded in transporting an admirable share of those commuting to and from downtown. But, despite the building of a costly downtown bus transit tunnel, recent years have witnessed faltering ridership not keeping pace with population and job growth, and falling significantly behind the rate of increase of car travel. A three-county proposal approved by voters in 1996 will concentrate light rail in a relatively short (given the expansiveness of the region) and extremely expensive tunnel and grade-separated segment in one Seattle corridor. A limited commuter rail service will be put into operation on existing tracks. The same plan will expend transit funds to build expensive HOV (high occupancy vehicle – transit and carpool) ramps and interchanges in the suburbs despite admonitions that such facilities generally do not work well for transit (Leman, Schiller and Pauly, 1994; Schiller, 1998). The transit plan will provide some much needed improvements; its new light rail line will likely attract good ridership, but at an enormous price and with limited regional coverage. The city of Seattle and the surrounding region appear to lack the leadership in transit improvements found in Portland. Years in advance of the construction of the light rail system, Seattle's downtown business leaders are warning the city against creating a surface bus mall once the current transit tunnel is converted to exclusive rail use because it might interfere with automobile access to downtown.

While Seattle has been a leader in the provision of pedestrian and bicycle facilities, and in some aspects of neighbourhood traffic calming and university transit pass programmes, it is still a difficult town for walking; fully one-third of its streets lack sidewalks. In 1995 Seattle's former mayor, Norm Rice, campaigned strenuously among his constituents for the reopening for motor vehicles of a one-block pedestrianized downtown street at the behest of Nordstrom's, a major retail interest. The city also rewarded the retailer with a twelve-storey, US$73 million 1200 stall parking garage (atop the downtown transit tunnel) paid for in large part by public funds, which had been intended to improve housing for low income families. Seattle is talking of focusing development in 'urban villages' and strengthening commercial areas. Unfortunately, many of the proposals are on such a vast scale and at such considerable cost that voters quickly become wary, resulting in their rejection (Schiller, 1994). Meanwhile, inexpensive and cost-effective extensions to highly popular and well used pedestrian and bicycle facilities are languishing.

The region's leaders are also preparing an additional costly runway for SeaTac Airport, while ignoring the extent to which an improved intercity passenger rail system and improved management of the current airport could divert many air passengers from the short distance and commuter flights to rail. Such flights consume 40 per cent of the airport's operations, a pattern common to US airports. Seattle is presently constructing two new large sports stadia. Both are much larger facilities than those in Portland, and both will entail parking expansions. Meanwhile, a moderate pace of road expansion continues.

Vancouver

Vancouver has benefited from a Canadian planning tradition that has been influenced by European thinking to a far greater extent than either Seattle or Portland. Vancouver and its region have chosen to strengthen central areas, whether in the city or in outlying cities (see Raad and Kenworthy, 1998). The extent of this commitment can be seen in the fact that since 1976, the population of the city-core of the region rose from 413,700 to 476,378 in 1991, the majority of that increase (41,626) occurring in just five years between 1986 and 1991. Much of the new housing to accommodate these population increases has occurred in urban village-style settings such as False Creek, where no motorized traffic is permitted through the housing area. Parking is underground and car access is from the rear. As a consequence, such developments are built on walkways and cycleways and are set within extensive gardens and natural areas, with local facilities such as shopping and entertainment only a short walk or ride away. Older areas near downtown, such as the West End, while built on a traditional street grid, offer excellent environments for walking and cycling because of the generous sidewalks, landscaped streets and short distances to extensive mixed uses lining the main streets. Small parks and gardens have been created by closing short sections of many streets. Electric trolley buses run every 6–8 minutes because of the high demand and provide a viable alternative for longer trips.

Suburban town centres are well defined, and many public facilities and amenities such as sidewalks and pedestrian signals are located in them as a matter of practice. Vancouver has electrified many of its bus routes within the city, and plans transit services that emphasize and strengthen its arterial grid system. As implied above, Vancouver has also planned its street and zoning system in order to foster commercial and mixed use development along arterials well served by transit adjacent to residential areas. Vancouver, unlike its neighbours to the south, has not allowed freeway construction within its city limits. It appears to be following a Toronto model of urban redevelopment; it is expanding the number of residents living in or near its centre, intensifying mixed use development and improving transit services for developed areas, rather than spreading transit services more thinly into less dense suburbs.

Indeed, the Vancouver region is strongly punctuated by high density, mixed use nodes of development at stations all along the Skytrain line. High-rise apartments and condominiums are built very close to the stations together with a variety of shops, workplaces and other facilities. Still within walking or cycling distance of stations, there are a range of other medium and low-rise compact housing projects and less intense mixed land uses. Each station has an effective bus interchange with many services feeding into it, and cycling to stations is encouraged through the provision of dedicated cycleways and locker facilities. The new urban development at station precincts such as Joyce, Patterson, Metrotown, Edmonds and New Westminster provide substantial demonstration projects of the way to exploit the land use advantages of investments in transit and how to make transit, walking and cycling central to the life of an area. They also show how this change towards transit-focused growth can be a very rapid process (Skytrain was only opened in 1986).

Since it was opened, Skytrain has been extended, and at present there is controversy over whether future rail transit extensions should be in the form of Skytrain or less costly light rail. The nature of this controversy is considerably different from many localities in the USA where rail transit in general is quite controversial. Unlike some transit planning in the USA, the planning system in Vancouver is firmly geared towards the creation of compact residential, mixed use, low auto use environments. Therefore, while there is still suburban sprawl, it is less dominant than in US cities. The popularity of transit and rail extensions, the provision and encouragement of non-motorized transportation and the effective integration of urban development and transportation planning indicate that Vancouver is the best prepared of the three cities and regions to develop more sustainable transportation should the will, leadership and determination to build on existing achievements be forthcoming.

Conclusions

In the Cascadia region, Vancouver seems to be leading in terms of sustainable transportation planning and practice. It also demonstrates how change can take place in a relatively short period of time given a favourable political and planning environment. Portland appears to offer some hope, especially in terms of planning directions and some of its transit practices as well as its commitment to an urban growth boundary and a healthy, liveable central area. Despite a relatively low urban density it has been able to increase its transit ridership significantly in the past decade. Seattle began the attempt to manage growth and integrate land use and transportation planning many years after its neighbours to the north and south. Its regional planning organization (the Puget Sound Regional Council) has developed much expertise in the area of transit and pedestrian-oriented development but lacks implementation authority. Despite having a population density considerably greater than that of Portland, Seattle has not been increasing its transit ridership. While there is proven success of neighbourhood traffic calming, bicycling and university transit pass programmes in the city, and an occasional bright pedestrian spot in the suburbs (such as the older suburb of Kirkland), Seattle seems to be going in the wrong direction in terms of many transportation performance measures. It seems to be unable to develop the political will to move progressive plans into practice – or even the consensus necessary to speak the language of sustainable transportation. Whether Seattle can be a 'late bloomer' or whether it is closing the stable door after the horse of sprawl and automobile dependency has fully bolted is uncertain.

Bright spots on the sustainable transport horizon of Cascadia include the friendly reception being afforded to proposals, led by Seattle and Washington State, to significantly upgrade the intercity passenger and freight rail system linking the three regions, and Vancouver's commitment to fund a new light rail system. Perhaps these will help generate sufficient enthusiasm for related improvements in public transportation and supportive land use practices in those parts of the region most heavily afflicted by automobile dependency.

Notes

1   This chapter was first published as a paper in *World Transport Policy & Practice*, vol 5, no 1, pp30–38.
2   The authors would like to express their appreciation to the following persons for their assistance in locating information for this article. Portland: David Horowitz, Bob Knight, Andrea Drury, Meeky Blizzard, Nancy Jarigese; Seattle: Norman Abbott, Ned Conroy, Bob Harvey, Nancy Tosta, Paul Gamble, Ray Deardorf, Leroy Chadwick; Vancouver: Clark Lim, Ryan So, Karoly Krajczar and Ross Long. All interpretations and conclusions are those of the authors.

References

Callenbach, E (1975) *Ecotopia: The Notebooks and Reports of William Weston Banyon*, Tree Books, Berkeley
Centre for Sustainable Transportation (1998) *Sustainable Transportation Monitor*, no 1, The Centre for Sustainable Transportation/Le Centre pour un Transport Durable, Toronto

Discovery Institute (ongoing) *Cascadia Project and Various Published Papers and Conference Proceedings, 1994–1998*, Discovery Institute, Seattle, http://www.discovery.org

Gakenheimer, R (ed) (1978) *The Automobile and the Environment: An International Perspective,* MIT Press, Cambridge, MA

Kenworthy, J R, Laube, F and Newman, P (1999*) An International Sourcebook of Automobile Dependence in Cities 1960–1990,* University Press of Colorado, Boulder

Leman, C K, Schiller, P L and Pauly, K (1994) *Re-thinking HOV: High Occupancy Vehicle Facilities and the Public Interest,* Chesapeake Bay Foundation, Annapolis

Newman, P W G and Kenworthy, J R (1989) *Cities and Automobile Dependence: An International Sourcebook,* Gower Publishing, Aldershot and Brookfield

Newman, P W G and Kenworthy, J R (1998) *Sustainability and Cities: Overcoming Automobile Dependence,* Island Press, Washington, DC

Newman, P W G, Kenworthy, J R and Laube, F (1997) *The Global City and Sustainability – Perspectives from Australian Cities and a Survey of 37 Global Cities*, presented at the Fifth International Workshop on Technological Change and Urban Form, 18–20 June, Jakarta

OECD (nd) *Environmentally Sustainable Transport,* Organisation for Economic Co-operation and Development, Paris

Puget Sound Regional Council (1998), *Cascadia Metropolitan Forum*, Puget Sound Regional Council, Seattle

Raad, T and Kenworthy, J R (1998) 'The US and us', *Alternatives Journal,* vol 24, no 1, pp14–22

Replogle, M (1995) 'What's sustainable?' in Zielinski, S and Laird, G (eds) *Beyond the Car: Essays on the Auto Culture,* Steel Rail Publishing/Transportation Options, Toronto

Schiller, P L (1994) *Transportation and Trade in the Corridor,* proceedings of the Georgia Basin–Puget Sound–Willamette Valley Building Bridges to Sustainable Communities International Conference, Western Washington University, Bellingham

Schiller, P L (1998) 'High occupancy vehicle (HOV) lanes: highway expansions in search of meaning', *World Transport Policy & Practice,* vol 4, no 2, pp32–38

Schiller, P L and Bruun, E C (1995) 'Learning and unlearning the car culture', *Urban Transport International,* no 2, pp20–21

Spaethling, D (1995) *Sustainable Transportation in the United States: An Examination of the Institutional Framework,* Federal Highway Administration, USDOT/Department of City and Regional Planning, University of Pennsylvania, Philadelphia

Stringer, P and Wenzel, H (eds) (1976) *Transportation Planning for a Better Environment,* Plenum Press, New York

Wixey, S and Lake, S (1998) 'Transport policy in the EU: a strategy for sustainable development?', *World Transport Policy & Practice,* vol 4, no 2, pp17–21

Zucker, M Y (1998) personal communication, 5 November, Portland

Part 8

Transport in the Middle East

22

Transport in the Middle East

Elaine Fletcher

Since antiquity, the Middle East has been a land bridge between Europe and Asia and Europe and Africa. Ancient roads running through this region carried countless armies on campaigns of conquest, as well as pilgrims to the holy sites of Jerusalem and Bethlehem, Mecca and Medina. Historically, therefore, the roads and transport systems that developed not only sought the safest and easiest geographical path through often difficult mountain and desert terrain, but they also served another goal. These same roads were important tools for preserving control over a region whose strategic and religious assets were the object of chronic rivalry and contest between regional powers and colonial empires. Particularly in the late 19th and early 20th century, extensive new railroads, asphalt highways and water roads, such as the Suez Canal, were designed and built with an eye to the geo-political needs of European governments or local rulers and dynasties under their protection and sponsorship.

Thus the Ottoman rulers of the late 19th century, and subsequent British and French mandate administrators, invested in an extensive regional rail network extending through Palestine and Lebanon, Egypt, Trans Jordan and Arabia in order to consolidate their power base and move men and materials in times of war. Subsequently, the early Zionist founders of Israel created an independent bus system to compete with the rail network, then perceived as a symbol of British colonial power in Mandate Palestine. Until today, buses are the dominant form of public transportation in modern-day Israel.

While development was often a byproduct of such transport projects, the needs of local populations were largely a secondary consideration to the *realpolitik* of transport planning decisions. Today, countries in the region continue to struggle with that legacy as they face a new millennium in which regional ethnic and religious conflicts still simmer, arable land and water resources are being rapidly degraded or diminished, and population growth rates are higher than almost anywhere else in the world.

Fifty years after the founding of the Israeli state, much of the grinding political battle between Israel and the Palestinian Authority takes place around road networks. Similarly, Israel has built an extensive network of so-called bypass roads in the West Bank to cement its control over some 200 West Bank settlements, at the same time bypassing existing Arab Palestinian villages. The network is bitterly resented by the Palestinian Authority, and Palestinian guerillas constantly carry out bloody attacks along the road arteries, transforming roads into a front line of military conflict. Inside pre-1967 Israel, meanwhile, the state is building a massive trans-Israel highway that was originally conceived as a means of boosting Jewish settlement in areas of the country bordering the Palestinian West Bank.

But even in Middle East regions and societies where political conflicts may be less acute, transport systems largely serve to underline and reinforce the deep and pervasive social gap that still exists between urban and rural populations, between the elites or middle classes and the masses of poor.

In a region awash with oil, and obsessed with Western symbols of status, the middle classes and the elites have found a simple solution to their day-to-day transport needs – the automobile, driven by a chauffeur if one's budget allows. Middle class women in particular, whose mobility is largely limited by social constraints, may feel uncomfortable travelling by any means other than a car, which may frequently be driven by a husband, uncle or brother. For many of those women, a driver's licence is a symbol of hard-won independence and new-found equality.

In peasant and rural societies, roads may be poorly maintained or virtually non-existent – unless they serve some larger aim such as connection to an air base, seawater port, etc. In such regions animal and pedestrian transport is still a common means of movement. Among the urban masses, bus and service taxi transport systems are the most common means of mass transport. But they are often poorly organized and maintained: 'Unlike many of the other countries of the world, the number of buses in Jordan is relatively low, and buses are not considered a major or popular transport mode' (Al-Suleiman and Al-Masaeid, 1992).

In addition, urban commuter rail and light rail systems are largely non-existent – the investments required for such endeavours are a low priority among the governments of the region, who are more concerned with their defence budgets than internal development. Even in Israel, which boasts the most affluent and westernized economy in the region, the planning of light rail systems for Tel Aviv and Jerusalem is only just now beginning to advance seriously, and Cairo, with a population of 8.5 million, is the only major city in the Middle East to host a subway system.

In both Egypt and Israel some remnants of the old British and Ottoman inter-urban rail systems still survive. Rail links Cairo with the Nile River destinations of Upper Egypt such as Luxor. In traffic-clogged Israel newly renovated rail lines running between Tel Aviv, Haifa and Beersheba are drawing record numbers of passengers.

But for the most part the great regional rail systems of the past that crisscrossed the Middle East region have been abandoned; their decaying tracks are a symbol of the region's political rivalry and official indifference. Regardless of the controversy over Jerusalem's political status, the fact that the city's rail link has been inoperative for several years is one more ironic comment on the low priority accorded to the rail system in the region.

It comes as no surprise, therefore, that the past two decades have seen the rapid construction of new inter-urban roads to accommodate the growing demand for the automobile. Highways lace modern city centres with little regard for non-motorized transport modes, such as bicycles and pedestrians. In terms of longer regional hauls or international journeys, airline links have replaced the old regional rail system, facilitating travel across international borders or across distances that are too great to be efficiently served by automobiles. But usually such airports serve little more than a select group of elites. An extreme example of this phenomenon is the Palestinian airport in Gaza, which opened several years ago with much ado because it also served as a symbol of Palestinian independence. But in fact the fragile airport connection, entirely under Israeli control, has done little to facilitate Palestinian travel between Gaza, the West Bank, Egypt and Jordan for more than a select few VIPs. A series of efficient rail links would have served the purpose of mass movements of goods and people far more efficiently.

The explosion of roads and vehicle transport modes has other far-reaching consequences for cities in the region. This is an era in which the Middle East, like other developing world regions, has witnessed a migration of rural agricultural populations to cities, drastically over-loading urban infrastructures. In Marrakech, Morocco, for instance, urban planners have bemoaned the demise of the city's green parks and oases, which once tempered the surrounding desert climate. The development of urban roads and highways – instead of more land-efficient pedestrian and rail alternatives – has only added to the dust and asphalt tones of urban life in such arid locales. In relatively new cities, such as Amman, Jordan, which developed primarily over the last century, cars and large highways have so profoundly shaped the ambience and infrastructure of the urban core that pedestrian activity is very slight, even in daytime, and cyclists are an even rarer sight.

In contrast, in older Middle Eastern city centres such as downtown Cairo, a traditional pedestrian ambience still survives, most markedly in districts that are home to traditional covered Middle Eastern *souks* or marketplaces. In days past, such *souks* served as the pulse of city life, and today they remain pedestrian paradises, an indigenous counterpoint to the shopping mall. Still, outside the defined limits of such areas, pedestrians must compete with the automobile on unequal terms. In Cairo, traffic lights, directional signs and sidewalks are almost non-existent; street crossings can be fatal.

Despite such problems, the limited efforts that are undertaken to re-pedestrianize ancient Arab urban areas often meet with local resistance among residents who may see walking as a sign of backwardness. Such was the case in Bethlehem in the West Bank, when the Palestinian Authority sought to renovate the city's ancient town centre in preparation for millennium celebrations, and close off several quarters around the famous Church of the Nativity to traffic. Although the renovations were completed nonetheless in time for the famous visit of Pope John Paul II in March 2000, the long term success of the redevelopment plan was predicated on the assumption that the area would become a popular tourist attraction. That scenario so far has failed to materialize due to the outbreak of renewed hostilities between Israelis and Palestinians in October 2000.

Amongst the countries of the region, it is in Israel, perhaps, where the awareness regarding the potential of green transport alternatives is most highly developed. Fledgling environmental movements have studied the experiences of European cities, and are actively pressing for greater government investment in rail travel, pedestrian and cycling networks, and fighting the expansion of new roads and highways.

However, here as elsewhere in the region, there is still little popular awareness at the grassroots or in government corridors as to how sustainable transport system development might be a useful tool for promoting urban quality of life or social equity.

Conversely, there is little understanding as to how new road development may reinforce existing social gaps by spurring a vicious cycle of accelerating car ownership and inappropriate land use development whereby new housing, educational and business centres develop along a US-style suburban model, accessible mostly to car-owning elites.

To use Israel and the Palestinian West Bank as case studies, it is noteworthy that in the West Bank, meanwhile, the number of Palestinian vehicles has increased more than ten-fold, from only 12,964 vehicles in 1975 to 133,386 vehicles in 1996. However, only about 23.2 per cent of Palestinian households today own cars.

Between the late 1980s and the late 1990s, the number of automobiles in Israel nearly doubled to over 234 cars per 1000 inhabitants, and car ownership is projected to reach 450 per 1000 by 2020. Yet some 40 per cent of Israeli households do not own a car at all. Car ownership per capita in poor Arab Israeli or Jewish Israeli cities such as Beersheba is half of that of the affluent suburbs of Tel Aviv such as Herzliya. That gap is expected to remain over the next 20 years, which means that while two- and three-car households will become the norm among affluent Israelis, poorer households will make do with one car or no car at all.

Despite relatively low per capita rates of car ownership, both Israel and the Palestinian Authority are already suffering from extremely high levels of traffic congestion and air pollution. Vehicle travel per km^2 in the portion of Israel north of the sparsely populated Negev region exceeds that of every country in Western Europe. Ozone pollution levels in the rural areas around Palestinian Bethlehem are roughly comparable to levels in moderately polluted US cities such as Newark, New Jersey. Particulate pollution in the urban centres of Tel Aviv and Jerusalem is comparable to rates in Los Angeles.

Such concentrations of pollution and congestion are partly due to the small size of both Palestinian and Israeli entities; together they cover less than $26,000km^2$, an area smaller than the entire Los Angeles metropolitan region. But the heavy dependence on motorized vehicle travel modes in and around urban areas is also a major factor.

For example, as of 1996, over 65 per cent of travel in Israeli Tel Aviv was by automobile, as compared to less than 30 per cent in Zurich (Switzerland), Delft (The Netherlands) or Milan (Italy).

In addition, 7–8 per cent of all passenger kilometres travelled in Denmark and The Netherlands are via bicycle, while another 7–11 per cent are via rail modes, which are both clean transport alternatives to the automobile. In comparison, in Israel and the Palestinian Authority, less than 2 per cent of travel is via such modes. Buses constitute the only real alternative to the automobile for either short urban trips or long distance inter-urban journeys, contributing heavily to road congestion and air pollution. Indeed, it is estimated that some 30 per cent of particulate pollution in the Tel Aviv area originates in diesel bus and truck emissions.

In terms of the social impact of transport patterns, Israel's annual investment in new road development (three times the investment in rail) reflects a clear preference of rich over poor and men over women in terms of development priorities (see Table 22.1). For instance, even though Israeli women enjoy greater social and professional mobility than women elsewhere in the Middle East, they are still concentrated in low wage earning professions, where owning an automobile is still a relative luxury. As recently as 1992, only 35 per cent of Israeli women held drivers' licences as compared to 65 per cent of men.

Moreover, Israeli men make nearly twice as many weekly inter-urban journeys as women, while women travel more within their local communities. Israeli business executives and professionals make two to three times as many inter-urban trips per week as sales clerks, teachers and nurses. Clearly, investments in road systems, and particularly inter-urban roads, benefit high wage earners, particularly men, more than low wage earners, who tend to be women. Alongside such roads, large commercial hypermarkets and new bedroom suburbs inevitably develop – services primarily accessible to the car-owning upper classes.

Table 22.1 *Israeli public transport infrastructure investments (2001)*

Inter-urban roads	Urban roads	Inter-urban rail	Urban mass transit/bus lanes
NIS1.811 billion	1.298 billion	NIS766 million	NIS412 million
Total road investment*	3.109 billion	Total rail/transit/bus lane investment	1.178 billion

Note: * Does not include urban road maintenance budgets, managed by municipalities, NIS equals New Israeli Shekels
Source: ADVA Institute (2001)

Conversely, public transport ridership is defined by socio-economic status, and most public transport patrons in Israel and the Palestinian Authority are in fact captive customers of the system. In Jerusalem, a city of both Israeli and Palestinian residents, only 59 per cent of men, as compared to 79 per cent of women, take the bus at least once a week, and bus ridership is over 30 per cent higher among low wage earners than among more affluent socio-economic groups.

Tragically, while Western governments have invested heavily in development projects and business partnerships in Israel, the Palestinian Territories and throughout the Middle East region, there has been virtually no examination of the interface between transport policy, land use and development goals in the Middle East region.

Europe, in particular, has much expertise and experience that it could share with Middle Eastern governments in the development of rail, pedestrian and cycle systems. Investment in simple, low budget networks of cycle and pedestrian systems, both rural and urban, would improve access among the poor to jobs and local services. Safer pedestrian and bicycle systems would also dramatically reduce traffic accident mortality among children, women and the elderly, who today can be seen picking their way dangerously through the traffic of almost any Middle Eastern city, and plodding miserably alongside the margins of major rural road systems.

But such efforts would require greater investments in planning, public education and local government coordination. In the absence of such initiatives, development budgets are routinely allocated to roads, or possibly airport projects, without any consideration of the alternatives.

Today, as in centuries past, an unholy alliance is sometimes evident between local Middle Eastern governments obsessed with their own military and strategic goals and

European or US governments and corporations who want to reap a relatively quick and easy profit from development investments in roads.

A Canadian-based corporation, Canadian Highways International (CHI), for instance, is a key partner in Israel's environmentally controversial trans-Israel highway project. As the price for CHI's participation in such a politically and financially risky endeavour, the Israeli government has offered to guarantee roughly 80 per cent of the firm's projected profits. The Canadian government has thus also given demonstrative support to the project, while remaining aloof to appeals by environmentalists and hydrologists, who note that the road corridor runs over one of Israel's major underground water aquifers and alongside hundreds of wells and springs. Those experts, who have appealed to Israel's Supreme Court, contend that the new highway will not only promote sprawl in a land-scarce region, but could very well contaminate one of Israel's last pristine water sources, which supplies some 2 million people in the Tel Aviv area with drinking water.

In the West Bank as well, international development organizations have failed to examine critically the broader impacts of road development plans, when such plans may result in lucrative business contracts for construction firms based in the home country of the sponsoring government agency.

Currently, the United States Agency for International Development (USAID) and the Palestinian Authority are involved in promoting a plan for a new Palestinian trans-West Bank highway project, which would serve as a political counterpoint to the 'Israeli' system of bypass roads already lacing the West Bank region. Environmentalist organizations have criticized the road plan, which cuts through one of the last remaining stretches of rural mountain landscape in the West Bank. But, in the destructive political competition over roads and land space, neither the Palestinian Authority nor USAID has ever considered the possibility of rail alternatives, or carried out a comprehensive study of Palestinian transport needs.

Today, following the 11 September 2001 airline terror attacks in New York and Washington, DC, the Middle East region, in all of its dimensions, has become the subject of heightened scrutiny again among US and European governments. Officials and experts in almost every field of endeavour are seeking to understand the root causes of social discontent in the region that contributed to attacks of an unprecedented scope and scale.

In this new and fast-changing world, Western governments may be well advised to re-examine the transport aspect of development policies in the Middle East region as well, and consider how those policies exacerbate existing social tensions that form the basis for unrest, alienation, poverty, and ultimately terrorism.

It may be worthwhile to note that in the new environment that has emerged since 11 September 2001, regional air transport systems in the Middle East may be particularly vulnerable to future hijacking and terror attacks which, if properly executed, could quickly trigger off a major regional war. Buses have already become a favourite target of terror attack inside Israel, further eroding ridership in an already declining system.

Certainly, rail systems are not immune to terror attacks either. But unlike airliners, train cabins operating on a fixed track can not easily be turned into a human-guided missile. Moreover, it has already become evident in Europe that rail systems can compete effectively with air travel even in regional journeys of several hundred kilometres or more. Reviving and developing the old regional rail systems of the past would be a bureaucratically and politically complicated task, but in the world of the Middle East it might be a worthwhile consideration. Such systems, were they developed on a country-by-country basis, could both help reduce the dependency on automobiles and at the same time enhance regional security.

As another first step towards a more sensible and holistic policy of transport investment, it is imperative that Western governments and aid organizations active in the Middle East region undertake comprehensive transport and land use evaluations of development plans in every country where they are active. Tragically, in most countries of this region, trips by pedestrians, cyclists and animal transport remain uncounted and unrecorded, and therefore invisible to the eyes of planners and bureaucrats. Only the movements of cars and vehicles are recorded in official annals and government bulletins.

A comprehensive reporting and analysis of all travel patterns, motorized and non-motorized, country by country, could go a long way towards including the millions of carless residents in planning considerations. In such a way, transport systems might eventually emerge that would truly advance the lives of peoples living in the region – and not just the political aims and financial gains of local government bureaucrats and European or US corporations.

References

ADVA Institute (2001) 'Analysis of transport investments in the Israel government budget, 2001', personal communication

Al-Suleiman, T I and Al-Masaeid, H R (1992) 'Descriptive model for fatality rates of traffic accidents in Jordan,' *ITE Journal*, April

Elhanany, S (2000) 'Israel hydrological service, risks of contamination to Israel's water aquifer from the trans-Israel highway', personal communication, December

Fletcher, E (1999a) 'Road transport, environment and social equity in Israel in the new millennium', *World Transport Policy & Practice*, vol 5, no 4, pp8–17

Fletcher, E (1999b) *Road Transport Environment and Equity in Israel*, ADVA Center, Institute on Equality and Social Justice in Israel, January, Jerusalem

Fletcher, E and Ginsberg, G (2001) *Road Transport Emissions and Their Impact on Health in Israel and Palestine*, Israel Palestine Center For Research and Information, Tel Aviv

International Road Federation (1994–1998) *World Road Statistics*, International Road Federation, Geneva

Maoh, H and Isaac, J (1999) 'The status of transportation in the West Bank', *World Transport Policy & Practice*, vol 5, no 4, pp18–20

Tel Aviv University (2001) *Road Development and Road Water Runoff*, symposium sponsored by the Committee for Public Transport, March 12, Tel Aviv University, Israel

Trans-Israel Highway Co (1994) 'Traffic analysis and economic evaluation', Matat, Tel Aviv-Jafo (in Hebrew)

23

How Many Shall Live? How Many Shall Die? Deaths Resulting from the Trans-Israel Highway and Alternatives: A Risk Assessment Revisited

Gary Ginsberg, Eli Ben-Michael, Stephen Reingold, Elaine Fletcher and Elihu Richter

Introduction

Public health officials and epidemiologists usually do not participate in assessments of risks for road deaths and injuries from highways before they are built. In Israel, such assessments were not part of the cost–benefit analysis that was central to the approval of the trans-Israel highway toll road (Route 6). The six-lane trans-Israel highway (320km length north–south) and its 16 east–west connecting roads, if built, will be the largest, most costly and most irreversible environmental modification ever undertaken in Israel. Its investors are advocates of high speed limits to attract more users – cars and commercial vehicles – and thereby maximize revenues.

The planners of Route 6 claimed there would be 'large savings in accident costs as a result of the construction of the highway' (Trans-Israel Highway Company, 1994). This chapter examines the validity of this assessment, using models that may be helpful elsewhere.[1] This examination could serve as a model for the pro-active assessment of public health impacts of economic and social decisions during the planning process, and not afterwards. Finally, the need for Code of Helsinki-type frameworks for carrying out such assessments is discussed.

Method

A spreadsheet model was constructed based on vehicle kilometres (vkm) travelled and road death data from 1995 to estimate the system-wide toll of road deaths for the year 2010. The results were then compared with two other possible scenarios: one in which the road was not built (Scenario 1: do nothing), and a second promoting the use of trains, bus lanes, congestion pricing, truck lanes and speed cameras (Scenario 2: sustainable transport). Estimates for Scenario 2 did not come from these calculations, but results from recent projects in other Western countries. The calculations used were based on (see Box 23.1):

- a current annual toll of 550 dead;
- the empirically demonstrated relationship between the fourth power of increases in travel speeds and increases in death tolls (Nilsson, 1979);
- projected increases in vehicle kilometres travelled (vkt) for the year 2010;
- speed increases of 6km per hour (kph) induced by Route 6 and connecting roads, because of a decrease in congestion; and
- the 'spill-over' or habituating effect of a raised maximum speed limit (110kph) on system-wide speeds on all roads (Schmidt and Tiffin, 1969; Mathews, 1978; Casey and Lund, 1987; 1992; Richter et al, 1997).

Box 23.1 *Calculations of predicted death toll on Route 6*

Based on the model presented in this chapter
291 passenger deaths on inter-urban roads ÷ 13.36 billion vkm (bvkm) × 0.58 risk factor = 12.63 deaths per bvkm (d/bvkm)
12.63d/bvkm × 6.73bvkm per year (bvkm/y) = 85 deaths per anticipated exposure on Route 6

But on Route 6, the risk increases as the fourth power of speed rises relative to the entire system: (68.1/58.5 to the fourth power = 1.83), which gives 152 deaths

Based on death rates per vkm on Israel's fast roads
(Using 1993 speed limit, 90km/h, and 1993 reported d/bvkm rate, 7.7)
7.7d/bvkm × (110/90 to the fourth power = 2.22) × 6.73bvkm/y = 115 deaths

Based on death rates per vkm on US inter-state highways
In the USA, d/bvkm was 10.6 with a speed limit of 65mph (105km/h)
10.6d/bvkm × (110/105 to the fourth power = 1.20) × 6.73bvkm/y = 85.6 deaths

---

Exposure – vkm travelled

The data sources used were Central Bureau of Statistics quarterly transportation reports (CBS, 1996), the International Road Federation (1994) and the Trans-Israel Highway Company (1994). The model (see Table 23.1) was used to project the total vkm travelled in the year 2010 (CBS, 1996) on urban roads, inter-urban roads and on Route 6

Table 23.1 *Modal parameters*

	Year	Inter-urban	Urban
Annual vkm (millions)	1995	13,375	17,258
Annual growth rate	1995–2000	3.90%	3.90%
Annual growth rate	2000–2010	2.96%	2.96%
Average system speed (km/h)	1995	58.5	22.0
Pedestrian fatalities	1995	35	132
Non-pedestrian fatalities	1995	291	92
Pedestrian fatalities/100 million km	1995	0.26	0.76
Non-pedestrian fatalities/100 million km	1995	2.19	0.53
Safety factor on Route 6	2010	58.33 %	

(see Table 23.2). Based on this data, two possible projections for each are included in the calculations: 6.6 per cent and 11.4 per cent increases in total vkm travelled.

Speed and estimated death risks

Data sources for speed (Richter et al, 1997) also include trans-Israel highway projections (Trans-Israel Highway Company, 1994). Calculations of death risks were based on the finding that non-pedestrian deaths vary with the fourth power (Nilsson, 1990; Gallager, 1989) of changes in average speeds (see Table 23.3). It was assumed that there were no changes in pedestrian deaths (Richter et al, 1997).

Route 6

On Route 6, the maximum speed limit will be raised to 110 kilometres per hour (kph). Based on latest reports from Israel (Derfner, 2000), the travel speeds of many vehicles will be much higher, in the range of 125–130kph. It is estimated that the risk of road deaths on Route 6 will be lower by 41.7 per cent compared with other inter-urban roads, based on comparisons of current death rates and vkm travelled on existing high speed and other inter-urban roads. The risks on roads with higher design speeds are lower than those on roads with lower design speeds. This difference in risks persists even though rises in death tolls on high speed as well as other roads follow rises in speed limits and travel speeds (National Research Council, 1984; Wagennar, 1984; Gallagher, 1989; Garber and Graham, 1990; Nilsson, 1990; Baum et al, 1991; Chang et al, 1993; Insurance Institute for Highway Safety, 1997). In an earlier paper (Ginsberg et al, 1997), calculations were presented showing that risks for deaths per vkt on major Israeli roads were already somewhat higher than those on US inter-state roads.

Table 23.2 *Additional vehicle kilometres travelled, system speeds and spill-over effects by scenario*

	1995	2010	2010 with Route 6
Additional vkm travelled (million km)			
Urban	17,258	26,716	26,893
Inter-urban	13,375	20,705	16,896
Route 6	0	0	6673
System speeds			
Average system speed, urban km/h	22.0	20.0	19.6
Average system speed, inter-urban km/h	58.5	53.2	63.2
Average system speed, Route 6 km/h	–	–	68.1
Spill-over effect			
Urban pedestrian fatality increase	–	0.00%	0.00%
Urban non-pedestrian fatality increase	–	6.35%	2.60%
Inter-urban pedestrian fatality increase	–	0.00%	0.00%
Inter-urban non-pedestrian fatality increase	–	27.03%	24.10%

Note: Assumes an additional 6.6 per cent kilometres travelled due to Route 6 being in place by 2010

Table 23.3 *Fatalities by type, cause and scenario (2010)*

Route 6 components	Route 6 occupant	Route 6 pedestrian	Inter-urban occupant	Inter-urban pedestrian	Urban occupant	Urban pedestrian	Total
Additional kilometres travelled							
With Route 6	85	0	370	44	143	206	848
Without Route 6	0	0	450	54	142	204	850
Difference	85	0	−80	−10	1	2	−2
Increased speed effects (from congestion relief) + additional kilometres travelled							
With Route 6	152	0	505	44	90	206	997
Without Route 6	0	0	309	54	98	204	665
Difference	152	0	196	−10	−8	2	332
Spill-over + additional kilometres travelled							
With Route 6	85	0	506	44	149	206	990
Without Route 6	0	0	450	54	142	204	850
Difference	85	0	56	−10	7	2	140
Spill-over effect + congestion relief + additional kilometres travelled							
With Route 6	152	0	641	44	96	206	1139
Without Route 6	0	0	309	54	98	204	665
Difference	152	0	332	−10	−2	2	474

All inter-urban roads

Baseline (1995) death rates for pedestrian and non-pedestrian urban and inter-urban routes per hundred million vkm (see Table 23.1) were multiplied by expected vkm travelled in year 2010, and the product multiplied by the fourth power of the ratio of new system-wide average speeds to current average speeds throughout the system. Higher average speeds result from congestion relief and spill-over (speed habituation from the higher travel speeds on Route 6, especially during off-peak hours). The estimated size of the spill-over effect (see Table 23.2) is based on 2.6 per cent and 24.1 per cent increases in urban and inter-urban deaths, respectively, directly following the increase in the speed limit (1 November 1993) on two major highways from 90kph to 100kph (Richter et al, 1997). These increases were presumed to apply only to non-pedestrian deaths (see Table 23.3), because impacts with pedestrians at existing speeds are already close to 100 per cent fatal.

Outcome – death tolls

Changes in road death tolls both with and without Route 6 were estimated using four different combinations for 1995 and 2010:

1 deaths from additional vkm travelled alone;
2 deaths from additional vkm travelled plus congestion relief;
3 deaths from additional vkm travelled plus spill-over effect; and
4 deaths from congestion relief plus spill-over effect.

Other scenarios not from the model

Building Route 6 was compared to the do-nothing scenario (Scenario 1) and alternative strategies (Scenario 2) to promote the use of trains, bus lanes, congestion pricing, truck lanes and speed cameras (see Figure 23.1).

Results

Effects from additional vkm travelled

Without Route 6, road death tolls could rise from 550 to as high as 850 during the period 1995–2010, solely as a result of additional vehicles generating additional vkt. If Route 6 were built, total deaths would show practically the same increase to 848 from additional vkt alone. This rise is offset by fewer pedestrian and non-pedestrian deaths from decreased vkt projected for inter-urban and urban roads.

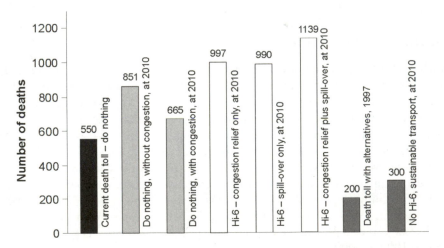

Figure 23.1 *Road death tolls for Highway 6 and alternatives*

Effects from additional vkt and congestion relief

Without Route 6, when congestion is also taken into account, deaths would drop by 185 (from 850 to 665), or 115 more than the current toll of 550. But with Route 6, the increase in system speeds would raise road deaths from 848 to 997, an increase of 149, or 332 more than the situation without Route 6 and without congestion relief. This rise in deaths would happen because large increases in death tolls on Route 6 and inter-urban roads combined offset the smaller reduction in deaths of urban non-pedestrians. The latter reduction in deaths is a consequence of the small decrease in urban speeds in all cities combined since 1995.

Effects from additional vkt and spill-over effect

Without Route 6, there would be no spill-over effect from its higher speeds (limit 110kph; expected 90 per cent travel speed 120kph), total deaths being 850. But with Route 6 and the spill-over effect alone, deaths would rise to 990, or an additional increase of 140, nearly all of which comes from the spill-over effect on inter-urban roads.

Effects from additional vkt, spill-over effect and congestion relief

With Route 6, the combined effects on speed from congestion relief and the spill-over effect, especially among inter-urban non-pedestrians, will increase death tolls to 1139 deaths, an increase of 474 deaths over the 665 fatalities in the non-Route 6 scenario.

Discussion

The nationwide increase in deaths from Route 6 ranges from 332 (congestion effect only) to 474 (congestion and spill-over effects) more than would occur if Route 6 were not built (by 2010, after congestion slowdowns, this would increase to 665). In a worst case scenario, without any congestion, these increases would produce annual nation-wide road death totals of 990–1139. A large majority of the rise in death tolls would occur on spill-over roads. The rise in deaths on the connecting and other inter-urban roads would offset the drop in risk per person vkt on the highway itself. There will be a rise in total deaths even if there is not one single death on the highway itself. Without congestion relief, over the years, much of the rise in death toll from increased speeds would be offset by slower speeds in ever expanding circles of congestion radiating out from the urban coastal area and the developed areas along the road corridor.

If congestion relief and spill-over both result in the same system-wide increases in travel speeds, then the second estimate will be more accurate. Table 23.4 and Figure 23.1 summarize these projections. Without Route 6, another strategy (Scenario 2 based on a nationwide network of speed cameras, lower speed limits and other measures) is estimated to provide a reduction in death tolls to under 200 per year now, and under 300 per year in 2010, provided that alternatives to private motor vehicles are introduced.

Table 23.4 *How many shall live? How many shall die?*

Scenario	Current deaths per year	Estimated deaths per year 2010
Route 6 no	550	665–850
Route 6 yes	–	990–1139
Alternatives	<200	<300

These alternatives rely on more trains, buses, dedicated bus lanes, congestion pricing and truck lanes.

Table 23.4 and Figure 23.1 present death tolls and differences from Route 6 and the alternatives in relation to two baselines: the current annual toll (550) and the toll after congestion (665–850) without Route 6 in 2010. With Route 6, the range of death toll estimates is 990–1139. Lower speeds could reduce all the above tolls for scenarios with and without Route 6. But lower speeds after the road's construction would undermine the stated reason for its construction: time savings caused by increases in speed.

The model is sensitive to changes in the estimates of both induced travel and increases in travel speeds, especially in inter-urban settings. If it is assumed that there will be an 11.4 per cent level of induced vkm travelled (CBS, 1996), then there will be 402–559 more deaths per annum system-wide from Route 6, not 332–474 more deaths based on a 6.6 per cent induced vkt. Table 23.5 presents a comparison of predicted death tolls based on these differing estimates of induced vkt. Furthermore, congestion from induced travel, by lowering travel speeds, would greatly reduce risks in peak hours of travel. But even so, such congestion without speed control cannot be expected to result in reductions in the absolute numbers of deaths (Richter and Berman, 2001).

Alternatives: immediate benefits, fewer deaths

An alternative policy for sustainable transportation can be suggested, based on more mobility (freezing road construction, more rail travel and buses, dedicated bus and truck lanes and congestion pricing) and speed control using cameras. The case for this policy reducing death tolls to fewer than 200 per year right now and fewer than 300 per year in 2010 is firmly based on reducing vehicle speed and providing alternatives to road travel. In Australia and the UK, 50–69 per cent reductions in death tolls have been achieved with recent speed camera projects (McDermott et al, 1996; West, 1998). Although speed cameras could also produce large drops in death even with Route 6, the reductions would be subtracted from higher death tolls and would not include the benefits of sustainable transportation. Previous experience has shown that there will be powerful (short term) financial pressures to mitigate speed control for the road, despite the huge costs of road injury (Friedman, 1997).

Is the estimate too high or too low?

Too high?
Defenders of the highway recycled erroneous statements, made by proponents of a previous raise in the speed limit from 90 to 100kph, that higher speeds do not result in

Table 23.5 *Effect of induced kilometrage on death tolls*

Effects from	Additional vkm travelled	Without R 6	With R 6	Difference in deaths
Additional vkm travelled	6.6%	850	848	−2
	11.35%	850	910	60
Difference				62
Additional vehicle + congestion relief	6.6%	665	997	332
	11.35%	665	1094	429
Difference				97
Extra kilometrage + spill-over effect	6.6%	850	990	140
	11.35%	850	1151	301
Difference				161
Extra kilometrage + congestion relief + spill-over effect	6.6%	665	1139	474
	11.35%	665	1260	595
Difference				121

increased road death tolls (Hocherman et al, 1996; Caspit, 1997). Their conclusions were based on government-funded studies of death trends over 100kph. These studies restricted themselves to a sample of roads, compared time frames that omitted the period immediately before and after raising the speed limit, and used rises in deaths on spill-over inter-urban roads – itself a direct effect of increased speed limits – to control for rises in deaths on high speed roads.

It is possible that the model used under-estimates the protective effects of congestion and counter-measures in reducing risks for deaths per vkt over the years. Road death tolls fell in Israel from 548 in 1998 to 476 in 1999 and then again to 461 in 2000. Some four-fifths of the drop in death tolls occurred in and around the large cities, where congestion worsened. More recent trends show that the death toll will again rise substantially in 2001, as speeds and case fatality increase on high speed out-of-town motorways, including recently widened roads that will feed into the trans-Israel highway, small sections of which have already opened. Elsewhere, drops in deaths per vkt in the USA represent the combined effects of counter-measures and congestion. Nevertheless, these measures have not resulted in a drop in death tolls in absolute numbers, owing to the rise in speed limits and case fatality rates. The latter are exquisitely sensitive to small changes in speeds.

Quite understandably, there is some intuitive resistance to the notion that just one road should increase road death tolls by such large numbers throughout the entire transportation system. But past work has shown that system-wide effects have already occurred in Israel following a less extreme measure: raising speed limits on 70km of inter-urban roads from 90 to 100kph (1 November 1993). This measure increased road deaths by roughly 40 (from 487 to 525) and case fatality by 15–20 per cent as a result of system-wide increases in speeds of 4–5 per cent (Livneh et al, 1993).

There is one other reason why the prediction may be too high: there are anecdotal indications that the first risk assessment itself served to alert the planners of the highway to the risks, and led them to invest more heavily in safeguards.

Too low?

In the case of Route 6, the estimated death tolls could be too low if its construction specifications include cost-cutting compromises on international standards ('value engineering'), which themselves are considered inadequate (Hauer, 1997). If, for example, the road is designed for peak travel speeds of 120kph and the speed limit is set at 110kph, as currently proposed, then, based on past observations in Israel, it is expected that 120kph will be the *median* speed in the fast lane (Richter et al, 1997). Actual travel speeds will far exceed those for which the road is designed. Currently, it has emerged that the police are already using 120kph as a threshold for enforcement, and so travel speeds may be higher than estimated during non-peak hours (Efrat, 2001).

Estimated costs

The average age of road death victims in 1995 was 38.6 years, meaning each road death cost 38.9 potential life years (CBS, 1996). Each death was valued at around US$307,000 using the gross national product (GNP) method of valuing human life and a 4 per cent discount rate as used in the Route 6 planning report. Therefore, the estimated 474 additional deaths in 2010 have mortality costs approximating US$146 million per annum. A higher valuation based on willingness-to-pay data would value mortality losses at around US$538 million per annum. The costs of road deaths, plus those from moderate and slight injury, would substantially undermine the projected net worth of Route 6. These estimates do not include costs from catastrophic chemical spills and air pollution.

The assessments indicate that Route 6 trades off tangible losses in human life and limb for esoteric and arbitrary valuations of increases in time savings. As already noted, injuries and deaths have been shown to rise exponentially as a function of the second and fourth powers of increases in average road traffic speeds respectively. These exponential relationships, which are rooted in Newtonian laws of mass and kinetic energy, create formidable barriers to injury reduction when speeds increase. These laws mean that with Route 6, there will be fewer deaths and injuries than predicted, but only if speeds drop from increases in congestion, ie, from conditions that nullify the justification for the road.

Policy implications: the alternatives

Alternative solutions (Scenario 2) are available that do not produce the expected large increases in road carnage from increased travel and faster speeds produced by Route 6. In European countries, for example, death risks per vkm and tonne-km travelled by rail are between one-half and one-tenth the risk of private car (European Federation for

Transport and Environment, 1993). Replacing the automobile with rail-based transportation will reduce the costs of operation, injury, deaths, pollution and time travelled. In addition, whereas toll roads only benefit those that can afford them, railways provide relatively cheap and safe transport for the entire population (Belin et al, 1997). But recent large train catastrophes in Europe call attention to the need for major investments in measures to further reduce the risks from train travel to zero. Another long term solution is the adoption of town planning modes that encourage the design and use of pedestrian and bicycle paths and rail networks as safer alternatives to motor vehicle use.

Shifting to safer modes that deliver mobility is preferable to relying on congestion to reduce road deaths. Freezes on road construction, dedicated bus and truck lanes, congestion pricing, lower speed limits (especially for trucks) and electronic speed camera networks are the elements of an alternative policy that would provide immediate relief and reduce death and injury tolls right away. Speed cameras have been shown to reduce death tolls by 50–70 per cent (Richter and Berman, 2001; West, 1998) while generating revenues that make detection and deterrence sustainable. These empirical findings mean there is a greater than 300 per cent difference in annual death tolls between the worst and best scenarios. The risk assessments in this chapter indicate that Route 6 is the worst scenario, and alternatives based on sustainable transportation packages offer the best scenario.

Cover up

Following the publication of the first version of this risk assessment, the authors discovered that the government suppressed the completion and examination of a model developed in the late 1990s by the Israel Institute for Transport Planning and Research as part of Israel's new transport master plan. The model compared traffic and travel loads on a transport network in which a rail service was intensively developed with a transport system anchored around the trans-Israel highway. According to the preliminary results of the model – which was never published – an intensive programme of urban and inter-urban rail development would reduce automobile travel in the metropolitan Tel Aviv area by more than 11 billion pkm annually, in comparison to the road-oriented development plan, of which the trans-Israel highway is the centrepiece. Intensive rail/public transport development would shift some 34 per cent of pkms to cleaner public transport modes in the metropolitan Tel Aviv area, as compared to only a 21 per cent share for public transport in the road-oriented model. Nationally, the intensive development of the rail-oriented system would cost US$10 billion less in capital costs than the road-oriented model, not including the enormous health savings such an alternative model would yield (Israel Institute for Transport Planning and Research, 1997).

Transport and the ethical framework of risk assessment

Route 6 and its connecting roads will not only result in more loss of life, but could also prevent the development of alternative, less hazardous modes of transport. In ethical terms, there is a quantifiable relationship between revenues for its operators and risks of death for its users, or what is termed a cash-for-carnage scenario. More speed means linear increases in revenues but exponential increases in deaths. More recently, Israeli transportation officials have characterized rises in speed limits as unethical exercises in human experimentation (Derfner, 2000).

These conclusions raise questions concerning the ethical integrity, independence and validity of the review process for major national projects in transportation. Such decisions, because of their major impacts on human health, should be subjected to the same kind of review process required for clinical trials and experiments involving human subjects. Therefore, Code of Helsinki-type institutional safeguards to protect the public from the risks of junk ethics and junk science guiding transport policy is required (Richter et al, 1999; Fishman, 1995).

The risk assessments outlined in this chapter require the application of the dictum: 'when someone saves a human life, it is as though (s)he has saved the whole world' (The Talmud, 1970). The question to be asked is: If not now, then when?

Note

1   This chapter was first published as a paper in *World Transport Policy & Practice*, vol 3, no 4, pp4–10. The opinions in this article are those of the authors and do not represent those of their institutions.

References

Baum, H M, Wells, J K and Lund, A K (1991) 'The fatality consequences of the 65mph speed limit', *Journal of Safety Research,* vol 22, pp171–177

Belin, M A, Johansson, R, Lindberg, J and Tingvall, C (1997) *The Vision Zero and its Consequences in Safety and the Environment in the 21st Century,* proceedings of the 4th International Conference on Safety in the Environment in 21st Century, 23–27 November, Tel Aviv

Casey, S M and Lund, A K (1987) 'Three field studies of driver speed adaptation', *Human Factors,* vol 29, pp541–550

Casey, S M and Lund, A K (1992) 'Changes in speed and speed adaptation following increase in national maximum speed limit', *Journal of Safety Research,* vol 23, pp135–46

Caspit, N, Mehalel, D and Livneh, M (1997) *Influence of Changed Speed Limits on Road Safety,* Report No 97-248, Technion-Israel Institute of Technology Research, Haifa (Hebrew)

CBS (1996) *Statistical Abstract of Israel No 47,* Central Bureau of Statistics, Government of Israel, Tel Aviv

Chang, G, Chen, C and Carter, E (1993) 'Intervention analysis for the impacts of the 65mph speed limit on rural interstate highway fatalities', *Journal of Safety Research,* vol 24, pp33–53

Derfner, L (2000) 'We take the high road', *Jerusalem Post,* 11 February, pp18–20

Efrat, Commander E (2001) 'Israel traffic police', personal communication, April

European Federation for Transport and Environment (1993) *Getting the Prices Right,* European Federation for Transport and Environment, Brussels, May, p28

Fishman, R H (1995) 'Anti-speeding Israeli doctors', *Lancet,* vol 345, p1040

Friedman, M S (1997) personal communication, 2 May. See 104 Western Alignment Corporation home page, email macloeosu@gov.ns.ca

Gallagher, S (1989) 'Effects of the 65mph speed limit on rural interstate fatalities in New Mexico', *JAMA*, vol 262, pp2243–2245

Garber, S and Graham, J D (1990) 'The effect of the new 65mph speed limit on rural highway fatalities: a state-by-state analysis', *Journal of Accident Analysis and Prevention*, vol 22, no 2, pp137–149

Ginsberg, G, Fletcher, E, Ben-Michael, E and Richter, E D (1997) 'How many shall live? How many shall die? Deaths resulting from the trans-Israel highway and alternatives: a risk assessment', *World Transport Policy & Practice*, vol 3, no 4, pp4–10

Hauer, E (1997) *Safety Review of Highway 407: Lessons and Uses*, fourth international conference on Safety and the Environment in the 21st Century, 23–27 November, Tel Aviv

Hocherman, I, Cohen, A and Dubeh, E (1996) 'Trends in speed and road accidents on fast roads in Israel', *Traffic and Transportation*, November, pp33–38 (Hebrew)

Insurance Institute for Highway Safety (1997) 'Limits up, speeds up, deaths up: status report', *Status Report*, vol 32, no 8, pp1–4

International Road Federation (1994) *World Road Statistics 1989–1993*, International Road Federation, Geneva

Israel Institute for Transport Planning and Research (1997) 'Table of modal split factors', personal communication, May

Livneh, M et al (1993) *Report of Expert Committee Appointed by Minister of Transportation Israel Kessar to Examine Maximum Permitted Speed Limits in Israel*, Minsistry of Transportation, Tel Aviv (Hebrew)

McDermott, J, Cordner, S M and Temanyne, A B (1996) 'Evaluation of the medical management and preventability of death in 137 road traffic fatalities in Victoria, Australia: an overview', *Journal of Trauma, Injury, Infection and Critical Care*, vol 40, no 4, pp520–535

Mathews, M L (1978) 'A field study of the effects of drivers' adaptation to automobile velocity', *Human Factors*, vol 20, pp709–716

National Research Council (1984) *55 MPH: A Decade of Experience*, National Research Council, Tel Aviv

Nilsson, G (1979*) The Effect of Speed Limits on Traffic Accidents in Sweden*, VTI Report 68, National Road and Traffic Institute, Linkoping, Sweden

Nilsson, G (1990) *Reduction in the Speed Limit from 110kph to 90kph During Summer 1989*, VTI Report 358, National Road and Traffic Institute, Linkoping, Sweden

Richter, E D, Barach, P, Krikler, S, Damian, D, Israeli, A, Ben-David, G and Weinberger, Z (1997) 'Do higher speed limits kill? The 100 KPH "experiment": an epidemiologic evaluation (abstract)', *Proceedings of the Israel Statistical Society*, Israel; Statistical Society, Jerusalem, based on Barach, P (1996) *100 KPH, What Have we Gained? Impact of Raising the Speed Limit on Inter-urban Highways on Accidents, Deaths and Injuries in Israel*, MPH thesis, Hebrew University—Hadassah, School of Public Health and Community Medicine, Jerusalem (Hebrew with English abstract)

Richter, E D et al (1999) *Junk Ethics and Junk Science in Transportation Risk Assessment (Abstract)*, Israel Society for Ecology and Environmental Quality Sciences 7th International Conference 'Environmental Challenges for the Next Millennium', 13–18 June, Jerusalem

Richter, E D and Berman, T (2001) 'Speed, air pollution and health: a neglected issue [editorial]', *Archives of Environmental Health*, July–August

Schmidt, D F and Tiffin, J (1969) 'Distortion of drivers' estimate of automobile speed as a function of speed adapation', *Journal of Applied Psychology*, vol 53, pp536–539

Standing Advisory Committee on Trunk Road Assessment (1994), *Trunk Roads and the Generation of Traffic*, SACTRA, Department of Transport, London

The Talmud (1970) *Sanhedriah 96b*, Soncino Press, London

Trans-Israel Highway Company (1994) *Vehicle Flow Analysis and Economic Evaluation*, Matat, Tel Aviv

Wagennar, A C (1984) 'Effects of macro-economic conditions on the incidence of motor vehicle crashes', *Journal of Accident Analysis and Prevention*, vol 16, pp191–205

West, R (1998) 'The effect of speed cameras on injuries from road accidents', *BMJ*, vol 316, pp5–6

24

The Status of Transportation in the West Bank

Hanna Maoh and Jad Isaac

Introduction

The varied, often mountainous topography of the West Bank's 5659.34km², as well as the region's hot and primarily dry climate, helped shape an ancient system of road links that was distinctively impacted by the natural geography of the land. Mountains or harsh desert regions separated many cities and villages that were in close proximity, requiring circuitous systems of access. High altitude cities such as Nablus or Hebron, which are 600–800m above sea level and might even receive snow in winter, are separated by steep mountain passes and ridges from low altitude areas in the Jordan Valley, which are at or below sea level and experience semi-tropical conditions. Access between major West Bank population centres, therefore, was via an historical road system that followed the mountainous contours of cultivated valleys or ancient desert river beds, known as *wadis*.

In recent years, however, the political conflict over the West Bank has become the major factor impacting on the modern development of transportation. During 30 years of Israeli occupation, large tracts of West Bank land were confiscated from Arab villages and private landowners for the establishment of Jewish settlements and, more recently, for the construction of an extensive system of bypass roads linking these settlements to each other and to Israel. Land use has thus been drastically altered in a relatively short period.

Another period of transition began in 1993, when the Israeli–Palestinian peace process commenced. Palestinians, for the first time, secured the right to develop lands in the major West Bank urban centres that came under their control. Since then, Palestinian institutions and agencies have begun to formulate plans for land use and natural resource development in both the West Bank and Gaza, where respectively 1,873,476 and 1,022,207 Palestinians live today (PCBS, 1997). One of the most pressing challenges facing Palestinians now is the planning of the current transportation system in both the West Bank and Gaza. This chapter focuses on the larger and more complex West Bank system, although many of the observations noted here may also be characteristic of Gaza.

Road transportation is the only mode of transport available in the West Bank, and motorized vehicles are by far the dominant mode on the network, while ancient forms of animal transport are gradually disappearing. Most West Bank roads suffered from a lack of maintenance for decades and were inferior in quality to those in neighbouring Israel. During more than 30 years of Israeli occupation, no serious attempt was made to plan for Palestinian future travel demands. The rapid growth of population – over 3 per cent annually in the West Bank and 4 per cent annually in Gaza – as well as the dependency on the automobile as the primary mode of travel, combined to create serious defects in the system on the eve of the new millennium. Increased rates of vehicle accidents, traffic congestion and air pollution, as well as disorder in systems of urban street signalling, etc, are just a few examples of the problems today.

The remainder of this chapter is in four parts.[1] The first section presents original data on the growth in the rate of motorization, the makeup of the car fleet, travel modes and trip destinations – data that have primarily been collected in surveys by the authors as part of an ongoing project designed to develop a comprehensive West Bank transport dataset that previously did not exist. The second part describes the land use composition in the West Bank in an attempt to show linkages between land use and transportation. Moreover, the section presents a preliminary model of pollution emissions for the Palestinian and Jewish settler car fleets in an attempt to test how the presence of settler cars affects air pollution in the West Bank. The third section presents the dual structure of the road network in the West Bank, both Palestinian and Israeli settler, and offers a case study of how that dual network worsens pollution levels, travel continuity and the Palestinian economy. Finally, the last section outlines the pressing problems in land use and transport planning that must be confronted in the system, and offers recommendations and scenarios for sustainable future development.

Basic Features of the Vehicle System

The number of motorized vehicles has increased in the West Bank by an average of 12 per cent per annum over the past two decades. In 1975, there were only 12,964 vehicles in the West Bank. By 1996, there were 133,386 vehicles registered in the names of Palestinians living in West Bank areas other than east Jerusalem (ARIJ, 1997a). There are, meanwhile, an estimated 25,000 cars for a population of 152,000 Israeli settlers who are residing in West Bank settlements other than east Jerusalem (ICBS, 1997).

Despite such growth, the motorization rate in the West Bank remains very low when compared to Israeli rates. In its 1997 census survey, the Palestinian Central Bureau of Statistics reported that there were 80,000 private cars in the West Bank, yielding a rate of 42.7 cars per 1000 Palestinians. In comparison, there were over 171 cars per 1000 for the Jewish inhabitants of the West Bank and over 208 cars per 1000 for Israel as a whole (ICBS, 1997). Approximately 23.2 per cent of Palestinian households own a car, reflecting the relatively low access to motor vehicles even among more affluent sectors of Palestinian society.

Rapid growth in Palestinian car ownership can be expected to continue under almost any transport development scenario, particularly in view of the fact that the median age of the Palestinian population is 17 years, and cars are increasingly viewed as a symbol of mobility and social status. Dependency on car transport in the West Bank urban centres is growing especially fast, as more and more Palestinians leave traditional vocations on farms and villages and commute to factory, construction and service employment in Palestinian cities or even in Israel.

The overall age of the Palestinian fleet has grave implications for pollution emissions. Approximately one-third of the private cars on the roads today were manufactured in the 1970s. About 60 per cent of the fleet is composed of cars manufactured between 1980 and 1989 and only 10 per cent are relatively new cars that were manufactured between 1990 and 1996 (ARIJ, 1997b). Comparing the age composition of the Palestinian car fleet to the Israeli car fleet, one can see that there is a huge difference. ICBS (1997) statistics indicate that 5.95 per cent of cars in Israel were built before 1981, 29.17 per cent between 1982 and 1989 and the majority of the fleet – about 64.88 per cent – are seven years old, having been built between 1990 and 1997.

Table 24.1 summarizes the distribution of vehicles over the major West Bank cities, excluding Jericho and Jerusalem. Despite the low motorization rate, there is a relatively high incidence of road traffic accidents (RTAs). The most recently available figures from 1993 indicate that 2781 accidents resulting in injuries occurred in that year, with 128 accidents resulting in fatalities. The relatively high rate of accidents – nearly 2 per cent of vehicles annually – is partly attributed to the poor quality of the road network, which is discussed below.

Table 24.1 *Motorized vehicles in the West Bank, 1997*

	Private cars	Trucks and commercial cars	Buses and minibuses	Taxis	Motorcycles and scooters	Tractors	Special services and other vehicles	Total
Jenin	7604	2262	46	72	6	952	4	10,946
Nablus	16,267	3791	165	556	23	520	16	21,338
Tulkarm	11,231	2654	14	102	25	416	11	14,453
Ramallah	14,083	3691	152	642	23	350	19	18,960
Bethlehem	10,816	1862	67	84	22	121	5	12,977
Hebron	18,161	4097	84	108	108	1006	15	23,579

Source: ARIJ (1997b)

Note: figures on motorized vehicles for Jerusalem and Jericho are not available in this dataset

The proportion of private cars to total vehicles varies widely among the various cities of the West Bank (see Table 24.2). Overall, those differences reflect a greater dependence on public transportation in the city of Ramallah, which is today's affluent centre of commerce, culture and political life, and the northern West Bank city of Nablus, which was a traditional economic and cultural stronghold in the pre-1967 period of Jordanian rule. Notably, Ramallah and Nablus contain 41 per cent and 35.5 per cent of the total number of taxis in the West Bank respectively. Some 24.7 per cent of the West Bank bus fleet is located in Ramallah and 30 per cent in Nablus.

Table 24.2 *Private cars as a proportion of the total vehicle fleet*

Jenin	Nablus	Tulkarm	Ramallah	Bethlehem	Hebron
69%	76%	77%	74%	83%	77%

Source: ARIJ (1997b)

Travel destinations

Results of a month-long traffic survey conducted by the authors indicate that a large majority of Palestinian intra-district trips are work trips. The exception noted is in the northern West Bank district of Jenin, where family farming is still a primary vocation. Special trips, such as family visits and recreational excursions, are the second most common type, while shopping ranks third, except for Jenin. Table 24.3 shows the distribution of these trips for each district.

Table 24.3 *Intra-district journeys by type for one month (%)*

Location	Work	Shopping	Official	Special
Jenin	35	41	0	23
Tulkarm	63	8	3	26
Bethlehem	60	10	0	29
Ramallah	63	8	3	27
Nablus	66	13	1	20
Jerusalem	61	8	5	25
Hebron	66	7	6	21

Source: ARIJ (1997b)

Land use and its impact on transport

The West Bank has a total area of $5659.34km^2$. Land use in this region is given in Table 24.4.

Table 24.4 *Land use in the West Bank*

Land use	%
Palestinian built-up area	6.53
Israeli built-up area	1.91
Palestinian cultivated land	28.31
Israeli cultivated land	0.95
Nature reserves and forests	5.84
Closed Israeli military areas and bases	22.14
Other (including grazing and unused land)	34.32

Source: ARIJ (1999)

Most Palestinian cities have been in existence since antiquity, and have developed around a traditional Middle Eastern *souk* (a mixed commercial and residential area noted for its narrow, winding streets and covered alleys) housing small shops, craftspeople and cottage industries that formed the basis for the traditional economy. Pedestrian transport was and is the dominant mode in this environment. Western-style business districts shaped along two-lane paved roads eventually developed around that core, gradually encroaching somewhat on the pedestrian areas. But the basic design of the Palestinian town and city today remains relatively compact, although higher rates of motorization are now generating new residential development on former farmland and orchards at the far-flung peripheries of cities.

Jewish settlements, unlike the traditional Palestinian cities and villages, are at most only 30 years old. With approximately 200 settlements and neighbourhoods around the West Bank, most settlements are marked by low population densities and function primarily as suburban satellites of existing Israeli cities. A marked feature of the settlements, therefore, has been their dependence on automobile transport due to the absence of employment and services within the settlements themselves. Per capita car ownership in the settlements reflects this far greater dependency on private car travel for work, shopping and recreational functions.

A comparison of the population densities of Palestinian and Jewish settlement built-up areas reflects the generally more dispersed and car-dependent pattern of the Jewish settlements on an approximate order of 2:1. There is approximately 369.55km^2 of built-up space for a population of 1.87m Palestinians as compared to 108.09km^2 of built space for a West Bank Jewish settlement community of 300,000, including east Jerusalem. That translates to a population density of 2775.46 Israelis per km^2 of built space in the Jewish settlements, as compared to 5069.61 Palestinians per km^2 of built space.

Congestion and pollution emissions

The rapid increase in motorization and the age of the car fleet have combined to create severe problems of traffic congestion and air pollution in and around major Palestinian cities over the past decade. Given the higher motorization rate of the settler population, settlement cars add to the pollution load disproportionately. A preliminary model of pollution emissions for the Palestinian and settler car fleets suggests that total emissions of major pollutants from cars may be 27–32 per cent higher in the West Bank due to the presence of the settler vehicles.

This preliminary model of pollution emissions is based on figures surveyed by the authors for the Palestinian car fleet and by the Israeli Census Bureau of Statistics (ICBS, 1997) for the Israeli settler car fleet. The model is sensitive to differences such as the older age of the Palestinian car fleet and the greater average annual travel distance per Palestinian vehicle. The pollutant values are based on the transportation air emission inventories (Economopoulos, 1993). These inventories provide the emission factors for carbon monoxide, sulphur oxides, nitrogen oxides, hydrocarbons and lead, and vary according to the age and engine capacity of a vehicle.

The values of harmful pollutants are summarized in Table 24.5 for both the Palestinian and Israeli settler car fleets. With regard to the Palestinian figures, emissions were calculated for cars in the following age categories: 1970–1979, 1980–1989 and 1990–1996. In all cases the authors assumed an engine capacity of 1.4l–2.0l. The annual average kilometrage per vehicle for the Palestinian cars is estimated to be 20,000km (ARIJ, 1997b). The same calculation was carried out for the Israeli car fleet according to the age composition. The 1997 Israeli statistics (ICBS, 1997) indicate that the annual average kilometrage per vehicle is approximately 17,000km. Moreover, the assumption was made that the average engine capacity for the settlers' cars is in the 1.4l–2.0l category.

Table 24.5 *Estimated emissions from private cars in the West Bank*

	Emissions (tonnes/year)			
	Emissions from Palestinian cars	Emissions from Israeli cars	Total emissions	% change in emissions due to presence of Israeli settlers' cars
Carbon monoxide	52,534	16,762	69,296	31.91
Sulphur oxides	2985	875	3860	29.31
Nitrogen oxides	2879	786	3666	27.31
Hydrocarbons	5015	1497	6512	29.84
Lead	198	60	257	29.74

The West Bank Road System: The Dual Israeli–Palestinian System

While Israel's road system is sometimes described by highway planners as relatively underdeveloped by North American and European standards, the West Bank system suffers from far greater deficiencies. There are 0.51km of road per km^2 in the West Bank, as compared to 0.70km per km^2 in Israel. The West Bank has 1.86km of road per thousand inhabitants as compared to 2.5km per thousand inhabitants inside Israel (ARIJ, 1997a). Moreover, the road system in the West Bank is essentially comprised of three systems, which at times duplicate each other and in other instances fail to provide adequate travel continuity. Some 1255km of main roads are shared by both Israelis and Palestinians but are usually under Israeli control; Israeli bypass roads comprising 225km link Jewish West Bank settlements and are used primarily by Israelis. Another 2556km of secondary roads are poorly maintained and are used primarily by Palestinians. Due to this multi-tiered system, road access and road development have become key issues in the political conflict.

Since signing the 1993 Oslo accords, Palestinians have wielded control over land use, road planning and maintenance only in the limited geographical area of seven major Palestinian urban areas, known as Area A. (Accessibility in the region is governed by the Oslo I and Oslo II agreements signed between the Palestinians and the Israelis in the early 1990s. The Oslo II agreement divided the land use of the West Bank into three major classes. These are Area A, Area B and Area C. Land in Area A covers the main cities of the West Bank, except for Hebron, which has a special agreement. The city of Hebron is divided into areas of different control called H1 and H2. Area H1 is defined as Area A and Area H2, which houses 400 settlers, and remains under Israeli control. In Area B, the Palestinians have full control over civil society except that Israel continues to have overriding responsibility for security. These areas comprise most of the Palestinian towns and villages. Area C covers the area that falls outside Areas A and B. In this area, the Palestinian Authority provides civil services. However, Israel retains full control over land, security, people and natural resources. The majority of Palestinian agricultural land lies in these areas.)

The Israeli bypass system, comprising some 25 roads today, is by far the most modern and well maintained part of the West Bank road system. The system is designed to improve accessibility between the different Jewish settlements in the West Bank and the rest of Israel. The bypass roads average 25–30m in width, with an average 120m-buffer zone around the road.

The bypass roads are located in Israeli-controlled Area C. Along with providing a traffic bypass around major Palestinian cities and communities in the West Bank, the roads also create a rigid boundary limiting Palestinian growth and development. This is particularly evident on the crowded urban outskirts of Jerusalem, ie Bethlehem and its environs. In rural areas, the bypass roads also consume open space as well as valuable farmland in fertile valleys and river beds, as well as fragmenting agricultural land use.

Although, technically, Palestinians may travel on the bypass roads, in most cases the system does not serve Palestinian travel destination needs efficiently, and Palestinians are also discouraged from travelling on the system by army roadblocks. The total land consumed by today's existing network of bypass roads is $27.8km^2$. Plans are underway, however, for the construction of another 14 bypass roads in the West Bank, extending 196.01km and consuming another area of $23.5km^2$ (ARIJ, 1999). Once constructed, bypass roads will comprise nearly 1 per cent of the West Bank's total land area.

The main roads in the West Bank were constructed during the British Mandate (1917–1948) and the period of Jordanian administration (1948–1967). Their primary function is to link major Palestinian urban areas with each other, even though these roads often provide intermediary links between different sectors of Israeli bypass roads as well. Typically, main roads in the Palestinian network average only 10–12m in width. Even after 1993, major Palestinian road works programmes became feasible only in areas under the jurisdiction of the Palestinian Authority, resulting in visible road improvements along limited stretches of urban systems. Access to the main roads is also sometimes blocked by Israeli military checkpoints, which control traffic to and from West Bank areas that remain under partial or full Israeli security control (Areas B and C).

Secondary roads are typically 4–8m in width, and most began as unpaved tracks. The curved structure of many roads follow ancient trails around mountains and hillsides making them dangerous for modern traffic. However, in cases where main roads are blocked by military checkpoints, secondary roads may become primary travel arteries, as can be seen in the case study of the Wadi Al-Nar route below.

Roads and Access – Wadi Al-Nar as a Case Study

Wadi Al-Nar became a critical commercial and passenger road link for Palestinians in the late 1980s, when Israel began to limit Palestinian access to Jerusalem's main north–south highway, blocking the historical road artery that links the northern West Bank cities of Nablus and Ramallah to the southern West Bank cities of Bethlehem and Hebron along a relatively flat mountain plateau.

Once a series of dirt tracks and footpaths, Wadi Al-Nar was paved by the Israelis as an improvisational move after direct access to Jerusalem was blocked in the early 1990s by repeated curfews. Today's two-lane road averages 4–5m width in total. The road descends from the northeastern Bethlehem hills into a steep mountain valley, and then ascends around another mountain in that area revealing many hidden curves along the route. The curved sections of the road are impassable to two-lane traffic when one lane is occupied by a freight vehicle. Due to the slopes, winter rain conditions enhance the risk of skidding and accidents. Such conditions impede trade between key West Bank economic centres such as Bethlehem and Ramallah, which lie in close geographical proximity to each other on the northern and southern outskirts of metropolitan Jerusalem. Although the Wadi Al-Nar road skirts the eastern outskirts of Jerusalem, it fails to serve the vital functions of a bypass road due both to design and trajectory.

The distance between Bethlehem and Ramallah on the Wadi Al-Nar road is 47km as compared to 26km on the main Jerusalem highway, and travel time as well as fuel consumption is nearly double, yielding increased travel costs as well as increased pollution emissions. Daily pollution emissions were estimated for cars travelling on both the Jerusalem road and Wadi Al-Nar from Bethlehem and Ramallah. Figure 24.1 indicates that amount of emissions increased by a rate of 2:1 on the Wadi Al-Nar road. The increased emissions might even be higher if factors such as road conditions and capacity were considered.

In terms of the economic toll, the total cost for one car travelling from Bethlehem to Ramallah on the Wadi Al-Nar route and the main Jerusalem highway is estimated at

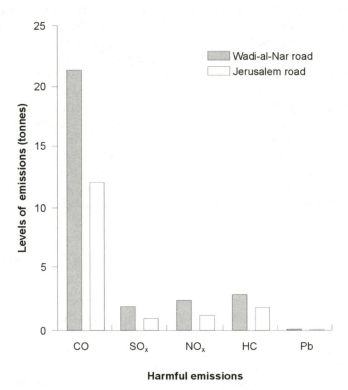

Figure 24.1 *Daily harmful emissions on Wadi Al-Nar and Jerusalem roads*

US$310 and US$120 respectively. Such an excess cost causes significant damage to the Palestinian gross national product (GNP), estimated at US$22.8m (Qattoush, 1999), considering the large amount of commercial traffic travelling between these two cities.

Transport and Land Use in Palestine – Dilemmas and Choices

While research so far has focused on the burning questions of travel discontinuity and Palestinian access to the present transport system, new issues loom on the horizon as the Palestinian Authority expands its jurisdictional authority over West Bank land use and transport systems, and simultaneously develops the planning mechanisms of a sovereign state.

The experience of the West has shown that the modern urban structure gains its formation from the linkage between urban land use and transport road systems. Historically, this change in shape began first with the onset of public transportation, when cities became more dispersed and greater separation between land uses such as commercial, industrial and residential became possible (Anderson et al, 1996). The post-World War Two construction of highways and expressways achieved another revolution, spawning vast new suburbs – particularly in the USA – and effectively turning the historic metropolitan core inside out (Hanson, 1986).

As noted earlier, during the Oslo peace process, land development in many areas on the outskirts of major West Bank Palestinian cities has remained under Israeli control (Area B or C), and thus tightly restricted. In addition, the bypass roads have created a physical obstacle to development. Yet even so, the trends of suburbanization are also beginning to make their impact in Palestine. In areas on the periphery of major Palestinian cities such as Bethlehem and Ramallah, the conversion of farmland to residential housing has accelerated. Fruit orchards and vineyards are giving way to residential housing, spurring sprawl as well as a high dependency on motor vehicles.

As Palestinians gain more control over their own urban periphery, residential and commercial land use development is likely to accelerate even more dramatically. The question then must be asked: how can this development be channelled or shaped to gain the widest benefit for millions of Palestinians? Recent political events in the region have brought an end to Palestinian control. This, and its associated problems of terror and intense military activity, now casts considerable doubts over the possibility of an independent Palestinian style of development.

In Palestine, most cities today still retain their monocentric urban form, where business is concentrated in the central core. Planners now must decide whether they want to encourage even greater urban centralization, or promote a polycentric development pattern. The first strategy would require decision-makers to strictly limit residential development in the outer suburbs and encourage the intensified development of inner suburbs and urban cores via the construction of high rises that could accommodate the growing population densities that can be forecast for the future. The second, polycentric option would create new nodes of commercial and residential development outside the traditional central business district.

In either scenario, however, forms of mixed land use and an employment–housing balance that offers people places to work in close proximity to where they live, and opportunities for walking or public transport, are essential to overcome growing problems of sprawl and commuting. However, more awareness of land use issues needs to be built at the municipal level and the national level before transport and land use planning can become effective development tools.

Whether the decision is for a centralized urban core or for a polycentric form, public transport planning is key to reducing the dependency on the private car. Improved public transport can make Palestinian society more equitable by offering transport solutions to social sectors with moderate incomes that cannot afford to own a private vehicle.

Shared taxis and small paratransit vehicles, accommodating 5–12 passengers, are the dominant modes of transportation in the West Bank today. One visible change evident since the arrival of the Palestinian Authority is the fact that multiple private taxi companies have come under a single regulatory agency. Service taxis and small vans that will accommodate 5–12 passengers have been painted a uniform bright yellow colour, allotted special licence plates, and are now readily identifiable in all areas of the West Bank as public transport vehicles. Paratransit vans are used not only in urban situations, but also in inter-urban transit as a mode of transport for workers crossing the Israeli border to work in Israel or for travellers moving from the northern part of the West Bank to the southern part. However, these privately run taxis and service vehicles – which do not run on a fixed schedule of stops and frequencies – are not a comprehensive alternative to a public bus system, which remains skeletal. Moreover, there is no organized system of route planning and control even for the paratransit vehicles.

Most of the new paratransit vehicles are also diesel-powered. As these types of vehicle are used increasingly in the cities, respirable particulate emissions can be expected to increase significantly (Whiteman, 1988). Yet given the far lower cost of diesel fuel in the West Bank, these vehicles also represent significant economic savings for the Palestinian economy. Environmental drawbacks thus are weighted against economic benefits.

Within Palestinian cities, there is a dearth of traffic signals and signs, as well as a lack of directional planning in the form of one-way roads and downtown bypasses. These features, together with a partial social disregard for traffic law, adds to the sense of disorder that permeates the transport system, as well as to the noise and congestion burden of the urban core.

Planning for the millennium has provided an opportunity to grapple with some of these problems, at least in the context of the Bethlehem 2000 project, which is revitalizing the ancient city's historic downtown area. Bethlehem 2000 has seen a major revamping of the traffic routes throughout the city to ease the flow of tourist vehicles, but particularly in the ancient city core.

One of the chief features of the project is the extensive re-pedestrianization of Bethlehem's Old City that is now underway, reversing a trend which saw narrow alleys of the Crusader and Byzantine period converted into streets for car access over the past several decades. The area around the famous Church of the Nativity, once a neglected parking lot, has been converted into a pedestrian plaza with elegant paving stones, benches and trees. The programme has already made a marked impact on residential quality of life in the core area and the benefits of reduced congestion, noise and air pollution should become even more apparent over time, as the centre city becomes more attractive for residential living as well as tourism.

Similar programmes should be undertaken in most of the core Palestinian urban areas, which share similar urban street patterns and contain buildings and facades of great historic and religious value even if they are not as well known as Bethlehem. Such pedestrian precincts would not only prove environmentally friendly, but would also improve living standards and provide better living amenities in the core, where restaurants, parks and leisure sites could become more readily available even to populations that do not own cars. Pedestrian districts would make other Palestinian cities more attractive and accessible to foreign tourists, and generate new economic growth by boosting open air markets, souvenir industries, hotels and restaurants.

In certain cases, where the terrain is not too hilly, cycling networks could even be integrated into such precincts as they have been in the West, and be supported as a cheap and low pollution alternative to motorized transport. Cycling is not a popular transport method among Palestinians today. Perhaps the greatest potential for cycling today lies in the flat Mediterranean seacoast area of Gaza where urban densities are also very high. While a thorough review of Gaza's transport system lies outside the scope of this chapter, it seems obvious that cycling should be supported by the Palestinian Authority as a transport mode in Gaza that holds great potential.

As mentioned earlier, road vehicles constitute the only mode of long distance transport in the West Bank and Gaza today. In a new era when Palestinian land is controlled by Palestinians, decision-makers should consider other modes as well. A rail link has already been proposed as a means of connecting the southern West Bank to Gaza, via Israel. A rail link should also be considered as a means to connect the major population centres of the West Bank along the north–south axis of Hebron, Bethlehem, Jerusalem, Ramallah, Nablus and Jenin, where population densities are highest, pollution and traffic are most intensive, and where a natural transport corridor already exists through otherwise mountainous terrain. Rail should be a travel mode available for both commercial and personal trips, and should eventually become part of a regional system connecting Israel, Jordan and Syria.

A Palestinian national rail system would help to promote economic growth and regional economic integration, and support the existence of a Palestinian state, not only by providing a link between Gaza and the West Bank, but also by increasing interaction between different sectors of the Palestinian economy and easing the passage of goods through border crossings. However, given the investment capital that would be required for basic infrastructure investment in rail, such a project could only become reality with the assistance of a coordinated effort from the world community. International donors, as well as the Palestinian Authority, should consider such a project as they look for solutions to the problems of high population density and land scarcity that a Palestinian state in the West Bank and Gaza will face in the first decades of the new millennium.

Conclusion

The transportation network in the West Bank suffers from years of neglect during three decades of Israeli occupation, and major investments will be needed in order to restructure the system, beginning with a greater investment in planning, as well as in travel demand modelling.

Congestion and pollution are becoming commonly observed phenomena in the West Bank cities and urban centres due to increases in motorization, the placement of Israeli military checkpoints and an inadequate system of roads, signalling and public transport. Traffic pollution is exacerbated by the presence of Israeli settlers' cars. The Israeli confiscation of land for settlements and bypass roads has created obstacles to rational land use and transport planning: such land confiscation and settlement expansion should cease. Other measures are imperative:

- Palestinian road access must be improved. Israeli checkpoints that still mark the entrances to West Bank Palestinian cities should be removed. Free access for Palestinians on the critical Jerusalem road axis must be ensured in order to facilitate traffic and commerce between various West Bank cities.
- Due to the sub-standard nature of the road system, and the rapid growth in population and motorization, the road network in the West Bank will have to be improved and expanded in the future. The natural geography of the region does not allow for the easy construction of roads. New technology using GIS techniques is essential to identify suitable corridors.
- More emphasis should also be placed on managed land use. Decision-makers should promote policies that reduce car dependency and long travel times and promote public transport, including alternatives to road transport. Current patterns of land use development must be assessed, and strategies promulgated for the prevention of urban sprawl through the development of mixed land uses and/or compact urban forms in city centres. These strategies will help to reduce air pollution and promote social equity by allowing easier access to education, jobs, services and shopping for women, children, the elderly and poor people, who typically do not have access to cars.
- Simultaneously, the Palestinian Authority should promote walking and cycling as a means of reducing air pollution.

Modern research on transport systems in Palestine is very meagre indeed. More studies will be required in transportation modelling and modelling of land use planning, in addition to utilizing modern methodology as well as the experience of developed countries in developing a more sustainable transportation system in Palestine.

Notes

1   This chapter was first published as a paper in *World Transport Policy & Practice*, vol 5, no 4, pp18–29. The authors would like to express their gratitude to the

Deutsche Forschungsgemeinschaft (DFG) for funding the Applied Research Institute at Jerusalem (ARIJ) to undertake research on transport planning and land use. Also to Elaine Fletcher for her useful comments, discussion and feedback. A thank you goes to Violette Qumsieh, Isam Ishaq and Nezar Qattoush for their useful comments.

References

Anderson, W, Kanaroglou, P and Miller, E (1996) 'Urban forms, energy and the environment: a review of issues, evidence and policy', *Urban Studies,* vol 33, pp7–35

ARIJ (1997a) *The Status of the Environment in the West Bank*, Applied Research Institute, Jerusalem

ARIJ (1997b) *Traffic Survey for the West Bank*, Applied Research Institute, Jerusalem

ARIJ (1999) *ARIJ GIS Database*, Applied Research Institute, Jerusalem

Economopoulos, A (1993) *Assessments of Sources of Air, Water and Land Pollution: A Guide to Rapid Source Inventory Techniques and their Use in Formulating Control Strategies, Part 1*, World Health Organization, Geneva

Hanson, S (1986) *The Geography of Urban Transportation,* The Guildford Press, New York

ICBS (1995) *Judea, Samaria and Gaza Area Statistics*, Israeli Central Bureau of Statistics, Jerusalem

ICBS (1997) *Statistical Abstract of Israel* (vol 48), Israeli Central Bureau of Statistics, Jerusalem

PCBS (1997) *Census Data for the West Bank and Gaza Palestinian*, Central Bureau of Statistics, Gaza

Qattoush, N (1999) 'Transportation difficulties: Wadi Al-Nar as a case study', unpublished report presented at the Applied Research Institute, Jerusalem

Whiteman, J (1988) *The Environment in Israel*, Environmental Protection Service, Ministry of the Interior, Jerusalem

Part 9

Visioning Change

25

New Directions in World Transport Policy and Practice

John Whitelegg and Gary Haq

Introduction

The first 24 chapters in this book have shown that there is a very significant transport problem in most parts of the world, and it is getting worse. The developed world is currently experiencing unprecedented levels of personal and freight mobility and the associated impacts on the environment, quality of life, human health and physical and social wellbeing. Although motorization rates in many developing countries are relatively low compared to the developed world, they are rapidly increasing and are not dissimilar to the levels of motorization that were experienced in Europe in the 1950s and 1960s. However, opportunities exist for the developing world to learn from rather than replicate the mistakes of auto-dependent societies of the developed world. Whether it be car-free days in Bogotá, public transport in Hong Kong or land use planning in Groningen, developed and developing countries can learn from each other's transport policies and best practice to adopt appropriate measures to deal with their own unique development problems.

Increasing world mobility and the over-dependence on motorized transportation poses the greatest challenge to achieving sustainable transport in the 21st century. This chapter outlines the key messages that can be taken from policy and practice in European and North American countries and explores what is required to re-set the default option of an auto-dependent society in both the developed and developing world.

Dimensions of the Global Tranport Problem

There are many dimensions to the global transport problem, which makes it one of greatest challenges to sustainable development.

- Car dependence and car ownership is still seen as a very desirable consumer expectation and objective supported by large global expenditures in marketing, advertising and the sale of images. The images are primarily sexual and status-oriented with strong links into power and mastery. Alternatives to the car have a very difficult time when set against this powerful imagery and association. Ultimately, taking a bus in Manchester, Seoul or México City is not associated with sexual and economic success and is not attractive to successive cohorts of young adults making their way through to fully independent mobility.

- Car dependence is supported and encouraged by very large allocations of tax dollars. This support from national and international administrations (eg the European Union (EU), development banks) takes place at the same time as resources for welfare, health and pensions are scaled down and includes: highway construction, high speed rail and aviation infrastructure construction (both of which encourage car use), direct support to car manufacturers, technological research and development (R&D), revenue foregone through generous taxation rules (eg company car taxation benefits and free car parking), costs directly associated with car use and not paid for by the user (eg health costs associated with deaths and injuries, the costs of policing, health damage from air and noise pollution) and the economic costs of climate change.
- Global, national and regional materials flows are imposing larger burdens on society and the environment through an increase in lorry numbers. The distances over which road freight is carried by truck are increasing over time in response to globalized industry and the locational behaviour of production units, which seek out low cost (in terms of labour and tax breaks) regions. The spatial structure of production is fragmenting to build in longer distance movements and to substitute 'far for near'. The movement of food products especially represents a 'food swap' operation where the possibility of meeting local demands with local production/ supply are foregone in a spatially irrational, distance maximizing strategy.
- Aviation is probably the best example of a heavily subsidized, distance maximizing consumer product. The growth of aviation is putting larger demands on cities and regions to meet this growth with new airports, new terminals and new runways. Aviation receives very large subsidies (infrastructure and air traffic control, the absence of a fuel tax and the absence of VAT on tickets). Aviation also benefits from very large R&D expenditures nationally and internationally, especially from military engine, air frame and materials development costs, all of which are simply transferred as zero-cost benefits to the civil airline industry. The consequences of the strong growth of aviation for global climate change and biodiversity as well as human health around airports are very significant indeed.

These dimensions of the transport problem vary in their intensity around the world. There is also a strong temporal dimension. The large scale engineering and infrastructure effects in Europe and North America (land-take, loss of biodiversity) are now impacting in India and China, but not yet at their full strength. The growth in demand for transport infrastructure of all kinds in these two countries alone has much further to go and will involve the complete re-modelling of cities like Mumbai and Kolkata in India, and Beijing and Shanghai in China. This re-modelling will also involve a very large transfer of resources and investment capital from the poorer groups to the richer groups, as tax dollars are allocated to major road and airport schemes. Next in line for this double hit of 'sequestered' tax dollars and major land-take are African cities. Africa is slightly behind Asia in its car ownership and use performance (with the exception of South Africa), but like Asia over the last 20 years it will strive very hard to make up this lost ground. This temporal dimension to auto dependency will guarantee a steady supply of new markets for truck and auto makers (indeed, these interest groups are actively involved in creating the demand) and a strong resistance to the European and North American realization that there are alternative futures to the one dominated by the car, truck and plane.

The spatial and temporal dimension is also overlain by an ethical dimension (Whitelegg, 2000). The allocation of significant financial resources to transport infrastructure projects transfers cash from general use (eg clean drinking water, public health, housing, community facilities) to narrowly defined, relatively wealthy groups (eg car users in Asia). The construction of new roads often involves the forcible relocation of local residents and/or the transfer of land from agricultural use to tarmac and concrete, causing distress and economic hardship to such groups. Relocation is an ethical problem, and reallocating land to car 'crops' as opposed to food crops is an ethical problem. These problems are increasingly concentrated in India and China and other parts of Asia, but the construction of motorways in the UK (eg the Birmingham Northern Relief Road) has caused distress to thousands of people and has been justified on grounds of relieving traffic congestion on adjacent motorways. Alternative ways of alleviating congestion (eg demand management) have been rejected.

The ethical dimension is ubiquitous in space and time. The affluent car commuter driving to work in central Liverpool in the UK imposes a significant environmental and health burden on poor communities in nearby Toxteth and Dingle. The wealthy residents of affluent villages in rural England drive regularly into towns and cities, destroying the environment of poorer groups while demanding better transport facilities for their own rural idylls. Local residents of all income groups around Heathrow airport in London suffer noise and health damage from thousands of aircraft movements every week. The loss of sleep and the loss of health is accepted by airport planners and governments as a reasonable price to pay for a cheap holiday in Spain or a short journey by air (when there are rail alternatives).

Transport has now become one of the most significant ethical problems in the world today. The daily damage to children, the elderly, the sick and local communities is routinely accepted everywhere as a price worth paying for a car trip for any purpose over any distance, even when that car trip is breaking the speed limit and terrorizing local neighbourhoods with anti-social driving behaviour. There is an official acceptance of the general principle that there should be no restriction on car use, and there is no mechanism for weighing the enormous advantages of a car trip of 500m to buy a packet of cigarettes over the small disadvantages of a dead child or a street that cannot be used by local residents because it so dangerous, noisy and polluted.

Re-setting the Default Option in Auto-dependent Societies

Notwithstanding the scale of the transport problem and the signs that the global problem is getting worse, there are a large number of well designed and highly effective projects in Europe and North America that are reversing these trends. These include the following:

- Zurich in Switzerland has held levels of auto ownership and traffic volumes constant for a decade whilst public transit use has soared.
- Houten in The Netherlands has developed a comprehensive bicycle/pedestrian network and cut car trips per household by 25 per cent.
- Swiss and German research on car-sharing shows that people who have joined a car-sharing scheme (not carpooling) and who have previously owned a car have reduced their car mileage by 50 per cent. The Federal Ministry of Transport in Germany estimates that car-sharing will reduce annual vehicle kilometres (vkm) by 7000 million. For Europe as a whole the figure is a reduction of 30,000 million vkm.
- In Aachen (Germany), traffic into the city centre has been reduced by 85 per cent over the last ten years, the car's share of transport has fallen from 44 per cent to 36 per cent and the emission of nitrogen oxides (NO_x) has been reduced by 50 per cent.
- In Bologna (Italy), a deliberate policy of traffic restraint involving the closing of streets and park and ride produced a 48 per cent reduction in motorized traffic entering the historic core and a 64 per cent reduction in cars (1982–1989).
- In Groningen (The Netherlands) in 1990, 48 per cent of all trips within the city were by bicycle, 17 per cent by foot, 5 per cent by public transport and 30 per cent by car.
- In Manchester (UK), the Metrolink tram has taken up to 50 per cent of car journeys off roads in the area it serves. It has replaced over 1 million car journeys into the city centre each year.
- Five per cent of car users switched to a new 'City Express' bus service in Belfast (Northern Ireland) in the first six months of operation.
- Edinburgh (UK) has set itself a traffic reduction target of 30 per cent.
- In Leicester (UK), 10 per cent more 7–9 year olds were allowed to walk to school after traffic calming.
- Levels of cycling in one of the 'Safe Routes to School' pilot projects at Horndean Community School in Hampshire (UK) have more than doubled even without the necessary infrastructure works being carried out. More than 120 pupils are regularly cycling to school, compared with about 50 the previous autumn and just 36 when the project began at the end of 1995.
- The 'Carte Orange' in Paris (France), covering all modes and introduced in 1975, led to a 36 per cent increase in bus patronage.
- The London travelcard (UK) led to a 16 per cent increase in public transport use at a time of decline elsewhere.
- The integration of land use planning and transport planning in Portland, Oregon (USA) has led to 30,000 more jobs and 40 per cent of commuters using public transport.
- In Zurich (Switzerland), substantial investment in public transport coupled with parking and access policies have led to the stabilization that will allow local authorities to do their work effectively.

One of the most remarkable transport projects in recent years has taken place in Perth (Western Australia). In a project funded by the state government and carried out by the German transport consultancy Socialdata, the number of vehicles on the roads of Perth has been reduced by 78,000 per day. The project is one of several similar projects that have been carried out in Australia, the UK, Germany and Austria, which are known as 'individualized marketing'. The central concept underpinning these projects is that individual travel choices currently being exercized in the direction of the car can be changed. The process of change involves direct contact with the individuals concerned (15,300 households containing 35,000 individuals in the case of South Perth). Individuals are contacted by phone and those responding to the request for a discussion about travel choice are presented with information and advice of direct relevance to their individual circumstances. Those requiring more information and a detailed discussion are visited in their own homes and offered sample tickets on public transport as well as advice on walking and cycling.

In Perth, the results of the project have been:

- a 10 per cent reduction in single occupancy vehicle (SOV) use;
- a 21 per cent increase in public transport use;
- a 91 per cent increase in cycling;
- a 16 per cent increase in walking; and
- a 14 per cent reduction in vkms.

These results reveal a great deal about transport problems, perceptions and psychology. The most significant implication is that people are prepared to change their behaviour when presented with enough information and discussion to facilitate the shift away from the car. Clearly, the degree of auto dependency in Western societies is the result of habitual behaviour and of a severe lack of detailed targeted information available exactly where and when it is needed. The car has become the default option, and attempts to improve public transport or make cycling more attractive will not have much impact if they are implemented at a general level in a context where individual choice-making is left to take its normal course. One could add that this normal course includes several hundred millions of dollars annually of advertising aimed at the car and targeting the most individual of individual preferences (sex, status, power, safety, security, instantaneous satisfaction of wants). The Perth project has been repeated in Brisbane, Australia with similar results and in Frome and Gloucester in the UK (results not yet available).

In the UK, there are now over 1000 transport plans in place at the level of individual organizations (offices, universities, hospitals, local authorities, government departments and airports). Many of these have been carried out at the individual initiative of the organization itself, while others have been carried out with direct governmental support through the supply of free consultancy to organizations expressing an interest in implementing one of these plans. The UK government programme is known as the Energy Best Practice Programme (EBPP), and the individual organizational activities as site-specific advice (SSA). In a manner that is directly analogous with the Perth project, these company transport plans have reduced SOV use or vkm by up to 20 per cent over a three-year plan period. Individuals have once again responded to the direct application of analysis and measures linked to personal circumstances to make a change in travel choice. A UK government report on the effectiveness of company transport plans (DTLR, 2002) concluded:

Averaged overall these organizations managed to reduce the numbers of cars arriving at their sites by more than 14 per 100 staff – more than an 18 per cent reduction in the number of cars that were previously there. Sixteen of the travel plans cut car use by more than 10 per cent, five by more than a fifth and two by more than 50 per cent.

In 2001, the USA-based multinational pharmaceutical company, Pfizer, carried out a three-year monitoring exercise on its transport plan at a large manufacturing and research facility in southeast England. A detailed survey of travel behaviour was carried out on 4000 staff and the results compared with a baseline survey from 1998. The 1998–2001 change in travel behaviour revealed:

- 11.8 per cent reduction in SOVs;
- 76 per cent increase in bus use;
- 15.2 per cent increase in car-sharing;
- 8.8 per cent reduction in bicycle use;
- 6.6 per cent reduction in walking; and
- 25 per cent increase in motorcycle use.

This level of change in a three-year period in a semi-rural area of southeast England by relatively well paid professional staff is very unusual in the UK. The geography of this area (Sandwich in Kent) is not conducive to walking and cycling and the distances travelled by staff to work are not easily accomplished by public transport.

The Pfizer project (Pfizer, 2000) was initiated by the company in 1997, developed by the transport consultants Eco-Logica Ltd and implemented by a designated transport officer working within the company. It involved no encouragement or persuasion from public bodies (city or regional authorities) and it received no funding from government at any level.

The detailed measures that were implemented to achieve this amount of change in travel behaviour are not particularly new or original. They include very efficient car-share database systems, reduced prices on buses and trains, company funded buses, large amounts of debate and discussion amongst all the staff about the objectives of the transport plan, the establishment of user groups, clear and widely available information about public transport options, journey planning information on the company intranet, improved internal bus movement possibilities, new cycle routes and bicycle parking facilities. What was new and original was the coordinated effort throughout the company to bring about change and the commitment of senior personnel in the company to the principle of reducing car use. This commitment includes guidance on how to run meetings so that the meetings start and finish to fit in with public transport/car-share arrangements.

In 2002, a survey of 1000 staff working for a medium sized city administration in central England showed that significant proportions of the staff were more than happy to move away from car use and towards different transport alternatives. The survey revealed a number of improvements in walking, cycling and public transport conditions that staff would like to see implemented, but none of the changes suggested were particularly difficult, time consuming or expensive. The survey asked the employees how many of them would use the alternative to the SOV three or more times a week if these improvements were put in place. The answers were:

- 38 per cent of employees would car-share;
- 20 per cent would cycle;
- 39 per cent would use public transport; and
- 20 per cent would walk.

Even allowing for the uncertainties around questionnaires and invitations to express multiple preferences, the scale of support for alternatives to SOVs is very large. Transport plans in the UK show that there is no problem with propensity to change. The only problem (which is very large) is the unwillingness of politicians at all levels to make the policy shift. Politicians still believe that the car is a politically sensitive question and that policies should not be capable of being interpreted as anti-car. As Werner Brög has shown (Brög, 2002), politicians fundamentally misread the views of members of public on the degree to which they would like to see car use curbed and policies shift in the direction of prioritizing alternatives to the car. Whilst this is primarily a European finding supported by Australian research, there are strong echoes in the well supported NGO movements in Mumbai and Kolkata. Transport advocacy work with NGOs in Kolkata (Whitelegg, 1999) revealed a huge groundswell of popular support for reducing car use, car access and vehicle pollution in that city and for improving the impressive but neglected walking, tram and rickshaw transport systems.

The significance of the Australian individualized marketing work and the transport plan work exemplified by Pfizer is that travel choices can and will change in response to carefully targeted information and well designed plans to encourage lower levels of car dependence.

These approaches have their origins in the USA and Europe and are not directly transferable to India, China or Africa. They do, however, have a global significance that goes far beyond their limited territorial application. They show that so-called advanced industrial and post-industrial societies can reduce car use. Hence car use and auto dependency is not a necessary consequence of a particular stage of development. Equally, it is not a model that can be exported everywhere in the world. We now have another model and one based on lower levels of car use. The default option is no longer the car.

Re-setting the Default Option: The Details

Notwithstanding the success of individualized marketing and the UK SSA programme, it would not be prudent to rely entirely on projects that work on perception, information and choices alone. Many of the chapters in this Reader have shown very powerfully the degree to which current transport policies in most parts of the world are working to shift choices even more strongly in the direction of car dependency. It follows that there has to be some unravelling of the perverse policy options currently near the top of the pile in most countries (including road building, taxation and airport expansion). A great deal of hard and creative work on SSAs and individualized marketing will not stop the flyovers currently under construction in cities in Asia to encourage higher levels of motorization.

Re-setting the default option requires a vision of where we want to get to (ie, what is the objective of transport policy?) and a management intervention model that can deal with transport issues on every front at the same time. At the very least we need to manage the demand for transport through nine inter-related policy programmes at the same time and in the same place, and with a very sensitive eye for geographical individuality. What might be a good idea in rural Wiltshire in southwest England might be totally irrelevant in Kolkata or rural West Bengal. We need to identify the principles, the ways of intervening and the successes and good news associated with intervention, and then leave the actual implementation to local and regional bodies near to the problem and as near as possible to local geography. The inter-related policy areas are:

- Land use planning to move local and regional spatial structures in the direction of reducing the demand for transport.
- Full internalization of external costs so that every trip by car, truck and air pays its full cost and pays its own way without requiring tax dollars from those not enjoying the benefits of the journey.
- Re-engineering of taxation systems to eradicate tax breaks and tax incentives that have the effect of encouraging more car/truck travel and transferring resources from poorer groups to richer groups.
- Re-engineering cities to make them safe havens for pedestrians and cyclists. This will mean effective speed and emission controls and highway space re-allocation (less space for cars/trucks and more for public transport, walking and cycling).
- An end to direct state funding of any aspect of car/truck/aircraft R&D and an end to any direct subsidy of manufacturing/job creation or regeneration involving these technologies.
- An ethical audit of all transport spending. Projects that transfer wealth from the poor to the rich or damage the health of groups other than those in the cars/trucks/ aircraft should not go ahead. Projects that damage children should not go ahead. A better way to solve accessibility and mobility requirements can be found.
- A very clear carbon reduction strategy for transport so that transport delivers its proportionate responsibility for a 60 per cent cut in greenhouse gas (GHG) emissions. The proportionate contribution should also be delivered within sub-sectors of transport (aviation, car travel and trucking).
- New ways of conceptualizing the transport product, enhancing accessibility and delivering mobility, eg community car-share clubs, smart card purchases of distance by a variety of modes, direct payment per kilometre travelled.
- Localization projects, where detailed audits and system-wide interventions increase the proportion of goods and services consumed from local sources. The intention here is to reduce vkms of trucking.

Land Use Planning to Move Local and Regional Spatial Structures in the Direction of Reducing the Demand for Transport: Full Internalization of External Cost

The work of Newman and Kenworthy (1989) in Australia shows that car use and fuel consumption decline as urban residential density increases. US cities are amongst the most spatially dispersed in the world, followed by a group of Australian cities and then a group of European cities. Density should not be regarded as the most important determinant of car use, but it does offer a number of possibilities for bringing about a better balance of land uses and transport choices.

In both the UK and the USA there is a well established debate about the potential of 'compact cities' and 'smart growth' for bringing about a better quality of life, with more travel destinations accessible within a smaller area, higher levels of non-motorized transport (NMT) use and investment in restoring a sense of community and vitality to city centres and older suburbs (see www.smartgrowth.org).

Large Asian cities (eg Kolkata) already perform very well on accessibility and NMT criteria. The problems in Indian cities are mainly related to air pollution and road traffic accidents (RTAs). Walking and cycling in Delhi or Kolkata will expose the road user to very high levels of particulate pollution, which cause respiratory diseases and can be fatal. The pedestrian footpaths are also often very sub-standard, with narrow width, numerous obstacles and inadequate crossing facilities.

There are numerous examples of good urban design and integrated land use and transport planning around the world, including the Curitiba (Brazil) bus-ways and the concentration of development on those corridors, and the train line to Joondaloup north of Perth in Western Australia, which has attracted many commuters from the roads and supported commercial and housing developments around railway stations. Both the Brazilian and Australian examples show the advantages of transit-oriented development.

Cities such as Curitiba, Bogotá (Colombia) and Copenhagen (Denmark) provide good practice examples where coordination of land use and transport planning can result in a reduction in car use, improved public transport use, walking and cycling and a better quality of life for all (O'Meara Sheehan, 2002).

John Robert (of the consultancy TEST) ran a comparison of Almere (The Netherlands) and Milton Keynes and demonstrated the extent to which land use and transport planning can influence the demand for motorized transport:

> the most obvious finding, and an important one, was the much higher percentage of trips made by car and the much lower level of bicycle use in Milton Keynes when compared to Almere (65.7 per cent of trips by car compared to 43.1 per cent, 5.8 per cent of trips by bicycle compared to 27.5 per cent respectively) (TEST, 1991).

The influence of compact cities on reducing motorized trips is reviewed in Smith, Whitelegg and Williams (1998). Physical land use planning is a tried and tested method of reducing the length of trips, increasing the use of NMT modes and reducing the demand for expensive road infrastructure.

Key Message: avoid low density sprawl and use every opportunity to develop transit-oriented development alongside new public transport infrastructure.

Cars, trucks and air traffic do not pay the full amount of the costs that they impose on non-users. Pollution, health damage, road building and maintenance, GHGs, policing and judicial systems all create costs that are paid by non-users (the general taxpayer). These sums are very large (Maddison et al, 1996). In Europe, the policy of the EU is clear: the user should pay the full amount of these costs (the internalization of external costs). However, legislation and taxation changes to implement this policy are seriously ineffective. Even more surprisingly there is still a substantial flow of public funds into the car industry and into aviation, which both boost demand for a polluting activity and widen the gap between what the user pays and what the full implementation of internalization would imply should be paid.

In road transport, a number of policies are in existence or about to be implemented (eg, in the UK, the London road pricing cordon) which move transport closer to full internalization. Road pricing and fuel taxation are attractive policy options, particularly if the revenues could be recycled into the local economy to support all the alternatives to the private car. According to the OECD (1995) survey of transport policy options, road pricing is being considered in some shape or form in most OECD countries. Plans are well advanced in Cambridge and Edinburgh (UK); toll systems exist in Bergen, Oslo and Trondheim in Norway; and Stockholm, Sweden is planning to introduce such a system. Since the early 1960s, the implementation of road pricing in London has been considered on several occasions. Road pricing is generally suggested for those locations where the growth rate in traffic is already the lowest across a number of geographical situations. The growth of traffic into and out of central London has been far lower than the growth in outer London or the growth on the M25 corridor. Road pricing is best seen as a strongly supportive measure alongside a battery of other measures including strong land use controls and modal preference.

The view of the OECD (1995, p154) is that 'The key to the sustainable development strand is a substantial and steadily increasing fuel tax coupled with (other) measures'. The UK already had a policy commitment to increase fuel tax by 6 per cent above the rate of inflation at each annual budget. This was abandoned in 1998 by the new Labour government. The OECD suggest that the impact of a 7 per cent per annum rise in fuel costs in real terms would be to 'quadruple fuel prices in 20 years … [leading] … to lower car ownership levels compared with what they would otherwise be, fewer car trips and shorter trip lengths'. An overall reduction in car trip-making of about 15 per cent, a reduction in trip length of about 25 per cent and an overall reduction of vkms of one-third is predicted if fuel prices rise by a factor of 2.5 (OECD, 1995, p156).

The Stockholm proposals provide a model for city authorities in Europe. Stockholm will be divided into ten zones covering the whole of the built-up area, served by 90 fee stations. Light vehicles (eg cars) would pay €0.45 or €0.55 per transit on weekdays between 6am and 7pm. The lower charge is for automatic debiting and the higher for manual systems. Heavy good vehicles (HGVs) would pay €1.10 per transit if fitted with noise-reduction technology and €1.40 if not. Once again, higher charges would apply to manual systems. The differential charge for noise indicates a real environmental benefit from road pricing. Vehicles can be charged on a number of different noise and pollution criteria to help achieve air and noise quality objectives as well as congestion targets.

The Stockholm scheme is estimated to result in approximately €140 million a year. 13 per cent is allocated to administrative costs, 79 per cent is refunded to residents and the rest set aside for noise reduction and public transport expenditures.

Key Message: apply the full force of internalization of all external costs so that the user pays the full cost of the chosen mode.

Re-engineering of Taxation

Taxation systems around the world reward car ownership, car use and trucking. This is very clearly the case in Australia (Laird et al, 2001). The authors of the Australian analysis suggest four basic areas for reform:

1   Bring the perceived cost of car use into line with the actual total costs by means of parking charges and congestion tolls on urban roads.
2   Reduce federal taxation benefits for car ownership and usage and increase tax benefits for public transport use.
3   Increase the aggregate road cost recovery from trucks and introduce distance differentiation (weight–distance tax).
4   Increase federal fuel excise duty so as to recover the external costs of road vehicle usage.

These measures are equally applicable in other countries. Best practice examples already exist in some countries. Denmark has one of the lowest car ownership rates in the EU, which is at least in part the result of a 160 per cent tax on the purchase of new vehicles. Taxation on vehicles in The Netherlands and Germany varies with the size of the engine so that larger, more polluting vehicles pay a higher tax.

Key Message: dismantle all taxation systems that work in favour of increased car ownership and use and re-structure taxation to reward sustainable transport choices. The same principle should be applied to freight.

Re-engineering Cities to Improve Conditions for Pedestrians, Cyclists and Public Transport Users

There are many isolated examples of successful policies in this area: the Manchester Metrolink; bus lanes in several UK cities; Zurich's prioritization of public transport (Switzerland); the Maidstone Integrated Sustainable Transport (MIST) project (UK); car-free residential and city centre areas (Lubeck, Amsterdam, Berlin, Edinburgh); building homes on car parks; bicycle priority schemes and planning in York and

Cambridge (UK), Delft and Groningen (The Netherlands) and Detmold and Rosen-heim (Germany); Copenhagen's cycling strategy (Denmark); Darmstadt's (Germany) encouragement of cyclists and pedestrians to share the same large car-free space in the city centre; SMART buses in Liverpool; new tram systems in Strasbourg; and innovative car-sharing initiatives (StattAuto) in Berlin, Bremen and Edinburgh (eg 3000 participants in the Berlin car-sharing scheme have removed 2000 cars from the roads of Berlin). Vienna (Austria) has adopted a policy of constructing several hundred extended pavements at crossings and tram stops to improve safety for pedestrians.

Groningen (The Netherlands) has developed a sector access model; Bochum (Germany) has prioritized its trams in preference to cars; Gothenburg (Sweden) has divided the central business district into five cells, which has had the effect of reducing car mobility by 50 per cent; Houten (The Netherlands, population 30,000) has given preference to bicycles, restricted access by sectors and restrained traffic. Over the last 20 years, Oxford has produced one of the lowest rates of traffic growth in the city centre of any UK city through parking controls and park and ride schemes.

The Institute for Transportation and Development Policy (ITDP) in New York has been actively involved in strengthening the human-powered vehicle industry in a number of developing countries (ITDP, 2001). In India, ITDP worked with bicycle manufacturers to modernize the cycle rickshaw, which resulted in over 500 modern cycle rickshaws operating in cities such as Delhi and Agra. The project demonstrated that modernized rickshaws were superior vehicles that attracted 19 per cent of their ridership from highly polluting two-stroke-engine vehicles. In addition, the incomes of the cycle rickshaw drivers increased by 20–50 per cent because they were able to attract new passengers. Based on the success in India, ITDP now plans to replicate the project in Indonesia. ITDP has been also involved in providing technical support and funding to the Afribike project in South Africa to increase bicycle use. Afribike receives most of its bicycles from European and US groups, which send used bikes to Africa. In 2000, Afribike became an independent organization and is now working to establish South Africa's first bicycle path network (see www.afribike.org).

Key Message: reallocate urban space away from the car and towards walking, cycling and public transport. Use the same principle to reward pedestrians, cyclists and public transport users with time advantages (shorter routes, priority at junctions etc).

An End to Direct State Funding of any Aspect of Car/ Truck/Aircraft R&D and the Subsidy of Manufacturing Activity

In March 2002 the EU launched an investigation into the direct subsidy of a BMW car manufacturing plant in Leipzig (Germany). The German government had declared its intention to make a grant of approximately €40 million to encourage BMW to build the factory in the former East Germany. This represents 35 per cent of the total cost of the project. Every car manufacturer in Europe has received similar assistance, and new vehicle manufacturing plants in India and China have received direct state subsidies. Similar subsidies have gone to truck manufacturers on the same arguments that regional or employment policy requires investment in factories to make vehicles. This generosity has not extended to walking, cycling and public transport investments.

In Rio Grande do Sul in southern Brazil, the state government has promised to build a new port, a dedicated canal link, utilities and road and rail links in order to lure in a US$600 million General Motors car plant. All of this expensive new infrastructure will be provided free of charge and for the exclusive use of General Motors. Because these expenditures are so large, basic services to the general population (energy, water and roads) are under threat.

Aviation receives equally large subsidies. Large amounts of public expenditure are devoted to military budgets and used in the development of new engines, new airframes and new material for aircraft. All this very expensive R&D is then provided at no cost to civil aviation. This represents a huge subsidy to one of the fastest growing sectors of transport.

Airlines receive large amounts of funds from their national governments for restructuring, and air traffic control costs are funded partly if not wholly from public funds (including EU R&D funds). These funds may be direct payments, as in the case of Air France and Olympic Airways, or indirect, as in the case of the slots at London's Heathrow Airport allocated to British Airways. Slots are a valuable commodity conferring historic rights to profitable routes and are not allocated by any market mechanism.

Aircraft R&D and manufacture are also subsidized, as in the March 2000 decision of the UK government to offer approximately UK£500 million to British Aerospace to develop the next generation of large aircraft. All these methods of shifting the costs of aviation away from users and on to the taxpayer, whether he or she flies or not, are economic distortions and should be ended together with fuel tax exemption and zero-rated VAT on airline tickets. The Dutch aviation campaigning group Right Price for Air Travel has calculated that EU taxpayers subsidize the aviation industry by €45 billion per annum (and this figure excludes surface access data, because they are not available).

The EU is deeply involved in funding the expansion of aviation facilities. The majority of this funding is from the European Investment Bank (EIB), which in 1998 provided €5.4 billion in loans to transport infrastructure projects of which €1.25 billion was for air and maritime transport. These loans funded increases in capacity at Hanover, Edinburgh, Heathrow, Gatwick, Bologna, Athens, Reunion and Madeira airports. They also funded airline fleet renewals in Austria, Spain, Portugal, Luxembourg and Sweden. These large sums of money are provided under very favourable terms and conditions to the aviation industry (EIB, 1998, p22):

> the bank is prepared to extend the terms of its loans and the grace periods in respect of repayment of principal, and even payment of interest, beyond the customary limits and arrange financial engineering to help reduce the risks incurred by the various players involved, for instance by means of refinancing facilities, making advance funding available or drawing up, also in advance, framework financing agreements. A growing number of projects, especially priority schemes, have already benefited from the measures provided for under this window such as … the new Milan-Malpensa airport and Athens Spata airport.

In the UK alone, €152 million (out of a total of €956 million) was provided for expansion and modernization at Edinburgh, Heathrow and Gatwick airports. The total of €956.9 million for aviation in one year is much larger than the total loans made to all small and medium enterprises in Europe in all sectors of the economy in one year (€600 million).

This system of favourable loans made in support of EU policies on transport and regional development acts as both an insulator from the normal rigours of free market financing and as a strong force pushing up the supply of infrastructure and stimulating growth in demand. In this sense, aviation does not conform in any way to a free market model of business development. The removal of these unnecessary privileges and subsidies is a key component of any strategy to reduce the demand for flying.

Key Message: end the practice of direct state subsidy to car, truck and aircraft manufacturers. The aviation industry should pay full commercial rates for the transfer of technology from military projects.

An Ethical Audit of Transport Spending

The current spate of flyover construction in Mumbai and Kolkata illustrates the significance of this issue. In both cities it has been very difficult to find the resources to improve public transport, develop cycling facilities and improve the pedestrian environment. In Kolkata, the subcontinent's last remaining tram system is in very poor physical condition and subject to repeated breakdowns. Tram system assets (road space, workshops, depots) are attracting interest from property developers and others who can offer the state of West Bengal financially rewarding arrangements linked to the removal of trams. Trams in Kolkata are safe and pleasant to use (especially for women and children) and much safer than the badly maintained and badly driven buses. Funding the tram system offers considerable benefits to every section of Kolkata society, but this option attracts very little political support. Funding the construction of flyovers offers large financial gains to the construction industry as well as bribes. Funding flyovers allocates 90 per cent of transport spending in a given geographical area for the benefit of 5 per cent of the population of Kolkata who own cars. This is unethical.

Ethics is not something that richer countries are good at, and poorer countries have misunderstood it. In the developed world the wealthier groups in society drive much more and fly much more than the poorer groups. These wealthier groups benefit disproportionately from public expenditures (they win a bigger share of available tax dollars) whilst at the same time imposing most of the pollution on poorer groups. In the UK, rich people do not tend to live on heavily trafficked streets. They can afford to live in more pleasant areas but they then enjoy the pleasures of driving on streets in Liverpool and London, imposing severe RTA, pollution and respiratory disease hazards on poorer people.

In a recent court judgement (October 2001) before the European Court of Human Rights (in the case of Hatton and Others versus the United Kingdom), the Court held that there had been a violation of Article 8 of the European Convention on Human

Rights. Article 8 guarantees the right to respect for private and family life and home. The case involved a group of residents around Heathrow Airport near London who argued that they could not sleep because of aircraft noise and that their family life had been disrupted. The Court agreed with the residents and found against the UK government which, it concluded, had not done enough to protect its citizens' rights. Importantly from a transport point of view the Court also concluded that it is not enough for a national government simply to assert that the night flights were essential to the efficient working of the UK economy.

This judgement is of some considerable significance in transport. Europe's most important human rights court has confirmed that citizens do have a right to environmental protection, that the state does have an obligation to protect this right and that general economic arguments are insufficient to overturn these rights. These ingredients are also in place along most heavily trafficked roads in Europe and in the vicinity of major examples of transport infrastructure including high speed rail links, all airports and freight/logistic centres. Transport has now been linked to human rights and a great deal more of this kind of legal struggle will occur in the future.

Key Message: develop a completely new ethical and human rights perspective on transport and test transport decisions and policy-making procedures on their ethical and human rights implications.

A Carbon Reduction Strategy for the Transport Sector

The conclusions of the Intergovernmental Panel on Climate Change (IPCC) are very clear. Global warming and climate change is being influenced by greenhouse gas (GHG) emissions from human activity, and the consequences over the next 50 years for an increasing likelihood of flooding, storm damage, loss of life, drought and damage to the fabric of life in developing countries is real and confirmed (IPCC, 2001). According to the UK Meteorological Office and the University of East Anglia, the year 2001 proved to be the second warmest year worldwide since records began in the mid-19th century (Tiempo, 2002).

The Kyoto process has agreed an international system for reducing emissions. The USA refused to ratify this agreement, and in February 2002 President George Bush announced a unilateral, voluntary plan to reduce GHG emissions by 18 per cent over the next ten years based on GHG intensity, compared to a 33 per cent reduction under the Kyoto Protocol. GHG intensity is the ratio of emissions to economic output. The Bush administration believes that by linking emissions to economic growth rates, adverse impacts on employment and the economy can be avoided. However, in actual emission reductions the Bush target represents a 4.5 per cent reduction below the 1990 baseline, as opposed to the Kyoto target for the USA of 7 per cent. The voluntary nature of the plan means that businesses can decide to opt into the GHG reduction programme. Tax breaks, together with an emissions trading programme, will be provided to act as incentives for GHG reduction (Tiempo, 2002). Australia has also been very reluctant and has now accepted that its GHG reduction target is an 8 per cent increase by 2012 on a 1990 base.

Through all of these discussion and at national level there is an assumption that transport is in some way difficult or expensive to include within specific sectoral reduction strategies. This is not the case and this view is not acceptable.

Even in Australian cities (low density, generous freeway provision, long distances) there is a 10/30/50 rule:

- 10 per cent of all trips by car are less than 1km in length;
- 30 per cent of all trips by car are less than 3km in length; and
- 50 per cent of all trips by car are less than 5km in length.

Transferring a proportion of these trips away from the car and towards NMT/public transport can reduce GHGs by 30 per cent. A 30 per cent reduction in vkms translates into an equivalent reduction in GHG.

Similarly, in trucking it is possible to reduce the distances travelled by truck (see the localization section below), and in aviation a combination of emission charges, fuel taxes and modal transfer from air travel to train travel over distances of up to 500km can reduce GHG emissions from this sector by 20–30 per cent.

Currently in Europe, North America and Australia, GHG emissions from the transport sector are 'excused' the rigours of reduction strategies. This has significant implications for the achievement of Kyoto targets overall, and the view of the European Environment Agency in Copenhagen is that the growth of GHG from transport may well result in the failure to achieve Kyoto targets to reduce GHGs. This is certainly the case in the UK where the national target is a 23 per cent reduction by 2010 on a 1990 base.

The absence of a sectoral target for transport also transfers the burden to other sectors (domestic heating, offices/commercial, industrial). In economic terms this may not be an efficient allocation of responsibilities. Why should we strive to reduce manufacturing industry GHG emissions below what has already been achieved in order to encourage people to use low cost airlines to fly from Liverpool to Barcelona for UK£20? The starting point for a sectoral reduction strategy has to be fair and efficient, ie equal burden sharing. If there is an argument for trucking and aviation to be excused then we have not yet heard it.

Implementing transport reduction strategies has to be seen as part of a wider global contraction and convergence strategy (see www.gci.org.uk). Global equity requires that all nations reduce their GHG emissions, but in a way that recognizes the needs of developing countries to move at a different rate towards a target figure (convergence). Transport reductions in North America and Europe should be greater per annum than those expected of India. This element of equity will allow the debate in India (and developing countries more generally) to embrace GHG reduction more enthusiastically within an equitable framework.

Key Message: introduce GHG reduction targets for transport as a whole and for cars, trucks and aviation. These reduction targets should be at least equivalent to the agreed Kyoto and/or national GHG reduction targets (eg 23 per cent in the UK) and should take on board the policy of contraction and convergence (rich countries reduce their GHG more than poor countries and we all end up at an agreed level of emissions).

New Ways of Conceptualizing the Transport Product

Transport is the consumption of distance for a particular purpose, and yet the development of transport over the last 100 years has seen this simple of act of consumption shift towards the purchase of a car (a thing rather than a quantity of distance). This shift of emphasis, motivation and organization is a major obstacle to shifting transport behaviour into mainstream sustainability delivery.

The city of Bremen (Germany) is currently leading the way in a radical re-conceptualizing of transport consumption. The city has developed a number of community car-share clubs where local residents have the option of buying into vehicles that they do not own but can book for use for particular purposes at particular times. More importantly, they can purchase access to vehicles (time and distance) through the use of smart cards (or stored value cards), which can also be used for purchasing trips on buses, trains and trams in Bremen. Bremen residents also have a high quality pedestrian and cycling infrastructure. Bremen residents can now think about transport in a radically different way to the citizens of almost every other city in the world. If they really need to use a car, then they can have access to a car. If they do not, then they have a number of alternatives and all the choices (including the car) can be paid for within a very simple, accessible, clear and affordable payment system (see www.bremen.de). This rearranges the building blocks of decision-making in people's heads with some interesting results:

- One community car-share car replaces ten individually owned cars.
- Those who buy into the car-share clubs use cars a lot less than those who do not.
- Those who use the full range of distance purchasing options spend less than those who continue to pay for an individually owned car.

New technology can now take the Bremen model further. Smart cards exist that do not have to be swiped in a reading device or even produced for a bus driver/tram driver to inspect. They can be retained in the pocket/wallet and they will be automatically read and debited on using a bus, train or tram. This makes a transport system even easier to use and transforms public transport into a near match of car use. When using a car the user does not have to find any cash, pay a driver, find the right change, have the right ticket, get the zonal system right, pass an intelligence test to use the ticket machines or the zonal system, or acquire the tickets in advance. All of these normal aspects of public transport are a nuisance to many people and discourage public transport use. If car use is similarly organized (eg electronic road pricing with automatic smart card debiting systems, which are currently in place on the motorways around Milan (Italy), on the Sydney Harbour bridge in Australia and in Singapore) then individuals can bring all distance consuming activities within a directly comparable and easy to assimilate mental model of access, barriers and cost comparisons.

Smart cards also permit governmental intervention to re-balance the system in favour of sustainability. It would be very easy to adjust the smart card systems on motorways and urban roads to charge the full internalization of external cost price, and equally easy to adjust smart card technology/pricing systems to reflect the wider societal advantages (eg GHG reduction) of getting people out of cars for short journeys.

Key Message: adopt and develop further the Bremen model of reconceptualizing the transport consumption process to shift perceptions away from things (the car) and towards distance. Use smart cards and similar technology to remove all barriers to using public transport and to bring car use and the alternatives into a direct comparable relationship at the time decisions are made.

Localization and Truck Kilometre Reduction Strategies

Large trucks are a longstanding problem in towns and cities, on trunk roads through villages and in or near national parks. In general, their impact is much greater than their numbers would suggest. Their impact on noise, road damage, pedestrians, cyclists and air quality is large, and there is a strong case for reduction in ways that can protect the economy of towns and cities and the consumer who has come to depend on goods and services supplied by heavy goods vehicles (HGVs). Considerable progress has been made in this area in mainland Europe, particularly Germany, whilst hardly any progress at all has been made in the UK. In Germany, HGV reduction strategies that pay attention to the commercial interests of the companies involved are generally referred to as 'City-Logistik' strategies.

City-Logistiks involves setting up new partnerships and styles of cooperation between all those involved in the logistics chain and in delivering/receiving goods in city centres. These partnerships offer significant reductions in vkms and truck numbers and are currently in existence in Germany and Switzerland. City-Logistiks is a very clear illustration of the importance of developing high quality organizational arrangements and inter-company cooperation agreements in addition to whatever new technology might be appropriate. It has taken transport operations into an area of development that builds links and emphasizes cooperation across all players and interest groups.

In Germany, partnerships between logistics contractors are reducing lorry numbers and improving the urban environment. These partnerships (known as City-Logistik companies in Germany) are in operation in Berlin, Bremen, Ulm, Kassel and Freiburg. The Freiburg example has several pointers to the future shape of freight transport in urban areas. There are currently 12 partners in the scheme. Three of the partners leave city centre deliveries at the premises of a fourth. The latter then delivers all the goods involved in the city centre area. A second group of five partners delivers all its goods to one depot located near the city centre. An independent contractor (City-Logistik) delivers them to city centre customers. A third group, this time with only two service providers, specializes in refrigerated fresh products. These partners form an unbroken relay chain, one partner collecting the goods from the other for delivery to the city centre.

The Freiburg scheme has reduced total journey times from 566 hours to 168 hours (per month), the monthly number of truck operations from 440 to 295 (a 33 per cent reduction) and the time spent by lorries in the city from 612 hours to 317 hours (per month). The number of customers supplied or shipments made has remained the same. The Kassel scheme showed a reduction in vkms travelled of 70 per cent and in the number of delivering trucks of 11 per cent. This has reduced the costs of all the companies involved and increased the amount of work that can be done by each vehicle/driver combination.

These reductions in vehicle numbers and in traffic levels have benefited the companies through higher levels of utilization of the vehicle stock. It is not in the interests of logistic companies to have expensive vehicles clogged up in city centres, one-way systems and circuitous ring roads. There are clear economic benefits arising from lorry traffic reductions.

City-Logistiks shows the potential for new forms of company and spatial organization. The current pattern of truck use does not necessarily represent economic logic, and there are economic gains to be won at the same time as GHG reductions and environmental improvements. Germany has also implemented a specific truck tax (*LKW Maut*) to implement internalization of external cost principles and shift freight from road to rail.

The potential for yet more reduction in truck activity also exists. The growth in road freight in Europe in recent years has been in the distance over which goods are transported and not in the weight or volume of the goods. Put very crudely, we are getting much better at moving a given amount of freight over ever greater distances and in a way that transports many goods (especially food products) over much longer distances than necessary (there are intermediate sources of exactly the same products, but more distant sources are preferred). The main area of unexplored potential lies in localization. Localization is a term that describes a new kind of transport and regional analysis that tries to work out the potential for substituting near for far. For example, in any given region, what is the potential for supplying food products from the local region, as opposed to supplying the UK market with carrots from South Africa (Sustain, 2001)? Localization is not anti-free trade, nor is it anti-development in developing countries. It simply seeks a re-balancing of local and regional economies to encourage an appropriate level of local sourcing.

Key Message: the growth of road freight is a major threat to sustainable development and quality of life. New taxation measures are needed to apply full internalization of external cost and to make sure that road freight is not subsidized by the general taxpayer or other road users.

Concluding Remarks

Transport brings most, if not all, of the issues around sustainability, environmental and social impacts and citizen participation into a very sharp focus. If we can get transport right then we can deliver a huge contribution to GHG reduction and a huge increase in social justice all in one go. In many ways, transport is a metaphor for the generality of environmental and pollution (including land-take) problems. Whilst very clear threats do exist to climate, biodiversity and human health, the same tendencies and forces that are pressurizing environmental systems are also putting an intolerable burden on the poor, the sick and the powerless. Current transport problems harm children and the elderly, and off-load environmental problems onto the poor.

Transport is also the key to global environmental and social justice. Transport problems are real and severe in European, Australian and North American cities but the threats to human health, environment and social justice in megacities in developing countries are far greater. This is because many poor people live at higher densities in close proximity to polluting traffic, and because many of the cities will have to undergo fundamental re-engineering to make room for cars if the growth in car use is going to continue at the same rate as the last few years. This re-engineering will destroy the high performing accessibility of cities such as Kolkata, where tens of thousands of people live within walking and cycling distance of thousands of jobs, shops, schools and other commonly accessed destinations. Once the accessibility is lost, the spatial structures will reinforce the non-sustainability of many sprawling developed world cities.

If Asian, African and Latin American cities move rapidly into the Western model of transport and land use, then many millions of residents will be exposed to air and noise pollution and physical relocation (to make way for new infrastructure), all of which damage human health and the environment and deny human rights. If China is to provide the road space required by the size of its car fleet in 2030, then thousands of hectares will be removed from food production and laid down for the final crop, which is tarmac and concrete. India, Bangladesh and China will be faced with a choice between land for food or land for cars, and the balance of probabilities is in favour of cars.

The chapters in this Reader have covered Asian, African and Latin American examples of transport failures and transport remedies, but the discussion here has been biased towards a European view of the world. This is not because Europe is better placed to provide good ideas or insights than other parts of the world. It is partly a function of data availability and evidence, but more importantly it is the result of a clear conviction on the part of the editors that the developed world has an urgent responsibility to reduce its demand for car, truck and aircraft activity as a contribution to the global policy debate about these issues. Europe and North America led the way in the first part of the 20th century in designing and promoting a technology that was intended to earn a lot of money for big business (eg Henry Ford), but was also intended to transform society into something that was modern, mobile and hooked on the consumption of material things and images. Henry Ford, writing in 1929, said:

> We are entering a new era. Old landmarks have disappeared. Our new thinking and new doing are bringing us a new world, a new heaven, and a new Earth, for which prophets have been looking from time immemorial (Ford, 1929, p13).

A mobile society was seen as a religious achievement and a major transformation for the better. This is the legacy of the developed world that is still being exported and heavily marketed to China by the company set up by Henry Ford. Our developed world bias is intended to make the point that the developed world has to reassess its 100 year old fascination with mobility and recast that set of objectives within a socially and environmentally just approach to sustainability. Put very simply, those parts of the world that led the transition to auto dependency must now lead the transition to sustainable mobility and a reduction in the demand for transport.

Sustainability can never be achieved on the basis of driving, trucking and flying 6 per cent more kilometres year on year without limit and without thought. Europe and

North America have to bring an effective closure to the Henry Ford dream and move into a new paradigm based on the economic, social, environmental and human rights illogicality of hyper-mobility. In so doing we will send the clearest message of all to developing countries such as India, China and Bangladesh about the wisdom of pursuing a business as usual strategy in transport. If we do not send this message then Henry Ford will have achieved his objectives on a scale even he could not have contemplated. The world will become motorized at current European/North American standards with similar levels of mobility in terms of kilometres driven each year, flown each year and per capita truck kilometres driven each year. The consequences for global climate change, environmental pollution, human health, social justice and land-take are clear. This vision of the future is within our reach, but so is the alternative vision so clearly captured by the chapters in this book. Only our grandchildren will know which path was taken.

References

Brög, W (2002) *Individuelles marketing - der homoopatische Weg zur Forderung einer nachhaltigen Mobilität*, paper delivered to the conference on 'Soft Policies', 22 March, Ministry of Transport, Berlin

DTLR (2002) *Making Travel Plans Work. Lessons from UK Case Studies*, Department of Transport, Local Government and the Regions, London

EIB (1998) *Annual Report*, European Investment Bank, Luxembourg

Ford, H (1929) *My Philosophy of Industry*, George C Harrap, London

IPCC (2001) *Climate Change 2001: The Scientific Basis*, Intergovernmental Panel on Climate Change/Cambridge University Press, Cambridge

ITDP (2001) *Sustainable Transport*, no 12, Fall, p7, www.itdp.org

Kenworthy, J and Laube, F (1999) *An International Sourcebook of Automobile Dependence in Cities 1960–1990*, University Press of Colorado, Colorado

Laird, P, Newman, P, Bachels, M and Kenworthy, J (2001) *Back on Track: Rethinking Transport Policy in Australia and New Zealand*, UNSW Press, Sydney

Maddison, D, Pearce, D, Johansson, O, Calthrop, E, Litman, T and Verhoef, E (1996) *Blueprint 5: The True Costs of Road Transport*, Earthscan, London

Newman, P and Kenworthy, J (1989) *Cities and Automobile Dependence: An International Sourcebook*, Gower, Aldershot

OECD (1995) *Urban Travel and Sustainable Development*, OECD, Paris

O'Meara Sheehan, M (2002) 'What will it take to halt sprawl?' *World Watch*, vol 15, no 1, January/February, pp12–23

Pfizer (2000) *The Future of Transport at Pfizer*, Pfizer, Sandwich, Kent

Smith, M, Whitelegg, J and Williams, N (1998) *Greening the Built Environment*, Earthscan, London

Sustain (2001) *Eating Oil: Food Supply in a Changing Climate*, Sustain, London

TEST (1991) *Changed Travel – Better World: A Study of Travel Patterns in Milton Keynes and Almere*, TEST, London

Tiempo (2002) *Tiempo: Global Warming and the Third World*, no 43, March, www.cru.uea.ac.uk/tiempo/

United Nations (2001) *World Urbanisation Prospects: The 1999 Revision*, Population Division, Department of Economic and Social Affairs, United Nations, New York

Whitelegg, J (1999) *Sustainable Transport in Calcutta*, Eco-Logica Ltd, Lancaster
Whitelegg, J (2000) 'Building ethics into the built environment' in Fox, W (ed) *Ethics and the Built Environment*, Routledge, London, pp31–43

Index